Taste of Home

COOK IT QUICK

All-time family classics in 10, 20 & 30 minutes

TASTE OF HOME BOOKS • RDA ENTHUSIAST BRANDS, LLC • MILWAUKEE, WI

© 2019 RDA Enthusiast Brands, LLC.
1610 N. 2nd St., Suite 102, Milwaukee WI 53212-3906
All rights reserved. Taste of Home is a registered
trademark of RDA Enthusiast Brands, LLC.

Visit us at tasteofhome.com for other Taste of Home
books and products.

ISBN: 978-1-61765-833-4
LOCC: 2019931314

Deputy Editor: Mark Hagen
Senior Art Director: Raeann Thompson
Editors: Amy Glander, Christine Rukavena,
Hazel Wheaton
Senior Designer: Courtney Lovetere
Designer: Jazmin Delgado
Copy Editor: Ann Walter

Cover photography: Taste of Home Photo Studio

Pictured on front cover: Grilled Banana Brownie
Sundaes, p. 129; Po'Boy Tacos, p. 236; Pumpkin
Hummus, p. 68; Basil-Tomato Grilled Cheese, p. 112;
Meatball Submarine Casserole, p. 217

Pictured on title page: Chocolate Peanut Cookies,
p. 342; Bacon, Lettuce & Tomato Pizza, p. 210;
Colorful Spiral Pasta Salad, p. 81; Greek Tilapia, p. 302;
Easy Chicken & Dumplings, p. 239

Spine credit:
Babyboom/Shutterstock

Pictured on back cover:
Makeover Mac & Cheese, p. 388;
Ginger-Orange Wings, p. 351;
Cake & Berry Campfire Cobbler, p. 334

Printed in China
1 3 5 7 9 10 8 6 4 2

CONTENTS

GET SOCIAL WITH US

TO FIND A RECIPE: tasteofhome.com
TO SUBMIT A RECIPE: tasteofhome.com/submit
TO FIND OUT ABOUT OTHER TASTE OF HOME
PRODUCTS: shoptasteofhome.com

COOK IT QUICK EVERY DAY

488 MOUTHWATERING FOODS IN A MATTER OF MINUTES

Think you don't have time to cook? Think again! Now you can savor delicious specialties no matter how little time you have. Grab your copy of *Taste of Home Cook It Quick,* and you'll be noshing on a new favorite in moments.

Simply turn to the section that fits your schedule best. For instance, you can whip up Mexicali Pork Chops (p. 39) in no time because it's from the "10 Minutes" chapter. Or flip to the handy "30 Minutes" section for 141 stir-fries, tacos, pizzas, dips, soups, casseroles, fruity cobblers and other mainstays that satisfy in half an hour.

Cook once and eat all week with the "Planned Overs" chapter. Here, you can serve a roast, ham or chicken—then try the recipes that use up the tasty leftovers. What a time-saver! You'll even find three handy icons to speed up meal planning:

- **5 INGREDIENT:** Set a satisfying dish on the table with only a handful of items (not including water, salt, pepper, oils and optional ingredients such as garnishes).

- **EAT SMART:** These recipes trim back calories, fat, sodium, carbs or sugar.

- **FREEZE IT:** Stock your freezer with meals that heat up in a flash.

Best of all, these dishes come from today's home cooks who know how to set a meal on the table even on their busiest nights. Now they're sharing their speedy recipes with you. With *Taste of Home Cook It Quick,* there's always time to create fantastic meals, enjoy delicious foods and make heartwarming memories at the table.

31

109

269

91

294

BROWNIE BATTER DIP

I'm all about the sweeter side of dips, and this brownie-flavored treat fits in with my life's philosophy: Chocolate makes anything better. Grab some fruit, cookies or salty snacks and start dunking.
—Mel Gunnell, Boise, ID

- -

Takes: 10 min.
Makes: 2½ cups (20 servings)

1 pkg. (8 oz.) cream cheese, softened
¼ cup butter, softened
2 cups confectioners' sugar
⅓ cup baking cocoa
¼ cup 2% milk
2 Tbsp. brown sugar
1 tsp. vanilla extract
¼ cup M&M's minis, optional
   Animal crackers, pretzels and/or
   sliced apples

In a bowl, beat cream cheese and butter until smooth. Beat in confectioners' sugar, cocoa, milk, brown sugar and vanilla until smooth. If desired, sprinkle with M&M's minis. Serve with dippers of your choice.
2 Tbsp.: 117 cal., 6g fat (4g sat. fat), 19mg chol., 62mg sod., 15g carb. (14g sugars, 0 fiber), 1g pro.

CANNELLINI BEAN HUMMUS

My version of hummus features a delightful nuttiness from tahini, a peanut butter-like paste made from ground sesame seeds. The beans pack a lot of protein so it's a healthy snack, too!
—Marina Castle Kelley, Canyon Country, CA

Takes: 5 min.
Makes: 1¼ cups (10 servings)

- 2 garlic cloves, peeled
- 1 can (15 oz.) cannellini beans, rinsed and drained
- ¼ cup tahini
- 3 Tbsp. lemon juice
- 1½ tsp. ground cumin
- ¼ tsp. salt
- ¼ tsp. crushed red pepper flakes
- 2 Tbsp. minced fresh parsley
  Pita breads, cut into wedges
  Assorted fresh vegetables

1. Place garlic in a food processor; cover and process until minced. Add the beans, tahini, lemon juice, cumin, salt and pepper flakes; cover and process until smooth.
2. Transfer to a small bowl; stir in parsley. Refrigerate until serving. Serve with pita wedges and assorted fresh vegetables.
2 Tbsp.: 78 cal., 4g fat (1g sat. fat), 0 chol., 114mg sod., 8g carb. (0 sugars, 2g fiber), 3g pro. **Diabetic exchanges:** 1 fat, ½ starch.

CARAMEL APPLE & BRIE SKEWERS

I'm a caterer, and these sweet treats rank among my best-sellers. Using prepared caramel makes them a snap to assemble. Who doesn't love a shortcut?
—Camille Ellis, Tampa, FL

Takes: 10 min. • **Makes:** 6 skewers

- 2 medium apples, cubed
- 1 log (6 oz.) Brie cheese, cubed
- ½ cup hot caramel ice cream topping
- ½ cup finely chopped macadamia nuts
- 2 Tbsp. dried cranberries

On each of six appetizer skewers, alternately thread apple and cheese cubes; place on a serving plate. Drizzle with caramel topping; sprinkle with the macadamia nuts and cranberries.

1 skewer: 272 cal., 16g fat (6g sat. fat), 29mg chol., 303mg sod., 27g carb. (7g sugars, 2g fiber), 7g pro.

SPEEDY SURPRISE
"This was a quick snack for a girls' night I hosted. Definitely a recipe that I'll keep as a go-to!"
—GINA.KAPFHAMMER, TASTEOFHOME.COM

LOADED BAKED POTATO DIP

I never thought of using waffle-cut fries as a scoop for dip until a friend of mine did at a baby shower. They're ideal for my cheesy bacon and chive dip, which tastes just like a baked potato topper.

—Nicholas J. King, Duluth, MN

- -

Takes: 10 min.
Makes: 2½ cups (10 servings)

- 2 cups reduced-fat sour cream
- 2 cups shredded reduced-fat cheddar cheese
- 8 center-cut bacon or turkey bacon strips, chopped and cooked
- ⅓ cup minced fresh chives
- 2 tsp. Louisiana-style hot sauce
  Hot cooked waffle-cut fries

In a small bowl, mix the first five ingredients until blended; refrigerate until serving. Serve with waffle fries.

¼ cup: 149 cal., 10g fat (6g sat. fat), 38mg chol., 260mg sod., 4g carb. (4g sugars, 0 fiber), 11g pro.

APPLE SNACK WEDGES

Break out these easy, fun apple bites before you head out the door. The protein in the peanut butter will help fill you up.
—Jacquie Berg, St. Cloud, WI

- -

Takes: 10 min. • **Makes:** 1 dozen

2	medium apples
1	cup Rice Chex, crushed
1½	tsp. packed brown sugar
2	Tbsp. reduced-fat creamy peanut butter

1. Core apples; cut each apple into six wedges. Pat dry with paper towels.
2. In a small shallow bowl, combine the cereal and brown sugar. Spread cut sides of apples with peanut butter; roll in cereal mixture. Serve immediately.

1 piece: 36 cal., 1g fat (0 sat. fat), 0 chol., 33mg sod., 6g carb. (3g sugars, 1g fiber), 1g pro. **Diabetic exchanges:** ½ starch.

TEST KITCHEN TIP
Apples make for a quick, easy and healthy snack. Be sure to buy your family the best by selecting those that are firm and have a smooth, unblemished skin free from any bruises.

TUNA CHEESE SPREAD

The flavor of tuna is very subtle in this thick and creamy spread. It's terrific on crackers or carrot and celery sticks, stuffed in a tomato or used for a sandwich.
—Dorothy Anderson, Ottawa, KS

- -

Takes: 5 min. • **Makes:** 2 cups (8 servings)

1	pkg. (8 oz.) cream cheese, softened
½	cup thinly sliced green onions
¼	cup mayonnaise
1	Tbsp. lemon juice
¾	tsp. curry powder
	Dash salt
1	can (6 oz.) tuna, drained and flaked
	Bread or crackers

In a bowl, combine the first six ingredients. Stir in tuna. Serve with bread or crackers.

¼ cup: 177 cal., 16g fat (7g sat. fat), 40mg chol., 213mg sod., 1g carb. (1g sugars, 0 fiber), 8g pro.

5 INGREDIENT

MARSHMALLOW FRUIT DIP

You can whip up this sweet and creamy dip in just 10 minutes. I like to serve it in a bowl surrounded by fresh-picked strawberries at spring brunches or luncheons.
—Cindy Steffen, Cedarburg, WI

Takes: 10 min.
Makes: 5 cups (40 servings)

1 pkg. (8 oz.) cream cheese, softened
¾ cup cherry yogurt
1 carton (8 oz.) frozen whipped topping, thawed
1 jar (7 oz.) marshmallow creme
Assorted fresh fruit

In a large bowl, beat cream cheese and yogurt until blended. Fold in whipped topping and marshmallow creme. Serve with fruit.
2 Tbsp.: 56 cal., 3g fat (2g sat. fat), 7mg chol., 24mg sod., 6g carb. (5g sugars, 0 fiber), 1g pro.

SPEEDY SURPRISE

"I made this for the first time for a dinner party. What a hit! We used it as dessert, and the kids loved it."
—KMARQUI, TASTEOFHOME.COM

5 INGREDIENT

PIZZA OYSTER CRACKERS

This quick and easy snack is a favorite of my kids. I like to include it in their lunch boxes.
—Carol S. Betz, Grand Rapids, MI

Takes: 10 min.
Makes: 12 cups (24 servings)

2 pkg. (9 oz. each) oyster crackers
½ cup canola oil
⅓ cup grated Parmesan cheese
¼ cup pizza seasoning or Italian seasoning
½ tsp. garlic powder

1. Preheat oven to 350°. Place crackers in a large bowl. In a small bowl, mix oil, cheese, pizza seasoning and garlic powder; pour over the crackers and toss gently to coat. Transfer to two ungreased 15x10x1-in. baking pans.
2. Bake 5-7 minutes, stirring once. Cool. Store in an airtight container.
½ cup: 135 cal., 7g fat (1g sat. fat), 1mg chol., 220mg sod., 16g carb. (0 sugars, 1g fiber), 2g pro.

10 MINUTE SIDES

SIMPLE WALDORF SALAD

This is my go-to salad when I need a snappy little something for a meal. Sometimes, when I want a sweeter flavor, I use whipped cream instead of yogurt.
—Wendy Masters, East Garafraxa, ON

Takes: 10 min. • **Makes:** 6 servings

- 2 large Gala or Honeycrisp apples, unpeeled and chopped (about 3 cups)
- 2 cups chopped celery
- ¼ cup raisins
- ¼ cup chopped walnuts, toasted
- ⅓ cup reduced-fat mayonnaise
- ⅓ cup plain yogurt

Combine apples, celery, raisins and walnuts. Add mayonnaise and yogurt; toss to coat. Refrigerate, covered, until serving.
Note: To toast nuts, bake in a shallow pan in a 350° oven for 5-10 minutes or cook in a skillet over low heat until lightly browned, stirring occasionally.
¾ cup: 140 cal., 8g fat (1g sat. fat), 6mg chol. 119mg sod., 17g carb. (12g sugars, 3g fiber), 2g pro. **Diabetic exchanges:** 1½ fat, 1 fruit.

SIMPLE LETTUCE SALAD

My mother often fixed this salad when I was a child. I grew up on a farm so most of our food came right from the garden. We especially liked this in the spring, when early leaf lettuce appeared. After a long winter of cooked vegetables, this was always a real treat.
—Susan Davis, Vale, NC

Takes: 10 min. • **Makes:** 2 servings

- 2 cups torn leaf lettuce
- 1 hard-boiled large egg, chopped
- 1 green onion, sliced
- 2 Tbsp. mayonnaise
- 1 tsp. cider vinegar
- ⅛ tsp. pepper

In a salad bowl, combine lettuce, egg and onion. In a small bowl, whisk mayonnaise, vinegar and pepper. Pour over salad and toss to coat.
1 cup: 150 cal., 14g fat (2g sat. fat), 111mg chol., 123mg sod., 3g carb. (1g sugars, 1g fiber), 4g pro.

TEST KITCHEN TIP

Save yourself a bit of time during the week by preparing several hard-boiled eggs at once. Unpeeled, the eggs stay fresh in the refrigerator for up to 1 week. Once shelled, however, the eggs should be used right away.

SPINACH & GORGONZOLA SALAD

This is a quick and easy recipe with a wonderful combination of flavors. Enjoy!
—Nadine Mesch, Mount Healthy, OH

- -

Takes: 10 min. • **Makes:** 6 servings

- 5   cups fresh baby spinach
- 1   cup sliced fresh strawberries
- ⅓   cup lightly salted cashews
- ¼   cup crumbled Gorgonzola cheese

VINAIGRETTE

- ⅓   cup olive oil
- ¼   cup balsamic vinegar
- 1   Tbsp. seedless raspberry jam
- 1½ tsp. Dijon mustard
- ¼   tsp. salt
- ¼   tsp. pepper

In a large bowl, combine the spinach, strawberries, cashews and cheese. In a small bowl, whisk remaining ingredients. Drizzle over salad; toss to coat.

1 cup: 199 cal., 17g fat (3g sat. fat), 4mg chol., 229mg sod., 9g carb. (5g sugars, 2g fiber), 4g pro.

CURRY-CRANBERRY SPINACH SALAD

I sometimes switch up this salad by using chopped dried apricots or pineapple and arugula or other sturdy greens.
—Trisha Kruse, Eagle, ID

- -

Takes: 10 min. • **Makes:** 5 servings

- 5   cups fresh baby spinach
- ¼   cup pine nuts
- 3   Tbsp. dried cranberries
- 1   Tbsp. sesame seeds
- ¼   cup packed brown sugar
- ¼   cup rice vinegar
- ¼   cup olive oil
- 1   Tbsp. soy sauce
- 2   tsp. dried minced onion
- ½   tsp. curry powder
- ¼   tsp. salt

In a salad bowl, combine the spinach, pine nuts, cranberries and sesame seeds. In a small bowl, whisk remaining ingredients. Drizzle over the salad and toss to coat. Serve immediately.

1 cup: 214 cal., 15g fat (2g sat.fat), 0 chol., 332mg sod., 19g carb. (14g sugars, 1g fiber), 3g pro.

TEST KITCHEN TIP

Olive oil can be stored tightly capped at room temperature or in the refrigerator for up to 1 year. When chilled, the oil turns cloudy and thick. Chilled olive oil will return to its original consistency when left at room temperature for a short time.

GREENS WITH ORANGE VINAIGRETTE

Like a string of pearls on a little black dress, a vinaigrette is a classic way to dress things up a bit. A little oil, a little vinegar, a tangy infusion of orange juice and a sprinkle of orange zest are just enough to turn a package of greens into something special.
—Kristin Bataille, Stamford, CT

- -

Takes: 10 minutes • **Makes:** 6 servings

- 2 Tbsp. olive oil
- 2 Tbsp. orange juice
- 1 Tbsp. cider vinegar
- 1 tsp. grated orange zest
  Dash salt
  Dash pepper
- 1 pkg. (5 oz.) spring mix salad greens

In a small bowl, whisk first six ingredients. Place salad greens in a large bowl. Drizzle with vinaigrette; toss to coat.

1 cup: 47 cal., 5g fat (1g sat. fat), 0 chol., 31mg sod., 1g carb. (1g sugars, 1g fiber), 0 pro. **Diabetic exchanges:** 1 fat.

SPEEDY SURPRISE
"This was delicious and super quick to make. I will definitely make it again."
—KATLAYDEE3, TASTEOFHOME.COM

EASY PEASY SLAW

I get tons of compliments when I bring out this slaw brightened up with peas, peanuts and poppy seed dressing. It's fresh and colorful with a satisfying crunch.
—Sue Ort, Des Moines, IA

- -

Takes: 5 min.
Makes: 12 servings

- 4 cups frozen peas (about 16 oz.), thawed
- 1 pkg. (14 oz.) coleslaw mix
- 4 green onions, chopped
- 1 cup poppy seed salad dressing
- 1 cup sweet and crunchy peanuts or honey-roasted peanuts

Place peas, coleslaw mix and green onions in a large bowl. Pour dressing over the salad and toss to coat. Stir in the peanuts just before serving.

⅔ cup: 202 cal., 12g fat (2g sat. fat), 7mg chol., 178mg sod., 20g carb. (14g sugars, 4g fiber), 4g pro. **Diabetic exchanges:** 2 fat, 1 starch, 1 vegetable.

BROILED PARMESAN & SWISS TOMATOES

Planning to serve steak or tenderloin? These cheesy tomatoes make the ideal accompaniment. Plus, the recipe is simple to double for guests.
—Mary Price, Youngstown, OH

Takes: 10 min. • **Makes:** 4 servings

- 2   medium tomatoes, halved
- 2   Tbsp. plus ¼ cup butter, divided
- 4   green onions, chopped
- 3   Tbsp. dry bread crumbs
- 1   Tbsp. grated Parmesan cheese
- ⅛   tsp. salt
- ⅛   tsp. garlic powder
- ¼   cup shredded Swiss cheese

1. Place the tomatoes, cut side up, in an ungreased 15x10x1-in. baking pan; dot with 2 Tbsp. butter. Broil 4 in. from heat until butter is melted, 4-6 minutes.
2. Meanwhile, in a small microwave-safe bowl, combine remaining butter and onions. Microwave, uncovered, on high until onions are tender, 2-3 minutes. Stir in the bread crumbs, Parmesan cheese, salt and garlic powder; spoon over tomatoes. Sprinkle with Swiss cheese. Broil until the cheese is melted, 1-2 minutes.

1 tomato half: 220 cal., 20g fat (12g sat. fat), 52mg chol., 275mg sod., 8g carb. (3g sugars, 2g fiber), 4g pro.

Broiled Italian Tomatoes: Substitute shredded mozzarella for the Swiss. Stir 1 Tbsp. chopped fresh basil into the crumb mixture.

HONEY MUSTARD COLESLAW

I switched up a family coleslaw recipe—using packaged shredded cabbage is a real time-saver. And now there's very little cleanup to deal with!
—Rebecca Anderson, Melissa, TX

Takes: 10 min. • **Makes:** 5 servings

- 1   pkg. (14 oz.) coleslaw mix
- ½   cup mayonnaise
- 2   Tbsp. honey
- 1   Tbsp. cider vinegar
- 1   Tbsp. spicy brown mustard
- ½   tsp. lemon-pepper seasoning
- ⅛   tsp. celery seed

Place coleslaw mix in a large bowl. Combine remaining ingredients. Pour over coleslaw mix and toss to coat. Chill until serving.
¾ cup: 216 cal., 18g fat (2g sat. fat), 8mg chol., 232mg sod., 12g carb. (10g sugars, 2g fiber), 1g pro.

5 INGREDIENT
IN-A-FLASH BEANS

No one will guess this recipe begins with a can. Chopped onion and green pepper lend a little crunch while barbecue sauce brings lots of home-cooked flavor.
—Linda Coleman, Cedar Rapids, IA

Takes: 10 min. • **Makes:** 4 servings

- 1   can (15¾ oz.) pork and beans
- ½   cup barbecue sauce
- ½   cup chopped onion
- ¼   cup chopped green pepper, optional

In a large saucepan, combine the beans, barbecue sauce, onion and green pepper if desired. Cook and stir over medium heat until heated through.

⅔ cup: 129 cal., 2g fat (0 sat. fat), 0 chol., 647mg sod., 26g carb. (11g sugars, 6g fiber), 6g pro.

CURRY RICE PILAF

Salted cashews add a nice crunch to this simple rice dish quickly flavored with curry and turmeric.
—Katie Rose, Pewaukee, WI

Takes: 10 min. • **Makes:** 5 servings

- 2   pkg. (8½ oz. each) ready-to-serve jasmine rice
- 2   Tbsp. butter
- 1   cup salted whole cashews
- 2   green onions, sliced
- ½   tsp. curry powder
- ¼   tsp. salt
- ¼   tsp. ground turmeric
- ¼   tsp. pepper

Heat rice according to package directions. Meanwhile, in a small skillet, melt butter over medium heat. Add cashews, onions and seasonings; cook and stir until the onions are tender, 2-3 minutes. Add rice; toss to coat.

¾ cup: 436 cal., 23g fat (6g sat. fat), 12mg chol., 362mg sod., 50g carb. (2g sugars, 2g fiber), 10g pro.

FRUIT & SPINACH SALAD

The combination of sweet fruit and salty feta cheese makes this salad a winner.
—Virginia Dack, Asheville, NC

Takes: 10 min. • **Makes:** 2 servings

- 2 cups fresh baby spinach
- 1 snack-size cup (4 oz.) mandarin oranges, drained
- ⅓ cup seedless red grapes, halved
- ¼ cup crumbled feta cheese
- 2 Tbsp. chopped walnuts, toasted
- 1 green onion, chopped
- ¼ cup oil and vinegar salad dressing

In a salad bowl, combine the spinach, oranges, grapes, cheese, walnuts and onion. Drizzle with dressing; toss to coat. Serve immediately.

1 serving: 235 cal., 16g fat (2g sat. fat), 8mg chol., 644mg sod., 19g carb. (16g sugars, 2g fiber), 6g pro. **Diabetic exchanges:** 3 fat, 1 vegetable, ½ fruit.

PARSLEYED RICE PILAF

I dress up instant rice with bouillon, minced onion and fresh parsley for this speedy side dish. I like to serve it alongside seafood, particularly salmon.
—Kathy Peltier, Kalispell, MT

- -

Takes: 10 min. • **Makes:** 4 servings

- 2 **cups water**
- ¼ **cup dried minced onion**
- 4 **tsp. butter**
- 2 **tsp. chicken bouillon granules**
- 2 **cups instant rice**
- ¼ **cup minced fresh parsley**

In a small saucepan, bring the water, onion, butter and bouillon to a boil. Stir in rice and parsley. Remove from the heat. Cover and let stand for 5 minutes. Fluff with a fork.
½ cup: 230 cal., 4g fat (2g sat. fat), 11mg chol., 464mg sod., 43g carb. (3g sugars, 1g fiber), 4g pro.

LEMON DATE COUSCOUS

Couscous is a perfect base for bold flavors, colors and textures.
—Roxanne Chan, Albany, CA

- -

Takes: 10 min. • **Makes:** 4 servings

- ¾ **cup uncooked couscous**
- ½ **cup fresh baby spinach**
- ½ **cup shredded carrots**
- ¼ **cup chopped dates**
- 2 **Tbsp. sliced almonds**
- 1 **tsp. lemon juice**
- ¼ **tsp. grated lemon zest**
- ⅛ **tsp. salt**
- ⅛ **tsp. lemon-pepper seasoning**
  Thinly sliced green onions

1. Cook the couscous according to the package directions.
2. Meanwhile, in a small bowl, combine the spinach, carrots, dates, almonds, lemon juice, zest, salt and lemon pepper. Stir in couscous. Garnish with green onions.
¾ cup: 179 cal., 2g fat (0 sat. fat), 0 chol., 104mg sod., 37g carb. (9g sugars, 3g fiber), 6g pro. **Diabetic exchanges:** 2½ starch.

RED, WHITE & BLUE SLAW

This all-time favorite salad is perfect for any occasion, though obviously it's a great choice for a patriotic feast. It's a refreshing blend of ingredients.
—Bonnie Hawkins, Elkhorn, WI

- -

Takes: 10 min. • **Makes:** 6 servings

6	cups angel hair coleslaw mix
12	cherry tomatoes, halved
¾	cup coleslaw salad dressing
¾	cup crumbled blue cheese, divided
½	cup real bacon bits

In a large bowl, combine the coleslaw mix, tomatoes, salad dressing and ½ cup blue cheese. Cover and refrigerate until serving. Just before serving, sprinkle with bacon bits and remaining cheese.

¾ cup: 245 cal., 18g fat (5g sat.fat), 34mg chol., 960mg sod., 13g carb. (11g sugars, 2g fiber), 8g pro.

SPEEDY SURPRISE

"This is a really fantastic slaw! My husband and I absolutely loved it. The sweetness of the tomatoes, the bittersweet cabbage, smoky bacon and tangy blue cheese was perfect with our favorite grilled pork tenderloin sandwiches. We will definitely be serving this slaw again and again!"

—MARY0806, TASTEOFHOME.COM

DILL & CHIVE PEAS

Growing my own herbs helps me keep things fresh in the kitchen. This springtime side is a breeze to prepare.
—Tanna Richard, Cedar Rapids, IA

- -

Takes: 10 min. • **Makes:** 4 servings

1	pkg. (16 oz.) frozen peas
¼	cup snipped fresh dill
2	Tbsp. minced fresh chives
1	Tbsp. butter
1	tsp. lemon-pepper seasoning
¼	tsp. kosher salt

Cook peas according to package directions. Stir in the remaining ingredients; serve the peas immediately.

¾ cup: 113 cal., 3g fat (2g sat. fat), 8mg chol., 346mg sod., 16g carb. (6g sugars, 5g fiber), 6g pro. **Diabetic exchanges:** 1 starch, ½ fat.

HONEY KALE CURRANT & ALMOND SALAD

This honey-flavored kale salad makes our taste buds tingle. It has a subtle sweetness from currants and a nutty almond crunch. Add grated Asiago and you've truly got a stellar side.

—Ally Phillips, Murrells Inlet, SC

Takes: 10 min. • **Makes:** 4 servings

- 4 cups thinly sliced fresh kale
- ¼ cup slivered almonds
- ¼ cup dried currants
- 2 Tbsp. grated Asiago cheese
- 1 Tbsp. balsamic vinegar
- 1 Tbsp. olive oil
- 1 Tbsp. honey mustard
- 1½ tsp. honey
- ¾ tsp. coarsely ground pepper
- ½ tsp. sea salt

Place kale, almonds and currants in a large bowl. In a small bowl, whisk the remaining ingredients until blended. Drizzle over salad; toss to coat.

1 cup: 135 cal., 8g fat (1g sat. fat), 3mg chol., 287mg sod., 15g carb. (11g sugars, 2g fiber), 3g pro. **Diabetic exchanges:** 1½ fat, 1 vegetable, ½ starch.

SPEEDY SURPRISE

"This is a delicious salad that can be made ahead because kale does not go limp as quickly as other greens. Loved the sweet, tart, crunchy and salty tastes in the salad. I will definitely put this in my keeper file."

—ANNRMS, TASTEOFHOME.COM

PEAR COTTAGE CHEESE SALAD

Perfect any time, this snack makes a tasty pack-along lunch, too!

—Jeannie Thomas, Dry Ridge, KY

Takes: 10 min. • **Makes:** 6 servings

- 2 cups 2% cottage cheese
- 2 medium pears, chopped
- 2 celery ribs, chopped
- ⅓ cup chopped pecans
- ½ tsp. ground ginger

In a large bowl, combine all ingredients. Chill until serving.

⅔ cup: 135 cal., 6g fat (1g sat. fat), 9mg chol., 255mg sod., 14g carb. (8g sugars, 3g fiber), 8g pro. **Diabetic exchanges:** 1 lean meat, 1 fat, ½ fruit.

YELLOW SQUASH TURKEY SALAD

This is my favorite fast recipe. With a wonderful mix of flavors, colors and textures, this impressive salad can be made in minutes for lunch with friends or as a light and lovely dinner on busy weeknights.
—Mildred Sherrer, Fort Worth, TX

- -

Takes: 10 min. • **Makes:** 2 servings

4	cups spring mix salad greens
¼	lb. thinly sliced deli smoked turkey, cut into 1-in. strips
1	small yellow summer squash, halved lengthwise and sliced
1	small pear, chopped
½	cup dried cranberries
⅓	cup honey-roasted sliced almonds
¼	cup cubed cheddar cheese
⅓	cup red wine vinaigrette

In a large bowl, combine the first seven ingredients. Drizzle with vinaigrette and toss to coat. Serve immediately.
2 cups: 490 cal., 17g fat (3g sat. fat), 37mg chol., 1170mg sod., 61g carb. (48g sugars, 7g fiber), 22g pro.

SPEEDY SURPRISE
"Wow, this is so refreshing! We used it as a meal—it had everything in it. So good!"
—BONITO15, TASTEOFHOME.COM

BART'S BLACK BEAN SOUP

This cozy, colorful soup is made in just a few minutes—really! Add a salad for a complete meal that's a busy-day lifesaver.
—Sharon Ullyot, London, ON

- -

Takes: 10 min. • **Makes:** 4 servings (1 qt.)

1	can (15 oz.) black beans, rinsed and drained
1½	cups chicken broth
¾	cup chunky salsa
½	cup canned whole kernel corn, drained
	Dash hot pepper sauce
2	tsp. lime juice
1	cup shredded cheddar cheese
2	Tbsp. chopped green onions

In a microwave-safe bowl, combine the first five ingredients. Cover and microwave on high until heated through, about 2 minutes. Pour into four serving bowls; drizzle each with lime juice. Sprinkle with cheese and green onions.
1 cup: 229 cal., 8g fat (6g sat. fat), 32mg chol., 1004mg sod., 23g carb. (4g sugars, 5g fiber), 12g pro.

TURKEY PITAS WITH CREAMY SLAW

Pack these pockets of fun for school, work or a weekend picnic—or just eat them at home. Toss in a few slices of red pepper for extra color and crunch.
—*Taste of Home* Test Kitchen

Takes: 10 min. • **Makes:** 4 servings

- 3 cups coleslaw mix
- ¼ cup golden raisins
- 3 Tbsp. chopped red onion
- ⅓ cup reduced-fat mayonnaise
- 3 Tbsp. mango chutney
- 8 pita pocket halves
- ½ lb. sliced deli turkey
- 8 ready-to-serve fully cooked bacon strips, warmed
- 1 medium cucumber, thinly sliced

In a large bowl, combine the coleslaw mix, raisins and onion. Add mayonnaise and chutney; toss to coat. Line pita halves with turkey, bacon and cucumber; fill with the coleslaw mixture.

2 filled pita halves: 427 cal., 12g fat (2g sat. fat), 27mg chol., 1257mg sod., 57g carb. (18g sugars, 3g fiber), 21g pro.

JAZZED-UP CLAM CHOWDER

No one ever guesses that my dressed-up and delicious chowder starts with canned ingredients! It takes only 10 minutes to put together start to finish.
—Josephine Piro, Easton, PA

Takes: 10 min. • **Makes:** 4 servings (1 qt.)

- 1 can (19 oz.) chunky New England clam chowder
- 1 can (8¼ oz.) cream-style corn
- ⅔ cup 2% milk
- 2 Tbsp. shredded cheddar cheese
- 2 Tbsp. bacon bits
- 2 Tbsp. minced chives

In a 1½-qt. microwave-safe dish, combine the clam chowder, corn and milk. Cover and microwave on high until heated through, 4-6 minutes, stirring every 2 minutes. Sprinkle individual servings with cheese, bacon and chives.

1 cup: 211 cal., 10g fat (5g sat. fat), 14mg chol., 780mg sod., 24g carb. (5g sugars, 2g fiber), 8g pro.

TOMATO & AVOCADO SANDWICHES

I'm a vegetarian, and this is a tasty, quick and healthy lunch I could eat for every meal. At my house, we call these "HATS": hummus, avocado, tomato and shallots. They're all ingredients I almost always have on hand.
—Sarah Jaraha, Moorestown, NJ

Takes: 10 min. • **Makes:** 2 servings

½   medium ripe avocado, peeled and mashed
4   slices whole wheat bread, toasted
1   medium tomato, sliced
2   Tbsp. finely chopped shallot
¼   cup hummus

Spread avocado over two slices of toast. Top with tomato and shallot. Spread hummus over the remaining toast; place on top of avocado toast.

1 sandwich: 278 cal., 11g fat (2g sat. fat), 0 chol., 379mg sod., 35g carb. (6g sugars, 9g fiber), 11g pro. **Diabetic exchanges:** 2 starch, 2 fat.

SMOKED SALMON BAGEL SANDWICHES

A memorable pesto salmon I tried in Hawaii inspired these super convenient sandwiches. Pack them in a lunch or serve them on a brunch buffet.
—Sherryl Vera, Hurlburt Field, FL

- -

Takes: 10 min. • **Makes:** 2 servings

- 2 Tbsp. prepared pesto
- 2 whole wheat bagels, split and toasted
- ⅛ tsp. coarsely ground pepper
- 4 to 5 oz. smoked salmon or lox
- 2 slices tomato
- 2 Bibb or Boston lettuce leaves

Spread pesto over bagel bottoms; sprinkle with pepper. Layer with salmon, tomato and lettuce leaves. Replace bagel tops.
1 sandwich: 295 cal., 10g fat (3g sat. fat), 18mg chol., 1551mg sod., 33g carb. (2g sugars, 6g fiber), 19g pro.

TEST KITCHEN TIP
Boston, Bibb and butter lettuce are nearly indistinguishable in taste, texture and appearance; the three are all classified butterhead lettuces and can be used interchangeably.

LEMON-BUTTER TILAPIA WITH ALMONDS

Sometimes I want a nice meal without a ton of effort or wait time. Thankfully, I've got this lemony, buttery fish that's super fast and totally tasty.
—Ramona Parris, Canton, GA

- -

Takes: 10 min. • **Makes:** 4 servings

- 4 tilapia fillets (4 oz. each)
- ½ tsp. salt
- ¼ tsp. pepper
- 1 Tbsp. olive oil
- ¼ cup butter, cubed
- ¼ cup white wine or chicken broth
- 2 Tbsp. lemon juice
- ¼ cup sliced almonds

1. Sprinkle fillets with salt and pepper. In a large nonstick skillet, heat oil over medium heat. Add fillets; cook until fish just begins to flake easily with a fork, 2-3 minutes on each side. Remove and keep warm.
2. Add butter, wine and lemon juice to same pan; cook and stir until the butter is melted. Serve with fish; sprinkle with almonds.
1 fillet with about 2 Tbsp. sauce and 2 Tbsp. almonds: 269 cal., 19g fat (8g sat. fat), 86mg chol., 427mg sod., 2g carb. (1g sugars, 1g fiber), 22g pro.

SESAME TUNA STEAKS

These sesame-crusted tuna steaks will have your taste buds doing cartwheels. This quick-to-fix recipe is just right for two.
—*Taste of Home* Test Kitchen

Takes: 10 min. • **Makes:** 2 servings

2	tuna steaks (1 in. thick and 6 oz. each)
¼	tsp. salt
¼	cup sesame seeds
2	tsp. sesame oil

Sprinkle both sides of the tuna steaks with salt; rub with sesame seeds. In a large skillet, cook the tuna in oil over medium heat until slightly pink in the center, 2-4 minutes on each side for medium-rare.

1 serving: 302 cal., 14g fat (1g sat. fat), 77mg chol., 363mg sod., 3g carb. (0 sugars, 0 fiber), 44g pro.

ZIPPY EGG SALAD

Egg salad is a refreshing, tasty change from lunchmeat or peanut butter sandwiches. The touch of mustard and lemon juice gives it extra zip.
—Annemarie Pietila, Farmington Hills, MI

Takes: 10 min. • **Makes:** 2 servings

3	Tbsp. mayonnaise
1½	tsp. prepared mustard
⅛	tsp. salt
⅛	tsp. pepper
⅛	tsp. lemon juice
3	hard-boiled large eggs, coarsely chopped
1	Tbsp. minced green onion
2	slices bread
	Diced tomato, optional

Mix the first five ingredients. Stir in eggs and green onion. Serve on bread. If desired, top with tomato.

1 open-faced sandwich: 332 cal., 24g fat (5g sat. fat), 281mg chol., 530mg sod., 16g carb. (3g sugars, 1g fiber), 12g pro.

CURRIED CHICKEN & PEACH SALAD

This healthy salad is so simple, even my non-cooking husband can whip it together in minutes. We've served it to friends over the years—they always ask for the recipe!
—Radelle Knappenberger, Oviedo, FL

Takes: 10 min. • **Makes:** 4 servings

- ½ cup fat-free mayonnaise
- 1 tsp. curry powder
- 2 cups cubed cooked chicken breasts
- ½ cup chopped walnuts
- ¼ cup raisins
- 2 medium peaches, sliced
- 1 pkg. (5 oz.) spring mix salad greens

Mix the mayonnaise and curry powder; toss gently with the chicken, walnuts and raisins. Serve the chicken mixture and peaches over greens.

1 serving: 286 cal., 12g fat (2g sat. fat), 54mg chol., 315mg sod., 23g carb. (14g sugars, 4g fiber), 24g pro. **Diabetic exchanges:** 3 lean meat, 1½ fat, 1 vegetable, 1 fruit.

TEST KITCHEN TIP
Buying skinned and boned chicken breasts can trim up to 15 minutes off your cooking time. Save money by buying larger-size packages, then rewrap and freeze individually or in family-size portions.

SESAME CILANTRO SHRIMP

On days when I don't feel like spending much time in the kitchen, I reach for shrimp. I can have a hot meal on the table in 10 minutes.
—Tami Penunuri, League City, TX

Takes: 10 min. • **Makes:** 4 servings

- 1 Tbsp. plus ½ cup reduced-fat Asian toasted sesame salad dressing, divided
- 1 lb. uncooked shrimp (31-40 per lb.), peeled and deveined
- Lime wedges
- ¼ cup chopped fresh cilantro
- 3 cups cooked brown rice, optional

1. In a large nonstick skillet, heat 1 Tbsp. dressing over medium heat. Add shrimp; cook and stir 1 minute.

2. Stir in the remaining dressing; cook, uncovered, until the shrimp turn pink, 1-2 minutes longer. To serve, squeeze lime juice over top; sprinkle with cilantro. Serve with rice if desired.

½ cup shrimp mixture: 153 cal., 4g fat (0 sat. fat), 138mg chol., 461mg sod., 9g carb. (7g sugars, 0 fiber), 20g pro. **Diabetic exchanges:** 3 lean meat, ½ starch, ½ fat.

BLACK BEAN BURRITOS

My neighbor and I discovered these fabulous low-fat burritos a few years ago. On nights my husband or I have a meeting, we can have a satisfying supper on the table in minutes.

—Angela Studebaker, Goshen, IN

- -

Takes: 10 min. • **Makes:** 4 servings

- 1 Tbsp. canola oil
- 3 Tbsp. chopped onion
- 3 Tbsp. chopped green pepper
- 1 can (15 oz.) black beans, rinsed and drained
- 4 flour tortillas (8 in.), warmed
- 1 cup shredded Mexican cheese blend
- 1 medium tomato, chopped
- 1 cup shredded lettuce
  Optional toppings: salsa, sour cream, minced fresh cilantro, cubed avocado

1. In a nonstick skillet, heat oil over medium heat; saute onion and green pepper until tender. Stir in beans; heat through.

2. Spoon about ½ cupful of the vegetable mixture off center on each tortilla. Sprinkle with cheese, tomato and lettuce. Fold the sides and ends of the tortilla over the filling and roll up. Serve with salsa, sour cream, cilantro and avocado if desired.

1 burrito: 346 cal., 13g fat (5g sat. fat), 25mg chol., 615mg sod., 43g carb. (2g sugars, 6g fiber), 15g pro. **Diabetic exchanges:** 2½ starch, 1 lean meat, 1 vegetable, 1 fat.

MEXICALI PORK CHOPS

Grab just a couple of pantry staples—taco seasoning and your favorite salsa—to cook up a super-quick dinner of tender pork chops smothered in fun flavors.
—Laura Cohen, Eau Claire, WI

Takes: 10 min. • **Makes:** 4 servings

1   envelope taco seasoning
4   boneless pork loin chops
    (½ in. thick)
1   Tbsp. canola oil
    Salsa

Rub taco seasoning over pork chops. In a large skillet over medium-high heat, cook the pork chops in oil until juices run clear, 4-5 minutes on each side. Serve with salsa.
1 serving: 211 cal., 10g fat (3g sat. fat), 55mg chol., 856mg sod., 8g carb. (0 sugars, 0 fiber), 22g pro.

TEST KITCHEN TIP
Add the salsa to the pan after turning the chops, and let it all cook together—it'll make for juicier pork chops and a heated salsa topping. Then sprinkle each serving with grated cheese, and let it melt!

TUNA DILL SPREAD

This tasty sandwich filling does double duty—we also like to slather it on crackers when we want a swift snack.
—Geraldine Grisdale, Mount Pleasant, MI

Takes: 10 min. • **Makes:** 5 servings

1   can (6 oz.) tuna, drained and flaked
3   oz. cream cheese, softened
⅓   cup finely chopped
    seeded cucumber
2   Tbsp. lemon juice
1   to 2 Tbsp. minced fresh dill
½   tsp. salt
¼   tsp. pepper

Combine all ingredients; mix well. Use as sandwich filling or spread on crackers.
¼ cup: 102 cal., 6g fat (4g sat. fat), 29mg chol., 402mg sod., 1g carb. (1g sugars, 0 fiber), 10g pro.

TUNA CIABATTA MELTS

Use any good crusty bread when compiling this tuna spread sandwich. Top with slices of crunchy cucumber for extra freshness.
—Barb Templin, Norwood, MN

- -

Takes: 10 min. • **Makes:** 4 servings

- 1 pouch (11 oz.) light tuna in water
- ⅓ cup each finely chopped celery, cucumber and red onion
- ¼ cup mayonnaise
- 2 tsp. dill weed
- 1 tsp. lemon juice
- ⅛ tsp. salt
- ⅛ tsp. pepper
- 4 ciabatta rolls, split
- 2 cups shredded cheddar cheese

1. In a small bowl, combine the tuna, celery, cucumber, onion, mayonnaise, dill, lemon juice, salt and pepper; mix well.

2. Place rolls on a baking sheet. Spread each half with tuna mixture; sprinkle with cheese. Broil 2-3 in. from the heat until the cheese is melted, 2-4 minutes.

2 open-faced sandwiches: 482 cal., 29g fat (14g sat. fat), 88mg chol., 898mg sod., 22g carb. (2g sugars, 1g fiber), 35g pro.

TEST KITCHEN TIP
If you like things spicy, add prepared horseradish with the mayonnaise. You can experiment endlessly with these sandwiches, using salmon instead of tuna, or adding tomatoes or other fresh veggies.

EAT SMART
CAESAR CHICKEN WITH FETA

My tomatoey chicken is the perfect answer on those crazy days when supper has to be on the table fast (doesn't hurt that it's delicious, too).
—Denise Chelpka, Phoenix, AZ

- -

Takes: 10 min. • **Makes:** 4 servings

- 4 boneless skinless chicken breast halves (4 oz. each)
- ½ tsp. salt
- ¼ tsp. pepper
- 2 tsp. olive oil
- 1 medium tomato, chopped
- ¼ cup creamy Caesar salad dressing
- ½ cup crumbled feta cheese

Sprinkle chicken with salt and pepper. In a large skillet, heat oil over medium-high heat. Brown chicken on one side. Turn chicken; add tomato and salad dressing to skillet. Cook, covered, until a thermometer inserted in the chicken reads 165°, 6-8 minutes. Sprinkle with cheese.

1 chicken breast half with 3 Tbsp. tomato mixture: 262 cal., 16g fat (4g sat. fat), 76mg chol., 664mg sod., 2g carb. (1g sugars, 1g fiber), 26g pro.

SPLIT-SECOND SHRIMP

I use my microwave to hurry along preparation of this super fast shrimp scampi that's buttery and full of garlic flavor. It's good as an elegant entree or as an appetizer for a special occasion.
—Jalayne Luckett, Marion, IL

- -

Takes: 10 min. • **Makes:** 4 servings

2 Tbsp. butter
1 large garlic clove, minced
⅛ to ¼ tsp. cayenne pepper
2 Tbsp. white wine or chicken broth
5 tsp. lemon juice
1 Tbsp. minced fresh parsley
½ tsp. salt
1 lb. uncooked shrimp (26-30 per lb.), peeled and deveined

1. Place butter, garlic and cayenne in a 9-in. microwave-safe pie plate. Microwave, covered, on high until butter is melted, about 1 minute. Stir in wine, lemon juice, parsley and salt. Add shrimp; toss to coat.
2. Microwave, covered, on high until the shrimp turns pink, 2½-3½ minutes. Stir before serving.

3 oz. cooked shrimp: 157 cal., 7g fat (4g sat. fat), 153mg chol., 476mg sod., 2g carb. (0 sugars, 0 fiber), 19g pro. **Diabetic exchanges:** 3 lean meat, 1½ fat.

PEANUT BUTTER, HONEY & PEAR OPEN-FACED SANDWICHES

I work a night shift at a hospital and when I come home, I don't feel like cooking a big breakfast. I love these sandwiches because they're versatile; sometimes I use apples instead of pears, and different cheeses, such as Brie or grated Parmesan.
—L.J. Washington, Carpinteria, CA

- -

Takes: 10 min. • **Makes:** 4 servings

¼ cup chunky peanut butter
4 slices honey whole wheat bread, toasted
1 medium pear, thinly sliced
¼ tsp. salt
4 tsp. honey
½ cup shredded cheddar cheese

Spread peanut butter over the toast slices. Top with pear, salt, honey and shredded cheese. Place on a microwave-safe plate; microwave on high until the cheese is melted, 20-25 seconds.

1 open-faced sandwich: 268 cal., 14g fat (4g sat. fat), 14mg chol., 446mg sod., 28g carb. (13g sugars, 4g fiber), 11g pro.

TILAPIA WITH CORN SALSA

My family loves fish, and this super fast and delicious dish is very popular at my house. Though it tastes like it takes a long time, it cooks in minutes under the broiler. We like it garnished with lemon wedges with couscous on the side.
—Brenda Coffey, Singer Island, FL

Takes: 10 min. • **Makes:** 4 servings

- 4 tilapia fillets (6 oz. each)
- 1 Tbsp. olive oil
- ¼ tsp. salt
- ¼ tsp. pepper
- 1 can (15 oz.) black beans, rinsed and drained
- 1 can (11 oz.) whole kernel corn, drained
- ½ cup Italian salad dressing
- 2 Tbsp. chopped green onion
- 2 Tbsp. chopped sweet red pepper

1. Drizzle both sides of the fillets with oil; sprinkle with salt and pepper.
2. Broil 4-6 in. from the heat until the fish flakes easily with a fork, 5-7 minutes. Meanwhile, in a small bowl, combine the remaining ingredients. Serve with the fish.
1 each: 370 cal., 21g fat (3g sat.fat), 21mg chol. 1334mg sod., 27g carb. (6g sugars, 6g fiber), 14g pro.

SOURDOUGH TURKEY MELTS

When days feel rushed, these sandwiches with turkey and green chiles are one of my favorite standbys. They stack up in just about 10 minutes.
—Leah Carter, San Pedro, CA

Takes: 10 min. • **Makes:** 2 servings

- 2 Tbsp. mayonnaise
- 4 slices sourdough bread
- ¼ cup canned chopped green chiles
- ¼ lb. thinly sliced deli turkey
- ¼ cup shredded Colby-Monterey Jack cheese
- 1 Tbsp. butter, softened

1. Spread mayonnaise over two slices of bread. Layer with green chiles, turkey and cheese. Top with remaining bread. Spread outsides of sandwiches with butter.
2. In a large skillet, toast sandwiches over medium heat until golden brown and cheese is melted, 1-2 minutes on each side.
1 sandwich: 428 cal., 23g fat (8g sat. fat), 53mg chol., 1146mg sod., 33g carb. (3g sugars, 2g fiber), 21g pro.
Havarti-Mushroom Grilled Cheese: Layer two slices rye bread with 3 oz. sliced Havarti with dill cheese; top with one sliced tomato, ½ cup sliced fresh mushrooms, another 3 oz. Havarti with dill, and two slices rye. Butter sandwiches and cook as directed.

5 INGREDIENT
APRICOT HAM STEAK

Ham is a versatile main menu item that's a standby with all country cooks. One of the best and easiest ways to serve ham slices is topped off with a slightly sweet glaze, like this apricot version.
—Scott Woodward, Shullsburg, WI

Takes: 10 min. • **Makes:** 4 servings

- 2 Tbsp. butter, divided
- 4 fully cooked boneless ham steaks (5 oz. each)
- ½ cup apricot preserves
- 1 Tbsp. cider vinegar
- ¼ tsp. ground ginger
  Dash salt

1. In a large skillet, heat 1 Tbsp. butter over medium heat. Cook ham on both sides until lightly browned and heated through. Remove from the pan; keep warm.
2. Add 1 Tbsp. butter and remaining ingredients to pan; cook and stir over medium heat until blended and heated through. Serve over ham.

1 ham steak: 299 cal., 11g fat (5g sat. fat), 88mg chol., 1899mg sod., 26g carb. (17g sugars, 0 fiber), 26g pro.

Grilled Apricot Ham Steaks: Melt 1 Tbsp. butter and brush over ham steaks. Grill, covered, over medium heat until lightly browned, 3-5 minutes on each side. Serve as directed.

SESAME SHRIMP & RICE

Just a handful of convenience items and a quick flash in the skillet allow you to put a delightfully flavorful, high-quality meal on the table in minutes.
—*Taste of Home* Test Kitchen

Takes: 10 min. • **Makes:** 4 servings

- 1 pkg. (8.8 oz.) ready-to-serve long grain rice
- 1 cup fresh or frozen snow peas, thawed
- 2 green onions, sliced
- 1 tsp. canola oil
- 1 lb. cooked medium shrimp, peeled and deveined
- 1 can (20 oz.) pineapple tidbits, drained
- 1 can (11 oz.) mandarin oranges, drained
- ¼ cup sesame ginger salad dressing
- 2 Tbsp. slivered almonds, toasted

1. Microwave rice according to package directions. Meanwhile, in a large skillet or wok, stir-fry the snow peas and onions in oil for 1 minute. Add the shrimp, pineapple, oranges and salad dressing; cook until heated through and the vegetables are crisp-tender.
2. Sprinkle with almonds. Serve with rice.

1½ cups: 407 cal., 11g fat (1g sat. fat), 172mg chol., 330mg sod., 49g carb. (24g sugars, 3g fiber), 28g pro.

TURKEY-CRANBERRY BAGELS

Take care of that leftover Thanksgiving turkey in a way your family will love. It's good with all sorts of cranberry sauces and chutneys, so have fun playing around.
—*Taste of Home* Test Kitchen

Takes: 10 min. • **Makes:** 4 servings

  4   plain bagels, split and toasted
  8   oz. thinly sliced cooked turkey
  8   slices provolone cheese
  ½   cup whole-berry cranberry sauce

Preheat broiler. Place bagel halves on a baking sheet; layer with turkey, cheese and cranberry sauce. Broil 4-6 in. from heat until the cheese is melted, 1-2 minutes.

2 bagel halves: 469 cal., 16g fat (8g sat. fat), 73mg chol., 645mg sod., 49g carb. (12g sugars, 2g fiber), 34g pro.

SPEEDY SURPRISE

"These are delicious! They're so simple—why didn't I think of that? I'm going to be making these all year long! Maybe add a little crispy bacon!"

—CYNANDTOM, TASTEOFHOME.COM

CANNOLI DIP

Ricotta is one of my family's favorite ingredients. I made up the cannoli filling and broke up some ice cream waffle shells to use as chips and dip—it was an instant hit! It's also good served slightly warm.
—Ann Marie Eberhart, Gig Harbor, WA

- -

Takes: 10 min. • **Makes:** 8 servings

- 1   carton (15 oz.) whole-milk ricotta cheese
- ¾   cup confectioners' sugar
- 1   Tbsp. finely chopped candied citron
- 1   Tbsp. grated lime zest
    Mini ice cream sugar cones, optional
    Miniature semisweet chocolate chips, optional

Beat together the ricotta cheese, sugar, candied citron and lime zest. If desired, scoop ricotta mixture into mini ice cream cones and sprinkle with chocolate chips.
¼ cup: 128 cal., 5g fat (3g sat. fat), 21mg chol., 70mg sod., 16g carb. (15g sugars, 0 fiber), 6g pro.

TEST KITCHEN TIP

Do not use a food processor to chop the citron for this recipe— it could make it too fine, and its flavor is more intense with slightly larger bits.

PUMPKIN MILK SHAKES

My son loved this festive milk shake growing up—it's nicely spiced and tastes like pumpkin pie. I like cutting off both ends of a licorice twist and serving it as a straw.
—Joan Hallford, North Richland Hills, TX

- -

Takes: 10 min. • **Makes:** 6 servings

- 1   cup orange juice
- 4   cups vanilla ice cream
- 1   cup canned pumpkin
- ½   cup packed brown sugar
- 1   tsp. ground cinnamon
- ½   tsp. ground ginger
- ½   tsp. ground nutmeg
    Black licorice twists, optional

In batches, place first seven ingredients in a blender. Cover and process until the mixture is smooth, 20-30 seconds. Serve immediately with licorice stirrers if desired.
1 cup: 287 cal., 10g fat (6g sat. fat), 39mg chol., 78mg sod., 47g carb. (42g sugars, 2g fiber), 4g pro.

NO-BAKE PEANUT BUTTER TREATS

This quick and tasty dessert is perfect for a road trip. The treats won't stick to your hands, so you'll crave more than one. Keep them on hand in the refrigerator for an easy snack.
—Sonia Rohda, Waverly, NE

- -

Takes: 10 min. • **Makes:** 15 treats

⅓ cup chunky peanut butter
¼ cup honey
½ tsp. vanilla extract
⅓ cup nonfat dry milk powder
⅓ cup quick-cooking oats
2 Tbsp. graham cracker crumbs

In a small bowl, combine the peanut butter, honey and vanilla. Stir in the milk powder, oats and graham cracker crumbs. Shape the mixture into 1-in. balls. Cover and refrigerate until serving.
1 treat: 70 cal., 3g fat (1g sat. fat), 1mg chol., 46mg sod., 9g carb. (6g sugars, 1g fiber), 3g pro. **Diabetic exchanges:** ½ starch, ½ fat.

LEMON MERINGUE FLOATS

I actually dreamed of this float idea one night, and woke up knowing I needed to make it. Thank you, Mr. Sandman!
—Cindy Reams, Philipsburg, PA

- -

Takes: 5 min. • **Makes:** 6 servings

3 cups vanilla ice cream, softened if necessary
18 miniature meringue cookies
6 cups cold pink lemonade

Place ½ cup ice cream and three cookies in each of six tall glasses. Top with lemonade. Serve immediately.
1½ cups with 3 cookies: 282 cal., 7g fat (4g sat. fat), 29mg chol., 77mg sod., 51g carb. (48g sugars, 0 fiber), 3g pro.

TEST KITCHEN TIP
Make your floats with frozen yogurt for a slimmed-down but still tempting treat.

DUNKED STRAWBERRIES

Dressed-up strawberries give any meal an elegant finish. With brown sugar and a hint of lime, they're sweet, tangy and so tasty, you'll want more!
—Jennifer Reid, Farmington, ME

- -

Takes: 5 min. • **Makes:** 4 servings

- ½ cup sour cream
- ½ tsp. grated lime zest
- ½ cup packed brown sugar
- 12 fresh strawberries

In a small bowl, combine the sour cream and lime zest. Place brown sugar in another small bowl. Dip strawberries in the sour cream mixture, then coat with brown sugar. Serve immediately.

3 dipped strawberries: 187 cal., 5g fat (4g sat. fat), 20mg chol., 21mg sod., 33g carb. (31g sugars, 1g fiber), 1g pro.

SPEEDY SURPRISE

"Don't let the sour cream scare you away...these are so creamy and delicious! The first time I made these, I was at my sister's house and neither she nor my brother-in-law like sour cream, but they must have had at least five each! These are creamy, cool, sweet (but not too sweet), with the right amount of tang from the lime zest."

—LMGRBGCAB, TASTEOFHOME.COM

HAZELNUT MOCHA SMOOTHIES

This smooth blend of coffee, cocoa and nutty flavors is better than any coffeehouse version we've tried. Try it, and we're sure you will agree.
—*Taste of Home* Test Kitchen

- -

Takes: 10 min. • **Makes:** 3 servings

- 1 cup whole milk
- ½ cup Nutella
- 4 tsp. instant espresso powder
- 6 ice cubes
- 2 cups vanilla ice cream
  Chocolate curls, optional

In a blender, combine the milk, Nutella and espresso powder; cover and process until blended. Add ice cubes; cover and process until smooth. Add ice cream; cover and process until smooth. Pour into chilled glasses; serve immediately. Garnish with chocolate curls if desired.

1 cup: 474 cal., 27g fat (10g sat. fat), 47mg chol., 124mg sod., 55g carb. (46g sugars, 2g fiber), 9g pro.

FRUIT & GRANOLA CRISP WITH YOGURT

Here's an easy dessert you'll be happy to serve. Blueberries and peaches are such a delightful flavor combination.
—Sue Schmidtke, Oro Valley, AZ

- -

Takes: 10 min. • **Makes:** 4 servings

- 3 **cups fresh or frozen sliced peaches, thawed**
- 1 **cup fresh or frozen blueberries, thawed**
- 4 **Tbsp. hot caramel ice cream topping**
- 4 **Tbsp. granola without raisins**
- 2 **cups low-fat frozen yogurt**

Divide the peaches and blueberries among four 8-oz. ramekins. Top each with caramel and granola. Microwave, uncovered, on high until bubbly, 1-2 minutes. Top each with a scoop of frozen yogurt.
1 serving: 251 cal., 3g fat (1g sat. fat), 5mg chol., 133mg sod., 54g carb. (33g sugars, 4g fiber), 7g pro.

MANGO SORBET DESSERT

Not only is this recipe easy to prepare, it's also packed with fruit so you can feel good while eating your cake and ice cream!
—Katie Rose, Pewaukee, WI

- -

Takes: 10 min. • **Makes:** 4 servings

- ½ **cup seedless raspberry preserves**
- 1 **Tbsp. orange juice**
- ¼ **tsp. almond extract**
- 4 **slices angel food cake**
- 4 **scoops mango sorbet**
- 1 **cup fresh raspberries**
- ¼ **cup sliced almonds**

1. In a small microwave-safe bowl, combine preserves and orange juice. Microwave, uncovered, on high until heated through, about 30 seconds. Stir in extract.
2. Divide cake slices among four dessert plates. Top each with sorbet, preserve mixture, raspberries and almonds.
1 serving: 376 cal., 3g fat (0 sat. fat), 0 chol., 212mg sod., 86g carb. (62g sugars, 3g fiber), 3g pro.

5 INGREDIENT

CHERRY-CHOCOLATE PUDGY PIE

Here's an ooey-gooey treat that's just right for campfires and cookouts.
—Josh Carter, Birmingham, AL

- -

Takes: 10 min. • **Makes:** 1 serving

- 2   slices white bread
- 3   Tbsp. cherry pie filling
- 1   Tbsp. chopped almonds
- 1   Tbsp. semisweet chocolate chips

1. Place one slice of bread in a greased sandwich iron. Spread with pie filling; top with almonds, chocolate chips and the remaining bread slice. Close iron.

2. Cook over a hot campfire until golden brown and heated through, 3-6 minutes, turning occasionally.

1 sandwich: 309 cal., 9g fat (3g sat. fat), 0 chol., 294mg sod., 51g carb. (9g sugars, 3g fiber), 7g pro.

CHOCOLATE CINNAMON TOAST

Looking for a fun dessert or snack? Toast cinnamon bread in a skillet and top with chocolate and fresh fruit. Add a small dollop of whipped cream to each slice to make it extra indulgent.
—Jeanne Ambrose, Milwaukee, WI

- -

Takes: 10 min. • **Makes:** 1 serving

- 1 slice cinnamon bread
- 1 tsp. butter, softened
- 2 Tbsp. 60% cacao bittersweet chocolate baking chips
  Sliced banana and strawberries, optional

Spread both sides of bread with butter. In a small skillet, toast bread over medium-high heat 2-3 minutes on each side, topping with chocolate chips after turning. Remove from heat; spread melted chocolate evenly over toast. If desired, top with fruit.

1 serving: 235 cal., 13g fat (8g sat. fat), 10mg chol., 131mg sod., 29g carb. (19g sugars, 3g fiber), 4g pro.

MARSHMALLOW WANDS

These marshmallow pops are a hit with the kids. Let them drizzle away with their favorite colors!
—James Schend, Pleasant Prairie, WI

- -

Takes: 10 min. • **Makes:** 12 pops

- 2 cups semisweet chocolate chips
- 2 Tbsp. shortening
- 36 large marshmallows
- 12 lollipop sticks
  Assorted colored candy coating, melted

In a microwave, melt chocolate chips and shortening; stir until smooth. Skewer three marshmallows on each stick. Spoon the chocolate mixture over the marshmallows; set on waxed paper until firm. Drizzle with the melted colored candy coating.

1 pop: 74 cal., 3g fat (2g sat. fat), 0 chol., 7mg sod., 12g carb. (9g sugars, 1g fiber), 1g pro.

TEST KITCHEN TIP

For a neat drizzle, transfer the melted candy coating to a resealable plastic bag and cut a small hole in one corner. While moving back and forth over the bars, gently squeeze out the melted candy coating.

CREAMY PINEAPPLE PIE

This light and refreshing dessert is quick to make and impressive to serve—it's one of our favorite ways to complete a summer meal.
—Sharon Bickett, Chester, SC

Takes: 10 min. • **Makes:** 8 servings

1 can (14 oz.) sweetened condensed milk
1 can (8 oz.) crushed pineapple, undrained
¼ cup lemon juice
1 carton (8 oz.) frozen whipped topping, thawed
1 prepared graham cracker crust (9 in.)
  Chopped toasted macadamia nuts and additional crushed pineapple, optional

Combine milk, pineapple and lemon juice; fold in whipped topping. Pour into prepared crust. Refrigerate until serving. If desired, serve with toasted macadamia nuts and additional crushed pineapple.

Note: To toast nuts, bake in a shallow pan in a 350° oven for 5-10 minutes or cook in a skillet over low heat until lightly browned, stirring occasionally.

1 piece: 367 cal., 14g fat (9g sat. fat), 17mg chol., 185mg sod., 54g carb. (46g sugars, 1g fiber), 5g pro.

---

5 INGREDIENT

APPLE YOGURT PARFAITS

Get the morning started right with this super simple four-ingredient parfait. Try chunky or flavored applesauce for easy variations.
—Rebekah Radewahn, Wauwatosa, WI

Takes: 10 min. • **Makes:** 4 servings

1 cup sweetened applesauce
  Dash ground nutmeg
½ cup granola with raisins
1⅓ cups vanilla yogurt

In a small bowl, combine the applesauce and nutmeg. Spoon 1 Tbsp. granola into each of four parfait glasses. Layer each glass with ⅓ cup yogurt and ¼ cup applesauce; sprinkle with the remaining granola. Serve immediately.

1 parfait: 158 cal., 2g fat (1g sat. fat), 4mg chol., 70mg sod., 30g carb. (24g sugars, 1g fiber), 5g pro.

20 MINUTES

20 MINUTE SNACKS

SPRUCED-UP CHEESE SPREAD

A neighbor, who's a wonderful cook, gave me the recipe for this tasty cracker spread. With only two quick steps, it's so easy but the flavor really packs a punch.
—Judy Grimes, Brandon, MS

Takes: 20 min.
Makes: 4 cups

- 1 cup mayonnaise
- 1 small onion, grated
- 1 to 2 Tbsp. prepared mustard
- 1 Tbsp. Worcestershire sauce
- 1 tsp. celery seed
- ½ tsp. paprika
- ¼ tsp. garlic salt
- 1 jar (4 oz.) diced pimientos, drained, divided
- 3 cups finely shredded sharp cheddar cheese
  Minced fresh parsley
- 2 Tbsp. finely chopped pecans
  Assorted crackers

1. Mix first seven ingredients and ⅓ cup pimientos. Stir in cheese.
2. Transfer to a serving dish. Sprinkle with parsley, pecans and remaining pimientos. Serve with crackers.

2 Tbsp. spread: 93 cal., 9g fat (3g sat. fat), 11mg chol., 131mg sod., 1g carb. (0 sugars, 0 fiber), 3g pro.

HERB-ROASTED OLIVES & TOMATOES

Serve these roasted veggies alongside a crunchy baguette or sliced cheeses. You can also double or triple the amounts and have leftovers to toss with spaghetti the next day for dinner.
—Anndrea Bailey, Huntington Beach, CA

Takes: 20 min. • **Makes:** 4 cups

- 2 cups cherry tomatoes
- 1 cup garlic-stuffed olives
- 1 cup Greek olives
- 1 cup pitted ripe olives
- 8 garlic cloves, peeled
- 3 Tbsp. olive oil
- 1 Tbsp. herbes de Provence
- ¼ tsp. pepper

Preheat oven to 425°. Combine the first five ingredients on a greased 15x10x1-in. baking pan. Add oil and seasonings; toss to coat. Roast until the tomatoes are softened, 15-20 minutes, stirring occasionally.
Note: Look for herbes de Provence in the spice aisle.
¼ cup: 71 cal., 7g fat (1g sat. fat), 0 chol., 380mg sod., 3g carb. (1g sugars, 1g fiber), 0 pro.

ARTICHOKE & SPINACH DIP PIZZA

When I have it in my pantry, I substitute garlic oil for regular olive oil to add just a little bit of excitement to this easy pizza.
—Shelly Bevington, Hermiston, OR

Takes: 20 min. • **Makes:** 24 pieces

1   prebaked 12-in. pizza crust
1   Tbsp. olive oil
1   cup spinach dip
1   cup shredded part-skim mozzarella cheese
1   jar (7½ oz.) marinated quartered artichoke hearts, drained
½   cup oil-packed sun-dried tomatoes, patted dry and chopped
¼   cup chopped red onion

1. Preheat oven to 450°. Place crust on an ungreased pizza pan; brush with oil. Spread spinach dip over top. Sprinkle with cheese, artichokes, tomatoes and onion.
2. Bake until the cheese is melted and edges are lightly browned, 8-10 minutes. Cut into 24 pieces.
1 piece: 127 cal., 9g fat (2g sat. fat), 6mg chol., 213mg sod., 10g carb. (1g sugars, 0 fiber), 3g pro.

5 INGREDIENT
SPICY EDAMAME

Edamame are young soybeans in their pods. In our Test Kitchen, we boiled and seasoned them with salt, ginger, garlic powder and red pepper flakes for a fast and easy snack.
—*Taste of Home* Test Kitchen

Takes: 20 min. • **Makes:** 6 servings

1   pkg. (16 oz.) frozen edamame pods
2   tsp. kosher salt
¾   tsp. ground ginger
½   tsp. garlic powder
¼   tsp. crushed red pepper flakes

Place edamame in a large saucepan and cover with water. Bring to a boil. Cover and cook until tender, 4-5 minutes; drain. Transfer to a large bowl. Add seasonings; toss to coat.
1 serving: 52 cal., 2g fat (0 sat. fat), 0 chol., 642mg sod., 5g carb. (1g sugars, 2g fiber), 4g pro.

FRUIT COMPOTE WITH BRIE

This yummy compote is so versatile. I stir it into yogurt or serve it over cheesecake, ice cream, blintzes and crepes. Of course, it makes Brie taste amazing!
—Clara Coulson Minney, Washington Court House, OH

- -

Takes: 15 min. • **Makes:** 8 servings

- 1   round (8 oz.) Brie cheese
- ⅔   cup golden raisins and cherries
- ⅓   cup unsweetened apple juice
- 1   tsp. vanilla extract
- 1   Tbsp. cherry preserves
     Assorted crackers

1. Place cheese on an ungreased oven-proof serving plate. Bake at 400° until cheese is softened, 8-10 minutes.
2. Meanwhile, in a small saucepan, combine the golden raisins and cherries, apple juice and vanilla; bring to a boil. Remove from the heat; stir in preserves. Spoon over cheese. Serve with crackers.

1 serving: 140 cal., 8g fat (5g sat. fat), 28mg chol., 179mg sod., 11g carb. (9g sugars, 1g fiber), 6g pro.

BEST DEVILED EGGS

Herbs lend amazing flavor, making these the best deviled eggs you can make!
—Jesse & Anne Foust, Bluefield, WV

- -

Takes: 15 min. • **Makes:** 2 dozen

- ½   cup mayonnaise
- 2   Tbsp. 2% milk
- 1   tsp. dried parsley flakes
- ½   tsp. dill weed
- ½   tsp. minced chives
- ½   tsp. ground mustard
- ¼   tsp. salt
- ¼   tsp. paprika
- ⅛   tsp. garlic powder
- ⅛   tsp. pepper
- 12   hard-boiled large eggs
     Minced fresh parsley and additional paprika

In a small bowl, combine the first 10 ingredients. Slice the eggs in half lengthwise; remove yolks and set whites aside. In another bowl, mash yolks; add to mayonnaise mixture, mixing well. Spoon or pipe filling into egg whites. Sprinkle with parsley and additional paprika. Refrigerate until serving.

1 stuffed egg half: 73 cal., 6g fat (1g sat. fat), 108mg chol., 81mg sod., 0 carb. (0 sugars, 0 fiber), 3g pro.

ASPARAGUS WITH BASIL PESTO SAUCE

Add zip to your appetizer platter with an easy asparagus dip that can also double as a full-flavored sandwich spread.
—Janie Colle, Hutchinson, KS

- -

Takes: 15 min. • **Makes:** 12 servings

- ¾ cup reduced-fat mayonnaise
- 2 Tbsp. prepared pesto
- 1 Tbsp. grated Parmesan cheese
- 1 Tbsp. minced fresh basil
- 1 tsp. lemon juice
- 1 garlic clove, minced
- 1½ lbs. fresh asparagus, trimmed

1. In a small bowl, mix first six ingredients until blended; refrigerate until serving.
2. In a Dutch oven, bring 12 cups water to a boil. Add asparagus in batches; cook, uncovered, until crisp-tender, 2-3 minutes. Remove and immediately drop into ice water. Drain and pat dry. Serve with sauce.
1 serving: 72 cal., 6g fat (1g sat. fat), 6mg chol., 149mg sod., 3g carb. (1g sugars, 1g fiber), 1g pro. **Diabetic exchanges:** 1½ fat.

SHRIMP TARTLETS

Mini tart shells are filled with a cream cheese mixture, then topped with seafood sauce and shrimp for this picture-perfect appetizer. You could also serve several as a fast, light meal alongside a salad.
—Gina Hutchison, Smithville, MO

- -

Takes: 20 min. • **Makes:** 2½ dozen

- 1 pkg. (8 oz.) cream cheese, softened
- 1½ tsp. Worcestershire sauce
- 1 to 2 tsp. grated onion
- 1 tsp. garlic salt
- ⅛ tsp. lemon juice
- 2 pkg. (1.9 oz. each) frozen miniature phyllo tart shells
- ½ cup seafood cocktail sauce
- 30 peeled and deveined cooked shrimp (31-40 per lb.), tails removed
  Minced fresh parsley and lemon wedges, optional

1. Beat first five ingredients until blended. Place tart shells on a serving plate. Fill with cream cheese mixture; top with cocktail sauce and shrimp.
2. Refrigerate until serving. If desired, sprinkle tartlets with parsley and serve with lemon wedges.
1 tartlet: 61 cal., 4g fat (2g sat. fat), 23mg chol., 143mg sod., 4g carb. (1g sugars, 0 fiber), 3g pro.

5 INGREDIENT
PESTO-GOAT CHEESE TOASTS

I came across this fast and easy recipe years ago. Everyone who tries these little toasts absolutely loves them. The pesto is easy to find in the grocery store, and it blends beautifully with the tangy, creamy goat cheese.
—Jennifer Kunz, Troy, MI

Takes: 20 min. • **Makes:** 16 servings

- 16 slices French bread (½ in. thick)
- 1 log (11 oz.) fresh goat cheese, cut into 16 slices
- 3 Tbsp. prepared pesto

1. Preheat oven to 425°. Place French bread slices on a baking sheet; top with cheese.
2. Bake until cheese begins to brown and bread is toasted, 10-12 minutes. Top with pesto. Serve warm.
1 toast: 74 cal., 4g fat (2g sat. fat), 13mg chol., 181mg sod., 7g carb. (0 sugars, 0 fiber), 3g pro.

TEST KITCHEN TIP

Dress up these no-fuss bites with diced tomatoes, thin slices of pepperoni, chopped chives, tiny strips of sweet red pepper, pimientos or a sprinkling of grated Parmesan cheese.

EAT SMART
FRESH CORN & AVOCADO DIP

I alter my sister's dip recipe by adding finely chopped jalapeno for a little heat. It's a different way of serving corn as a dip that can be made ahead of time and then refrigerated until serving.
—Pat Roberts, Thornton, ON

Takes: 20 min. • **Makes:** 4 cups

- 2 cups fresh or frozen corn, thawed
- 1 medium ripe avocado, peeled and diced
- 1 small peach, peeled and chopped
- 1 small sweet red pepper, chopped
- 1 small red onion, chopped
- 2 Tbsp. olive oil
- 2 Tbsp. white wine vinegar
- 1 Tbsp. lime juice
- 1½ tsp. ground cumin
- 1 tsp. minced fresh oregano
- 1 garlic clove, crushed
   Salt and pepper to taste
- 1 minced and seeded jalapeno pepper, optional
   Baked tortilla chips

Combine first 11 ingredients; add salt and pepper and, if desired, jalapeno. Serve with tortilla chips.
¼ cup: 52 cal., 3g fat (0 sat. fat), 0 chol., 4mg sod., 6g carb. (2g sugars, 1g fiber), 1g pro.
Diabetic exchanges: ½ starch, ½ fat.

SHRIMP SALAD APPETIZERS

This refreshing hors d'oeuvre has gained a big following since a friend shared her family recipe with me. My 7-year-old son says it best: "The celery and shrimp are so yummy together."
—Solie Kimble, Kanata, ON

- -

Takes: 15 min. • **Makes:** 2 dozen

- 1 lb. peeled and deveined cooked shrimp, chopped
- 1 can (6 oz.) lump crabmeat, drained
- 2 celery ribs, finely chopped
- ¼ cup Dijon-mayonnaise blend
- 24 Belgian endive leaves (3-4 heads) or small butterhead lettuce leaves

In a large bowl, combine shrimp, crab and celery. Add mayonnaise blend; toss to coat. To serve, top each leaf with about 2 Tbsp. shrimp mixture.

1 appetizer: 31 cal., 0 fat (0 sat. fat), 35mg chol., 115mg sod., 1g carb. (0 sugars, 0 fiber), 5g pro.

SPEEDY SURPRISE

"I made this delicious appetizer and declare it a five-star winner. It's delicious and super simple to prepare. The lettuce leaf makes a nice presentation, but I baked bread in a scalloped bread tube yesterday and sliced it for the shrimp salad. It made a very pretty appetizer."

—MARINEMOM_TEXAS, TASTEOFHOME.COM

ARTICHOKE CAPRESE PLATTER

I dressed up the classic Italian trio of mozzarella, tomatoes and basil with marinated artichokes. It looks so fantastic on a pretty platter set out on a buffet. I think that using fresh mozzarella is the key to its great flavor.
—Margaret Wilson, San Bernardino, CA

- -

Takes: 15 min. • **Makes:** 12 servings

- 2 jars (7½ oz. each) marinated artichoke hearts
- 2 Tbsp. red wine vinegar
- 2 Tbsp. olive oil
- 6 plum tomatoes, sliced
- 1 lb. fresh mozzarella cheese, sliced
- 2 cups loosely packed fresh basil leaves
  Coarsely ground pepper, optional

1. Drain the artichokes, reserving ½ cup marinade. In a small bowl, whisk vinegar, oil and reserved marinade.

2. On a large serving platter, arrange the artichokes, tomatoes, mozzarella cheese and basil. Drizzle with vinaigrette. If desired, sprinkle with coarsely ground pepper.

Note: Fresh mozzarella can be found in the deli section of most grocery stores.

½ cup: 192 cal., 16g fat (7g sat. fat), 30mg chol., 179mg sod., 5g carb. (2g sugars, 1g fiber), 7g pro.

PIMIENTO CHEESE DEVILED EGGS

For my mother's 92nd birthday, we had deviled eggs topped with pimientos as part of the spread. They're quick, timeless and always in good taste.
—Linda Foreman, Locust Grove, OK

Takes: 15 min. • **Makes:** 1 dozen

- 6 hard-boiled large eggs
- ¼ cup finely shredded sharp cheddar cheese
- 2 Tbsp. mayonnaise
- 4 tsp. diced pimientos, drained
- 2 tsp. finely chopped sweet onion
- 1 tsp. Dijon mustard
- 1 small garlic clove, minced
- ¼ tsp. salt
- ⅛ tsp. pepper
   Additional diced pimientos and finely shredded sharp cheddar cheese

Cut eggs lengthwise in half. Remove yolks, reserving whites. In a bowl, mash yolks. Stir in cheese, mayonnaise, pimientos, onion, mustard, garlic, salt and pepper. Spoon or pipe into the egg whites. Sprinkle with additional pimientos and cheese. Refrigerate, covered, until serving.

1 stuffed egg half: 67 cal., 5g fat (2g sat. fat), 96mg chol., 128mg sod., 1g carb. (0 sugars, 0 fiber), 4g pro.

HAWAIIAN CRAB CANAPES

Treat your guests to a taste of paradise with crab, macadamia nuts, pineapple preserves and coconut. The sweet, crunchy canapes are a breeze to make and a joy to eat.

—Jamie Miller, Maple Grove, MN

Takes: 20 min. • **Makes:** about 4 dozen

- 1 carton (8 oz.) spreadable chive and onion cream cheese
- 1 pkg. (3.2 oz.) teriyaki rice crackers
- 1 can (6 oz.) lump crabmeat, drained
- 1 jar (12 oz.) pineapple preserves
- ¾ cup sweetened shredded coconut, toasted
- ½ cup chopped macadamia nuts, toasted
- 2 Tbsp. minced chives

Spread cream cheese over crackers. Top with the crab, preserves, coconut, nuts and chives.

1 appetizer: 58 cal., 3g fat (1g sat. fat), 6mg chol., 53mg sod., 7g carb. (5g sugars, 0 fiber), 1g pro.

TEST KITCHEN TIP

Macadamia nuts lend incredible taste and texture to these easy appetizers, but feel free to swap them with chopped peanuts or cashews or simply leave them out altogether.

PUMPKIN HUMMUS

Our home economists give traditional hummus an autumn appeal with the addition of canned pumpkin. Hot pepper sauce lends just the right amount of heat.

—*Taste of Home* Test Kitchen

Takes: 15 min. • **Makes:** 4 cups

- 2 cans (15 oz. each) garbanzo beans or chickpeas, rinsed and drained
- 1 can (15 oz.) solid-pack pumpkin
- ½ cup olive oil
- ⅓ cup tahini
- 5 Tbsp. lemon juice
- 2 tsp. hot pepper sauce
- 2 garlic cloves, minced
- 1 tsp. salt
  Baked pita chips
  Assorted fresh vegetables, optional

Place the first eight ingredients in a food processor; cover and process until blended. Serve with chips and vegetables as desired.

¼ cup: 173 cal., 13g fat (2g sat. fat), 0 chol., 243mg sod., 12g carb. (2g sugars, 4g fiber), 5g pro.

5 INGREDIENT
APRICOT KIELBASA SLICES

These satisfying sausage bites are coated in a thick, zesty sauce with just the right amount of sweetness. You'll love 'em!
—Barbara McCalley, Allison Park, PA

Takes: 15 min.
Makes: 12 servings

- 1   lb. fully cooked kielbasa or Polish sausage, cut into ¼-in. slices
- 1   jar (12 oz.) apricot preserves
- 2   Tbsp. lemon juice
- 2   tsp. Dijon mustard
- ¼   tsp. ground ginger

1. In a large cast-iron skillet, cook and stir sausage until browned. Remove from pan; discard drippings.
2. Add remaining ingredients to skillet; cook and stir over low heat until heated through, 2-3 minutes. Stir in sausage; heat through.
4 slices: 47 cal., 3g fat (1g sat. fat), 6mg chol., 110mg sod., 5g carb. (4g sugars, 0 fiber), 1g pro.

5 INGREDIENT
GOUDA MELT WITH BAGUETTE SLICES

This fun appetizer is guaranteed to wow guests. It takes just moments to whip up the melty delight.
—Susan Lewis, Leland, NC

Takes: 20 min. • **Makes:** 4 servings

- 1   French bread baguette (4 oz.), sliced
- 1   round (7 oz.) Gouda cheese
- 1   plum tomato, seeded and chopped
- 1   Tbsp. minced fresh basil

1. Place baguette slices on an ungreased baking sheet. Broil 3-4 in. from the heat until toasted, 1-2 minutes on each side.
2. Meanwhile, carefully remove waxed coating from cheese round. Using a 3-in. biscuit cutter, press into the center of cheese, but not all the way through. Scoop out the center, leaving a ¼-in. shell; set the shell aside.
3. Place tomato, basil and removed cheese in a small microwave-safe bowl. Cover and microwave on high until cheese is melted, about 1 minute. Stir until combined; pour into shell. Serve with baguette toasts.
1 serving: 303 cal., 17g fat (9g sat. fat), 57mg chol., 578mg sod., 24g carb. (2g sugars, 2g fiber), 15g pro.

GARBANZO-STUFFED MINI PEPPERS

Mini peppers are so colorful, and they're the perfect size for a two-bite appetizer. They have all the crunch of a pita chip, without the extra calories.
—Christine Hanover, Lewiston, CA

Takes: 20 min. • **Makes:** 32 appetizers

- 1 tsp. cumin seeds
- 1 can (15 oz.) garbanzo beans or chickpeas, rinsed and drained
- ¼ cup fresh cilantro leaves
- 3 Tbsp. water
- 3 Tbsp. cider vinegar
- ¼ tsp. salt
- 16 miniature sweet peppers, halved lengthwise
  Additional fresh cilantro leaves

1. In a dry small skillet, toast cumin seeds over medium heat until aromatic, stirring frequently, 1-2 minutes. Transfer to a food processor. Add garbanzo beans, cilantro, water, vinegar and salt; pulse until blended.
2. Spoon into pepper halves. Top with the additional cilantro. Refrigerate until serving.
1 appetizer: 15 cal., 0 fat (0 sat. fat), 0 chol., 36mg sod., 3g carb. (1g sugars, 1g fiber), 1g pro.

> ### SPEEDY SURPRISE
> *"I absolutely loved this recipe. Delicious—such great flavor!"*
> —CINDIHARTLINE, TASTEOFHOME.COM

BEER & CHEDDAR FONDUE

This great-tasting fondue is my mom's favorite, so I make it for her birthday every year. I like to serve it with apple slices, rye bread cubes and chunks of carrots, celery, zucchini, broccoli and even squash.
—Amanda Wentz, Virginia Beach, VA

Takes: 15 min. • **Makes:** 2 cups

- 4 cups shredded cheddar cheese
- 1 Tbsp. all-purpose flour
- 1 cup beer or nonalcoholic beer
- 3 garlic cloves, minced
- 1½ tsp. ground mustard
- ¼ tsp. coarsely ground pepper
  Radishes, sliced apples and breadsticks

1. In a large bowl, combine cheese and flour. In a small saucepan, heat the beer, garlic, mustard and pepper over medium heat until bubbles form around sides of pan.
2. Reduce heat to medium-low; add a handful of cheese mixture. Stir constantly, using a figure-eight motion, until almost completely melted. Continue adding cheese, one handful at a time, allowing cheese to almost completely melt between additions. Keep warm. Serve with radishes, sliced apples and breadsticks.
¼ cup fondue: 221 cal., 16g fat (12g sat. fat), 60mg chol., 341mg sod., 4g carb. (1g sugars, 0 fiber), 12g pro.

20 MINUTE SIDES

SPRING PEA & RADISH SALAD

Winters can be very long here in New Hampshire. I always look forward to the first veggies of spring and making some lighter dishes like this fresh salad.
—Jolene Martinelli, Fremont, NH

Takes: 20 min. • **Makes:** 6 servings

- ½ lb. fresh wax or green beans
- ½ lb. fresh sugar snap peas
- 2 cups water
- 6 large radishes, thinly sliced
- 2 Tbsp. honey
- 1 tsp. dried tarragon
- ¼ tsp. kosher salt
- ¼ tsp. coarsely ground pepper

1. Snip ends off beans and sugar snap peas; remove strings from snap peas. In a large saucepan, bring water to a boil over high heat. Add the beans, reduce heat; simmer, covered, 4-5 minutes. Add sugar snap peas; simmer, covered, until both the beans and sugar snap peas are crisp-tender, another 2-3 minutes. Drain.

2. Toss beans and peas with radishes. Stir together honey, tarragon, salt and pepper. Drizzle over vegetables.

⅔ cup: 50 cal., 0 fat (0 sat. fat), 0 chol., 86mg sod., 11g carb. (8g sugars, 2g fiber), 2g pro. **Diabetic exchanges:** 1 vegetable, ½ starch.

CHEESE & GARLIC BISCUITS

My biscuits won the title Best Quick Bread at my county fair. One of the judges liked it so much, she asked for the recipe! You'll see that these buttery, savory biscuits go with just about anything.
—Gloria Jarrett, Loveland, OH

Takes: 20 min. • **Makes:** 2½ dozen

- 2½ cups biscuit/baking mix
- ¾ cup shredded sharp cheddar cheese
- 1 tsp. garlic powder
- 1 tsp. ranch salad dressing mix
- 1 cup buttermilk

TOPPING

- ½ cup butter, melted
- 1 Tbsp. minced chives
- ½ tsp. garlic powder
- ½ tsp. ranch salad dressing mix
- ¼ tsp. pepper

1. In a large bowl, combine the baking mix, cheese, garlic powder and salad dressing mix. Stir in buttermilk just until moistened. Drop by tablespoonfuls onto greased baking sheets.

2. Bake at 450° until biscuits are golden brown, 6-8 minutes. Meanwhile, combine topping ingredients. Brush over biscuits.

1 biscuit: 81 cal., 5g fat (3g sat. fat), 11mg chol., 176mg sod., 7g carb. (1g sugars, 0 fiber), 2g pro.

5 INGREDIENT
ROMANO STICKS

It's hard to stop at just one of these yummy breadsticks. I can make them quickly using puff pastry and just a few other items.
—Viki Ailport, West Lakeland, MN

- -

Takes: 20 min. • **Makes:** 20 pastry sticks

- 1 pkg. (17.3 oz.) frozen puff pastry, thawed
- 1 large egg, lightly beaten
- 1½ cups grated Romano cheese
- 1 Tbsp. dried basil

1. Brush one side of each puff pastry sheet with egg; sprinkle with cheese and basil. Cut each sheet into ten 1-in. strips. Place 1 in. apart on greased baking sheets.
2. Bake at 400° until the sticks are golden brown, 10-13 minutes.
1 pastry stick: 160 cal., 10g fat (3g sat. fat), 20mg chol., 237mg sod., 14g carb. (0 sugars, 2g fiber), 6g pro.

TEST KITCHEN TIP
Only brush the egg on the top of the puff pastry—not the edges. If the edges are brushed, the layers of dough may stick together and the pastry won't rise as it should while baking.

GREEN SALAD WITH BAKED GOAT CHEESE

I combined my favorite parts of a variety of salads to create this masterpiece. The warm baked cheese and crunchy croutons are wonderful complements to the crisp salad greens.
—Deb Morris, Wevertown, NY

- -

Takes: 20 min. • **Makes:** 8 servings

- 1 log (4 oz.) fresh goat cheese
- 1 Tbsp. olive oil
- ¼ cup seasoned bread crumbs
- 1 pkg. (5 oz.) spring mix salad greens
- ½ cup dried cranberries
- ½ cup chopped walnuts, toasted
- 4 bacon strips, cooked and crumbled
- ½ cup Caesar salad croutons
  Salad dressing of your choice

1. Preheat oven to 350°. Cut goat cheese into eight slices; brush both sides with olive oil and coat with bread crumbs. Place on an ungreased baking sheet. Bake until cheese is bubbly, 5-6 minutes.
2. In a large bowl, combine salad greens, cranberries, walnuts and bacon; transfer to a platter. Top with cheese and croutons. Serve with dressing of your choice.
1 cup salad with 1 slice breaded goat cheese: 148 cal., 10g fat (2g sat. fat), 13mg chol., 192mg sod., 11g carb. (5g sugars, 1g fiber), 5g pro.

FIESTA COLESLAW

Coleslaw with a touch of heat makes a zesty side for barbecued chicken or pork. I also pile it on fish tacos and po'boy sandwiches.
—Fay Moreland, Wichita Falls, TX

Takes: 20 min. • **Makes:** 10 servings

- 1 pkg. (14 oz.) coleslaw mix
- 1 cup chopped peeled jicama
- 6 radishes, halved and sliced
- 4 jalapeno peppers, seeded and finely chopped
- 1 medium onion, chopped
- ⅓ cup minced fresh cilantro
- ½ cup mayonnaise
- ¼ cup cider vinegar
- 2 Tbsp. sugar
- ½ tsp. salt
- ½ tsp. celery salt
- ¼ tsp. coarsely ground pepper
  Lime wedges, optional

1. In a large bowl, combine the first six ingredients. In a small bowl, whisk the mayonnaise, vinegar, sugar and seasonings. Pour over coleslaw mixture; toss to coat.
2. Refrigerate, covered, until serving. If desired, serve with lime wedges.
Note: Wear disposable gloves when cutting hot peppers; the oils can burn skin. Avoid touching your face.
¾ cup: 114 cal., 9g fat (1g sat. fat), 4mg chol., 242mg sod., 8g carb. (5g sugars, 2g fiber), 1g pro. **Diabetic exchanges:** 2 fat, 1 vegetable.

YELLOW SQUASH & WATERMELON SALAD

I always like to bring this healthy option to parties and potlucks, and people seem to really appreciate that. No oil is necessary for this salad; the lemon juice combines with the feta to lightly coat the lovely, bright, fresh ingredients.
—Camille Parker, Chicago, IL

Takes: 20 min.
Makes: 12 servings

- 6 cups cubed seedless watermelon
- 2 medium yellow summer squash, chopped
- 2 medium zucchini, chopped
- ½ cup lemon juice
- 12 fresh mint leaves, torn
- 1 tsp. salt
- 8 cups fresh arugula or baby spinach
- 1 cup (4 oz.) crumbled feta cheese

1. In a large bowl, combine the first six ingredients. Just before serving, add arugula and cheese; toss gently to combine.
1 cup: 60 cal., 2g fat (1g sat. fat), 5mg chol., 297mg sod., 11g carb. (8g sugars, 2g fiber), 3g pro. **Diabetic exchanges:** 1 vegetable, ½ fruit.

SPEEDY SURPRISE

"Excellent flavors. I halved the recipe and served it as an entree for three. I thought we'd have a lot left over but we polished it off in one meal, served with a hearty bread."

AMEISTER423, TASTEOFHOME.COM

SAVORY BISCUIT-BREADSTICKS

I love to experiment in the kitchen with simple ingredients like refrigerated biscuits. The results usually are a big hit, as was the case with these super fast breadsticks.
—Billy Hensley, Mount Carmel, TN

Takes: 20 min. • **Makes:** 10 breadsticks

- ½ cup grated Parmesan cheese
- 2 tsp. dried minced garlic
- ¼ tsp. crushed red pepper flakes
- 1 tube (12 oz.) refrigerated buttermilk biscuits
- 2 Tbsp. olive oil

Preheat oven to 400°. In a shallow bowl, mix cheese, garlic and pepper flakes. Roll each biscuit into a 6-in. rope. Brush lightly with oil; roll in the cheese mixture. Place on a greased baking sheet. Bake until golden brown, 8-10 minutes.
1 breadstick: 142 cal., 8g fat (2g sat. fat), 3mg chol., 353mg sod., 16g carb. (2g sugars, 0 fiber), 3g pro.

5 INGREDIENT

GARLIC-ROASTED BRUSSELS SPROUTS WITH MUSTARD SAUCE

Don't be afraid to serve up this hearty side of Brussels sprouts! Mellowed by roasting and tossed with mustard sauce, they may just delight even the most skeptical folks.
—Becky Walch, Orland, CA

- -

Takes: 20 min. • **Makes:** 6 servings

1½ lbs. fresh Brussels sprouts, halved
2 Tbsp. olive oil
3 garlic cloves, minced
½ cup heavy whipping cream
3 Tbsp. Dijon mustard
⅛ tsp. white pepper
Dash salt

1. Place Brussels sprouts in an ungreased 15x10x1-in. baking pan. Combine the oil and garlic; drizzle over sprouts and toss to coat.
2. Bake, uncovered, at 450° until tender, stirring occasionally, 10-15 minutes.
3. Meanwhile, in a small saucepan, combine the cream, mustard, pepper and salt. Bring to a gentle boil; cook until slightly thickened, 1-2 minutes. Spoon the mixture over the Brussels sprouts.
¾ cup: 167 cal., 12g fat (5g sat. fat), 27mg chol., 241mg sod., 13g carb. (3g sugars, 4g fiber), 4g pro.

5 INGREDIENT

ONION CRESCENT ROLLS

Here's a deliciously easy way to dress up a tube of crescent roll dough. These savory bites are one of our favorite recipes—and a nice addition to any buffet. We like them so much, I usually triple the recipe.
—Barbara Nowakowski,
North Tonawanda, NY

- -

Takes: 20 min. • **Makes:** 8 servings

1 tube (8 oz.) refrigerated crescent rolls
1⅓ cups french-fried onions, divided
1 large egg
1 Tbsp. water

1. Unroll crescent dough and separate into triangles. Sprinkle each with about 2 Tbsp. onions. Roll up each from the wide end; place on an ungreased foil-lined baking sheet. Curve ends down to form crescents.
2. Beat the egg and water; brush over dough. Sprinkle with remaining onions. Bake at 400° until rolls are golden brown, 10-12 minutes. Serve warm.
1 roll: 181 cal., 11g fat (3g sat. fat), 27mg chol., 311mg sod., 15g carb. (2g sugars, 0 fiber), 3g pro.

NUTTY GOUDA ROLLS

Here's a quick take on crescents that feels special enough for company. With Gouda, pecans and honey, these very simple rolls complement a variety of meals, including last-minute weeknight dinners.
—*Taste of Home* Test Kitchen

Takes: 20 min. • **Makes:** 8 servings

- 2 oz. Gouda cheese
- 1 tube (8 oz.) refrigerated crescent rolls
- 2 Tbsp. finely chopped pecans
- 1 Tbsp. honey

1. Preheat oven to 375°. Cut cheese into eight ½-in.-wide strips. Separate crescent dough into eight triangles; sprinkle with pecans. Place a cheese strip on the shortest side of each triangle; roll up, starting with the side with the cheese. Pinch ends to seal.
2. Place on an ungreased baking sheet. Bake until rolls are golden brown, 10-12 minutes. Immediately brush with honey. Serve warm.
1 roll: 158 cal., 9g fat (3g sat. fat), 8mg chol., 281mg sod., 14g carb. (4g sugars, 0 fiber), 4g pro.

LEMON-ROASTED ASPARAGUS

When it comes to fixing asparagus, I think it's hard to go wrong. The springy flavors in this side dish burst with every bite.
—Jenn Tidwell, Fair Oaks, CA

Takes: 20 min. • **Makes:** 8 servings

- 2 lbs. fresh asparagus, trimmed
- ¼ cup olive oil
- 4 tsp. grated lemon zest
- 2 garlic cloves, minced
- ½ tsp. salt
- ½ tsp. pepper

Preheat oven to 425°. Place asparagus in a greased 15x10x1-in. baking pan. Mix remaining ingredients; drizzle over asparagus. Toss to coat. Roast until crisp-tender, 8-12 minutes.
1 serving: 75 cal., 7g fat (1g sat. fat), 0 chol., 154mg sod., 3g carb. (1g sugars, 1g fiber), 2g pro. **Diabetic exchanges:** 1½ fat, 1 vegetable.

5 INGREDIENT
COLORFUL SPIRAL PASTA SALAD

You can never go wrong with pasta salad when it comes to potluck contributions. Give this one a try!
—Amanda Cable, Boxford, MA

- -

Takes: 20 min. • **Makes:** 14 servings

- 1   pkg. (12 oz.) tricolor spiral pasta
- 4   cups fresh broccoli florets
- 1   pint grape tomatoes
- 1   can (6 oz.) pitted ripe olives, drained
- ⅛   tsp. salt
- ⅛   tsp. pepper
- 1½ cups Italian salad dressing with roasted red pepper and Parmesan

1. In a Dutch oven, cook pasta according to package directions, adding broccoli during the last 2 minutes of cooking. Drain and rinse in cold water.

2. Transfer to a large bowl. Add tomatoes, olives, salt and pepper. Drizzle with salad dressing; toss to coat. Chill until serving.

¾ cup: 149 cal., 4g fat (0 sat. fat), 0 chol., 513mg sod., 24g carb. (4g sugars, 2g fiber), 4g pro.

CREAMY SWEET CORN WITH OKRA

The whole family will love how a little cream and a few bacon crumbles jazz up these delightful veggies.
—*Taste of Home* Test Kitchen

- -

Takes: 20 min. • **Makes:** 4 servings

- 1   small onion, chopped
- 2   Tbsp. butter
- 1   garlic clove, minced
- 3   cups frozen corn, thawed
- 1   cup frozen sliced okra, thawed
- ¼   cup half-and-half cream
- 2   slices ready-to-serve fully cooked bacon, chopped
- 1   Tbsp. sugar
- ½   tsp. salt
- ¼   tsp. pepper

In a large skillet, saute onion in butter until tender. Add garlic; cook 1 minute longer. Stir in remaining ingredients; heat through.

¾ cup: 211 cal., 9g fat (5g sat. fat), 23mg chol., 384mg sod., 31g carb. (7g sugars, 3g fiber), 5g pro.

TEST KITCHEN TIP
Don't have okra in the freezer? Try replacing it with green beans or simply stir in an additional cup of corn.

WEDGE SALAD WITH BLUE CHEESE DRESSING

A wedge salad gets the creamy treatment when topped with blue cheese dressing. Keep the dressing as a topper, or make it as a dip for Buffalo wings.
—Jenn Smith, Rumford, RI

Takes: 20 min. • **Makes:** 6 servings

- ⅔ cup crumbled blue cheese
- ⅔ cup mayonnaise
- ⅓ cup reduced-fat sour cream
- 2 tsp. water
- 1½ tsp. red wine vinegar
- ⅛ tsp. Worcestershire sauce
  Dash cayenne pepper
- 1 large head iceberg lettuce
- 2 cups chopped assorted tomatoes
- 6 bacon strips, cooked and crumbled

In a small bowl, mix first seven ingredients. Cut lettuce into six wedges. To serve, top wedges with dressing, tomatoes and bacon.

1 serving: 313 cal., 28g fat (7g sat. fat), 33mg chol., 473mg sod., 6g carb. (4g sugars, 2g fiber), 8g pro.

SNAPPY GARLIC BREAD

A garlic lover's dream, this zesty loaf is perfect with pizza. Plus, it's a breeze to put together at the last minute.
—Mary Ann Lee, Clifton Park, NY

- -

Takes: 20 min. • **Makes:** 16 slices

- 1 loaf (1 lb.) Italian bread
- 5 Tbsp. butter, softened
- 4 garlic cloves, minced
- ½ cup finely shredded part-skim mozzarella cheese
- ¼ cup grated Parmesan cheese
- 1 tsp. dried basil
- 1 tsp. dried parsley flakes
- ½ tsp. crushed red pepper flakes

1. Cut loaf of bread in half lengthwise. Combine butter and garlic; spread over both halves of bread. Top with mozzarella cheese. Combine the Parmesan cheese, basil, parsley and pepper flakes; sprinkle over mozzarella.
2. Place in a 15x10x1-in. baking pan. Bake at 350° until cheese is melted and edges are golden brown, 10-13 minutes. Slice and serve warm.
1 slice: 124 cal., 5g fat (3g sat. fat), 13mg chol., 227mg sod., 15g carb. (0 sugars, 1g fiber), 4g pro.

5 INGREDIENT | EAT SMART
SAUTEED SQUASH WITH TOMATOES & ONIONS

My favorite meals show a love of family and food. Featuring tomatoes, this healthy side dish is like a scaled-down ratatouille.
—Adan Franco, Milwaukee, WI

- -

Takes: 20 min. • **Makes:** 8 servings

- 2 Tbsp. olive oil
- 1 medium onion, finely chopped
- 4 medium zucchini, chopped
- 2 large tomatoes, finely chopped
- 1 tsp. salt
- ¼ tsp. pepper

1. In a large skillet, heat oil over medium-high heat. Add onion; cook and stir until tender, 2-4 minutes. Add zucchini; cook and stir 3 minutes.
2. Stir in tomatoes, salt and pepper; cook and stir until squash is tender, 4-6 minutes longer. Serve with a slotted spoon.
¾ cup: 60 cal., 4g fat (1g sat. fat), 0 chol., 306mg sod., 6g carb. (4g sugars, 2g fiber), 2g pro. **Diabetic exchanges:** 1 vegetable, ½ fat.

LEMON PARMESAN ORZO

A splash of lemon and a bit of chopped parsley make this orzo one of my family's most requested sides. It's fantastic with chicken, pork and fish, or you can eat it on its own as light lunch.
—Leslie Palmer, Swampscott, MA

Takes: 20 min. • **Makes:** 4 servings

- 1 cup uncooked whole wheat orzo pasta
- 1 Tbsp. olive oil
- ¼ cup grated Parmesan cheese
- 2 Tbsp. minced fresh parsley
- ½ tsp. grated lemon zest
- ¼ tsp. salt
- ¼ tsp. pepper

Cook orzo according to package directions; drain. Transfer to a small bowl; drizzle with oil. Stir in remaining ingredients.
½ cup: 191 cal., 6g fat (1g sat. fat), 4mg chol., 225mg sod., 28g carb. (0 sugars, 7g fiber), 7g pro. **Diabetic exchanges:** 2 starch, ½ fat.

SPEEDY SURPRISE
"This is a nice, easy side dish. I toasted the orzo first for a bit more flavor."
—JSTOWELLSUPERMOM,
TASTEOFHOME.COM

TANGY POPPY SEED FRUIT SALAD

For a fruit salad that's delightful, I combine berries and citrus with a honey lime dressing flecked with poppy seeds.
—Carrie Howell, Lehi, UT

Takes: 20 min. • **Makes:** 10 servings

- 1 can (20 oz.) unsweetened pineapple chunks, drained
- 1 lb. fresh strawberries, quartered
- 2 cups fresh blueberries
- 2 cups fresh raspberries
- 2 medium navel oranges, peeled and sectioned
- 2 medium kiwifruit, peeled, halved and sliced

DRESSING
- 2 to 4 Tbsp. honey
- ½ tsp. grated lime zest
- 2 Tbsp. lime juice
- 2 tsp. poppy seeds

Place all fruit in a large bowl. In a small bowl, whisk dressing ingredients. Drizzle over fruit; toss gently to combine.
⅔ cup: 117 cal., 1g fat (0 sat. fat), 0 chol., 3mg sod., 29g carb. (21g sugars, 5g fiber), 2g pro. **Diabetic exchanges:** 2 fruit.

EAT SMART

HAVARTI TURKEY HERO

This is not just your ordinary sandwich! Everyone loves the combination of chutney and chopped peanuts. I like to make the bites for afternoon guests or for my evening card club.

—Agnes Ward, Stratford, ON

- -

Takes: 15 min. • **Makes:** 8 servings

- ⅓ cup mango chutney
- 2 Tbsp. reduced-fat mayonnaise
- 2 Tbsp. chopped unsalted peanuts
  Dash cayenne pepper
- 1 loaf (1 lb.) French bread, halved lengthwise
- ¾ lb. thinly sliced deli turkey
- 6 lettuce leaves
- 2 oz. thinly sliced Havarti cheese
- 1 medium Red Delicious apple, cored and cut into thin rings

In a small bowl, combine mango chutney, mayonnaise, peanuts and cayenne; spread evenly over the cut side of bread bottom. Layer with turkey, lettuce, cheese and apple. Replace bread top. Cut into eight slices.
1 serving: 302 cal., 7g fat (2g sat. fat), 27mg chol., 973mg sod., 45g carb. (9g sugars, 2g fiber), 16g pro. **Diabetic exchanges:** 3 starch, 1 lean meat, ½ fat.

TEST KITCHEN TIP
Apple wedges add a burst of unexpected flavor to this hearty sandwich. Feel free to mix it up with slices of pear instead, and replace the peanuts with walnuts or almonds.

GNOCCHI CHICKEN SKILLET

Potato gnocchi are little dumplings made from a dough of potatoes, flour and sometimes eggs. Look for gnocchi in the pasta, ethnic or frozen section of your grocery store.
—*Taste of Home* Test Kitchen

- -

Takes: 20 min. • **Makes:** 4 servings

- 1 pkg. (16 oz.) potato gnocchi
- 1 lb. ground chicken
- ½ cup chopped onion
- 2 Tbsp. olive oil
- 1 jar (26 oz.) spaghetti sauce
- ¼ tsp. salt
- ¼ to ½ tsp. dried oregano
  Shredded Parmesan cheese, optional

1. Cook gnocchi according to package directions. Meanwhile, in a large skillet, cook chicken and onion in oil over medium heat until chicken is no longer pink; drain if necessary. Stir in the spaghetti sauce, salt and oregano; cook until heated through, 5-10 minutes.

2. Drain gnocchi; gently stir into skillet. Garnish servings with cheese if desired.
1½ cups: 598 cal., 24g fat (6g sat. fat), 88mg chol., 1632mg sod., 66g carb. (19g sugars, 6g fiber), 30g pro.

GRILLED BRATS WITH SRIRACHA MAYO

I am a Sriracha fanatic, so that's what inspired this dish. You can boil the brats in your favorite beer to reduce the fat and give them flavor before grilling, or spread garlic butter on lightly toasted buns.
—Quincie Ball, Olympia, WA

Takes: 20 min. • **Makes:** 4 servings

- ½   cup mayonnaise
- ⅓   cup minced roasted
      sweet red peppers
- 3   Tbsp. Sriracha Asian hot chili sauce
- 1   tsp. hot pepper sauce
- 4   fully cooked bratwurst links
- 4   brat buns or hot dog buns, split
- ½   cup dill pickle relish
- ½   cup finely chopped red onion
      Ketchup, optional

Mix first four ingredients. Grill bratwursts, covered, over medium-low heat until browned and heated through, 7-10 minutes, turning occasionally. Serve in buns with mayonnaise mixture, relish, onion and, if desired, ketchup.

1 bratwurst: 742 cal., 49g fat (13g sat. fat), 65mg chol., 2020mg sod., 54g carb. (10g sugars, 2g fiber), 20g pro.

TEST KITCHEN TIP
Cut back on the sodium in this recipe by skipping the pickle relish and using half of the homemade sweet-spicy sauce. In the end, you'll save slightly more than 600 milligrams of sodium per serving.

MUSHROOM HUNTER'S SAUCE

Hunter sauce is a quick and easy wine sauce with an accent of tomato.
—*Taste of Home* Test Kitchen

Takes: 20 min. • **Makes:** 4 servings

- 4   cups uncooked
       extra-wide egg noodles
- 1½ lbs. sliced fresh mushrooms
- 3   Tbsp. butter
- 1   cup dry red wine
- 1   Tbsp. cornstarch
- 1¼ cups vegetable broth
- 3   Tbsp. tomato paste

1. Cook noodles according to the package directions. Meanwhile, in a large skillet, saute the mushrooms in butter until tender. Add wine. Bring to a boil; cook until sauce is reduced by half, about 5 minutes.
2. In a small bowl, combine the cornstarch, broth and tomato paste until smooth. Add to mushroom mixture. Bring to a boil; cook and stir until thickened, about 2 minutes. Drain noodles; serve with mushroom sauce.
1 cup: 330 cal., 11g fat (6g sat. fat), 59mg chol., 427mg sod., 40g carb. (6g sugars, 4g fiber), 11g pro.

SPINACH & TORTELLINI SOUP

My tomato-y broth is perfect for cheese tortellini and fresh spinach. Add extra garlic and Italian seasoning to suit your taste.
—Debbie Wilson, Burlington, NC

- -

Takes: 20 min. • **Makes:** 6 servings (2 qt.)

1 tsp. olive oil
2 garlic cloves, minced
1 can (14½ oz.) no-salt-added diced tomatoes, undrained
3 cans (14½ oz. each) vegetable broth
2 tsp. Italian seasoning
1 pkg. (9 oz.) refrigerated cheese tortellini
4 cups fresh baby spinach
Shredded Parmesan cheese and freshly ground pepper

1. In a large saucepan, heat oil over medium heat. Add garlic; cook and stir 1 minute. Stir in tomatoes, broth and Italian seasoning; bring to a boil. Add tortellini; bring to a gentle boil. Cook, uncovered, just until tortellini are tender, 7-9 minutes.
2. Stir in spinach. Sprinkle servings with cheese and pepper.
1⅓ cups: 164 cal., 5g fat (2g sat. fat), 18mg chol., 799mg sod., 25g carb. (4g sugars, 2g fiber), 7g pro.

EAT SMART
CHICKEN WITH PINEAPPLE

I'm always on the lookout for scrumptious low-fat recipes—like this one! In this main dish, quick-cooking chicken breasts get a wonderful sweet flavor from pineapple, honey and teriyaki sauce.
—Jenny Reece, Lowry, MN

- -

Takes: 20 min. • **Makes:** 4 servings

4 boneless skinless chicken breast halves (4 oz. each)
1 Tbsp. all-purpose flour
1 Tbsp. canola oil
2 cans (8 oz. each) unsweetened pineapple chunks
1 tsp. cornstarch
1 Tbsp. honey
1 Tbsp. reduced-sodium teriyaki sauce or reduced-sodium soy sauce
⅛ tsp. pepper
Hot cooked rice

1. Flatten the chicken to ¼-in. thickness. Place flour in a large shallow dish; add chicken and turn to coat.
2. In a large skillet, brown the chicken over medium heat in the oil until juices run clear, 3-5 minutes on each side. Remove and keep warm. Drain pineapple, reserving ¼ cup juice. (Discard remaining juice or save for another use.)
3. In a small bowl, combine cornstarch and reserved juice until smooth. Gradually add to skillet. Stir in the honey, teriyaki sauce and pepper. Bring to a boil. Cook and stir until thickened, about 30 seconds. Add the pineapple and chicken; heat through. Serve with hot cooked rice.
1 serving: 247 cal., 6g fat (1g sat. fat), 63mg chol., 135mg sod., 22g carb. (19g sugars, 1g fiber), 24g pro. **Diabetic exchanges:** 3 lean meat, 1 fruit, ½ starch, ½ fat.

AVOCADO CRAB BOATS

These boats are wonderful with tortilla chips, beans or rice. You can also cover them, pack them on ice, and take them to a picnic or potluck. Served warm or cold, they're always delicious.
—Frances Benthin, Scio, OR

Takes: 20 min. • **Makes:** 8 servings

- 5 medium ripe avocados, peeled and halved
- ½ cup mayonnaise
- 2 Tbsp. lemon juice
- 2 cans (6 oz. each) lump crabmeat, drained
- ¼ cup chopped fresh cilantro, divided
- 2 Tbsp. minced chives
- 1 serrano pepper, seeded and minced
- 1 Tbsp. capers, drained
- ¼ tsp. pepper
- 1 cup shredded pepper jack cheese
- ½ tsp. paprika
  Lemon wedges

1. Preheat broiler. Place two avocado halves in a large bowl; mash lightly with a fork. Add mayonnaise and lemon juice; mix until well blended. Stir in the crab, 3 Tbsp. cilantro, chives, serrano pepper, capers and pepper. Spoon into remaining avocado halves.
2. Transfer to a 15x10x1-in. baking pan. Sprinkle with the cheese and paprika. Broil 4-5 in. from heat until the cheese is melted, 3-5 minutes. Sprinkle with the remaining cilantro; serve with lemon wedges.
Note: Wear disposable gloves when cutting hot peppers; the oils can burn skin. Avoid touching your face.
1 filled avocado half: 325 cal., 28g fat (6g sat. fat), 57mg chol., 427mg sod., 8g carb. (0 sugars, 6g fiber), 13g pro.

OKTOBERFEST BRATS WITH MUSTARD SAUCE

I come from a town with a big German heritage, so we have a huge celebration each year for Oktoberfest. This recipe packs in all the traditional German flavors everyone just loves.
—Deborah Pennington, Cullman, AL

Takes: 20 min. • **Makes:** 4 servings

- ⅓ cup half-and-half cream
- 2 Tbsp. stone-ground mustard
- ½ tsp. dried minced onion
- ¼ tsp. pepper
  Dash paprika
- 4 fully cooked bratwurst links (about 12 oz.)
- 1 can (14 oz.) sauerkraut, rinsed and drained, warmed

1. For sauce, mix first five ingredients. Cut each bratwurst into thirds; thread onto four metal or soaked wooden skewers.
2. Grill brats, covered, over medium heat until golden brown and heated through, 7-10 minutes, turning occasionally. Serve with sauerkraut and sauce.
1 serving: 341 cal., 28g fat (10g sat. fat), 73mg chol., 1539mg sod., 9g carb. (3g sugars, 3g fiber), 14g pro.

ROTISSERIE CHICKEN PANINI

This ooey-gooey, melty delight is packed with bacon, chicken, cheese and just enough lemon to tickle your taste buds.
—Terri McCarty, Oro Grande, CA

Takes: 20 min. • **Makes:** 2 servings

- 3 Tbsp. mayonnaise
- 4½ tsp. grated Parmesan cheese
- 1 tsp. lemon juice
- ½ tsp. prepared pesto
- ¼ tsp. grated lemon zest
  Dash pepper
- 4 slices sourdough bread
- ¼ lb. sliced rotisserie chicken
- 4 slices ready-to-serve fully cooked bacon
- 2 slices smoked part-skim mozzarella cheese
- 2 slices red onion, separated into rings
- 4 slices tomato
- 2 Tbsp. butter, melted

1. In a small bowl, combine the first six ingredients; spread half over two bread slices. Layer with the chicken, bacon, mozzarella, onion and tomato. Spread remaining mayonnaise mixture over the remaining bread slices; place over top. Brush outsides of sandwiches with butter.
2. Cook on a panini maker or indoor grill until bread is browned and cheese is melted, 3-4 minutes.
1 sandwich: 653 cal., 42g fat (16g sat. fat), 80mg chol., 996mg sod., 40g carb. (3g sugars, 2g fiber), 28g pro.

ASIAN SALMON TACOS

This Asian/Mexican fusion dish is ready in minutes—perfect for on-the-run-meals! If the salmon fillets begin to stick, add 2-3 tablespoons of water and continue cooking through.

—Marisa Raponi, Vaughan, ON

Takes: 20 min. • **Makes:** 4 servings

1	lb. salmon fillet, skin removed, cut into 1-in. cubes
2	Tbsp. hoisin sauce
1	Tbsp. olive oil
	Shredded lettuce
8	corn tortillas (6 in.), warmed
1½	tsp. black sesame seeds
	Mango salsa, optional

1. Toss salmon with hoisin sauce. In a large nonstick skillet, heat oil over medium-high heat. Cook salmon until it begins to flake easily with a fork, 3-5 minutes, turning gently to brown all sides.

2. Serve salmon and lettuce in tortillas; sprinkle with sesame seeds. If desired, top with mango salsa.

2 tacos: 335 cal., 16g fat (3g sat. fat), 57mg chol., 208mg sod., 25g carb. (3g sugars, 3g fiber), 22g pro. **Diabetic exchanges:** 3 lean meat, 2 starch, 1 fat.

GARLIC TOAST PIZZAS

Between working full time, going to school and raising three children, finding those time-saving recipes my family actually enjoys is one of my biggest challenges. These quick little pizzas pack a huge amount of flavor in no time.

—Amy Grim, Chillicothe, OH

Takes: 15 min. • **Makes:** 8 slices

1	pkg. (11¼ oz.) frozen garlic Texas toast
½	cup pizza sauce
1	pkg. (3½ oz.) sliced regular or turkey pepperoni
2	cups shredded part-skim mozzarella cheese

1. Preheat oven to 425°. Place Texas toast in a 15x10x1-in. baking pan. Bake 5 minutes.

2. Spread toast with pizza sauce; top with pepperoni and cheese. Bake until cheese is melted, 4-5 minutes longer.

1 slice: 281 cal., 20g fat (8g sat. fat), 58mg chol., 610mg sod., 14g carb. (3g sugars, 1g fiber), 12g pro.

SPEEDY SURPRISE

"These yummy treats are great as a quick main dish or as a savory appetizer at a party. Fast and delicious!"

—PAGERD, TASTEOFHOME.COM

LEMON-PARSLEY TILAPIA

I like to include seafood in our weekly dinner rotation but don't want to bother with anything complicated. In addition, it had better taste good or the family will riot! This herbed fish does the trick.
—Trisha Kruse, Eagle, ID

Takes: 20 min. • **Makes:** 4 servings

- 4 tilapia fillets (about 4 oz. each)
- 2 Tbsp. lemon juice
- 1 Tbsp. butter, melted
- 2 Tbsp. minced fresh parsley
- 2 garlic cloves, minced
- 2 tsp. grated lemon zest
- ½ tsp. salt
- ¼ tsp. pepper

1. Preheat oven to 375°. Place tilapia in a parchment-lined 15x10x1-in. pan. Drizzle with lemon juice, then melted butter.

2. Bake until fish just begins to flake easily with a fork, 11-13 minutes. Meanwhile, mix remaining ingredients. Remove fish from oven; sprinkle with parsley mixture.

1 fillet: 124 cal., 4g fat (2g sat. fat), 63mg chol., 359mg sod., 1g carb. (0 sugars, 0 fiber), 21g pro. **Diabetic exchanges:** 3 lean meat, 1 fat.

SPICE-RUBBED CHICKEN THIGHS

Our go-to meal has always been baked chicken thighs. However, this easy grilled version takes things outside with a zesty rub of turmeric, paprika and chili powder.
—Bill Staley, Monroeville, PA

Takes: 20 min. • **Makes:** 6 servings

- 1 tsp. salt
- 1 tsp. garlic powder
- 1 tsp. onion powder
- 1 tsp. dried oregano
- ½ tsp. ground turmeric
- ½ tsp. paprika
- ¼ tsp. chili powder
- ¼ tsp. pepper
- 6 boneless skinless chicken thighs (about 1½ lbs.)

1. In a small bowl, mix the first eight ingredients. Sprinkle over both sides of chicken thighs.

2. On a lightly greased grill rack, grill chicken, covered, over medium heat or broil 4 in. from heat until a thermometer reads 170°, 6-8 minutes on each side.

1 chicken thigh: 169 cal., 8g fat (2g sat. fat), 76mg chol., 460mg sod., 1g carb. (0 sugars, 0 fiber), 21g pro. **Diabetic exchanges:** 3 lean meat.

PIEROGI QUESADILLAS

When I had my hungry gang in the kitchen and nothing but leftovers in the fridge, I invented these quesadillas. Now it's how we always use up our potatoes, meats and sometimes even veggies.
—Andrea Dibble, Solon, IA

Takes: 15 min. • **Makes:** 4 servings

- 1 pkg. (24 oz.) refrigerated sour cream and chive mashed potatoes
  Butter-flavored cooking spray
- 8 flour tortillas (8 in.)
- 1 cup chopped fully cooked ham
- ½ cup shredded cheddar cheese

1. Heat mashed potatoes according to package directions.
2. Spritz cooking spray over one side of each tortilla. Place half of the tortillas on a griddle, greased side down. Spread with mashed potatoes; top with ham, cheese and remaining tortillas, greased side up. Cook over medium heat until golden brown and cheese is melted, 2-3 minutes on each side.
1 quesadilla: 630 cal., 22g fat (8g sat. fat), 49mg chol., 1559mg sod., 82g carb. (1g sugars, 6g fiber), 24g pro.

GRILLED HUMMUS TURKEY SANDWICH

I created this toasted sandwich last summer using homemade hummus and veggies from our garden. We really can't get enough!
—Gunjan Gilbert, Franklin, ME

Takes: 15 min. • **Makes:** 2 servings

- ½ cup hummus
- 4 slices whole wheat bread
- 4 oz. thinly sliced deli turkey
- 4 slices tomato
- 2 slices pepper jack cheese
- 4 tsp. butter, softened

1. Spread hummus on two bread slices; top with turkey, tomato, cheese and remaining bread. Spread outsides of the sandwiches with butter.
2. In a large skillet, toast sandwiches over medium heat until golden brown and cheese is melted, 2-3 minutes per side.
1 sandwich: 458 cal., 23g fat (10g sat. fat), 63mg chol., 1183mg sod., 36g carb. (3g sugars, 7g fiber), 28g pro.

CASHEW CHICKEN WITH NOODLES

I tried this recipe for a get-together with some friends one night. We were smitten! It's quick, easy and so delicious!
—Anita Beachy, Bealeton, VA

- -

Takes: 20 min. • **Makes:** 4 servings

- 8 oz. uncooked thick rice noodles
- ¼ cup reduced-sodium soy sauce
- 2 Tbsp. cornstarch
- 3 garlic cloves, minced
- 1 lb. boneless skinless chicken breasts, cubed
- 1 Tbsp. peanut oil
- 1 Tbsp. sesame oil
- 6 green onions, cut into 2-in. pieces
- 1 cup unsalted cashews
- 2 Tbsp. sweet chili sauce
   Toasted sesame seeds, optional

1. Cook the rice noodles according to package directions.
2. Meanwhile, in a small bowl, combine the soy sauce, cornstarch and garlic. Add chicken. In a large skillet, saute chicken mixture in peanut and sesame oils until no longer pink. Add green onions; cook 1 minute longer.
3. Drain noodles; stir into skillet. Add cashews and chili sauce and heat through. If desired, top with toasted sesame seeds.
1½ cups: 638 cal., 26g fat (5g sat. fat), 63mg chol., 870mg sod., 68g carb. (6g sugars, 3g fiber), 33g pro.

MEXICAN HOT DOGS

My stepmom was born in Mexico and introduced us to hot dogs with avocado and bacon. We were instantly hooked. Now our whole family makes them.
—Amanda Brandenburg, Hamilton, OH

- -

Takes: 20 min. • **Makes:** 6 servings

- ½ medium ripe avocado, peeled
- 1 Tbsp. lime juice
- ¼ tsp. salt
- ⅛ tsp. pepper
- 6 hot dogs
- 6 hot dog buns, split
- 1 small tomato, chopped
- 3 Tbsp. finely chopped red onion
- 3 bacon strips, cooked and crumbled

1. In a small bowl, mash avocado with a fork, stirring in lime juice, salt and pepper. Grill the hot dogs, covered, over medium heat until heated through, 7-9 minutes, turning occasionally.
2. Serve in buns. Top with avocado mixture, tomato, onion and bacon.

1 hot dog: 310 cal., 19g fat (7g sat. fat), 29mg chol., 844mg sod., 25g carb. (4g sugars, 2g fiber), 11g pro.

SPEEDY SURPRISE

"These were a big hit with the whole family! I put all of the toppings on a plate and let my kids add them on their own. You really can't go wrong with avocado and bacon."

—CURLYLIS85, TASTEOFHOME.COM

---

5 INGREDIENT | EAT SMART
GRILLED SALMON WITH NECTARINES

My family liked this recipe so much, I doubled it and made it for a potluck the next day. Everyone raved about it, even people who aren't particularly fond of fish.
—Kerin Benjamin, Citrus Heights, CA

- -

Takes: 15 min. • **Makes:** 4 servings

- 4 salmon fillets (4 oz. each)
- ½ tsp. salt, divided
- ⅛ tsp. pepper
- 1 Tbsp. honey
- 1 Tbsp. lemon juice
- 1 Tbsp. olive oil
- 3 medium nectarines, thinly sliced
- 1 Tbsp. minced fresh basil

1. Sprinkle salmon with ¼ tsp. salt and pepper. Place on an oiled grill, skin side down. Grill, covered, over medium heat until fish just begins to flakes easily with a fork, 8-10 minutes.
2. Meanwhile, in a bowl, mix honey, lemon juice, oil and remaining salt. Stir in the nectarines and basil. Serve with salmon.

1 fillet with ⅓ cup nectarines: 307 cal., 16g fat (3g sat. fat), 67mg chol., 507mg sod., 17g carb. (13g sugars, 2g fiber), 23g pro.
Diabetic exchanges: 3 lean meat, 1½ fat, 1 fruit.

GUMBO IN A JIFFY

This is a yummy entree. My husband loves the kick that Italian sausage gives this gumbo, and it's such a cinch to assemble.
—Amy Flack, Homer City, PA

- -

Takes: 20 min. • **Makes:** 6 servings (1½ qt.)

- 1 pkg. (12 oz.) smoked sausage
- 1 can (14½ oz.) diced tomatoes with green peppers and onions, undrained
- 1 can (14½ oz.) chicken broth
- ½ cup water
- 1 cup uncooked instant rice
- 1 can (7 oz.) whole kernel corn, drained
  Sliced green onions, optional

In a large saucepan, cook sliced sausage until browned on both sides. Stir in the tomatoes, broth and water; bring to a boil. Stir in rice and corn; cover and remove from the heat. Let stand for 5 minutes. If desired, top with sliced green onions.

1 cup: 280 cal., 16g fat (7g sat. fat), 38mg chol., 1098mg sod., 22g carb. (6g sugars, 2g fiber), 11g pro.

SPEEDY SURPRISE
"Super easy recipe with a lot of flavor. Would make again! Perhaps next time we'll add some okra and cooked shrimp or chicken, too!"
—JGA2595176, TASTEOFHOME.COM

HADDOCK WITH LIME-CILANTRO BUTTER

In Louisiana the good times roll when we broil fish and serve it with lots of lime juice, cilantro and butter.
—Darlene Morris, Franklinton, LA

- -

Takes: 15 min. • **Makes:** 4 servings

- 4 haddock fillets (6 oz. each)
- ½ tsp. salt
- ¼ tsp. pepper
- 3 Tbsp. butter, melted
- 2 Tbsp. minced fresh cilantro
- 1 Tbsp. lime juice
- 1 tsp. grated lime zest

1. Preheat broiler. Sprinkle fillets with salt and pepper. Place on a greased broiler pan. Broil 4-5 in. from heat until fish flakes easily with a fork, 5-6 minutes.
2. In a small bowl, mix remaining ingredients. Serve over fish.

1 fillet with 1 Tbsp. butter mixture:
227 cal., 10g fat (6g sat. fat), 121mg chol., 479mg sod., 1g carb. (0 sugars, 0 fiber), 32g pro. **Diabetic exchanges:** 4 lean meat, 2 fat.

GRILLED GREEK PITA PIZZAS

This easy flatbread pizza captures classic Mediterranean flavors in every bite. It works equally well as a speedy main dish or an appetizer.
—Kristen Heigl, Staten Island, NY

Takes: 20 min. • **Makes:** 4 servings

- 1 jar (12 oz.) marinated quartered artichoke hearts, drained and chopped
- 1 cup grape tomatoes, halved
- ½ cup pitted Greek olives, halved
- ⅓ cup chopped fresh parsley
- 2 Tbsp. olive oil
- ¼ tsp. pepper
- ¾ cup hummus
- 4 whole pita breads
- 1 cup crumbled feta cheese

Place the first six ingredients in a small bowl; toss to combine. Spread hummus over pita breads. Top with artichoke mixture; sprinkle with cheese. Grill the pizzas, covered, over medium heat until the bottoms are golden brown, 4-5 minutes.

1 pizza: 585 cal., 34g fat (8g sat. fat), 15mg chol., 1336mg sod., 50g carb. (7g sugars, 6g fiber), 15g pro.

PUMPKIN SOUP

While this creamy, elegant soup is special enough for a weekend meal, the recipe is simple to prepare. My husband was skeptical at first, but after one bowl, he quickly asked for a second helping!
—Elizabeth Montgomery, Allston, MA

Takes: 20 min. • **Makes:** 6 servings (1½ qt.)

- ½ cup finely chopped onion
- 2 Tbsp. butter
- 1 Tbsp. all-purpose flour
- 2 cans (14½ oz. each) chicken broth
- 1 can (15 oz.) solid-pack pumpkin
- 1 tsp. brown sugar
- ¼ tsp. salt
- ⅛ tsp. pepper
- ⅛ tsp. ground nutmeg
- 1 cup heavy whipping cream

In a large saucepan, saute onion in butter until tender. Remove from the heat; stir in flour until smooth. Gradually stir in the broth, pumpkin, brown sugar, salt, pepper and nutmeg; bring to a boil. Reduce heat and simmer for 5 minutes. Add cream; cook until heated through, about 2 minutes.

1 cup: 212 cal., 19g fat (12g sat. fat), 65mg chol., 427mg sod., 10g carb. (5g sugars, 3g fiber), 3g pro.

CRISPY DILL TILAPIA

Every week I try to serve a new healthy fish dish. This tilapia recipe is a winner with its fresh dill and delicious panko bread crumb herb crust.
—Tamara Huron, New Market, AL

- -

Takes: 20 min. • **Makes:** 4 servings

1	cup panko (Japanese) bread crumbs
2	Tbsp. olive oil
2	Tbsp. snipped fresh dill
¼	tsp. salt
⅛	tsp. pepper
4	tilapia fillets (6 oz. each)
1	Tbsp. lemon juice
	Lemon wedges

1. Preheat oven to 400°. Toss together first five ingredients.
2. Place tilapia in a 15x10x1-in. baking pan coated with cooking spray; brush with lemon juice. Top with crumb mixture, patting to help adhere.
3. Bake, uncovered, on an upper oven rack until the fish just begins to flake easily with a fork, 12-15 minutes. Serve tilapia with lemon wedges.

1 fillet: 256 cal., 9g fat (2g sat. fat), 83mg chol., 251mg sod., 10g carb. (1g sugars, 1g fiber), 34g pro. **Diabetic exchanges:** 5 lean meat, 1½ fat, ½ starch.

GAME-NIGHT NACHO PIZZA

Some like it hot with jalapenos; others like it cool with a dollop of sour cream. But one thing's for sure: This is "nacho" ordinary pizza night.

—Jamie Jones, Madison, GA

- -

Takes: 20 min. • **Makes:** 6 slices

- 1   prebaked 12-in. pizza crust
- 1   Tbsp. olive oil
- 1   cup refried beans
- 1   cup refrigerated fully cooked barbecued shredded beef
- ½   cup chopped seeded tomatoes
- ½   cup pickled jalapeno slices
- 1   cup shredded Colby-Monterey Jack cheese
     Optional toppings: shredded lettuce, sour cream and salsa

1. Place crust on an ungreased pizza pan. Brush with oil. Spread beans over crust. Top with beef, tomatoes, jalapenos and cheese.
2. Bake at 450° until cheese is melted, 10-15 minutes. Serve with lettuce, sour cream and salsa if desired.
1 slice: 370 cal., 13g fat (5g sat. fat), 30mg chol., 1103mg sod., 46g carb. (6g sugars, 3g fiber), 18g pro.

SPEEDY SURPRISE
"Sooo good! And so very quick and easy to make! This will be going into my regular rotation of recipes."

—ASABOT, TASTEOFHOME.COM

GARLIC BREAD TUNA MELTS

There's something extra comforting about a tuna melt on a chilly day. Take it up a few notches with garlic, dill and tomatoes.

—Aimee Bachmann, North Bend, WA

- -

Takes: 20 min. • **Makes:** 4 servings

- ¼   cup butter, cubed
- 3   garlic cloves, minced
- 4   French rolls or hoagie buns, split
- 2   cans (one 12 oz., one 5 oz.) albacore white tuna in water, drained and flaked
- ¼   cup reduced-fat mayonnaise
- 1¼ tsp. dill weed, divided
- 8   slices cheddar cheese
- 8   slices tomato

1. Preheat broiler. In a microwave, melt butter with garlic. Place rolls on a baking sheet, cut side up; brush with the butter mixture. Broil 2-3 in. from heat until lightly browned, 2-3 minutes.
2. In a small bowl, mix tuna, mayonnaise and 1 tsp. dill. Layer roll bottoms with tuna mixture and cheese. Broil until cheese is melted, 1-2 minutes longer. Top with the tomato; sprinkle with remaining dill. Replace tops; serve immediately.
1 sandwich: 704 cal., 41g fat (19g sat. fat), 146mg chol., 1314mg sod., 36g carb. (3g sugars, 2g fiber), 49g pro.

5 INGREDIENT | EAT SMART
MEDITERRANEAN TILAPIA

I recently became a fan of tilapia. Its mild taste makes it easy to top with my favorite ingredients. Plus, it's low in calories and fat. What's not to love?
—Robin Brenneman, Hilliard, OH

- -

Takes: 20 min. • **Makes:** 6 servings

- 6 tilapia fillets (6 oz. each)
- 1 cup canned Italian diced tomatoes
- ½ cup water-packed artichoke hearts, chopped
- ½ cup sliced ripe olives
- ½ cup crumbled feta cheese

Preheat oven to 400°. Place the fillets in a 15x10x1-in. baking pan coated with cooking spray. Top with tomatoes, artichoke hearts, olives and cheese. Bake, uncovered, until fish flakes easily with a fork, 15-20 minutes.

1 fillet: 197 cal., 4g fat (2g sat. fat), 88mg chol., 446mg sod., 5g carb. (2g sugars, 1g fiber), 34g pro. **Diabetic exchanges:** 5 lean meat, ½ fat.

Italian Tilapia: Follow method as directed but top fillets with 1 cup diced tomatoes with roasted garlic, ½ cup each julienned roasted sweet red pepper, sliced fresh mushrooms, diced fresh mozzarella cheese and ½ tsp. dried basil.

Southwest Tilapia: Follow method as directed but top fillets with 1 cup diced tomatoes with mild green chiles, ½ each cup cubed avocado, thawed corn, cubed cheddar cheese and ½ tsp. dried cilantro.

EAT SMART
SPINACH DIP BURGERS

Every Friday night is burger night at our house. Here, tomatoes add fresh flavor to patties, and the cool spinach dip brings it all together. We often skip the buns and serve these over a bed of grilled cabbage.
—Courtney Stultz, Weir, KS

- -

Takes: 20 min. • **Makes:** 4 servings

- 1 large egg, lightly beaten
- 2 Tbsp. fat-free milk
- ½ cup soft bread crumbs
- 1 tsp. dried basil
- ½ tsp. salt
- ¼ tsp. pepper
- 1 lb. lean ground beef (90% lean)
- 4 whole wheat hamburger buns, split
- ¼ cup spinach dip
- ¼ cup julienned soft sun-dried tomatoes (not packed in oil)
     Lettuce leaves

1. Combine first six ingredients. Add beef; mix lightly but thoroughly. Shape into four ½-in.-thick patties.

2. Place burgers on an oiled grill rack or in a greased 15x10x1-in. pan. Grill, covered, over medium heat or broil 4-5 in. from heat until a thermometer reads 160°, 4-5 minutes per side. Grill buns, cut side down, over medium heat until toasted. Serve burgers on buns; top with spinach dip, tomatoes and lettuce.

Note: To make soft bread crumbs, tear the bread into pieces and place them in a food processor or blender. Cover and pulse until crumbs form. One slice of bread yields ½ to ¾ cup crumbs. This recipe was tested with sun-dried tomatoes that do not need to be soaked before use.

1 burger: 389 cal., 17g fat (6g sat. fat), 125mg chol., 737mg sod., 29g carb. (7g sugars, 4g fiber), 29g pro. **Diabetic exchanges:** 3 lean meat, 2 starch, 1½ fat.

ASIAN CHICKEN RICE BOWL

This super flavorful, nutrient-packed dish makes use of supermarket conveniences like coleslaw mix and rotisserie chicken. This recipe is easily doubled or tripled for large families.

—Christianna Gozzi, Astoria, NY

Takes: 20 min. • **Makes:** 4 servings

- ¼ cup rice vinegar
- 1 green onion, minced
- 2 Tbsp. reduced-sodium soy sauce
- 1 Tbsp. toasted sesame seeds
- 1 Tbsp. sesame oil
- 1 Tbsp. honey
- 1 tsp. minced fresh gingerroot
- 1 pkg. (8.8 oz.) ready-to-serve brown rice
- 4 cups coleslaw mix (about 9 oz.)
- 2 cups shredded rotisserie chicken, chilled
- 2 cups frozen shelled edamame, thawed

1. For dressing, whisk together first seven ingredients. Cook rice according to package directions. Divide among four bowls.

2. In a large bowl, toss the coleslaw mix and chicken with half of the dressing. Serve the edamame and slaw mixture over rice; drizzle with remaining dressing.

1 serving: 429 cal., 15g fat (2g sat. fat), 62mg chol., 616mg sod., 38g carb. (13g sugars, 5g fiber), 32g pro. **Diabetic exchanges:** 3 lean meat, 2 starch, 1 vegetable, 1 fat.

FREEZE IT
PICO DE GALLO BLACK BEAN SOUP

Everyone at my table goes for this feel-good soup. It's quick when you are pressed for time and beats fast food, hands down.
—Darlis Wilfer, West Bend, WI

- -

Takes: 20 min. • **Makes:** 6 servings (2 qt.)

- **4** cans (15 oz. each) black beans, rinsed and drained
- **2** cups vegetable broth
- **2** cups pico de gallo
- **½** cup water
- **2** tsp. ground cumin

TOPPINGS
- Chopped fresh cilantro
- Additional pico de gallo, optional

1. In a Dutch oven, combine the first five ingredients; bring to a boil over medium heat, stirring occasionally. Reduce heat; simmer, uncovered, until vegetables in pico de gallo are softened, 5-7 minutes, stirring occasionally.
2. Puree soup using an immersion blender, or cool soup slightly and puree in batches in a blender. Return to pan and heat through. Serve with toppings as desired.

Freeze option: Freeze cooled soup in freezer containers. To use, partially thaw in refrigerator overnight. Heat through in a saucepan, stirring occasionally; add a little broth or water if necessary. Top as desired.

1¼ cups: 241 cal., 0 fat (0 sat. fat), 0 chol., 856mg sod., 44g carb. (4g sugars, 12g fiber), 14g pro.

5 INGREDIENT
PESTO FISH WITH PINE NUTS

I love fish, and Italian flavors are my favorite. This is a tasty, healthy way to enjoy them both!
—Valery Anderson, Sterling Heights, MI

- -

Takes: 15 min. • **Makes:** 4 servings

- **2** envelopes pesto sauce mix, divided
- **4** cod fillets (6 oz. each)
- **¼** cup olive oil
- **½** cup shredded Parmesan or Romano cheese
- **½** cup pine nuts, toasted

1. Prepare one envelope pesto sauce mix according to package directions; set aside. Sprinkle fillets with remaining pesto mix, patting to help adhere.
2. In a large skillet, heat oil over medium heat. Add fillets; cook until fish just begins to flake easily with a fork, 4-5 minutes on each side. Remove from heat. Sprinkle with shredded cheese and pine nuts. Serve with pesto sauce.

Note: To toast nuts, bake in a shallow pan in a 350° oven for 5-10 minutes or cook in a skillet over low heat until lightly browned, stirring occasionally.

1 fillet with scant 3 Tbsp. pesto sauce: 560 cal., 39g fat (5g sat. fat), 72mg chol., 1522mg sod., 17g carb. (7g sugars, 1g fiber), 35g pro.

Pesto Chicken with Pine Nuts: Substitute four boneless skinless chicken breasts (6 oz. each) for cod. Cook until a thermometer reads 165°, 6-8 minutes on each side.

SWEET CHILI & ORANGE CHICKEN

My husband loves this simple chicken dish so much that he often requests it when he comes home from deployment. The sweet chili sauce adds just the right amount of heat to the bright, citrusy sauce.
—Jessica Eastman, Bremerton, WA

- -

Takes: 20 min. • **Makes:** 4 servings

- 1 lb. boneless skinless chicken breasts, cut into 1-in. pieces
- ¼ tsp. salt
- ¼ tsp. pepper
- 2 Tbsp. butter
- ¾ cup sweet chili sauce
- ⅓ cup thawed orange juice concentrate
  Hot cooked jasmine or other rice
  Minced fresh basil

1. Toss chicken with salt and pepper. In a large skillet, heat butter over medium-high heat; stir-fry chicken until no longer pink, 5-7 minutes. Remove from pan; keep warm.
2. Add chili sauce and juice concentrate to skillet; cook and stir until heated through. Stir in chicken. Serve with rice; sprinkle with minced basil.
½ cup chicken mixture: 309 cal., 9g fat (4g sat. fat), 78mg chol., 1014mg sod., 33g carb. (31g sugars, 1g fiber), 24g pro.

BASIL-TOMATO GRILLED CHEESE

Enjoy the taste of summer all year long with my Italian-style grilled cheese sandwich. It tastes fresh and comforting all in one bite, and it is super fast to make on busy days.
—Sylvia Schmitt, Sun City, AZ

- -

Takes: 20 min. • **Makes:** 4 servings

- 8 slices Italian bread (¾ in. thick)
- 8 slices part-skim mozzarella cheese
- 2 large plum tomatoes, sliced
- 2 Tbsp. minced fresh basil
- 2 tsp. balsamic vinegar
  Salt and pepper to taste
- ¼ cup olive oil
- 3 Tbsp. grated Parmesan cheese
- ¼ tsp. garlic powder

1. On four slices of bread, layer mozzarella cheese and tomatoes; sprinkle with the basil, vinegar, salt and pepper. Top with remaining bread.
2. In a small bowl, combine the olive oil, Parmesan cheese and garlic powder; brush over the outsides of each sandwich.
3. In a skillet over medium heat, toast sandwiches until golden brown on both sides and cheese is melted.
1 sandwich: 467 cal., 27g fat (9g sat. fat), 34mg chol., 723mg sod., 34g carb. (4g sugars, 2g fiber), 23g pro.

PESTO HALIBUT

The mildness of halibut contrasts perfectly with the robust flavor of pesto in this easy recipe. It takes only minutes to get the fish ready for the oven, so you can start quickly on your side dishes. Nearly anything goes well with this entree.
—April Showalter, Indianapolis, IN

Takes: 20 min. • **Makes:** 6 servings

- 2 Tbsp. olive oil
- 1 envelope pesto sauce mix
- 1 Tbsp. lemon juice
- 6 halibut fillets (4 oz. each)

1. Preheat oven to 450°. In a small bowl, combine oil, sauce mix and lemon juice; brush over both sides of fillets. Place in a greased 13x9-in. baking dish.
2. Bake, uncovered, until fish just begins to flake easily with a fork, 12-15 minutes.
1 fillet: 188 cal., 7g fat (1g sat. fat), 36mg chol., 481mg sod., 5g carb. (2g sugars, 0 fiber), 24g pro. **Diabetic exchanges:** 3 lean meat, 1 fat.

SPEEDY SURPRISE
"I made this tonight with salmon, and my family loved it—even my pickiest eater!"
—CHEFNICOLE, TASTEOFHOME.COM

BUFFALO CHICKEN TENDERS

These chicken tenders get a spicy kick thanks to homemade Buffalo sauce. They taste like they're from a restaurant, but are so easy to make at home.
—Dahlia Abrams, Detroit, MI

Takes: 20 min. • **Makes:** 4 servings

- 1 lb. chicken tenderloins
- 2 Tbsp. all-purpose flour
- ¼ tsp. pepper
- 2 Tbsp. butter, divided
- ⅓ cup Louisiana-style hot sauce
- 1¼ tsp. Worcestershire sauce
- 1 tsp. minced fresh oregano
- ½ tsp. garlic powder
   Blue cheese salad dressing, optional

1. Toss chicken with flour and pepper. In a large skillet, heat 1 Tbsp. butter over medium heat. Add chicken; cook until no longer pink, 4-6 minutes per side. Remove from pan.
2. Mix hot sauce, Worcestershire sauce, oregano and garlic powder. In same skillet, melt remaining butter; stir in sauce mixture. Add chicken; heat through, turning to coat. If desired, serve with blue cheese dressing.
1 serving: 184 cal., 7g fat (4g sat. fat), 71mg chol., 801mg sod., 5g carb. (1g sugars, 0 fiber), 27g pro. **Diabetic exchanges:** 3 lean meat, 1½ fat.

SESAME-ORANGE SALMON

We're always on the lookout for new and interesting ways to prepare salmon. This Asian-inspired butter will be a new favorite for citrus lovers. Using reduced-fat butter saves 40 calories and 4 grams of fat per serving, but still adds a generous coating to the fish.
—*Taste of Home* Test Kitchen

- -

Takes: 15 min. • **Makes:** 2 servings

- 2 salmon fillets (4 oz. each)
- 5 tsp. reduced-fat butter, melted
- 1½ tsp. reduced-sodium soy sauce
- ¾ tsp. grated orange zest
- ½ tsp. sesame seeds

Place salmon skin side down on a broiler pan. Combine butter, soy sauce, orange zest and sesame seeds. Brush one-third of mixture over salmon. Broil 3-4 in. from the heat until fish flakes easily with a fork, 7-9 minutes, basting occasionally with remaining butter mixture.

Note: This recipe was tested with Land O'Lakes light stick butter.

1 fillet: 225 cal., 16g fat (5g sat. fat), 69mg chol., 288mg sod., 1g carb. (0 sugars, 0 fiber), 20g pro. **Diabetic exchanges:** 3 lean meat, 1½ fat.

ITALIAN PATTIES

While trying to think of a new way to fix hamburgers with the same old ground beef, I came up with this Italian twist. They're perfect with a side salad or fresh green beans.
—Rebekah Beyer, Sabetha, KS

- -

Takes: 20 min. • **Makes:** 4 servings

- 1 cup shredded part-skim mozzarella cheese, divided
- 1 tsp. Worcestershire sauce
- ¼ tsp. Italian seasoning
- ⅛ tsp. salt
- ⅛ tsp. pepper
- 1 lb. ground beef
  Marinara or spaghetti sauce, warmed

1. In a large bowl, combine ½ cup cheese and Worcestershire sauce and seasonings. Add beef; mix lightly but thoroughly. Shape into four ½-in.-thick patties.

2. Grill burgers, covered, over medium heat or broil 4 in. from heat until a thermometer reads 160°, 4-5 minutes on each side. Sprinkle with the remaining cheese; grill, covered, until cheese is melted, 1-2 minutes longer. Serve with marinara sauce.

1 burger: 279 cal., 18g fat (8g sat. fat), 86mg chol., 282mg sod., 1g carb. (1g sugars, 0 fiber), 27g pro.

ASIAN RAMEN SHRIMP SOUP

A package of store-bought ramen noodles speeds up assembly of this colorful broth with shrimp and carrots. My mother passed the recipe on to me. It's delicious and so quick to make.
—Donna Hellinger, Lorain, OH

- -

Takes: 15 min. • **Makes:** 4 servings

3½ cups water
1 pkg. (3 oz.) Oriental ramen noodles
1 cup cooked small shrimp, peeled and deveined
½ cup chopped green onions
1 medium carrot, julienned
2 Tbsp. soy sauce

1. In a large saucepan, bring water to a boil. Set aside seasoning packet from noodles. Add the noodles to boiling water; cook and stir for 3 minutes.

2. Add the shrimp, onions, carrot, soy sauce and contents of the seasoning packet. Cook until heated through, 3-4 minutes longer.

1 cup: 148 cal., 4g fat (2g sat. fat), 83mg chol., 857mg sod., 17g carb. (2g sugars, 1g fiber), 12g pro. **Diabetic exchanges:** 1 starch, 1 lean meat.

5 INGREDIENT | EAT SMART

GINGER-GLAZED GRILLED SALMON

Our family loves salmon prepared this way, and it's a real treat to make on a warm summer evening. These fillets may be baked in the oven at 450 degrees for 18 minutes, basting occasionally.
—Wanda Toews, Cromer, MB

- -

Takes: 15 min. • **Makes:** 4 servings

- 2 Tbsp. reduced-sodium soy sauce
- 2 Tbsp. maple syrup
- 2 tsp. minced fresh gingerroot
- 2 garlic cloves, minced
- 4 salmon fillets (6 oz. each)

1. For glaze, mix first four ingredients.
2. Place salmon on an oiled grill rack over medium heat, skin side up. Grill, covered, until fish just begins to flake easily with a fork, 4-5 minutes per side; brush top with half of the glaze after turning. Brush with remaining glaze before serving.

1 fillet: 299 cal., 16g fat (3g sat. fat), 85mg chol., 374mg sod., 8g carb. (6g sugars, 0 fiber), 29g pro. **Diabetic exchanges:** 4 lean meat, ½ starch.

TEST KITCHEN TIP

Consider this easy glaze the next time you're grilling pork or chicken as well. It's also great brushed over grilled vegetables or meaty kabobs.

FREEZE IT

SLOPPY CHEESESTEAKS

Sloppy joes are a favorite go-to dish for many busy families, and my spin with melty provolone, green pepper and onions makes for a fun, unexpected twist on the classic!
—Mandy Rivers, Lexington, SC

- -

Takes: 20 min. • **Makes:** 6 servings

- 1 lb. ground beef
- 1 medium green pepper, chopped
- 1 medium onion, chopped
- 1 tsp. garlic powder
- ½ tsp. salt
- ½ tsp. pepper
- 6 French rolls
- 6 slices provolone cheese
  Mayonnaise, optional

1. Preheat broiler. In a large skillet, cook and crumble beef with pepper and onion over medium-high heat until no longer pink, 5-7 minutes; drain. Stir in seasonings.
2. Cut rolls horizontally in half. Place bottoms on a baking sheet; broil 3-4 in. from heat until toasted, about 30 seconds. Top with beef mixture, then with cheese. Broil until cheese is melted, 45-60 seconds.
3. Place roll tops on a baking sheet; broil 3-4 in. from heat until toasted, about 30 seconds. Spread with mayonnaise if desired. Close sandwiches.
Freeze option: Freeze cooled beef mixture in freezer containers. To use, partially thaw in refrigerator overnight. Microwave, covered, on high in a microwave-safe dish until heated through, stirring occasionally. Prepare the sandwiches as directed.
1 sandwich: 417 cal., 19g fat (9g sat. fat), 66mg chol., 798mg sod., 34g carb. (2g sugars, 2g fiber), 27g pro.

EASY ASIAN GLAZED MEATBALLS

As a writer and busy mom of three boys, I need tasty meals on the quick. I like to serve these yummy glazed meatballs over a steaming bed of rice.
—Amy Dong, Woodbury, MN

Takes: 20 min. • **Makes:** 4 servings

- ½ cup hoisin sauce
- 2 Tbsp. rice vinegar
- 4 tsp. brown sugar
- 1 tsp. garlic powder
- 1 tsp. Sriracha Asian hot chili sauce
- ½ tsp. ground ginger
- 1 pkg. (12 oz.) frozen fully cooked homestyle or Italian meatballs, thawed
  Thinly sliced green onions and toasted sesame seeds, optional
  Hot cooked rice

1. In a large saucepan, mix the first six ingredients until blended. Add meatballs, stirring to coat; cook, covered, over medium-low heat until heated through, 12-15 minutes, stirring occasionally.
2. If desired, sprinkle with green onions and sesame seeds. Serve with rice.
1 serving: 376 cal., 23g fat (10g sat. fat), 36mg chol., 1296mg sod., 29g carb. (17g sugars, 2g fiber), 13g pro.

COPYCAT CHICKEN SALAD

This copycat Chik-fil-A chicken salad recipe is incredibly easy to make, and your family will love it. The sweet pickle relish gives it its signature taste. I like to use a thick crusty oat bread.
—Julie Peterson, Crofton, MD

Takes: 20 min. • **Makes:** 2 servings

- ½ cup reduced-fat mayonnaise
- ⅓ cup sweet pickle relish
- ⅓ cup finely chopped celery
- ½ tsp. sugar
- ¼ tsp. salt
- ¼ tsp. pepper
- 1 hard-boiled large egg, cooled and minced
- 2 cups chopped cooked chicken breast
- 4 slices whole wheat bread, toasted
- 2 romaine leaves

Mix first seven ingredients; stir in chicken. Line two slices of toast with lettuce. Top with chicken salad and remaining toast.
1 sandwich: 651 cal., 29g fat (5g sat. fat), 222mg chol., 1386mg sod., 45g carb. (18g sugars, 4g fiber), 51g pro.

TEST KITCHEN TIP
If you're cooking your own bird for this recipe, you'll need roughly half a pound of raw chicken for every cup of cooked chopped breast meat. Double the chicken mixture for lunch during the week, and use it as a sandwich filling or even serve it over salad greens.

SKILLET PORK CHOPS WITH APPLES & ONION

Simple recipes that land on the table fast are a lifesaver. I serve skillet pork chops with veggies and, when there's time, cornbread stuffing.
—Tracey Karst, Ponderay, ID

Takes: 20 min. • **Makes:** 4 servings

- 4 **boneless pork loin chops (6 oz. each)**
- 3 **medium apples, cut into wedges**
- 1 **large onion, cut into thin wedges**
- ¼ **cup water**
- ⅓ **cup balsamic vinaigrette**
- ½ **tsp. salt**
- ¼ **tsp. pepper**

1. Place a large nonstick skillet over medium heat; brown pork chops on both sides, about 4 minutes. Remove from pan.

2. In same skillet, combine apples, onion and water. Place pork chops over apple mixture; drizzle chops with vinaigrette. Sprinkle with salt and pepper. Reduce heat; simmer, covered, until a thermometer inserted in chops reads 145°, 3-5 minutes.

1 pork chop with ¾ cup apple mixture: 360 cal., 15g fat (4g sat. fat), 82mg chol., 545mg sod., 22g carb. (15g sugars, 3g fiber), 33g pro. **Diabetic exchanges:** 5 lean meat, 1 fruit, 1 fat.

EAT SMART
CURRIED CHICKEN SALAD

Curry and mustard complement the sweet fruit and crunchy nuts in this guilt-free salad. I also like it on whole wheat toast or scooped up with apple slices.

—Joanna Perdomo, Chicago, IL

Takes: 15 min. • **Makes:** 4 servings

- 3 cups cubed cooked chicken breast
- 1 medium apple, finely chopped
- ¼ cup slivered almonds, toasted
- 2 Tbsp. golden raisins
- 2 Tbsp. dried cranberries
- ½ cup fat-free plain Greek yogurt
- ¼ cup apricot preserves
- 2 Tbsp. curry powder
- 1 Tbsp. Dijon mustard
- ½ tsp. salt
- ¼ to ½ tsp. pepper
  Lettuce leaves

In a small bowl, combine the first five ingredients. In a small bowl, whisk the yogurt, preserves, curry, mustard, salt and pepper; pour over chicken mixture and toss to coat. Serve on lettuce leaves.

Note: If Greek yogurt is not available in your area, line a strainer with a coffee filter and place over a bowl. Place 1 cup fat-free yogurt in prepared strainer; refrigerate overnight. Discard liquid from bowl; proceed with the recipe as directed.

1 cup: 323 cal., 7g fat (1g sat. fat), 81mg chol., 477mg sod., 30g carb. (18g sugars, 3g fiber), 36g pro. **Diabetic exchanges:** 4 lean meat, 1 starch, ½ fruit, ½ fat.

5 INGREDIENT | EAT SMART
SHRIMP ASPARAGUS FETTUCCINE

Fettuccine lovers rejoice! This is a quick and healthy way to enjoy your favorite pasta. You could also use leftover chicken instead of shrimp in this versatile dinner.

—*Taste of Home* Test Kitchen

Takes: 20 min. • **Makes:** 4 servings

- 1 pkg. (9 oz.) refrigerated fettuccine
- 1 cup cut fresh asparagus (1-in. pieces)
- 1 lb. uncooked medium shrimp, peeled and deveined
- 3 Tbsp. olive oil, divided
- 2 garlic cloves, minced
- ¾ tsp. dried basil
- ¼ tsp. salt
- ¼ tsp. pepper

1. Bring 4 qt. water to a boil. Add fettuccine and asparagus. Boil until the pasta is tender, 2-3 minutes.

2. In a large nonstick skillet, saute shrimp in 2 Tbsp. oil for 2 minutes. Add garlic; cook until shrimp turn pink, 1-2 minutes longer.

3. Drain fettuccine mixture; add to skillet. Stir in the basil, salt, pepper and remaining oil; toss to coat.

1½ cups: 394 cal., 17g fat (4g sat. fat), 165mg chol., 519mg sod., 32g carb. (2g sugars, 2g fiber), 28g pro. **Diabetic exchanges:** 3 lean meat, 2½ starch, 2 fat.

5 INGREDIENT | EAT SMART
LEMON-GARLIC PORK CHOPS

My son James created these zesty chops spiced with paprika and cayenne. He keeps lemon juice and the seasonings on hand, using them for chops or even chicken at a moment's notice. It's also a smart way to flavor foods without a lot of additional calories, fat and sodium.
—Molly Seidel, Edgewood, NM

- -

Takes: 20 min. • **Makes:** 4 servings

2	Tbsp. lemon juice
2	garlic cloves, minced
1	tsp. salt
1	tsp. paprika
½	tsp. pepper
¼	tsp. cayenne pepper
4	boneless pork loin chops (6 oz. each)

1. Preheat broiler. In a small bowl, mix the first six ingredients; brush over pork chops. Place in a 15x10x1-in. baking pan.
2. Broil 4-5 in. from heat 4-5 minutes on each side or until a thermometer reads 145°. Let stand 5 minutes before serving.
1 pork chop: 233 cal., 10g fat (4g sat. fat), 82mg chol., 638mg sod., 2g carb. (0 sugars, 0 fiber), 33g pro. **Diabetic exchanges:** 5 lean meat.

5 INGREDIENT
GARLIC BREAD PIZZA SANDWICHES

I love inventing new ways to make grilled cheese sandwiches for my children. This version tastes like pizza. Using frozen garlic bread is a huge time-saver.
—Courtney Stultz, Weir, KS

- -

Takes: 20 min. • **Makes:** 4 servings

1	pkg. (11¼ oz.) frozen garlic Texas toast
¼	cup pasta sauce
4	slices provolone cheese
16	slices pepperoni
8	slices thinly sliced hard salami
	Additional pasta sauce, warmed, optional

1. Preheat griddle over medium-low heat. Add garlic toast; cook until lightly browned, 3-4 minutes per side.
2. Spoon 1 Tbsp. sauce over each of four pieces of toast. Top with cheese, pepperoni, salami and remaining toast. Cook until crisp and cheese is melted, 3-5 minutes, turning as necessary. Serve with additional pasta sauce if desired.
1 sandwich: 456 cal., 28g fat (10g sat. fat), 50mg chol., 1177mg sod., 36g carb. (4g sugars, 2g fiber), 19g pro.

TOMATO-ARTICHOKE TILAPIA

My mom and I really like tomatoes, capers and artichokes, so I used them together in this one-pan meal. The best part is that, on a busy night, I have all of the ingredients ready and waiting.
—Denise Klibert, Shreveport, LA

- -

Takes: 15 min. • **Makes:** 4 servings

- 1 Tbsp. olive oil
- 1 can (14½ oz.) diced tomatoes with roasted garlic, drained
- 1 can (14 oz.) water-packed quartered artichoke hearts, drained
- 2 Tbsp. drained capers
- 4 tilapia fillets (6 oz. each)

1. In a large skillet, heat oil over medium heat. Add tomatoes, artichoke hearts and capers; cook until heated through, stirring occasionally, 3-5 minutes.

2. Arrange tilapia over tomato mixture. Cook, covered, until fish begins to flake easily with a fork, 6-8 minutes.

1 fillet with ¾ cup sauce: 246 cal., 5g fat (1g sat. fat), 83mg chol., 886mg sod., 15g carb. (6g sugars, 1g fiber), 35g pro.

Italian Fish Fillets: Substitute 1 medium julienned green pepper, 1 small julienned onion, ½ cup Italian salad dressing and ½ tsp. Italian seasoning for first four ingredients. Cook 5 minutes or until tender. Add 2 cans (14½ oz. each) diced tomatoes; bring to a boil. Add fish and cook as directed.

EASY CARIBBEAN CHICKEN

This is a simple recipe that uses easy-to-find ingredients. Serve with some steamed vegetables for a complete meal. Use cubes of cooked pork or even shrimp instead of the chicken.
—Courtney Stultz, Weir, KS

- -

Takes: 20 min. • **Makes:** 4 servings

- 1 Tbsp. olive oil
- 1 lb. boneless skinless chicken breasts, cut into 1-in. pieces
- 2 tsp. garlic-herb seasoning blend
- 1 can (14½ oz.) fire-roasted diced tomatoes
- 1 can (8 oz.) unsweetened pineapple chunks
- ¼ cup barbecue sauce
    Hot cooked rice
    Fresh cilantro leaves, optional

In a large nonstick skillet, heat oil over medium-high heat. Add chicken and seasoning; saute until chicken is lightly browned and no longer pink, about 5 minutes. Add tomatoes, pineapple and barbecue sauce. Bring to a boil; cook and stir until flavors are blended and chicken is cooked through, 5-7 minutes. Serve with rice and, if desired, cilantro.

1 cup chicken mixture: 242 cal., 6g fat (1g sat. fat), 63mg chol., 605mg sod., 20g carb. (15g sugars, 1g fiber), 24g pro. **Diabetic exchanges:** 3 lean meat, 1 starch, ½ fat.

GRILLED BANANA BROWNIE SUNDAES

My niece Amanda Jean and I have a lot of fun in the kitchen creating different dishes. One of us will start with a recipe idea and it just grows from there—and so does the mess. That's exactly what happened with this incredible brownie sundae.
—Carol Farnsworth, Greenwood, IN

- -

Takes: 15 min. • **Makes:** 8 servings

- 2 medium bananas, unpeeled
- 4 oz. cream cheese, softened
- ¼ cup packed brown sugar
- 3 Tbsp. creamy peanut butter
- 8 prepared brownies (2-in. squares)
- 4 cups vanilla ice cream
- ½ cup hot fudge ice cream topping, warmed
- ½ cup chopped salted peanuts

1. Cut unpeeled bananas crosswise in half, then lengthwise in half. Place quartered bananas on an oiled grill rack, cut side down. Grill, covered, over medium-high heat on each side until lightly browned, 2-3 minutes. Cool slightly.
2. In a small bowl, beat the cream cheese, brown sugar and creamy peanut butter until smooth.
3. To serve, remove bananas from peel; place over brownies. Top with the cream cheese mixture, ice cream, fudge topping and peanuts.
1 sundae: 505 cal., 28g fat (11g sat. fat), 62mg chol., 277mg sod., 57g carb. (33g sugars, 3g fiber), 10g pro.

CHEESECAKE STRAWBERRY TRIFLE

The only drawback to this lovely dessert is that there's never any left! For a patriotic look, simply replace one of the layers of strawberry pie filling with blueberry—or use whatever filling you prefer.
—Lori Thorp, Frazee, MN

- -

Takes: 20 min. • **Makes:** 16 servings

- 1 pkg. (8 oz.) cream cheese, softened
- 1 cup sour cream
- ½ cup cold whole milk
- 1 pkg. (3.4 oz.) instant vanilla pudding mix
- 1 carton (12 oz.) frozen whipped topping, thawed
- 1½ cups crushed butter-flavored crackers (about 38 crackers)
- ¼ cup butter, melted
- 2 cans (21 oz. each) strawberry pie filling

1. In a large bowl, beat cream cheese until smooth. Beat in the sour cream; mix well.
2. In a small bowl, beat milk and pudding mix on low speed for 2 minutes. Stir into cream cheese mixture. Fold in whipped topping.
3. In a small bowl, combine the crackers and butter.
4. In a 2½-qt. trifle bowl, layer half of the cream cheese mixture, crumbs and the strawberry pie filling. Repeat the layers. Refrigerate until serving.
1 serving: 369 cal., 22g fat (14g sat. fat), 46mg chol., 333mg sod., 37g carb. (21g sugars, 1g fiber), 4g pro.

5 INGREDIENT
CINNAMON APPLE PAN BETTY

I found this recipe soon after I was married. You'll need just a few ingredients, which you probably already have on hand. It's super quick to put together, too. I make it often during fall and winter, when apples are at their best.
—Shirley Leister, West Chester, PA

- -

Takes: 15 min. • **Makes:** 6 servings

- 3   medium apples, peeled and cubed
- ½   cup butter
- 3   cups cubed bread
- ½   cup sugar
- ¾   tsp. ground cinnamon

In a large skillet, saute apples in butter until tender, 4-5 minutes. Add bread cubes. Stir together sugar and cinnamon; sprinkle over apple mixture and toss to coat. Saute until bread is warmed.

½ cup: 279 cal., 16g fat (10g sat. fat), 41mg chol., 208mg sod., 34g carb. (25g sugars, 2g fiber), 2g pro.

CANTALOUPE A LA MODE

This special dessert is a refreshing finale to a warm-weather meal.
—Nancy Walker, Granite City, IL

- -

Takes: 15 min.
Makes: 4 servings (1 cup sauce)

- ½   cup water
- ½   cup sugar
- 2   Tbsp. lemon juice
- 1   Tbsp. cornstarch
- 1   tsp. grated lemon zest
- 1   cup fresh or frozen blueberries
- 2   small cantaloupes, halved and seeded
- 4   scoops vanilla ice cream
     Fresh mint, optional

In a small saucepan, combine the first five ingredients; bring to a boil over medium heat. Boil and stir until thickened, about 2 minutes. Add blueberries; cook until heated through. Fill cantaloupe with ice cream; top with sauce. Garnish with fresh mint if desired.

1 serving: 337 cal., 8g fat (5g sat. fat), 29mg chol., 74mg sod., 67g carb. (56g sugars, 3g fiber), 5g pro.

TEST KITCHEN TIP
Frozen blueberries give off more juice than fresh berries. While this shouldn't affect this particular recipe, you may need to add a pinch more cornstarch to get the consistency you desire in the sauce.

HOMEMADE CHERRY CRISP

Only a few moments for a heartwarming dessert? It's true! This tasty treat relies on canned pie filling and takes mere minutes to heat up in the microwave.
—Laurie Todd, Columbus, MS

Takes: 15 min. • **Makes:** 4 servings

1	can (21 oz.) cherry pie filling
1	tsp. lemon juice
1	cup all-purpose flour
¼	cup packed brown sugar
¾	tsp. ground cinnamon
¼	tsp. ground allspice
⅓	cup cold butter, cubed
½	cup chopped walnuts
	Vanilla ice cream

1. Combine the pie filling and lemon juice in an ungreased 1½-qt. microwave-safe dish; set aside.
2. In a small bowl, combine flour, brown sugar, cinnamon and allspice; cut in butter until mixture resembles coarse crumbs. Add walnuts. Sprinkle over filling.
3. Microwave, uncovered, on high until bubbly, 3-4 minutes. Serve warm with vanilla ice cream.
1 cup: 567 cal., 24g fat (10g sat. fat), 41mg chol., 187mg sod., 81g carb. (50g sugars, 3g fiber), 8g pro.

5 INGREDIENT
ICE CREAM CONE TREATS

I came up with this recipe as a way for my grandkids to enjoy Rice Krispies treats without getting sticky hands. You can also insert a wooden pop stick into the cereal mixture balls and to create cute pops.
—Mabel Nolan, Vancouver, WA

- -

Takes: 20 min. • **Makes:** 12 servings

- 12 ice cream sugar cones
     Melted semisweet chocolate, optional
     Colored sprinkles
- 4 cups miniature marshmallows
- 3 Tbsp. butter
- 6 cups Rice Krispies

1. If desired, dip ice cream cones in melted chocolate to coat the edges; stand in juice glasses or coffee mugs.
2. Place the sprinkles in a shallow bowl. In a microwave or in a large saucepan over low heat, melt marshmallows and butter; stir until smooth. Remove from heat; stir in Rice Krispies.
3. Working quickly, use buttered hands to shape mixture into 12 balls; pack firmly into cones. Dip tops in sprinkles.
1 treat: 174 cal., 4g fat (2g sat. fat), 8mg chol., 142mg sod., 34g carb. (14g sugars, 0 fiber), 2g pro.

5 INGREDIENT | EAT SMART
STAR-SPANGLED PARFAITS

The best time for this dessert is mid-summer, when the blueberries are thick in our northern woods. Red raspberries can be added to the mixed berries, too, to brighten up the patriotic colors.
—Anne Theriault, Wellesley, MA

- -

Takes: 15 min. • **Makes:** 4 servings

- 2 cups fresh strawberries, cut into ½-in. pieces
- 2 cups fresh blueberries
- 4 tsp. reduced-fat raspberry walnut vinaigrette
- ¾ cup fat-free vanilla or strawberry Greek yogurt
- 2 tsp. minced fresh mint
     Unsweetened shredded coconut, optional

1. Place strawberries and blueberries in separate bowls. Drizzle each with 2 tsp. vinaigrette; toss to coat. In a small bowl, mix yogurt and mint.
2. Spoon the strawberries into four parfait glasses. Layer each with yogurt mixture and blueberries. If desired, top with coconut.
Note: Look for unsweetened coconut in the baking or health food section.
1 parfait: 172 cal., 7g fat (5g sat. fat), 0 chol., 41mg sod., 24g carb. (17g sugars, 5g fiber), 5g pro. **Diabetic exchanges:** 1 fruit, 1 fat, ½ starch.

CHOCOLATE CHERRY CREPES

No one suspects crepes can be this quick and easy. Try preparing the crepes and filling in advance. Then assemble them and add the topping just before serving.
—*Taste of Home* Test Kitchen

Takes: 20 min. • **Makes:** 6 servings

- 1 can (21 oz.) cherry pie filling
- 1 tsp. almond extract
- ⅔ cup whole milk
- 2 large eggs
- 2 Tbsp. butter, melted
- ¼ cup blanched almonds, ground
- ¼ cup all-purpose flour

FILLING

- 1 cup heavy whipping cream
- 3 oz. semisweet chocolate, melted and cooled
- ¼ cup slivered almonds, toasted

1. In a small bowl, combine pie filling and almond extract; cover and refrigerate until chilled. For crepes, place the milk, eggs, butter, almonds and flour in a blender; cover and process until smooth.

2. Heat a lightly greased 8-in. nonstick skillet; pour about 2 Tbsp. batter into center of skillet. Lift and tilt pan to coat bottom evenly. Cook until the top appears dry and the bottom is golden brown; turn and cook 15-20 seconds longer. Remove to a wire rack. Repeat with remaining batter, greasing skillet as needed. Stack cooled crepes with waxed paper or paper towels in between.

3. For the filling, in a mixing bowl, beat the cream and melted chocolate until soft peaks form. Spoon about 2 Tbsp. over each crepe; roll up. Top with cherry mixture and sprinkle with slivered almonds.

2 crepes: 433 cal., 28g fat (14g sat. fat), 139mg chol., 108mg sod., 39g carb. (29g sugars, 2g fiber), 7g pro.

5 INGREDIENT | EAT SMART

EASY LEMON BERRY TARTLETS

These flaky, sweet little treats filled with raspberries are a fun ending to a great weeknight meal. And they come together in mere minutes.
—Elizabeth Dehart, West Jordan, UT

Takes: 15 min. • **Makes:** 15 tartlets

- ⅔ cup frozen unsweetened raspberries, thawed and drained
- 1 tsp. confectioners' sugar
- 1 pkg. (1.9 oz.) frozen miniature phyllo tart shells
- 4 oz. reduced-fat cream cheese
- 2 Tbsp. lemon curd
  Fresh raspberries, optional

1. In a small bowl, combine the raspberries and confectioners' sugar; mash with a fork. Spoon into tart shells.

2. In a small bowl, combine cream cheese and lemon curd. Pipe or spoon over filling. Top with fresh raspberries if desired.

1 tartlet: 51 cal., 3g fat (1g sat. fat), 7mg chol., 43mg sod., 5g carb. (2g sugars, 0 fiber), 1g pro. **Diabetic exchanges:** ½ starch, ½ fat.

PEAR-BLUEBERRY AMBROSIA WITH CREAMY LIME DRESSING

This dessert is creamy and decadent, yet is chock-full of healthy fruit; the blueberries provide a pop of color.
—Laura Stricklin, Jackson, MS

- -

Takes: 20 min. • **Makes:** 10 servings

- 1 carton (8 oz.) mascarpone cheese
- 2 Tbsp. sugar
- 2 tsp. grated lime zest
- 2 Tbsp. lime juice
- 3 medium ripe pears, peeled and chopped
- 3 medium ripe bananas, sliced
- 1½ cups fresh blueberries
- ½ cup chopped hazelnuts

In a small bowl, mix mascarpone cheese, sugar, lime zest and lime juice. In a large bowl, combine the pears, bananas and blueberries. Spoon cheese mixture over fruit; gently toss to coat. Sprinkle with hazelnuts. Refrigerate leftovers.

¾ cup: 218 cal., 14g fat (6g sat. fat), 28mg chol., 13mg sod., 23g carb. (14g sugars, 4g fiber), 3g pro.

TEST KITCHEN TIP
A sprinkling of toasted coconut tops off this dessert quickly and with extra flair.

PUMPKIN PECAN SUNDAES

My family enjoys anything with pumpkin so I knew this recipe would be well-received. Butter pecan ice cream is a perfect partner for the spiced pumpkin sauce.
—Fancheon Resler, Albion, IN

Takes: 20 min. • **Makes:** 6 servings

- ⅓ cup sugar
- 2 tsp. cornstarch
- ¼ tsp. each ground ginger, cinnamon and nutmeg
- 1 cup canned pumpkin
- ⅔ cup 2% milk
- 1½ tsp. vanilla extract, divided
- 1 cup heavy whipping cream
- 3 Tbsp. confectioners' sugar
- 3 cups butter pecan ice cream
- 6 Tbsp. chopped pecans, toasted

1. In a small saucepan, combine the sugar, cornstarch and spices. Stir in the pumpkin and milk until smooth. Bring to a boil; cook and stir until thickened, about 2 minutes. Remove from the heat; stir in 1 tsp. vanilla.
2. In a small bowl, beat cream until it begins to thicken. Add confectioners' sugar and remaining vanilla; beat until stiff peaks form.
3. Scoop ice cream into six dessert dishes. Top each with ¼ cup pumpkin sauce and ⅓ cup whipped cream. Sprinkle with the chopped pecans.
1 sundae: 444 cal., 32g fat (15g sat. fat), 81mg chol., 140mg sod., 36g carb. (31g sugars, 2g fiber), 6g pro.

QUICK APPLE CRISP

This is the perfect ending to any meal. It's as quick as a boxed cake mix but it's a bit of a healthier dessert choice. It's ideal in fall when it seems that everyone has a bag of fresh apples to give away!
—Terri Wetzel, Roseburg, OR

Takes: 20 min. • **Makes:** 6 servings

- 4 medium tart apples, peeled and thinly sliced
- ¼ cup sugar
- 1 Tbsp. all-purpose flour
- 2 tsp. lemon juice
- ¼ tsp. ground cinnamon
TOPPING
- ⅔ cup old-fashioned oats
- ½ cup packed brown sugar
- ¼ cup all-purpose flour
- ½ tsp. ground cinnamon
- 3 Tbsp. cold butter
  Vanilla ice cream, optional

1. Toss apples with the sugar, flour, lemon juice and cinnamon. Transfer to a greased microwave-safe 9-in. deep-dish pie plate.
2. Mix first four topping ingredients. Cut in butter until crumbly; sprinkle over filling.
3. Cover with waxed paper. Microwave on high until apples are tender, 5-7 minutes. If desired, serve with ice cream.
1 cup: 252 cal., 7g fat (4g sat. fat), 15mg chol., 66mg sod., 49g carb. (35g sugars, 3g fiber), 2g pro.

BANANAS FOSTER SUNDAES

I have wonderful memories of eating bananas Foster in New Orleans, and as a dietitian, I wanted to find a healthier version. I combined the best of two recipes and added my own tweaks to create this southern treat.
—Lisa Varner, El Paso, TX

- -

Takes: 15 min. • **Makes:** 6 servings

- 1 Tbsp. butter
- 3 Tbsp. brown sugar
- 1 Tbsp. orange juice
- ¼ tsp. ground cinnamon
- ¼ tsp. ground nutmeg
- 3 large firm bananas, sliced
- 2 Tbsp. chopped pecans, toasted
- ½ tsp. rum extract
- 3 cups reduced-fat vanilla ice cream

1. In an 8- or 9-in. cast-iron or other ovenproof skillet, melt the butter over medium-low heat. Stir in brown sugar, orange juice, cinnamon and nutmeg until blended. Add bananas and pecans; cook until bananas are glazed and slightly softened, 2-3 minutes, stirring gently.
2. Remove from heat; stir in extract. Serve with ice cream.

Note: To toast nuts, cook in a skillet over low heat until nuts are lightly browned, stirring occasionally.

1 sundae: 233 cal., 7g fat (3g sat. fat), 23mg chol., 66mg sod., 40g carb. (30g sugars, 2g fiber), 4g pro.

BLUEBERRY GRAHAM DESSERT

When you're short on time but longing for cheesecake, try this fruity dessert. Ricotta and cream cheeses give every bit as much flavor as the classic dessert but without the effort. Instead of making individual servings, try laying the ingredients in a large serving bowl.
—*Taste of Home* Test Kitchen

- -

Takes: 15 min. • **Makes:** 4 servings

- ¾ cup graham cracker crumbs (about 12 squares)
- ¼ cup chopped walnuts
- 2 Tbsp. sugar
- ¼ tsp. ground cinnamon
- 2 Tbsp. butter
- 3 oz. cream cheese, softened
- ⅓ cup confectioners' sugar
- ½ cup ricotta cheese
- 2 tsp. lemon juice
- 4 cups fresh blueberries
  Whipped cream, optional

1. In a large bowl, combine the graham cracker crumbs, chopped walnuts, sugar and cinnamon. Stir in the butter; set aside. In another large bowl, beat cream cheese and confectioners' sugar until smooth. Beat in ricotta cheese and lemon juice.
2. Place ½ cup blueberries in each in four dessert dishes. Top with cream cheese mixture, crumbs and remaining blueberries. Garnish with whipped cream if desired. Refrigerate until serving.

½ cup: 430 cal., 23g fat (11g sat. fat), 51mg chol., 255mg sod., 53g carb. (35g sugars, 4g fiber), 9g pro.

5 INGREDIENT
NUTTY RICE KRISPIE COOKIES

My mom and I used to make these treats for Christmas every year. Making them with just the microwave means they're super easy and fun to mix up with little ones.
—Savanna Chapdelaine, Orlando, FL

- -

Takes: 15 min. • **Makes:** about 2 dozen

- 1 pkg. (10 to 12 oz.) white baking chips
- ¼ cup creamy peanut butter
- 1 cup miniature marshmallows
- 1 cup Rice Krispies
- 1 cup salted peanuts

In a large microwave-safe bowl, melt baking chips; stir until smooth. Stir in the peanut butter until blended. Add marshmallows, Rice Krispies and peanuts. Drop by heaping tablespoonfuls onto waxed paper-lined baking sheets. Cool completely. Store in an airtight container.

1 cookie: 127 cal., 8g fat (3g sat. fat), 2mg chol., 49mg sod., 11g carb. (9g sugars, 1g fiber), 3g pro.

TEST KITCHEN TIP
For extra fun, trying using chunky peanut butter instead of the creamy. You can also substitute chopped or slivered almonds for the salted peanuts.

5 INGREDIENT
FLUFFY HOT CHOCOLATE

This is our daughter's favorite recipe for hot chocolate. It may look like ordinary cocoa, but a touch of vanilla truly sets it apart from the rest. Best of all, the melted marshmallows give it a frothy body you just don't get from a cocoa packet.
—Jo Ann Schimcek, Weimar, TX

- -

Takes: 15 min. • **Makes:** 4 servings

- 8 tsp. sugar
- 4 tsp. baking cocoa
- 4 cups 2% milk
- 1½ cups miniature marshmallows
- 1 tsp. vanilla extract

In a small saucepan, combine the first four ingredients. Cook and stir over medium heat until marshmallows are melted, about 8 minutes. Remove from the heat; stir in vanilla. Ladle into mugs.

1 cup: 249 cal., 8g fat (5g sat. fat), 33mg chol., 128mg sod., 36g carb. (30g sugars, 0 fiber), 9g pro.

PRESSURE-COOKER CHERRY & SPICE RICE PUDDING

I love cherries, and this treat is a great way to showcase them. Best of all, it comes together fast in my one-pot pressure cooker. What could be easier? The rice pudding recipe always turns out wonderful.
—Deb Perry, Traverse City, MI

Takes: 20 min. • **Makes:** 12 servings

  4   cups cooked rice
  1   can (12 oz.) evaporated milk
  1   cup 2% milk
 ⅓   cup sugar
 ¼   cup water
 ¾   cup dried cherries
  3   Tbsp. butter, softened
  2   tsp. vanilla extract
 ½   tsp. ground cinnamon
 ¼   tsp. ground nutmeg

1. Generously grease a 6-qt. electric pressure cooker. Add rice, milks, sugar and water; stir to combine. Stir in the remaining ingredients.
2. Lock lid; make sure vent is closed. Select manual setting; adjust pressure to high and set the time for 3 minutes. When finished cooking, allow pressure to naturally release for 5 minutes, then quick-release any remaining pressure according to the manufacturer's directions. Stir lightly. Serve warm or cold. Refrigerate leftovers.
1 serving: 202 cal., 6g fat (4g sat. fat), 19mg chol., 64mg sod., 33g carb. (16g sugars, 1g fiber), 4g pro.

SNOWMEN COOKIES

These cute snowmen cookies make fun treats for children's parties. Kids are always willing to chip in and help decorate them.
—Sherri Johnson, Burns, TN

Takes: 20 min. • **Makes:** 32 cookies

  1   pkg. (16 oz.) Nutter Butter cookies
1¼   lbs. white candy coating, melted
      Miniature chocolate chips
      M&M's minis
      Pretzel sticks, halved
      Decorating gel or frosting

1. Using tongs, dip cookies in candy coating; allow the excess to drip off. Place on waxed paper. Place two chocolate chips on one end of each cookie for eyes. Place M&M's minis down middle for the buttons and between eyes for the nose.
2. For arms, dip ends of two pretzel stick halves into coating; attach one to each side of snowmen. Let stand until set. Pipe mouth and scarf with gel or frosting.
1 cookie: 180 cal., 9g fat (6g sat. fat), 0 chol., 67mg sod., 23g carb. (17g sugars, 1g fiber), 1g pro.

30 MINUTES

30 MINUTE SNACKS

FRUIT CHARCUTERIE BOARD

Who says cheese and sausage get to have all the fun? Make this a go-to party plate with any fruits that are in season.
—*Taste of Home* Test Kitchen

Takes: 25 minutes
Makes: 14 servings

- 10 fresh strawberries, halved
- 8 fresh or dried figs, halved
- 2 small navel oranges, thinly sliced
- 12 oz. seedless red grapes, about 1½ cups
- 1 medium mango, halved and scored
- ½ cup fresh blueberries
- 1 cup fresh blackberries
- ½ cup dried banana chips
- 2 large kiwifruit, peeled, halved, and thinly sliced
- 12 oz. seedless watermelon, about six slices
- ½ cup unblanched almonds
- 8 oz. Brie cheese
- 8 oz. mascarpone cheese
- ½ cup honey

On a large platter or cutting board, arrange the fruit, almonds, cheeses and honey. If desired, drizzle some of the honey over the mascarpone cheese before serving.

1 serving: 304 cal., 17g fat (8g sat. fat), 36mg chol., 116mg sod., 36g carb. (30g sugars, 4g fiber), 7g pro.

5 INGREDIENT
EASY BUFFALO CHICKEN DIP

Everyone will simply devour this savory and delicious dip with shredded chicken throughout. The spicy kick makes it perfect football-watching food, and the recipe always brings raves.
—Janice Foltz, Hershey, PA

Takes: 30 min. • **Makes:** 4 cups

- 1 pkg. (8 oz.) reduced-fat cream cheese
- 1 cup reduced-fat sour cream
- ½ cup Louisiana-style hot sauce
- 3 cups shredded cooked chicken breast
  Assorted crackers

1. Preheat oven to 350°. In a large bowl, beat the cream cheese, sour cream and hot sauce until smooth; stir in chicken.

2. Transfer to an 8-in. square baking dish coated with cooking spray. Cover and bake until heated through, 18-22 minutes. Serve warm with crackers.

3 Tbsp.: 77 cal., 4g fat (2g sat. fat), 28mg chol., 71mg sod., 1g carb. (1g sugars, 0 fiber), 8g pro.

CRANBERRY MEATBALLS & SAUSAGE

Years ago, I found a version of this recipe in a cookbook. At first taste, my family judged it a keeper. The tangy, saucy meatballs are requested by our friends whenever I host card night. We also take the yummy dish on camping trips.
—Marybell Lintott, Vernon, BC

- -

Takes: 30 min. • **Makes:** 16 servings

- 1 large egg, lightly beaten
- 1 small onion, finely chopped
- ¾ cup dry bread crumbs
- 1 Tbsp. dried parsley flakes
- 1 Tbsp. Worcestershire sauce
- ¼ tsp. salt
- 1 lb. bulk pork sausage
- 1 can (14 oz.) jellied cranberry sauce
- 3 Tbsp. cider vinegar
- 2 Tbsp. brown sugar
- 1 Tbsp. prepared mustard
- 1 pkg. (1 lb.) miniature smoked sausage links

1. In a large bowl, combine the first six ingredients. Crumble bulk sausage over the mixture and mix well. Shape into 1-in. balls. In a large skillet, cook the meatballs over medium heat until a thermometer reads 160°; drain.
2. In a large saucepan, combine cranberry sauce, vinegar, brown sugar and mustard. Cook and stir over medium heat until the cranberry sauce is melted. Add the meatballs and sausage links. Bring to a boil. Reduce heat; simmer, uncovered, until the sausage links are no longer pink and the sauce is slightly thickened, 10-15 minutes.
1 serving: 218 cal., 14g fat (5g sat. fat), 41mg chol., 514mg sod., 18g carb. (10g sugars, 1g fiber), 7g pro.

EAT SMART
SWEET PEA PESTO CROSTINI

I made a healthier spin on my favorite celebrity chef's pesto by using vegetable broth and going easy on the cheese. The thick consistency is perfect for topping crostini. If you're using it with pasta, add more broth for a sauce-like pesto.
—Amber Massey, Argyle, TX

- -

Takes: 25 min. • **Makes:** 20 pieces

- 12 oz. fresh or frozen peas, thawed
- 4 garlic cloves, halved
- 1 tsp. rice vinegar
- ½ tsp. salt
- ⅛ tsp. lemon-pepper seasoning
- 3 Tbsp. olive oil
- ¼ cup shredded Parmesan cheese
- ⅓ cup vegetable broth
- 1 whole wheat French bread demi-baguette (about 6 oz. and 12 in. long)
- 2 cups cherry tomatoes (about 10 oz.), halved or quartered

1. Preheat the broiler. Place the peas, garlic, vinegar, salt and lemon pepper in a blender or food processor; pulse until well blended. Continue processing while gradually adding oil in a steady stream. Add cheese; pulse just until blended. Add broth; pulse until mixture reaches the desired consistency.
2. Cut baguette into 20 slices, each ½ in. thick. Place slices on ungreased baking sheet. Broil 4-5 in. from heat until golden brown, 45-60 seconds per side. Remove to a wire rack to cool.
3. To assemble crostini, spread each slice with about 1 Tbsp. of the pesto mixture; top with tomato pieces.
1 piece: 77 cal., 2g fat (trace sat. fat), 1mg chol., 190mg sod., 11g carb. (2g sugars, 1g fiber), 3g pro. **Diabetic exchanges:** ½ starch, ½ fat.

5 INGREDIENT
BROCCOLI & CHIVE-STUFFED MINI PEPPERS

There's plenty of both crunch and cream in these party appetizers. Fresh chives help them really stand out.
—Jean McKenzie, Vancouver, WA

- -

Takes: 30 min. • **Makes:** 2 dozen

12	miniature sweet peppers
1	pkg. (8 oz.) cream cheese, softened
⅓	cup minced fresh chives
⅛	tsp. salt
⅛	tsp. pepper
⅔	cup finely chopped fresh broccoli
⅔	cup shredded cheddar cheese

1. Preheat oven to 400°. Cut the peppers lengthwise in half; remove seeds. In a bowl, mix cream cheese, chives, salt and pepper; stir in broccoli. Spoon into pepper halves.
2. Place on a foil-lined baking sheet; bake until heated through, 9-11 minutes. Sprinkle with cheddar cheese. Bake until the cheese is melted, 3-4 minutes longer. Cool slightly before serving.
1 stuffed pepper half: 48 cal., 4g fat (2g sat. fat), 14mg chol., 68mg sod., 1g carb. (1g sugars, 0 fiber), 1g pro.

SPEEDY SURPRISE
"I love these little poppers! Sometimes, I'll switch it up to add just a little more spice, and use jalapenos instead of sweet peppers. They have different flavors but both are always a big hit to bring as an appetizer to any event!"
—GINA.KAPFHAMER, TASTEOFHOME.COM

ROAST BEEF AIOLI BUNDLES

Everyone will want to try these delicious, dainty bundles. And while they look impressive, they're actually quite easy!
—*Taste of Home* Test Kitchen

Takes: 30 min. • **Makes:** 16 appetizers

16   fresh asparagus spears, trimmed
⅓   cup mayonnaise
1   garlic clove, minced
1   tsp. Dijon mustard
1   tsp. lemon juice
⅛   tsp. ground cumin
8   thin slices deli roast beef, cut in half lengthwise
1   medium sweet yellow pepper, thinly sliced
1   medium sweet orange pepper, thinly sliced
1   medium sweet red pepper, thinly sliced
16   whole chives

1. In a large skillet, bring 1 in. of water to a boil. Add asparagus; cover and cook for 3 minutes. Drain and immediately place in ice water. Drain and pat dry.
2. For the aioli, combine the mayonnaise, garlic, mustard, lemon juice and cumin in a small bowl. Place roast beef slices on a work surface; spread each slice with 1 tsp. aioli. Top each with an asparagus spear and the pepper strips. Roll up tightly; tie bundles with chives. Serve immediately.
1 appetizer: 52 cal., 4g fat (1g sat. fat), 6mg chol., 74mg sod., 2g carb. (1g sugars, 1g fiber), 2g pro. **Diabetic exchanges:** 1 fat.

BLUE CHEESE-STUFFED STRAWBERRIES

I was enjoying a salad with strawberries and blue cheese when the idea hit me to stuff the strawberries and serve them as an appetizer. It worked out perfectly, and the flavors blend so nicely.
—Diane Nemitz, Ludington, MI

Takes: 25 min. • **Makes:** 16 appetizers

½   cup balsamic vinegar
3   oz. fat-free cream cheese
½   cup crumbled blue cheese
16   large fresh strawberries
3   Tbsp. finely chopped pecans, toasted

1. Place vinegar in a small saucepan. Bring to a boil; cook until the liquid is reduced by half. Cool to room temperature.
2. Meanwhile, in a small bowl, beat cream cheese until smooth. Beat in blue cheese. Remove stems from the strawberries and scoop out the centers; fill each with about 2 tsp. of the cheese mixture. Sprinkle the pecans over the filling, pressing lightly. Chill until serving. Drizzle with balsamic vinegar.
1 stuffed strawberry: 36 cal., 2g fat (1g sat. fat), 3mg chol., 80mg sod., 3g carb. (2g sugars, 0 fiber), 2g pro. **Diabetic exchanges:** ½ fat.

QUICK & EASY SWEDISH MEATBALLS

Rich and creamy, this classic meatball sauce is a must in your recipe box.
—*Taste of Home* Test Kitchen

- -

Takes: 30 min. • **Makes:** 20 servings

1   pkg. (22 oz.) frozen fully cooked Angus beef meatballs
2   Tbsp. butter
2   Tbsp. all-purpose flour
1   cup beef broth
½   cup heavy whipping cream
¼   tsp. dill weed
¼   cup minced fresh parsley, optional

1. Prepare the meatballs according to the package directions.
2. Meanwhile, in a large saucepan, melt butter. Stir in flour until smooth; gradually add broth. Bring to a boil; cook and stir until thickened, 1-2 minutes. Stir in cream and dill; simmer for 1 minute. Stir in meatballs; heat through. Garnish with minced fresh parsley if desired.
1 meatball: 115 cal., 10g fat (5g sat. fat), 26mg chol., 253mg sod., 2g carb. (1g sugars, 0 fiber), 4g pro.

TEST KITCHEN TIP
You can use homemade meatballs and still turn out this recipe in record time. Make your meatballs ahead of time and freeze them; once cooked, they'll keep in an airtight container for up to three months.

WATERMELON CUPS

This lovely appetizer is almost too pretty to eat! Sweet watermelon cubes hold a refreshing topping that showcases cucumber, red onion and fresh herbs.
—*Taste of Home* Test Kitchen

- -

Takes: 25 min. • **Makes:** 16 appetizers

16   seedless watermelon cubes (1 in.)
⅓   cup finely chopped cucumber
5   tsp. finely chopped red onion
2   tsp. minced fresh mint
2   tsp. minced fresh cilantro
½   to 1 tsp. lime juice

1. Using a small melon baller or measuring spoon, scoop out the center of each watermelon cube, leaving a ¼-in. shell (save the pulp for another use).
2. In a small bowl, combine remaining ingredients; spoon the filling into the watermelon cubes.
1 serving: 7 cal., 0 fat (0 sat. fat), 0 chol., 1mg sod., 2g carb. (2g sugars, 0 fiber), 0 pro.

5 INGREDIENT
APPLE-GOUDA PIGS IN A BLANKET

For New Year's Eve, I used to make beef and cheddar pigs in a blanket, but I think apple and Gouda make an even better flavor celebration.
—Megan Weiss, Menomonie, WI

- -

Takes: 30 min. • **Makes:** 2 dozen

- 1 tube (8 oz.) refrigerated crescent rolls
- 1 small apple, peeled and cut into 24 thin slices
- 6 thin slices Gouda cheese, quartered
- 24 miniature smoked sausages
  Honey mustard salad dressing, optional

1. Preheat oven to 375°. Unroll the crescent dough and separate into eight triangles; cut each lengthwise into three thin triangles. On the wide end of each triangle, place one slice of apple, one folded piece of cheese and one sausage; roll up tightly.
2. Place 1 in. apart on parchment-lined baking sheets, point side down. Bake until golden brown, 10-12 minutes. If desired, serve with dressing.
1 appetizer: 82 cal., 6g fat (2g sat. fat), 11mg chol., 203mg sod., 5g carb. (1g sugars, 0 fiber), 3g pro.

HOT CHEESE DIP

When a colleague brought this cheesy dip to school for a teachers' potluck, I immediately gave it an A+. I had to have this irresistibly creamy recipe!
—Ardyce Piehl, Poynette, WI

- -

Takes: 30 min. • **Makes:** 3 cups

- 2 cups shredded part-skim mozzarella cheese
- 2 cups shredded cheddar cheese
- 2 cups mayonnaise
- 1 medium onion, minced
- 1 can (4 to 4½ oz.) chopped green chiles, drained
- ½ cup sliced ripe olives
- 1½ oz. sliced pepperoni
  Assorted crackers and fresh vegetables

Preheat oven to 325°. Combine the first five ingredients; spread into a greased shallow baking dish or pie plate. Top with olives and pepperoni. Bake until bubbly, about 25 minutes. Serve with crackers and fresh vegetables.
2 Tbsp.: 201 cal., 19g fat (5g sat. fat), 18mg chol., 285mg sod., 2g carb. (0 sugars, 0 fiber), 5g pro.

CILANTRO TOMATO BRUSCHETTA

All my family and friends love this easy tomato appetizer. The flavors blend for a great-tasting hors d'oeuvre that goes well with many different main dishes.
—Lisa Kane, Milwaukee, WI

- -

Takes: 25 min. • **Makes:** about 2 dozen

1 loaf (1 lb.) French bread, cut into 1-in. slices
½ cup olive oil, divided
1 Tbsp. balsamic vinegar
3 small tomatoes, seeded and chopped
¼ cup finely chopped onion
¼ cup fresh cilantro leaves, coarsely chopped
¼ tsp. salt
¼ tsp. pepper
¼ cup shredded part-skim mozzarella cheese

1. Preheat oven to 325°. Place the bread slices on ungreased baking sheets; brush with ¼ cup of oil. Bake until golden brown, 10-12 minutes.
2. In a small bowl, whisk together vinegar and the remaining oil. Stir in tomatoes, onion, cilantro, salt and pepper.
3. To serve, spoon scant 1 Tbsp. of the tomato mixture onto each slice of bread. Top with cheese.
1 piece: 98 cal., 5g fat (1g sat. fat), 1mg chol., 147mg sod., 11g carb. (1g sugars, 1g fiber), 2g pro. **Diabetic exchanges:** 1 starch, 1 fat.

ITALIAN-STYLE PIZZAS

With prepared pesto and crusts, these little tasty pizzas come together in a flash. I like to complete this satisfying meal with a salad and fresh fruit.
—Trisha Kruse, Eagle, ID

- -

Takes: 25 min. • **Makes:** 2 pizzas

2 prebaked mini pizza crusts
½ cup prepared pesto
⅔ cup shredded part-skim mozzarella cheese
½ cup sliced sweet onion
½ cup thinly sliced fresh mushrooms
¼ cup roasted sweet red peppers, drained
2 Tbsp. grated Parmesan cheese

Preheat oven to 400°. Place crusts on an ungreased baking sheet; spread with pesto. Layer with the mozzarella cheese, onion, mushrooms and peppers; sprinkle with Parmesan cheese. Bake until the cheese is melted, 10-12 minutes.
½ pizza: 429 cal., 23g fat (7g sat. fat), 23mg chol., 820mg sod., 37g carb. (3g sugars, 2g fiber), 19g pro.

5 INGREDIENT
BAKED ASPARAGUS DIP

Since I'm from Wisconsin, I thought it was only natural to put together a vegetable and a cheese—two of the foods my state produces in abundance!
—Sandra Baratka, Phillips, WI

Takes: 30 min. • **Makes:** about 2 cups

- 1 lb. diced cooked fresh asparagus, drained
- 1 cup grated Parmesan cheese
- 1 cup mayonnaise
  Baked pita chips

In a large bowl, combine the asparagus, cheese and mayonnaise. Place in a 2-cup ovenproof bowl. Bake at 375° until heated through, about 20 minutes. Serve warm with pita chips.

2 Tbsp.: 120 cal., 11g fat (2g sat. fat), 5mg chol., 162mg sod., 2g carb. (1g sugars, 0 fiber), 2g pro.

5 INGREDIENT
BOURBON MEATBALLS

Kick up your meatballs with a splash of bourbon and vinegar for punchy sweet-and-sour flavor.
—Kimla Carsten, Grand Junction, CO

Takes: 30 min. • **Makes:** about 3½ dozen

- 2 pkg. (22 oz. each) frozen fully cooked angus beef meatballs
- ¾ cup packed brown sugar
- ¼ cup white vinegar
- ¼ cup bourbon
- 2 tsp. spicy brown mustard

Prepare the meatballs according to package directions. In a large skillet, whisk together the remaining ingredients. Bring mixture to a simmer; cook 5 minutes. Stir in the meatballs; simmer until heated through, about 5 minutes.

1 meatball: 95 cal., 6g fat (3g sat. fat), 16mg chol., 192mg sod., 5g carb. (4g sugars, 0 fiber), 4g pro.

BACON CHEDDAR POTATO SKINS

Both crisp and hearty, this restaurant-quality snack is one that my family requests often—and I'm always happy to oblige!
—Trish Perrin, Keizer, OR

- -

Takes: 30 min. • **Makes:** 8 servings

4	large baking potatoes, baked
3	Tbsp. canola oil
1	Tbsp. grated Parmesan cheese
½	tsp. salt
¼	tsp. garlic powder
¼	tsp. paprika
⅛	tsp. pepper
8	bacon strips, cooked and crumbled
1½	cups shredded cheddar cheese
½	cup sour cream
4	green onions, sliced

1. Preheat oven to 475°. Cut the potatoes in half lengthwise; scoop out the pulp, leaving a ¼-in. shell (save the pulp for another use). Place the eight potato skins on a greased baking sheet.

2. Combine the next six ingredients; brush over both sides of skins.

3. Bake until crisp, about 7 minutes on each side. Sprinkle bacon and cheddar cheese inside the skins. Bake until the cheese is melted, about 2 minutes longer. Top with sour cream and onions. Serve immediately.

1 potato skin: 350 cal., 19g fat (7g sat. fat), 33mg chol., 460mg sod., 34g carb. (2g sugars, 4g fiber), 12g pro.

5 INGREDIENT

APRICOT-GLAZED BACON SPIRALS

Here's a real crowd-pleaser for an appetizer table or brunch buffet. Each spiral boasts a whole piece of crispy bacon, which contrasts with the apricot preserves for a sweet-and-salty treat.
—Kellie Mulleavy, Lambertville, MI

- -

Takes: 25 min. • **Makes:** 15 servings

1	Tbsp. butter
½	cup finely chopped onion
3	Tbsp. apricot preserves
1	tube (8 oz.) refrigerated crescent rolls
1	pkg. (2.1 oz.) ready-to-serve fully cooked bacon

1. Preheat oven to 375°. In a small skillet, heat butter over medium heat. Add onion; cook and stir until tender, 3-5 minutes. Reduce heat to low; add preserves. Cook and stir until melted. Remove from heat.
2. Unroll crescent dough into one long rectangle. Roll into a 15x9-in. rectangle, sealing seams and perforations. Cut crosswise into fifteen 1-in. strips; top each strip with a piece of bacon. Roll up jelly-roll style, starting with a short side; pinch seam to seal. Place on an ungreased baking sheet, cut side down.
3. Spoon apricot mixture over each spiral. Bake until golden brown, 12-15 minutes. Let stand for 5 minutes before serving. Refrigerate leftovers.
1 piece: 97 cal., 5g fat (2g sat. fat), 2mg chol., 185mg sod., 9g carb. (3g sugars, 0 fiber), 3g pro.

EAT SMART

GREEK SANDWICH BITES

Here's an appetizer that tastes like traditional spanakopita, but is much easier to make.
—Lynn Scully, Rancho Santa Fe, CA

- -

Takes: 25 min. • **Makes:** 16 appetizers

1	medium onion, finely chopped
1	Tbsp. olive oil
2	garlic cloves, minced
1	lb. fresh baby spinach
1	cup crumbled feta cheese
¼	cup pine nuts, toasted
¼	tsp. salt
¼	tsp. pepper
⅛	tsp. ground nutmeg
8	slices Italian bread (½ in. thick)
4	tsp. butter, softened

1. In a large nonstick skillet, saute onion in oil until tender. Add garlic; cook 1 minute longer. Stir in the spinach; cook and stir until wilted. Drain. Stir in the feta, pine nuts, salt, pepper and nutmeg.
2. Spread over four bread slices; top with the remaining bread slices. Spread outsides of the sandwiches with butter. Grill the sandwiches, uncovered, over medium heat until the bread is browned and the cheese is melted, turning once, 3-4 minutes. Cut each sandwich into quarters.
1 appetizer: 87 cal., 5g fat (2g sat. fat), 6mg chol., 200mg sod., 8g carb. (1g sugars, 1g fiber), 4g pro. **Diabetic exchanges:** 1 fat, ½ starch.

A KICK & A TWIST ARTICHOKE DIP

Some warm cream cheese-based dips are too salty for me, but this one has a nice balance. I developed the recipe for a co-worker's going-away party. If you want a little more zing, try adding black pepper or lemon pepper.

—Susan Hein, Burlington, WI

Takes: 25 min. • Makes: 8 cups

- 1 Tbsp. olive oil
- 10 to 12 green onions, chopped
- 6 garlic cloves, pureed
- 1 jalapeno pepper, seeded and chopped
- ¼ cup minced fresh parsley
- 3 Tbsp. lemon juice
- 4 pkg. (8 oz. each) cream cheese, softened
- 1 cup sour cream
- 1 cup mayonnaise
- 2 tsp. cracked fennel seed
- 1 to 2 tsp. crushed red pepper flakes
- 2 cups shredded Parmesan cheese
- 2 cans (14 oz. each) water-packed artichoke hearts, drained and coarsely chopped
  French bread baguette, sliced

1. In a large skillet, heat oil over medium heat. Add onions, garlic and jalapeno; cook and stir until soft, 4-6 minutes. Reduce heat; stir in parsley and lemon juice.
2. Add the cream cheese and cover, stirring every few minutes, until cream cheese is melted. Stir in sour cream, mayonnaise, fennel and pepper flakes. Remove from heat. Add Parmesan cheese and artichoke hearts, stirring gently to prevent the artichokes from breaking up.
3. Transfer to a 3- or 4-qt. slow cooker; turn heat to low. Serve warm on baguette slices. May be refrigerated until serving.
¼ cup: 197 cal., 18g fat (8g sat. fat), 34mg chol., 275mg sod., 4g carb. (2g sugars, 0 fiber), 5g pro.

GREEK PINWHEELS

I really like Greek-style food and appetizers, so I made up this recipe for a baby shower. It's a simple combination of puff pastry, cream cheese and tasty fillings. I just love sharing it with others.

—Veronica Worlund, Pasco, WA

Takes: 30 min. • Makes: 20 appetizers

- 1 sheet frozen puff pastry, thawed
- 1 Tbsp. beaten egg
- ¾ tsp. water
- ½ cup cream cheese, softened
- ⅓ cup marinated quartered artichoke hearts, drained and finely chopped
- ¼ cup crumbled feta cheese
- 1 Tbsp. finely chopped drained oil-packed sun-dried tomatoes
- 3 Greek olives, finely chopped
- 1 tsp. Greek seasoning

1. Preheat oven to 425°. Unfold puff pastry. Whisk egg and water; brush over pastry. Combine the remaining ingredients; spread over pastry to within ½ in. of edges. Roll up jelly-roll style. Cut into twenty ½-in. slices.
2. Place pinwheels 2 in. apart on greased baking sheets. Bake until puffed and golden brown, 9-11 minutes. Serve warm.
1 serving: 92 cal., 6g fat (2g sat. fat), 9mg chol., 142mg sod., 7g carb. (0 sugars, 1g fiber), 2g pro.

5 INGREDIENT
MEATBALLS WITH CHIMICHURRI SAUCE

Chimichurri is a delicious South American herb sauce featuring fresh cilantro and parsley. When you serve these meatballs, make sure you set out a bowl of the sauce on the side—your guests will want some for extra dipping!
—Amy Chase, Vanderhoof, BC

- -

Takes: 30 min.
Makes: about 20 (⅔ cup sauce)

- 1   pkg. (22 oz.) frozen fully cooked Angus beef meatballs
- 3   garlic cloves, peeled
- 1   cup packed Italian flat leaf parsley
- ¼   cup packed fresh cilantro leaves
- 1   tsp. salt
- ¼   tsp. coarsely ground pepper
- 2   Tbsp. red wine vinegar
- ½   cup extra virgin olive oil

1. Prepare the meatballs according to the package directions.
2. Meanwhile, place the garlic in a small food processor; pulse until chopped. Add the parsley, cilantro, salt and pepper; pulse until finely chopped. Add the vinegar. While processing, gradually add oil to the mixture in a steady stream.
3. In a large bowl, toss the meatballs with a little more than half of the chimichurri sauce. Transfer to a platter. Serve with remaining sauce for dipping.
1 meatball with about 2 tsp. sauce: 130 cal., 12g fat (4g sat. fat), 17mg chol., 318mg sod., 2g carb. (0 sugars, 0 fiber), 4g pro.

5 INGREDIENT
KICKIN' CAULIFLOWER

Try these savory bites for a kickin' appetizer that's healthy, too!
—Emily Tyra, Traverse City, MI

- -

Takes: 25 min. • **Makes:** 8 servings

- 1   medium head cauliflower (about 2¼ lbs.), cut into florets
- 1   Tbsp. canola oil
- ½   cup Buffalo wing sauce
-    Blue cheese salad dressing

1. Preheat oven to 400°. Toss cauliflower florets with oil; spread in a 15x10x1-in. pan. Roast until tender and lightly browned, 20-25 minutes, stirring once.
2. Transfer to a bowl; toss with the wing sauce. Serve with dressing on the side.
⅓ cup: 39 cal., 2g fat (0 sat. fat), 0 chol., 474mg sod., 5g carb. (2g sugars, 2g fiber), 2g pro.

30 MINUTE SIDES

AU GRATIN PEAS & POTATOES

While this delicious potato skillet is a wonderful side dish, it's satisfying enough to be a main course. The skillet prep takes less time than it does to bake an au gratin casserole or scalloped potatoes—but it's still good, old-fashioned comfort food at its best!
—Marie Peterson, DeForest, WI

Takes: 30 min. • **Makes:** 6 servings

- 6 bacon strips, diced
- 1 medium onion, chopped
- 4 cups sliced peeled cooked potatoes
- ½ tsp. salt
- 1 pkg. (10 oz.) frozen peas, cooked and drained
- 2 cups shredded sharp cheddar cheese, divided
- ½ cup mayonnaise
- ½ cup whole milk

1. In a large skillet, cook bacon until crisp. Remove with a slotted spoon to paper towels. Drain, reserving 1 Tbsp. of drippings in the pan. Saute onion in the drippings until tender.
2. Layer with potatoes, salt, peas, 1 cup of the cheese and the bacon. Reduce heat; cover and simmer until heated through, about 10 minutes.
3. Combine the mayonnaise and milk until smooth; pour over bacon. Sprinkle with the remaining cheese. Remove from heat; let stand for 5 minutes before serving.

1 cup: 473 cal., 31g fat (11g sat. fat), 52mg chol., 794mg sod., 31g carb. (5g sugars, 4g fiber), 18g pro.

EAT SMART
HONEYDEW & PROSCIUTTO SALAD

For parties, I turn melon and prosciutto into an easy salad with a honey mustard dressing. To add zip, stir in fresh basil and mint.
—Julie Merriman, Seattle, WA

Takes: 30 min. • **Makes:** 12 servings

- ⅓ cup olive oil
- ½ tsp. grated lime zest
- 2 Tbsp. lime juice
- 2 Tbsp. white wine vinegar
- 2 Tbsp. honey
- 1 tsp. Dijon mustard
- ¼ tsp. salt
- ¾ cup fresh cilantro leaves

SALAD
- 8 cups fresh arugula or baby spinach (about 5 oz.)
- ½ medium red onion, thinly sliced
- ¼ cup thinly sliced fresh mint leaves
- ¼ cup thinly sliced fresh basil leaves
- 8 cups diced honeydew melon
- 1 pkg. (8 oz.) fresh mozzarella cheese pearls
- ¼ lb. thinly sliced prosciutto, cut into wide strips

1. Place the first eight ingredients in a blender; cover and process until smooth. Place the arugula, onion and herbs in a large bowl. Drizzle with ⅓ cup of the vinaigrette and toss lightly to coat.
2. In large serving bowl, layer ¼ of each of the arugula mixture, honeydew, cheese and prosciutto. Repeat the layers 3 times. Serve with the remaining vinaigrette.

1 serving: 186 cal., 12g fat (4g sat. fat), 23mg chol., 294mg sod., 15g carb. (13g sugars, 1g fiber), 7g pro. **Diabetic exchanges:** 1 medium-fat meat, 1 vegetable, 1 fruit, 1 fat.

SWISS CHEESE BREAD

This bread will receive rave reviews, whether you serve it as an appetizer or with a meal. For real convenience, make it ahead of time and freeze it!
—Karla Boice, Mahtomedi, MN

- -

Takes: 30 min. • **Makes:** 24 servings

1	loaf (18-20 in.) French bread
8	oz. (2 sticks) butter, softened
2	cups shredded Swiss cheese
¾	tsp. celery seed
¾	tsp. garlic powder
3	Tbsp. dehydrated parsley flakes

1. Preheat oven to 425°. Cut bread in half crosswise. Make diagonal cuts, 1 in. thick, into bread but not through the bottom crust. Combine all remaining ingredients. Spread half the butter mixture between the bread slices. Spread remaining mixture over top and sides of bread.
2. Place the bread on double thickness of foil; cover loosely with more foil. Bake for 20-30 minutes. For the last 5 minutes, remove the foil covering bread to allow it to brown.
1 piece: 154 cal., 11g fat (6g sat. fat), 29mg chol., 217mg sod., 10g carb. (1g sugars, 1g fiber), 4g pro.

TEST KITCHEN TIP
You can make a smaller version of this recipe using fresh Italian rolls. You'll need half a stick of butter and a cup of shredded Swiss to make six rolls. Cheesy rolls go great alongside a cup of soup or chili!

EAT SMART
PUMPKIN & CAULIFLOWER GARLIC MASH

I wanted healthy alternatives to my family's favorite recipes. Pumpkin, cauliflower and thyme make an amazing dish. You'll never miss those plain old mashed potatoes!
—Kari Wheaton, South Beloit, IL

- -

Takes: 25 min. • **Makes:** 6 servings

1	medium head cauliflower, broken into florets (about 6 cups)
3	garlic cloves
⅓	cup spreadable cream cheese
1	can (15 oz.) solid-pack pumpkin
1	Tbsp. minced fresh thyme
1	tsp. salt
¼	tsp. cayenne pepper
¼	tsp. pepper

1. Place 1 in. of water in a large saucepan; bring to a boil. Add the cauliflower florets and garlic cloves; cook, covered, until tender, 8-10 minutes. Drain; transfer to a food processor.
2. Add the remaining ingredients; process until smooth. Return to pan; heat through, stirring occasionally.
⅔ cup: 87 cal., 4g fat (2g sat. fat), 9mg chol., 482mg sod., 12g carb. (5g sugars, 4g fiber), 4g pro. **Diabetic exchanges:** 1 vegetable, ½ starch, ½ fat.

PARMESAN SNAP PEA PASTA

My family loves pasta! This simple dish is always welcome on our table, especially during the spring when sugar snap peas are at their sweetest. To keep us from getting in a rut, I change up the flavors.
—Crystal Jo Bruns, Iliff, CO

Takes: 30 min.
Makes: 12 servings

- 1 lb. fresh sugar snap peas (about 5 cups), trimmed
- 1 pkg. (16 oz.) angel hair pasta
- 5 Tbsp. olive oil, divided
- 1 medium red onion, finely chopped
- 3 garlic cloves, minced
- ½ tsp. salt
- ¼ tsp. crushed red pepper flakes
- ⅛ tsp. coarsely ground pepper
- 1¼ cups grated Parmesan cheese, divided

1. In a 6-qt. stockpot, bring 16 cups water to a boil. Add peas; cook, uncovered, just until crisp-tender, 3-4 minutes. Using a strainer, remove peas from pot.

2. In the same pot, add pasta to the boiling water; cook according to the package directions. Drain, reserving 1 cup of the cooking water; return to pot. Toss with 3 Tbsp. oil.

3. In a large skillet, heat the remaining oil over medium heat; saute onion until tender, 2-3 minutes. Add the garlic and seasonings; cook and stir for 1 minute. Stir in the peas; heat through.

4. Toss with pasta, adding 1 cup of cheese and the reserved cooking water as desired. Sprinkle with the remaining cheese.

¾ cup: 258 cal., 9g fat (2g sat. fat), 7mg chol., 254mg sod., 35g carb. (4g sugars, 3g fiber), 10g pro.

SPINACH & BACON SALAD WITH PEACHES

Peaches with bacon? Oh, yeah! I made this family favorite for a summer party. It was so easy to prep the parts separately, then toss it all together right before chow time.
—Megan Riofski, Frankfort, IL

Takes: 25 min.
Makes: 8 servings (1½ cups dressing)

- 1 cup olive oil
- ⅓ cup cider vinegar
- ¼ cup sugar
- 1 tsp. celery seed
- 1 tsp. ground mustard
- ½ tsp. salt

SALAD
- 6 cups fresh baby spinach (about 6 oz.)
- 2 medium peaches, sliced
- 1¾ cups sliced fresh mushrooms
- 3 large hard-boiled large eggs, halved and sliced
- ½ lb. bacon strips, cooked and crumbled
- 1 small red onion, halved and thinly sliced
- ¼ cup sliced almonds, toasted
  Grated Parmesan cheese

Place the first six ingredients in a blender; cover and process until blended. In a large bowl, combine the spinach, peaches, mushrooms, eggs, bacon, onion and almonds. Serve with dressing and cheese.

1½ cups salad with 3 Tbsp. dressing: 391 cal., 35g fat (6g sat. fat), 80mg chol., 372mg sod., 13g carb. (10g sugars, 2g fiber), 8g pro.

BACON-PIMIENTO CHEESE CORN MUFFINS

Cornbread is essential at our family dinners. With the addition of bacon and pimiento cheese, you'll have requests for more long after the get-together!
—Holly Jones, Kennesaw, GA

Takes: 25 min. • **Makes:** 10 muffins

    1   jar (5 oz.) pimiento cheese spread
    ¼   cup butter, melted
    ¼   cup sour cream
    1   large egg
    1   pkg. (8½ oz.) cornbread/muffin
        mix
    4   bacon strips, cooked and crumbled

1. Preheat oven to 400°. Whisk together cheese spread, butter, sour cream and egg until blended. Add muffin mix; stir just until moistened. Fold in bacon.
2. Fill 10 greased or paper-lined muffin cups three-fourths full. Bake until a toothpick inserted in the center of a muffin comes out clean, 10-12 minutes. Cool muffins for 5 minutes before removing from pan to a wire rack. Serve warm.
1 muffin: 212 cal., 13g fat (7g sat. fat), 47mg chol., 376mg sod., 18g carb. (6g sugars, 2g fiber), 5g pro.

CRUNCHY RAMEN SALAD

For potlucks and picnics, this salad is a knockout. I tote the veggies in a bowl, the dressing in a jar and the noodles in a bag— then shake them up together when it's time to eat.
—LJ Porter, Bauxite, AR

Takes: 25 min. • **Makes:** 16 servings

    1   Tbsp. plus ½ cup olive oil, divided
    ½   cup slivered almonds
    ½   cup sunflower kernels
    2   pkg. (14 oz. each) coleslaw mix
   12   green onions, chopped
        (about 1½ cups)
    1   medium sweet red pepper,
        chopped
    ⅓   cup cider vinegar
    ¼   cup sugar
    ⅛   tsp. pepper
    2   pkg. (3 oz. each) chicken-
        flavored ramen noodles

1. In a large skillet, heat 1 Tbsp. oil over medium heat. Add the slivered almonds and sunflower kernels; cook until toasted, about 4 minutes. Cool.
2. In a large bowl, combine the coleslaw mix, onions and red pepper. In a small bowl, whisk vinegar, sugar, pepper, the contents of the ramen seasoning packets and the remaining oil. Pour over salad; toss to coat. Refrigerate until serving. Break noodles into small pieces. Just before serving, stir in noodles, almonds and sunflower kernels.
¾ cup: 189 cal., 13g fat (2g sat. fat), 0 chol., 250mg sod., 16g carb. (6g sugars, 3g fiber), 4g pro.

5 INGREDIENT

SPINACH-PARM CASSEROLE

For those who ignore Popeye and won't eat their spinach, I find that spinach with garlicky butter and Parmesan helps to change their minds.

—Judy Batson, Tampa, FL

- -

Takes: 25 min. • **Makes:** 6 servings

2   lbs. fresh baby spinach
5   Tbsp. butter
3   Tbsp. olive oil
3   garlic cloves, minced
1   Tbsp. Italian seasoning
¾   tsp. salt
1   cup grated Parmesan cheese

1. Preheat oven to 400°. In a stockpot, bring 5 cups water to a boil. Add spinach; cook, covered, 1 minute or just until wilted. Drain well.

2. In a small skillet, heat butter and oil over medium-low heat. Add the garlic, Italian seasoning and salt; cook and stir until the garlic is tender, 1-2 minutes.

3. Spread the spinach in a greased 8-in. square or 1½-qt. baking dish. Drizzle with the butter mixture; sprinkle with cheese. Bake, uncovered, until the cheese is lightly browned, 10-15 minutes.

⅔ cup: 239 cal., 21g fat (9g sat. fat), 37mg chol., 703mg sod., 7g carb. (1g sugars, 3g fiber), 10g pro.

GRANDMA'S POTATO DUMPLINGS

Day-old rolls and leftover spuds are scrumptious the second time around when you turn them into buttery potato dumplings. Once you've tried this recipe, don't be surprised if you regularly make too many mashed potatoes on purpose!
—Wendy Stenman, Germantown, WI

- -

Takes: 25 min. • **Makes:** 4 servings

2 day-old hard rolls
½ cup water
2 tsp. canola oil
½ cup leftover mashed potatoes
1 large egg, lightly beaten
  Dash ground nutmeg
1 to 2 Tbsp. all-purpose flour
¼ cup butter, cubed

1. Tear rolls into ½-in. pieces; place in a 15x10x1-in. baking pan. Drizzle with water and squeeze dry.
2. In a large skillet, heat oil over medium-high heat. Add torn rolls; cook and stir until lightly toasted, 1-2 minutes.
3. In a small bowl, combine potatoes, egg, nutmeg and bread. Add enough flour to achieve a shaping consistency. With floured hands, shape mixture into 3-in. balls.
4. Fill a Dutch oven two-thirds full with water; bring to a boil. Carefully add the dumplings. Reduce the heat; simmer, uncovered, until a toothpick inserted in center of dumplings comes out clean, 8-10 minutes. Meanwhile, in a small heavy saucepan, melt butter over medium heat. Heat until golden brown, 4-6 minutes[.
5. Serve warm dumplings with butter.
1 dumpling with 1 Tbsp. butter: 255 cal., 17g fat (8g sat. fat), 84mg chol., 322mg sod., 22g carb. (1g sugars, 1g fiber), 5g pro.

5 INGREDIENT | EAT SMART
SLICED TOMATO SALAD

This treasured recipe is from my grandmother. It's a perfect platter to serve with burgers or hot sandwiches.
—Kendal Tangedal, Plentywood, MT

- -

Takes: 25 min. • **Makes:** 12 servings

8 large tomatoes, cut into ¼-in. slices
2 large sweet onions, halved and thinly sliced
⅓ cup olive oil
2 Tbsp. lemon juice
1 tsp. dried oregano
¾ tsp. salt
¼ tsp. pepper
2 Tbsp. minced fresh parsley

Arrange tomatoes and onions on a large rimmed serving platter. In a small bowl, whisk the oil, lemon juice, oregano, salt and pepper. Drizzle over top. Sprinkle with parsley.
1 serving: 94 cal., 6g fat (1g sat. fat), 0 chol., 159mg sod., 9g carb. (6g sugars, 2g fiber), 2g pro. **Diabetic exchanges:** 2 vegetable, 1 fat.

TEST KITCHEN TIP
Make the most of the bounty from a summer garden by adding in sliced zucchini, cucumbers or peppers—red, yellow or green. Or for a little creaminess, add slices of fresh mozzarella cheese.

HONEY-GARLIC BRUSSELS SPROUTS

At a holiday dinner recently, I had the best Brussels sprouts ever! They were seasoned to perfection and lightly sweetened. I've tried to re-create the dish, and this comes very close. It has just the right amount of garlic and sweetness.

—Robin Haas, Jamaica Plain, MA

Takes: 25 min. • **Makes:** 6 servings

- 2   lbs. Brussels sprouts, trimmed and halved
- 2   Tbsp. honey
- 1   Tbsp. lemon juice
- 1   Tbsp. olive oil
- 2   tsp. garlic salt

Preheat oven to 425°. Toss all ingredients; spread in a foil-lined 15x10x1-in. baking pan. Bake, stirring halfway through cooking, until the sprouts are tender and lightly browned, 15-20 minutes.

⅔ cup: 100 cal., 3g fat (0 sat. fat), 0 chol., 357mg sod., 18g carb. (9g sugars, 5g fiber), 5g pro. **Diabetic exchanges:** 1 vegetable, ½ starch, ½ fat.

TEST KITCHEN TIP
These same ingredients make an awesome slaw. Core and chop the raw Brussels sprouts, then toss them with the rest of the ingredients. For a fall twist, use maple syrup instead of honey.

BLUE CHEESE GARLIC BREAD

This is a great way to dress up an ordinary loaf of bread. Serve slices as an appetizer or with a meal.

—Kevalyn Henderson, Hayward, WI

Takes: 30 min. • **Makes:** 10 servings

- ½   cup butter, softened
- 4   oz. crumbled blue cheese
- 2   Tbsp. grated Parmesan cheese
- 1   Tbsp. minced chives
- 1   tsp. garlic powder
- 1   loaf (1 lb.) unsliced French bread

1. Preheat oven to 350°. In a small bowl, combine the first five ingredients. Cut into the bread to make 1-in.-thick slices, but don't cut all the way through the bottom crust; leave slices attached at the bottom. Spread the cheese mixture between slices.
2. Wrap loaf in a large piece of heavy-duty foil (about 28x18 in.). Fold the foil around the bread and seal tightly. Bake until heated through, about 20 minutes. Serve warm.
1 slice: 250 cal., 14g fat (8g sat. fat), 34mg chol., 546mg sod., 24g carb. (1g sugars, 1g fiber), 7g pro.

ROASTED CARROTS WITH THYME

Cutting the carrots lengthwise makes this dish look extra pretty.
—Deirdre Cox, Kansas City, MO

Takes: 30 min. • **Makes:** 4 servings

1   lb. medium carrots, peeled and halved lengthwise
2   tsp. minced fresh thyme or ½ tsp. dried thyme
2   tsp. canola oil
1   tsp. honey
¼   tsp. salt

Preheat oven to 400°. Place the carrots in a greased 15x10x1-in. baking pan. In a small bowl, mix the thyme, oil, honey and salt; brush over the carrots. Roast until tender, 20-25 minutes.

1 serving: 73 cal., 3g fat (0 sat. fat), 0 chol., 226mg sod., 12g carb. (7g sugars, 3g fiber), 1g pro. **Diabetic exchanges:** 1 vegetable, ½ fat.

SPEEDY SURPRISE

"This recipe is flavorful and so easy. It's a pretty dish you can prep ahead of time then simply toss in the oven when it's time to bake. The fresh thyme makes it special."

—EBRAMKAMP, TASTEOFHOME.COM

FRENCH ONION CASSEROLE

Fans of French onion soup will gobble up this comforting casserole. The 30-minute side dish would be a nice accompaniment to beef entrees.
—Margaret McClatchey, Loveland, CO

Takes: 30 min. • **Makes:** 8 servings

8   medium onions, sliced
5   Tbsp. butter, divided
2   Tbsp. all-purpose flour
       Dash pepper
¾   cup beef broth
¼   cup sherry or additional beef broth
1½   cups salad croutons
½   cup shredded Swiss cheese
3   Tbsp. grated Parmesan cheese

1. Preheat broiler. In a large cast-iron or other ovenproof skillet, saute onions in 3 Tbsp. butter until tender. Stir in flour and pepper until blended; gradually add broth and sherry. Bring to a boil; cook and stir until thickened, about 2 minutes.

2. In a microwave, melt remaining butter. Add croutons; toss to coat. Spoon over onion mixture. Sprinkle with cheeses.

3. Broil 3-4 in. from the heat until cheese is melted, 1-2 minutes.

½ cup: 205 cal., 11g fat (6g sat. fat), 27mg chol., 279mg sod., 21g carb. (10g sugars, 3g fiber), 6g pro.

HONEY-THYME BUTTERNUT SQUASH

This golden, honey-sweetened squash is just as hearty and comforting as your favorite potato dish. With its bright color, it makes an attractive side for special autumn meals.

—Bianca Noiseux, Bristol, CT

Takes: 30 min. • **Makes:** 10 servings

- 1 large butternut squash (about 5 lbs.), peeled and cubed
- ¼ cup butter, cubed
- 3 Tbsp. half-and-half cream
- 2 Tbsp. honey
- 2 tsp. dried parsley flakes
- ½ tsp. salt
- ⅛ tsp. dried thyme
- ⅛ tsp. coarsely ground pepper

In a large saucepan, bring 1 in. of water to a boil. Add the squash; cover and cook for 10-15 minutes or until tender. Drain and mash with the remaining ingredients.

¾ cup: 145 cal., 5g fat (3g sat. fat), 14mg chol., 161mg sod., 26g carb. (9g sugars, 7g fiber), 2g pro. **Diabetic exchanges:** 1½ starch, 1 fat.

SPEEDY SURPRISE

"Very good, very easy. If you cut the squash in half, place it in a dish with water and microwave it on high for 20-30 minutes, the skin peels right off."

—WISCOOK, TASTEOFHOME.COM

PEAR & POMEGRANATE SALAD

Pomegranate and Boursin add zip to this cool salad of Bosc pears over lettuce. Look for the 5-ounce Boursin with a firmer texture than the spreadable version.

—Erika Monroe-Williams, Scottsdale, AZ

Takes: 25 min. • **Makes:** 4 servings

- ¼ cup apple juice
- 2 Tbsp. canola oil
- 1 Tbsp. cider vinegar
- 1 Tbsp. white balsamic vinegar or white wine vinegar
- ⅛ tsp. onion powder
- ⅛ tsp. coarsely ground pepper
  Dash salt
- 3 medium Bosc pears
- 1 head Boston or Bibb lettuce (about 6 oz.), torn
- 1 cup pomegranate seeds
- 1 cup coarsely chopped pecans, toasted
- ¾ cup crumbled Boursin garlic and fine herbs cheese (half of a 5.2-oz. pkg.) or garlic and herb feta cheese

1. In a blender, combine the first seven ingredients. Cut one pear lengthwise in half; peel, core and coarsely chop one pear half. Add chopped pear to blender; cover and process until blended. Cut remaining pears and pear half lengthwise into ¼-in. slices.
2. Arrange lettuce on four plates. Top with the pears, pomegranate seeds and pecans; sprinkle with cheese. Drizzle with dressing; serve immediately.

Note: Boursin garlic and fine herbs cheese, sold in a 5.2-oz. package, has a firmer texture than the spreadable cheese product. To toast nuts, bake in a shallow pan at 350° for 5-10 minutes or cook in a skillet over low heat until lightly browned, stirring occasionally.

1 serving: 388 cal., 29g fat (4g sat. fat), 6mg chol., 74mg sod., 34g carb. (23g sugars, 7g fiber), 4g pro.

VEGGIE CHOPPED SALAD

My husband's aunt gave me this recipe back in the 1980s, and it's been a staple at our house ever since. I like to make it a day ahead because some time in the fridge makes it even better.
—Madeline Etzkorn, Burien, WA

Takes: 25 min.
Makes: 12 servings

- 3 cups finely chopped fresh broccoli
- 3 cups finely chopped cauliflower
- 3 cups finely chopped celery
- 2 cups frozen peas (about 8 oz.), thawed
- 6 bacon strips, cooked and crumbled
- 1⅓ cups mayonnaise
- ¼ cup sugar
- 2 Tbsp. grated Parmesan cheese
- 1 Tbsp. cider vinegar
- ¼ tsp. salt
- ¾ cup salted peanuts

In a large bowl, combine the first five ingredients. In a small bowl, mix the mayonnaise, sugar, cheese, vinegar and salt until blended. Add to the salad and toss to coat. Just before serving, stir in peanuts. Refrigerate any leftovers.

¾ cup: 308 cal., 26g fat (4g sat. fat), 14mg chol., 357mg sod., 12g carb. (7g sugars, 3g fiber), 7g pro.

ZUCCHINI CHEDDAR SAUTE

When the zucchini in your garden ripens all at once, try my saute method and sprinkle with cheese and toppings. We sometimes add other quick-cooking veggies.
—Margaret Drye, Plainfield, NH

Takes: 25 min. • **Makes:** 4 servings

- 3 Tbsp. butter
- ¾ cup chopped onion
- 1½ tsp. dried basil
- 4 cups coarsely shredded zucchini
- 1 large garlic clove, minced
- ¾ tsp. salt
- ¼ tsp. pepper
- 1 cup shredded cheddar cheese
- 2 medium tomatoes, cut into ¾-in. pieces
- 3 Tbsp. sliced ripe olives

1. In a large skillet, heat butter over medium heat. Add onion and basil; cook and stir until the onion is tender, 4-5 minutes. Add the zucchini and garlic; cook and stir over medium-high heat just until zucchini is tender, 2-3 minutes. Stir in salt and pepper.
2. Top with cheese, tomatoes and olives. Cook, covered, on low until the cheese is melted, about 1 minute.

¾ cup: 244 cal., 19g fat (12g sat. fat), 53mg chol., 747mg sod., 10g carb. (6g sugars, 3g fiber), 10g pro.

SPICY CHUCK WAGON BEANS

Baked beans don't get any easier! All you have to do is open some cans, chop a pepper and an onion, and add a dash (or two) of hot sauce. They'll simmer to perfection in minutes.
—James Schend, Pleasant Prairie, WI

Takes: 30 min. • **Makes:** 24 servings

- 1 Tbsp. canola oil
- 1 medium onion, chopped
- 2 cans (28 oz. each) baked beans
- 3 cans (15 oz. each) chili beans, undrained
- 2 cans (15 oz. each) black beans, rinsed and drained
- 2 pkg. (7 oz. each) frozen fully cooked breakfast sausage links, thawed and cut into ½-in. pieces
- 1 cup beer or reduced-sodium chicken broth
- 2 chipotle peppers in adobo sauce, minced
- 1 to 2 Tbsp. hot pepper sauce

In a Dutch oven, heat oil over medium-high heat; saute onion until tender, 3-5 minutes. Stir in remaining ingredients; bring to a boil. Reduce heat; simmer, uncovered, until thickened and flavors are blended, about 15 minutes, stirring occasionally.

⅔ cup: 221 cal., 8g fat (3g sat. fat), 15mg chol., 663mg sod., 30g carb. (2g sugars, 8g fiber), 10g pro.

Slow cooker option: In a greased 6-qt. slow cooker, combine all ingredients, omitting oil. Cook, covered, on low until heated through, 6-8 hours.

5 INGREDIENT
CORN FRITTER PATTIES

These five-ingredient fritters are a thrifty way to enjoy a beloved southern staple without having to leave home.
—Megan Hamilton, Pineville, MO

Takes: 30 min. • **Makes:** 4 servings

- 1 cup pancake mix
- 1 large egg, lightly beaten
- ¼ cup plus 2 Tbsp. 2% milk
- 1 can (7 oz.) whole kernel corn, drained
- 2 cups canola oil

1. In a small bowl, combine the pancake mix, egg and milk just until moistened. Stir in the whole kernel corn.
2. In a cast-iron or electric skillet, heat ¼ in. of oil to 375°. Drop batter by ¼ cupfuls into the oil; press lightly to flatten. Cook until patties are golden brown, about 2 minutes on each side.

2 fritters : 228 cal., 11g fat (1g sat. fat), 48mg chol., 590mg sod., 26g carb. (5g sugars, 3g fiber), 6g pro.

CHIVE-CHEESE CORNBREAD

This cornbread goes well with any main dish. The chives and sharp cheddar cheese give it a special flavor.
—Sybil Eades, Gainesville, GA

Takes: 30 min. • **Makes:** 15 servings

1 cup cornmeal
1 cup all-purpose flour
¼ cup sugar
4 tsp. baking powder
2 large eggs, room temperature
1 cup whole milk
¼ cup butter, melted
1 cup shredded sharp
   cheddar cheese
3 Tbsp. minced chives

1. Preheat oven to 400°. In a large bowl, combine cornmeal, flour, sugar and baking powder. In another bowl, whisk the eggs, milk and butter. Stir into the dry ingredients just until moistened. Gently fold in cheese and chives.

2. Pour into a greased 13x9-in. baking pan. Bake until golden brown, about 18 minutes. Cut into strips; serve warm.

1 piece: 150 cal., 7g fat (4g sat. fat), 47mg chol., 200mg sod., 18g carb. (4g sugars, 1g fiber), 5g pro.

QUICK BARBECUED BEANS

Cooking on the grill introduces a subtle flavor to this simple, classic recipe. This dish features a nice blend of beans and preparation time is minimal.
—Millie Vickery, Lena, IL

Takes: 25 min. • **Makes:** 5 servings

1 can (16 oz.) kidney beans, rinsed
   and drained
1 can (15½ oz.) great northern
   beans, rinsed and drained
1 can (15 oz.) pork and beans
½ cup barbecue sauce
2 Tbsp. brown sugar
2 tsp. prepared mustard

In an ungreased 8-in. square disposable foil pan, combine all ingredients. Grill, covered, over medium heat until heated through, 15-20 minutes, stirring occasionally.

¾ cup: 264 cal., 2g fat (0 sat. fat), 0 chol., 877mg sod., 51g carb. (15g sugars, 13g fiber), 14g pro.

OLD-FASHIONED GREEN BEANS

Mom would prepare homegrown green beans using this recipe. Boy, did they ever taste good! The bacon provides rich flavor and the brown sugar a touch of sweetness. This is one irresistible side dish.

—Willa Govoro, St. Clair, MO

- -

Takes: 30 min. • **Makes:** 6-8 servings

6   bacon strips, cut into ½-in. pieces
2   lbs. fresh green beans
3   Tbsp. brown sugar
½   cup water

In a large skillet, cook bacon over medium heat until crisp, about 5 minutes. Add the beans, brown sugar and water. Stir gently; bring to a boil. Reduce the heat; cover and simmer for 15 minutes or until beans are crisp-tender. Remove to a serving bowl with a slotted spoon.

¾ cup: 145 cal., 10g fat (4g sat. fat), 11mg chol., 132mg sod., 12g carb. (8g sugars, 3g fiber), 3g pro.

VEGETABLE & BARLEY PILAF

This hearty, colorful dish has the added benefit of being good for you. Barley has a healthy amount of soluble fiber, which aids digestion—and it can help to lower cholesterol, too! You can easily substitute other fresh veggies you have on hand.
—Jesse Klausmeier, Burbank, CA

- -

Takes: 30 min. • **Makes:** 4 servings

- 1   large zucchini, quartered and sliced
- 1   large carrot, chopped
- 1   Tbsp. butter
- 2   cups reduced-sodium chicken broth
- 1   cup quick-cooking barley
- 2   green onions, chopped
- ½   tsp. dried marjoram
- ¼   tsp. salt
- ⅛   tsp. pepper

1. In a large saucepan, saute zucchini and carrot in butter until crisp-tender. Add the broth; bring to a boil. Stir in the barley. Reduce heat; cover and simmer until the barley is tender, 10-12 minutes.
2. Stir in onions, marjoram, salt and pepper. Remove from the heat; cover and let stand for 5 minutes.
¾ cup: 219 cal., 4g fat (2g sat. fat), 8mg chol., 480mg sod., 39g carb. (3g sugars, 10g fiber), 9g pro.
Spinach Barley Pilaf: With the onions, stir in 1 cup chopped fresh spinach.

EAT SMART
CHOCOLATE BANANA BRAN MUFFINS

So easy to make, these treats are healthy but still satisfy my chocolate-loving family. Stir in raisin bran instead of bran flakes for a little extra flavorful fun.
—Tracy Chappell, Hamiota, MB

- -

Takes: 25 min. • **Makes:** 1 dozen

- 1   cup all-purpose flour
- ½   cup sugar
- 2   Tbsp. baking cocoa
- 1   tsp. baking powder
- 1   tsp. baking soda
- ½   tsp. salt
- 1   cup bran flakes
- 2   large eggs, room temperature
- 1   cup mashed ripe bananas (about 2 medium)
- ⅓   cup canola oil
- ¼   cup buttermilk

1. Preheat oven to 400°. In a large bowl, whisk the first six ingredients. Stir in bran flakes. In another bowl, whisk the eggs, mashed bananas, oil and buttermilk until blended. Add to the flour mixture; stir just until moistened.
2. Fill foil-lined muffin cups three-fourths full. Bake until a toothpick inserted in center comes out clean, 12-14 minutes. Cool the muffins for 5 minutes before removing from pan to a wire rack. Serve warm.
1 muffin: 169 cal., 7g fat (1g sat. fat), 35mg chol., 278mg sod., 24g carb. (12g sugars, 2g fiber), 3g pro. **Diabetic exchanges:** 1½ starch, 1½ fat.

5 INGREDIENT
GRANDMA'S BISCUITS

My grandmother makes these homemade biscuits to go with her seafood chowder, but they taste great with almost any dish.
—Melissa Obernesser, Utica, NY

- -

Takes: 25 min. • **Makes:** 10 biscuits

- 2 cups all-purpose flour
- 3 tsp. baking powder
- 1 tsp. salt
- ⅓ cup shortening
- ⅔ cup 2% milk
- 1 large egg, lightly beaten

1. Preheat oven to 450°. In a large bowl, whisk flour, baking powder and salt. Cut in shortening until mixture resembles coarse crumbs. Add milk; stir just until moistened.
2. Turn onto a lightly floured surface; knead gently 8-10 times. Pat dough into a 10x4-in. rectangle. Cut rectangle lengthwise in half; cut crosswise to make 10 squares.
3. Place squares 1 in. apart on an ungreased baking sheet; brush the tops with egg. Bake biscuits until golden brown, 8-10 minutes. Serve warm.

1 biscuit: 165 cal., 7g fat (2g sat. fat), 20mg chol., 371mg sod., 20g carb. (1g sugars, 1g fiber), 4g pro.

EAT SMART
GARLIC GREEN BEANS

If you've got side-dish duty, change up the usual green bean casserole. These beans travel well, too.
—Christine Bergman, Suwanee, GA

- -

Takes: 25 min. • **Makes:** 10 servings

- 2 Tbsp. oil from oil-packed sun-dried tomatoes
- 1 cup sliced sweet onion
- ½ cup oil-packed sun-dried tomatoes, chopped
- 3 garlic cloves, minced
- 1½ tsp. lemon-pepper seasoning
- 2 pkg. (16 oz. each) frozen french-style green beans

1. In a Dutch oven, heat oil over medium heat. Add onion; cook and stir until tender, 3-4 minutes. Add the tomatoes, garlic and lemon-pepper seasoning; cook and stir 2 minutes longer.
2. Stir in frozen green beans; cook, covered, until heated through, stirring occasionally, 7-9 minutes. Uncover; cook until liquid is almost evaporated, 2-3 minutes longer.
⅔ cup: 76 cal., 3g fat (0 sat. fat), 0 chol., 85mg sod., 9g carb. (3g sugars, 3g fiber), 2g pro. **Diabetic exchanges:** 1 vegetable, 1 fat.

ZUCCHINI RICE PILAF

I created this colorful rice and veggie side dish one night by combining a few ingredients I had on hand. My husband and I have been making it ever since.
—Lori Blevins, Douglasville, GA

Takes: 25 min. • **Makes:** 4 servings

- ½ tsp. dried basil
- 2 Tbsp. butter
- 2¼ cups hot water
- 1¼ tsp. chicken bouillon granules
- 1 cup uncooked long grain rice
- ½ cup shredded carrot
- 1 small zucchini, halved and thinly sliced

1. In a large skillet, saute basil in butter for 2 minutes. Add water and bouillon; bring to a boil. Stir in rice and carrot. Reduce heat; cover and simmer for 10 minutes.
2. Add the zucchini; cover and simmer until the rice is tender, about 5 minutes longer.
1 cup: 231 cal., 6g fat (4g sat. fat), 15mg chol., 318mg sod., 40g carb. (1g sugars, 1g fiber), 4g pro. **Diabetic exchanges:** 2 starch, 2 vegetable, ½ fat.

TEST KITCHEN TIP
To pick the freshest zucchini, look for a firm heavy squash with a moist stem end and a shiny skin. Store zucchini in a plastic bag in the refrigerator crisper for 4 to 5 days. Do not wash until ready to use.

ROASTED PARMESAN CARROTS

Mom always said, "Eat your carrots, help your eyes." Rich in beta carotene, carrots are not only healthy but also taste amazing when roasted and tossed with Parmesan.
—*Taste of Home* Test Kitchen

Takes: 25 min. • **Makes:** 4 servings

- 1 lb. fresh carrots, peeled
- 1 tsp. olive oil
- ½ tsp. kosher salt
- ¼ tsp. freshly ground pepper
- ¼ tsp. dried thyme
- 3 Tbsp. grated Parmesan cheese

1. Preheat oven to 450°. Cut the carrots crosswise in half and then lengthwise into ½-in.-thick sticks. Toss carrots with the oil, salt, pepper and thyme; spread evenly in a greased 15x10x10-in. baking pan.
2. Roast until tender and lightly browned, stirring once, 12-15 minutes. Toss with the Parmesan cheese.
1 serving: 72 cal., 2g fat (1g sat. fat), 3mg chol., 386mg sod., 11g carb. (5g sugars, 3g fiber), 2g pro. **Diabetic exchanges:** 1 vegetable, ½ fat.

ZUCCHINI PARMESAN

You'll knock their socks off with this easy-to-prep side that's absolutely delicious. My favorite time to make it is when the veggies are fresh out of the garden.

—Sandi Guettler, Bay City, MI

- -

Takes: 25 min. • **Makes:** 6 servings

4	medium zucchini, cut into ¼-in. slices
1	Tbsp. olive oil
½	to 1 tsp. minced garlic
1	can (14½ oz.) Italian diced tomatoes, undrained
1	tsp. seasoned salt
¼	tsp. pepper
¼	cup grated Parmesan cheese

1. In a large skillet, saute the zucchini in oil until crisp-tender. Add garlic; cook for 1 minute longer.

2. Stir in the tomatoes, seasoned salt and pepper. Simmer, uncovered, until the liquid is evaporated, 9-10 minutes. Sprinkle with the grated Parmesan cheese. Serve with a slotted spoon.

½ cup: 81 cal., 3g fat (1g sat. fat), 3mg chol., 581mg sod., 10g carb. (6g sugars, 2g fiber), 3g pro. **Diabetic exchanges:** 2 vegetable, ½ fat.

SPEEDY SURPRISE

"Yum! So easy and tasty. I used zucchini and cherry tomatoes from our garden—fantastic! I also added Italian sausage to make this a main dish."

—DANAB1925, TASTEOFHOME.COM

MOM'S BUTTERMILK BISCUITS

These fluffy biscuits are so tasty served warm, slathered with butter or used to mop every last drop of gravy off your plate. I can still see Mom pulling these tender biscuits out of the oven.

—Vera Reid, Laramie, WY

- -

Takes: 30 min. • **Makes:** 10 servings

2	cups all-purpose flour
2	tsp. baking powder
½	tsp. baking soda
½	tsp. salt
¼	cup shortening
¾	cup buttermilk

Preheat oven to 450°. In a bowl, combine flour, baking powder, baking soda and salt; cut in shortening until mixture resembles coarse crumbs. Stir in buttermilk; knead dough gently. Roll out to ½-in. thickness. Cut with a 2½-in. biscuit cutter and place on a lightly greased baking sheet. Bake until golden brown, 10-15 minutes.

Freeze option: Freeze cooled biscuits in a resealable freezer container. To use, heat in a preheated 350° oven 15-20 minutes.

1 biscuit: 142 cal., 5g fat (1g sat. fat), 1mg chol., 281mg sod., 20g carb. (1g sugars, 1g fiber), 3g pro.

Herb Biscuits: To buttermilk, add 2 Tbsp. minced fresh basil and 2 tsp. minced fresh rosemary. Bake as directed above.

Parmesan-Chive Biscuits: To buttermilk, add 2 Tbsp. minced fresh chives. Beat one egg white with 1 Tbsp. water. Brush over the tops of the biscuits. Sprinkle with 3-4 tsp. of grated Parmesan. Bake at 425° for 10-15 minutes.

30 MINUTE MAINS

ITALIAN SAUSAGE & ZUCCHINI SOUP

Everyone in my family likes this half-hour soup. Sometimes I use mini farfalle pasta because my grandchildren say it looks like tiny butterflies. The recipe also works in a slow cooker.

—Nancy Murphy, Mount Dora, FL

- -

Takes: 30 min. • **Makes:** 6 servings (2 qt.)

½	lb. bulk Italian sausage
1	medium onion, chopped
1	medium green pepper, chopped
3	cups beef broth
1	can (14½ oz.) diced tomatoes, undrained
1	Tbsp. minced fresh basil or 1 tsp. dried basil
1	Tbsp. minced fresh parsley or 1 tsp. dried parsley flakes
1	medium zucchini, cut into ½-in. pieces
½	cup uncooked orzo pasta

1. In a large saucepan, cook sausage, onion and pepper over medium heat until sausage is no longer pink and vegetables are tender, 4-6 minutes, breaking up the sausage into crumbles; drain.

2. Add broth, tomatoes, basil and parsley; bring to a boil. Stir in the zucchini and orzo; return to a boil. Cook, covered, until the zucchini and orzo are tender, 10-12 minutes.

1¼ cups: 191 cal., 9g fat (3g sat. fat), 20mg chol., 789mg sod., 20g carb. (5g sugars, 2g fiber), 9g pro.

MEDITERRANEAN SHRIMP ORZO SALAD

This pretty crowd-pleaser always stands out on the buffet table because it's a tasty change of pace from other pasta salads. I like to use a from-scratch vinaigrette, but bottled dressing works just fine.

—Ginger Johnson, Pottstown, PA

- -

Takes: 30 min. • **Makes:** 8 servings

1	pkg. (16 oz.) orzo pasta
¾	lb. peeled and deveined cooked shrimp (31-40 per lb.), cut into thirds
1	can (14 oz.) water-packed quartered artichoke hearts, rinsed and drained
1	cup finely chopped green pepper
1	cup finely chopped sweet red pepper
¾	cup finely chopped red onion
½	cup pitted Greek olives
½	cup minced fresh parsley
⅓	cup chopped fresh dill
¾	cup Greek vinaigrette

1. Cook the orzo according to package directions. Drain; rinse with cold water and drain well.

2. In a large bowl, combine orzo, shrimp, vegetables, olives and herbs. Add the vinaigrette; toss to coat. Refrigerate, covered, until serving.

1½ cups: 397 cal., 12g fat (2g sat. fat), 65mg chol., 574mg sod., 52g carb. (4g sugars, 3g fiber), 18g pro.

ROASTED SWEET POTATO & CHICKPEA PITAS

Here's a quick yet hearty take on a favorite Mediterranean food—this time with sweet potatoes tucked inside.
—Beth Jacobson, Milwaukee, WI

- -

Takes: 30 min. • **Makes:** 6 servings

2	medium sweet potatoes (about 1¼ lbs.), peeled and cubed
2	cans (15 oz. each) chickpeas or garbanzo beans, rinsed and drained
1	medium red onion, chopped
3	Tbsp. canola oil, divided
2	tsp. garam masala
½	tsp. salt, divided
2	garlic cloves, minced
1	cup plain Greek yogurt
1	Tbsp. lemon juice
1	tsp. ground cumin
2	cups arugula or baby spinach
12	whole wheat pita pocket halves, warmed
¼	cup minced fresh cilantro

1. Preheat oven to 400°. Place potatoes in a large microwave-safe bowl; microwave, covered, on high 5 minutes. Stir in the chickpeas and onion; toss with 2 Tbsp. oil, garam masala and ¼ tsp. salt.
2. Spread into a 15x10x1-in. pan. Roast until the potatoes are tender, about 15 minutes. Cool slightly.
3. Place the garlic and remaining oil in a small microwave-safe bowl; microwave on high until the garlic is lightly browned, 1-1½ minutes. Stir in yogurt, lemon juice, cumin and remaining salt.
4. Toss potato mixture with arugula. Spoon into pitas; top with sauce and cilantro.

2 filled pita halves: 462 cal., 15g fat (3g sat. fat), 10mg chol., 662mg sod., 72g carb. (13g sugars, 12g fiber), 14g pro.

QUINOA & BLACK BEAN-STUFFED PEPPERS

If you're thinking about a meatless meal, give these no-fuss peppers a try. They come together with just few ingredients and put a tasty spin on dinner.
—Cindy Reams, Philipsburg, PA

- -

Takes: 30 min. • **Makes:** 4 servings

1½	cups water
1	cup quinoa, rinsed
4	large green peppers
1	jar (16 oz.) chunky salsa, divided
1	can (15 oz.) black beans, rinsed and drained
½	cup reduced-fat ricotta cheese
½	cup shredded Monterey Jack cheese, divided

1. Preheat oven to 400°. In a saucepan, bring water to a boil. Add quinoa. Reduce heat; simmer, covered, until the water is absorbed, 10-12 minutes.
2. Meanwhile, cut and discard tops from peppers; remove seeds. Place in a greased 8-in. square baking dish, cut side down. Microwave, uncovered, on high until crisp-tender, 3-4 minutes. Carefully turn peppers cut side up.
3. Reserve ⅓ cup salsa; add remaining salsa to quinoa. Stir in beans, ricotta cheese and ¼ cup Jack cheese. Spoon mixture into peppers; sprinkle with remaining cheese. Bake, uncovered, until the filling is heated through, 10-15 minutes. Top with the reserved salsa.

1 stuffed pepper: 393 cal., 8g fat (4g sat. fat), 20mg chol., 774mg sod., 59g carb. (10g sugars, 10g fiber), 18g pro.

GLAZED SMOKED CHOPS WITH PEARS

My husband would eat pork chops every day if he could. Lucky for me they're tasty no matter how you make them—even with pears!
—Lynn Moretti, Oconomowoc, WI

Takes: 30 min. • **Makes:** 4 servings

- 4 smoked boneless pork chops
- 1 Tbsp. olive oil
- 1 large sweet onion, cut into thin wedges
- ½ cup dry red wine or reduced-sodium chicken broth
- 2 Tbsp. balsamic vinegar
- 2 Tbsp. honey
- 2 large ripe pears, cut into 1-in. wedges

1. Preheat oven to 350°. In an ovenproof skillet over medium-high heat, brown pork chops on both sides; remove from pan.
2. In same pan, heat oil over medium heat; saute the onion until tender, 3-5 minutes. Add wine, vinegar and honey; bring to a boil, stirring to loosen browned bits from pan. Reduce the heat; simmer, uncovered, until slightly thickened, about 5 minutes, stirring occasionally.
3. Return chops to pan; top with pears. Transfer to oven; bake until the pears are tender, 10-15 minutes.
1 serving: 313 cal., 4g fat (6g sat. fat), 41mg chol., 1056mg sod., 34g carb. (26g sugars, 4g fiber), 22g pro.

EASY SWEET-AND-SOUR MEATBALLS

Frozen meatballs can help jump-start supper on a busy night, or you can use homemade meatballs if you have time.
—Ruth Andrewson, Leavenworth, WA

Takes: 30 min. • **Makes:** 6 servings

- 1 can (20 oz.) unsweetened pineapple chunks
- 1 pkg. (12 oz.) frozen fully cooked homestyle or Swedish meatballs, thawed
- 1 large green pepper, cut into 1-in. pieces
- 3 Tbsp. cornstarch
- ⅓ cup cold water
- 3 Tbsp. cider vinegar
- 1 Tbsp. soy sauce
- ½ cup packed brown sugar
  Optional: Hot cooked rice, thinly sliced green onions

1. Drain pineapple, reserving juice. Set the pineapple aside. Add enough water to juice if needed to measure 1 cup. In a large skillet over medium heat, cook the meatballs, green pepper and juice mixture until heated through.
2. In a small bowl, combine the cornstarch, cold water, vinegar and soy sauce until smooth. Add brown sugar and reserved pineapple to the pan; stir in cornstarch mixture. Bring to a boil; cook and stir until thickened, about 2 minutes. If desired, serve with rice and top with green onions.
1 serving: 330 cal., 15g fat (7g sat. fat), 24mg chol., 572mg sod., 40g carb. (31g sugars, 2g fiber), 9g pro.

EAT SMART
COD & ASPARAGUS BAKE

Lemon pulls this flavorful and healthy dish together. You can use a bit of grated Parmesan cheese instead of Romano.
—Thomas Faglon, Somerset, NJ

- -

Takes: 30 min. • **Makes:** 4 servings

- 4   cod fillets (4 oz. each)
- 1   lb. fresh thin asparagus, trimmed
- 1   pint cherry tomatoes, halved
- 2   Tbsp. lemon juice
- 1½ tsp. grated lemon zest
- ¼   cup grated Romano cheese

1. Preheat oven to 375°. Place cod and asparagus in a 15x10x1-in. baking pan brushed with oil. Add tomatoes, cut side down. Brush fish with lemon juice; sprinkle with the lemon zest. Sprinkle the fish and vegetables with Romano cheese. Bake until fish just begins to flake easily with a fork, about 12 minutes.
2. Remove pan from oven; preheat broiler. Broil cod mixture 3-4 in. from heat until vegetables are lightly browned, 2-3 minutes.
1 serving: 141 cal., 3g fat (2g sat. fat), 45mg chol., 184mg sod., 6g carb. (3g sugars, 2g fiber), 23g pro. **Diabetic exchanges:** 3 lean meat, 1 vegetable.

TEST KITCHEN TIP
If asparagus isn't in season, fresh green beans make a great substitution and will cook in about the same amount of time. We tested with cod fillets that were about ¾ in. thick. You'll need to adjust the bake time up or down if your fillets are thicker or thinner.

JAMAICAN HAM & BEAN SOUP

"An island vacation in a bowl" might be the best way to describe this hearty soup. A splash of lime juice and a hint of jerk seasoning add a bit of tropical flair.
—Mary Lou Timpson, Colorado City, AZ

- -

Takes: 30 min. • **Makes:** 7 servings (2¾ qt.)

- 1   small onion, chopped
- 1   Tbsp. canola oil
- 3   cups cubed fully cooked ham
- 2   cans (16 oz. each) vegetarian refried beans
- 1   can (14½ oz.) chicken broth
- 1   can (11 oz.) Mexicorn, drained
- 1   can (7 oz.) white or shoepeg corn, drained
- 1   can (4 oz.) chopped green chiles
- ½   cup salsa
- 1   tsp. Caribbean jerk seasoning
- 1   can (2¼ oz.) sliced ripe olives, drained
- ⅓   cup lime juice
      Sour cream and lime slices

1. In a Dutch oven, saute onion in oil until tender, 3-4 minutes. Stir in the ham, refried beans, broth, corn, chiles, salsa and jerk seasoning; bring to a boil. Reduce heat; simmer, uncovered, for 5 minutes, stirring occasionally.
2. Stir in the olives and lime juice; heat through. Garnish servings with sour cream and lime slices.
1½ cups: 312 cal., 9g fat (2g sat. fat), 33mg chol., 2211mg sod., 38g carb. (7g sugars, 9g fiber), 20g pro.

GRILLED GARDEN PIZZA

Dazzle your family and friends with pizzas fresh off the grill. We top them with Asiago, Parmesan, veggies and fresh basil. Pile on the toppings you love.

—Teri Rasey, Cadillac, MI

- -

Takes: 30 min. • **Makes:** 6 servings

- 2 plum tomatoes, thinly sliced
- ½ tsp. sea salt or kosher salt
- 1 loaf (1 lb.) frozen pizza dough, thawed
- 2 Tbsp. olive oil, divided
- ½ cup shredded Parmesan or Asiago cheese
- ½ cup fresh or frozen corn, thawed
- ¼ cup thinly sliced red onion
- 8 oz. fresh mozzarella cheese, sliced
- ½ cup thinly sliced fresh spinach
- 3 Tbsp. chopped fresh basil

1. Sprinkle tomatoes with salt; set aside. On a lightly floured surface, divide dough in half. Roll or press each to ¼-in. thickness; place each on a greased sheet of foil (about 10 in. square). Brush tops with 1 Tbsp. oil.
2. Carefully invert crusts onto a grill rack, removing foil. Brush tops with remaining oil. Grill, covered, over medium heat until crust bottoms are golden brown, 2-3 minutes. Remove crusts from grill; reduce the grill temperature to low.
3. Top grilled sides of crusts with Parmesan or Asiago cheese, tomatoes, corn, onion and mozzarella cheese. Grill, covered, on low heat until cheese is melted, 4-6 minutes. Sprinkle with spinach and basil.
1 piece: 375 cal., 16g fat (7g sat. fat), 35mg chol., 680mg sod., 40g carb. (4g sugars, 1g fiber), 15g pro.

PULLED PORK GRILLED CHEESE

My family combined two of our favorite things: pulled pork and grilled cheese sandwiches. This recipe is super fast and easy when you use a carton of store-bought pulled pork.

—Crystal Jo Bruns, Iliff, CO

- -

Takes: 30 min. • **Makes:** 4 servings

- 1 carton (16 oz.) refrigerated fully cooked barbecued shredded pork
- 1 garlic clove, minced
- 8 slices country white bread
- 6 oz. sliced Manchego cheese or
- 8 slices Monterey Jack cheese
- 1 small red onion, thinly sliced
- ¼ cup mayonnaise

1. Heat the shredded pork according to package directions. Stir in garlic. Layer four slices of bread with cheese, onion, pork mixture and remaining bread. Spread outsides of sandwiches with mayonnaise.
2. In a large nonstick skillet, toast the sandwiches in batches over medium-low heat until golden brown and cheese is melted, 2-3 minutes per side.
1 sandwich: 605 cal., 29g fat (13g sat. fat), 74mg chol., 1406mg sod., 53g carb. (22g sugars, 2g fiber), 29g pro.

SKILLET NACHOS

My mom gave me a fundraiser cookbook, and this is the recipe I've used most. My whole family is on board. For toppings, think sour cream, tomatoes, jalapeno and red onion.

—Judy Hughes, Waverly, KS

Takes: 30 min. • **Makes:** 6 servings

- 1 **lb. ground beef**
- 1 **can (14½ oz.) diced tomatoes, undrained**
- 1 **cup fresh or frozen corn, thawed**
- ¾ **cup uncooked instant rice**
- ½ **cup water**
- 1 **envelope taco seasoning**
- ½ **tsp. salt**
- 1 **cup shredded Colby-Monterey Jack cheese**
- 1 **pkg. (16 oz.) tortilla chips**
  Optional toppings: Sour cream, sliced fresh jalapenos, shredded lettuce and lime wedges

1. In a large skillet, cook beef over medium heat until no longer pink, 6-8 minutes, breaking into crumbles; drain. Stir in the tomatoes, corn, rice, water, taco seasoning and salt. Bring to a boil. Reduce the heat; simmer, covered, until rice is tender and mixture is slightly thickened, 8-10 minutes.
2. Remove from heat; sprinkle with cheese. Let stand, covered, until cheese is melted, about 5 minutes. Divide tortilla chips among six plates; spoon beef mixture over chips. Serve with toppings as desired.

1 serving: 676 cal., 31g fat (10g sat. fat), 63mg chol., 1293mg sod., 74g carb. (4g sugars, 4g fiber), 25g pro.

CREAMY LENTILS WITH KALE ARTICHOKE SAUTE

I've been trying to eat more meatless meals, so I experimented with this hearty saute and served it over brown rice. It was so good that even those who aren't big fans of kale gobbled it up quickly.
—Teri Rasey, Cadillac, MI

- -

Takes: 30 min. • **Makes:** 4 servings

- ½ cup dried red lentils, rinsed and sorted
- ¼ tsp. dried oregano
- ⅛ tsp. pepper
- 1¼ cups vegetable broth
- ¼ tsp. sea salt, divided
- 1 Tbsp. olive oil or grapeseed oil
- 16 cups chopped fresh kale (about 12 oz.)
- 1 can (14 oz.) water-packed artichoke hearts, drained and chopped
- 3 garlic cloves, minced
- ½ tsp. Italian seasoning
- 2 Tbsp. grated Romano cheese
- 2 cups hot cooked brown or basmati rice

1. Place first four ingredients and ⅛ tsp. salt in a small saucepan; bring to a boil. Reduce heat; simmer, covered, until the lentils are tender and the liquid is almost absorbed, 12-15 minutes. Remove from heat.
2. In a 6-qt. stockpot, heat oil over medium heat. Add kale and remaining salt; cook, covered, until kale is wilted, 4-5 minutes, stirring occasionally. Add artichoke hearts, garlic and Italian seasoning; cook and stir 3 minutes. Remove from heat; stir in cheese.
3. Serve lentils and kale mixture over rice.
1 serving: 321 cal., 6g fat (2g sat. fat), 1mg chol., 661mg sod., 53g carb. (1g sugars, 5g fiber), 15g pro.

BLT SKILLET SUPPER

Here, the "L" stands for linguine! Chunks of bacon and tomato adorn this weeknight meal that is a pasta lover's take on the beloved BLT sandwich.
—Edrie O'Brien, Denver, CO

- -

Takes: 30 min. • **Makes:** 4 servings

- 8 oz. uncooked linguine or whole wheat linguine
- 8 bacon strips, cut into 1½-in. pieces
- 2 plum tomatoes, cut into 1-in. pieces
- 2 garlic cloves, minced
- 1 Tbsp. lemon juice
- ½ tsp. salt
- ½ tsp. pepper
- ¼ cup grated Parmesan cheese
- 2 Tbsp. minced fresh parsley

1. Cook linguine according to package directions. Meanwhile, in a large skillet, cook bacon over medium heat until crisp. Remove to paper towels; drain, reserving 2 tsp. drippings.
2. In the drippings, cook and stir tomatoes and garlic until heated through, 2-3 minutes. Stir in bacon, lemon juice, salt and pepper.
3. Drain linguine; add to skillet. Sprinkle with cheese and parsley; toss to coat.
1½ cups: 335 cal., 11g fat (4g sat. fat), 23mg chol., 685mg sod., 44g carb. (3g sugars, 2g fiber), 15g pro.

TEST KITCHEN TIP
When a recipe calls for grated Parmesan, use the finely grated cheese sold in containers with shaker/pourer tops. This type works well in lasagna and casseroles.

SALSA VERDE CHICKEN CASSEROLE

This is a rich and tasty rendition of all the Tex-Mex dishes molded into one beautiful casserole. Best of all, it's ready in no time!
—Janet McCormick, Proctorville, OH

Takes: 30 min. • **Makes:** 6 servings

2 cups shredded rotisserie chicken
1 cup sour cream
1½ cups salsa verde, divided
8 corn tortillas (6 in.)
2 cups chopped tomatoes
¼ cup minced fresh cilantro
2 cups shredded Monterey
   Jack cheese
   Optional toppings: Avocado slices,
   thinly sliced green onions or fresh
   cilantro leaves

1. In a small bowl, combine the chicken, sour cream and ¾ cup salsa. Spread ¼ cup salsa on the bottom of a greased 8-in. square baking dish.
2. Layer with half of the tortillas and chicken mixture; sprinkle with half the tomatoes, minced cilantro and half of the cheese. Repeat layers with remaining tortillas, chicken mixture, tomatoes and cheese.
3. Bake, uncovered, at 400° until bubbly, 20-25 minutes. Serve with remaining salsa and toppings as desired.
1 serving: 400 cal., 23g fat (13g sat. fat), 102mg chol., 637mg sod., 22g carb. (5g sugars, 3g fiber), 26g pro.

ASIAN BARBECUE CHICKEN SLAW

When it's springtime in the South, cabbage is plentiful, and we take advantage of that. One of our favorite recipes is this combo of Asian slaw and barbecued chicken. Plus, it's easy to halve or double the servings.
—Paula Todora, Maple Valley, WA

Takes: 25 min. • **Makes:** 4 servings

¼ cup reduced-sodium soy sauce
¼ cup honey
4 Tbsp. canola oil, divided
2 Tbsp. rice vinegar
½ cup barbecue sauce
1 lb. boneless skinless chicken
   breasts, cut into strips
¼ tsp. pepper
¼ cup honey mustard salad dressing
1 pkg. (14 oz.) coleslaw mix
3 green onions, chopped
4 Tbsp. sliced almonds,
   toasted, divided
3 tsp. sesame seeds, toasted, divided

1. In a large bowl, whisk soy sauce, honey, 3 Tbsp. oil and vinegar until blended. Pour half of the honey mixture into a small bowl; stir in barbecue sauce. Sprinkle chicken with pepper. In a large nonstick skillet, heat the remaining oil over medium-high heat. Add chicken; cook and stir until no longer pink, 4-6 minutes. Add barbecue sauce mixture; heat through.
2. Meanwhile, whisk salad dressing into remaining honey mixture until blended. Add coleslaw mix, green onions, 3 Tbsp. almonds and 2 tsp. sesame seeds; toss to coat. Serve with chicken. Sprinkle servings with remaining almonds and sesame seeds.
Note: To toast nuts, bake in a shallow pan in a 350° oven for 5-10 minutes or cook in a skillet over low heat until lightly browned, stirring occasionally.
½ cup chicken mixture with 1¼ cups slaw: 531 cal., 27g fat (3g sat. fat), 67mg chol., 1202mg sod., 47g carb. (37g sugars, 4g fiber), 27g pro.

EAT SMART
CASHEW MANGO GRILLED CHICKEN

This sweet and nutty chicken hits all the right spots for flavor, speed and family appeal. On a rainy day, you can bake it, then finish it under the broiler.
—Trisha Kruse, Eagle, ID

Takes: 25 min. • **Makes:** 8 servings

¼ cup mango chutney
¼ cup cashew butter
2 Tbsp. reduced-sodium soy sauce
2 Tbsp. rice vinegar
8 boneless skinless chicken thighs
½ tsp. salt
½ tsp. crushed red pepper flakes
1 large mango, peeled
   and thinly sliced
⅓ cup lightly salted cashews, chopped
   Additional mango chutney, optional

1. Mix together the first four ingredients until blended.
2. Sprinkle chicken with salt and pepper flakes; place on an oiled grill rack over medium heat. Grill chicken, covered, until a thermometer reads 170°, 6-8 minutes per side, brushing with chutney mixture during the last 5 minutes. Serve with mango; top with chopped cashews and, if desired, additional chutney.
1 serving: 308 cal., 16g fat (4g sat. fat), 76mg chol., 537mg sod., 18g carb. (12g sugars, 1g fiber), 24g pro. **Diabetic exchanges:** 3 lean meat, 2½ fat, 1 starch.

FAST REFRIED BEAN SOUP

I think you will just love the way this recipe combines the ease of canned ingredients with the heartiness of chili. It's a perfect filler-upper on cold afternoons and a great last-minute lunch. If you like it spicier, use hot green chiles instead of mild.
—Darlene Brenden, Salem, OR

Takes: 25 min. • **Makes:** 8 servings (2 qt.)

1 can (16 oz.) spicy fat-free
   refried beans
1 can (15¼ oz.) whole kernel
   corn, drained
1 can (15 oz.) black beans,
   rinsed and drained
1 can (14½ oz.) chicken broth
1 can (14½ oz.) stewed
   tomatoes, cut up
½ cup water
1 can (4 oz.) chopped green chiles
¼ cup salsa
   Tortilla chips

In a large saucepan, combine the first eight ingredients. Bring to a boil. Reduce heat; simmer, uncovered, until heated through, 8-10 minutes. Serve with the tortilla chips.
1 cup: 117 cal., 1g fat (0 sat. fat), 1mg chol., 720mg sod., 21g carb. (6g sugars, 4g fiber), 5g pro.

ONE-PAN CHICKEN RICE CURRY

I've been loving the subtle spice from curry lately, so I incorporated it into this saucy chicken and rice dish. It's a one-pan meal that's become a go-to dinnertime favorite.
—Mary Lou Timpson, Colorado City, AZ

Takes: 30 min. • **Makes:** 4 servings

- 2 Tbsp. butter, divided
- 1 medium onion, halved and thinly sliced
- 2 Tbsp. all-purpose flour
- 3 tsp. curry powder
- ½ tsp. salt
- ½ tsp. pepper
- 1 lb. boneless skinless chicken breasts, cut into 1-in. pieces
- 1 can (14½ oz.) reduced-sodium chicken broth
- 1 cup uncooked instant rice
  Chopped fresh cilantro leaves, optional

1. In a large nonstick skillet, heat 1 Tbsp. butter over medium-high heat; saute the onion until tender and lightly browned, 3-5 minutes. Remove from pan.
2. In a bowl, mix flour and seasonings; toss with chicken. In same skillet, heat remaining butter over medium-high heat. Add chicken; cook just until no longer pink, 4-6 minutes, turning occasionally.
3. Stir in broth and onion; bring to a boil. Stir in rice. Remove from heat; let stand, covered, 5 minutes (mixture will be saucy). If desired, sprinkle with cilantro.
1 cup: 300 cal., 9g fat (4g sat. fat), 78mg chol., 658mg sod., 27g carb. (2g sugars, 2g fiber), 27g pro. **Diabetic exchanges:** 3 lean meat, 2 starch, 1½ fat.

BACON, LETTUCE & TOMATO PIZZA

I bring together two all-time favorites with this recipe—pizza and BLT sandwiches. I brought this fun mashup to a ladies lunch and was met with oohs and ahhs.
—Bonnie Hawkins, Elkhorn, WI

Takes: 30 min. • **Makes:** 6 servings

- 1 tube (13.8 oz.) refrigerated pizza crust
- 2 Tbsp. olive oil
- 2 Tbsp. grated Parmesan cheese
- 1 tsp. garlic salt
- ½ cup mayonnaise
- 2 tsp. ranch dip mix
- 4 cups shredded romaine
- 3 to 4 plum tomatoes, chopped
- ½ lb. bacon strips, cooked and crumbled

1. Preheat oven to 425°. Unroll and press the dough onto bottom of a greased 15x10x1-in. baking pan. Brush with oil; top with the cheese and garlic salt. Bake until golden brown, 15-18 minutes; cool crust slightly.
2. Meanwhile, combine the mayonnaise and ranch mix. Spread over pizza crust; top with lettuce, tomatoes and bacon.
1 piece: 389 cal., 23g fat (5g sat. fat), 16mg chol., 1236mg sod., 34g carb. (5g sugars, 2g fiber), 11g pro.

HAMBURGER STEAKS WITH MUSHROOM GRAVY

Here's a meat-and-potatoes meal that no one will want to miss. It makes for a hearty dish the whole family will cozy up to any night of the week.
—Denise Wheeler, Newaygo, MI

Takes: 25 min. • **Makes:** 4 servings

- 1 large egg
- ½ cup dry bread crumbs
- 1 envelope onion soup mix, divided
  Dash pepper
- 1 lb. ground beef
- 3 Tbsp. all-purpose flour
- 1¾ cups cold water
- 1 tsp. Worcestershire sauce
- 1 jar (4½ oz.) whole mushrooms, drained
  Hot cooked mashed potatoes

1. In a large bowl, combine the egg, bread crumbs, 2 Tbsp. soup mix and pepper. Crumble beef over mixture and mix well. Shape into four patties.

2. In a large cast-iron or other heavy skillet, cook patties over medium heat until a thermometer reads 160°, and juices run clear, 4-5 minutes on each side. Set aside and keep warm.

3. Combine the flour, water, Worcestershire sauce and remaining soup mix until blended; stir into skillet. Add mushrooms. Bring to a boil; cook and stir until thickened, about 5 minutes. Serve sauce with patties and mashed potatoes.

1 patty with ½ cup gravy: 325 cal., 15g fat (6g sat. fat), 123mg chol., 920mg sod., 20g carb. (2g sugars, 2g fiber), 25g pro.

EAT SMART
COUNTRY CHICKEN WITH GRAVY

Here's a lightened-up take on classic southern comfort food. It's been a hit at our house since the first time we tried it.
—Ruth Helmuth, Abbeville, SC

Takes: 30 min. • **Makes:** 4 servings

- ¾ cup crushed cornflakes
- ½ tsp. poultry seasoning
- ½ tsp. paprika
- ¼ tsp. salt
- ¼ tsp. dried thyme
- ¼ tsp. pepper
- 2 Tbsp. fat-free evaporated milk
- 4 boneless skinless chicken breast halves (4 oz. each)
- 2 tsp. canola oil

GRAVY

- 1 Tbsp. butter
- 1 Tbsp. all-purpose flour
- ¼ tsp. pepper
- ⅛ tsp. salt
- ½ cup fat-free evaporated milk
- ¼ cup condensed chicken broth, undiluted
- 1 tsp. sherry or additional condensed chicken broth
- 2 Tbsp. minced chives

1. In a shallow bowl, combine the first six ingredients. Place milk in another shallow bowl. Dip the chicken in milk, then roll in cornflake mixture.

2. In a large nonstick skillet, cook chicken in oil over medium heat until a thermometer reads 170°, 6-8 minutes on each side.

3. In a small saucepan, melt butter. Stir in flour, pepper and salt until smooth. Stir in the milk, broth and sherry. Bring to a boil; cook and stir until thickened, 1-2 minutes. Stir in chives. Serve with chicken.

1 chicken breast half with 2 Tbsp. gravy: 274 cal., 8g fat (3g sat. fat), 72mg chol., 569mg sod., 20g carb. (6g sugars, 0 fiber), 28g pro. **Diabetic exchanges:** 3 lean meat, 1 starch, ½ fat.

EAT SMART
PRESSURE-COOKER LENTIL PUMPKIN SOUP

Plenty of herbs and spices brighten up my hearty pumpkin soup. It's just the thing we need on chilly days and nights, and it comes together easily in my electric all-in-one pressure cooker.

—Laura Magee, Houlton, WI

- -

Takes: 25 min. • **Makes:** 6 servings (2¼ qt.)

1 lb. medium red potatoes (about 4 medium), cut into ½-in. pieces
1 can (15 oz.) canned pumpkin
1 cup dried lentils, rinsed
1 medium onion, chopped
3 garlic cloves, minced
½ tsp. ground ginger
½ tsp. pepper
⅛ tsp. salt
2 cans (14½ oz. each) vegetable broth
1½ cups water
   Minced fresh cilantro, optional

In a 6-qt. electric pressure cooker, combine first 10 ingredients. Lock lid; make sure vent is closed. Select manual setting; adjust pressure to high and set the time for 12 minutes. When finished cooking, quick-release pressure according to manufacturer's directions. If desired, sprinkle servings with cilantro.

1½ cups: 210 cal., 1g fat (0 sat. fat), 0 chol., 463mg sod., 42g carb. (5g sugars, 7g fiber), 11g pro. **Diabetic exchanges:** 2½ starch, 1 lean meat.

EAT SMART
ASIAN PORK LINGUINE

If I have fresh ginger on hand, I grate a quarter teaspoon to use in place of the ground ginger in this tasty pasta entree.

—Lisa Varner, El Paso, TX

- -

Takes: 30 min. • **Makes:** 5 servings

6 oz. uncooked linguine
2 tsp. cornstarch
½ cup water
¼ cup reduced-fat creamy peanut butter
2 Tbsp. reduced-sodium soy sauce
1 Tbsp. honey
½ tsp. garlic powder
⅛ tsp. ground ginger
1 lb. boneless pork loin chops, cubed
3 tsp. sesame oil, divided
2 medium carrots, sliced
1 medium onion, halved and sliced

1. Cook linguine according to package directions. For sauce, in a small bowl, combine cornstarch and water until smooth. Whisk in the peanut butter, soy sauce, honey, garlic powder and ginger until blended; set aside.

2. In a large nonstick skillet or wok, stir-fry pork in 2 tsp. oil until meat is no longer pink. Remove and keep warm. Stir-fry carrots and onion in the remaining oil until crisp-tender. Stir the sauce and add to the pan. Bring to a boil; cook and stir until sauce is thickened, about 2 minutes.

3. Return pork to the pan. Drain linguine; add to the pan and stir to coat.

1 cup: 376 cal., 13g fat (3g sat. fat), 44mg chol., 358mg sod., 39g carb. (9g sugars, 3g fiber), 27g pro. **Diabetic exchanges:** 3 lean meat, 2½ starch, 2 fat.

EAT SMART | FREEZE IT
SOUTHWEST TURKEY BURGERS

I made these burgers with corn, green chiles and taco spice for my parents, who loved them!
—Katie Ring, Menasha, WI

- -

Takes: 30 min. • **Makes:** 6 servings

½ cup seasoned bread crumbs
½ cup frozen corn, thawed
1 can (4 oz.) chopped green chiles
1 Tbsp. reduced-sodium taco seasoning
1 lb. lean ground turkey
4 tsp. canola oil
6 whole wheat hamburger buns, split
6 wedges queso fresco chipotle cheese, halved
Lettuce leaves, optional

1. Preheat broiler. Mix first four ingredients. Add the turkey; mix lightly but thoroughly. Shape into six ½-in.-thick patties.

2. In a large nonstick skillet, heat 2 tsp. oil over medium heat. Cook the burgers in batches, adding more oil as needed, until a thermometer reads 165°, 4-6 minutes per side. Keep warm.

3. Meanwhile, place buns on a baking sheet, cut side up. Broil 3-4 in. from heat until toasted, about 30 seconds. Spread tops with cheese. Serve burgers in buns with lettuce, if desired.

Note: This recipe was tested with The Laughing Cow Queso Fresco Chiptole Cheese.

Freeze option: Place uncooked patties on a waxed paper-lined baking sheet; cover and freeze until firm. Remove from pan and transfer to a large freezer container; return to freezer. To use, cook frozen patties in a nonstick skillet with 2 tsp. oil over medium-low heat until a thermometer reads 165°, 6-8 minutes per side.

1 burger: 340 cal., 13g fat (3g sat. fat), 57mg chol., 796mg sod., 35g carb. (6g sugars, 4g fiber), 22g pro. **Diabetic exchanges:** 3 lean meat, 2 starch, ½ fat.

EAT SMART
LEMON-DILL SALMON PACKETS

Grilling in foil is an easy technique I use with foods that cook quickly, including salmon, shrimp, bite-sized meats and fresh veggies. The options are endless—and the cleanup is super easy.
—A.J. Weinhold, McArthur, CA

- -

Takes: 25 min. • **Makes:** 4 servings

1 Tbsp. butter, softened
4 salmon fillets (6 oz. each)
½ tsp. salt
¼ tsp. pepper
½ medium onion, sliced
4 garlic cloves, sliced
4 fresh dill sprigs
1 Tbsp. minced fresh basil
1 medium lemon, sliced

1. Prepare campfire or grill for medium heat. Spread butter in the center of each of four pieces of a double thickness of foil (about 12 in. square). Place one salmon fillet in the center of each; sprinkle with salt and pepper. Top with onion, garlic, dill, basil and lemon. Fold foil around fillets; seal.

2. Place the packets on a grill grate over a campfire or grill. Cook until fish just begins to flake easily with a fork, 8-10 minutes. Open carefully to allow steam to escape.

1 fillet: 305 cal., 19g fat (5g sat. fat), 93mg chol., 405mg sod., 4g carb. (1g sugars, 1g fiber), 29g pro. **Diabetic exchanges:** 5 lean meat, 1 fat.

MEATBALL SUBMARINE CASSEROLE

We were hosting a bunch of friends, and after a comedy of errors, I had to come up with a plan B for dinner. Much-loved meatball subs are even better as a hearty casserole—so delicious!
—Rick Friedman, Palm Springs, CA

- -

Takes: 30 min. • **Makes:** 4 servings

- 1 pkg. (12 oz.) frozen fully cooked Italian meatballs
- 4 slices sourdough bread
- 1½ tsp. olive oil
- 1 garlic clove, halved
- 1½ cups pasta sauce with mushrooms
- ½ cup shredded part-skim mozzarella cheese, divided
- ½ cup grated Parmesan cheese, divided

1. Preheat broiler. Microwave meatballs, covered, on high until heated through, 4-6 minutes. Meanwhile, place bread on an ungreased baking sheet; brush one side of bread with oil. Broil 4-6 in. from heat until golden brown, 1-2 minutes. Rub bread with cut surface of garlic; discard garlic. Tear bread into bite-sized pieces; transfer to a greased 11x7-in. baking dish. Reduce oven setting to 350°.

2. Add pasta sauce, ¼ cup mozzarella cheese and ¼ cup Parmesan cheese to meatballs; toss to combine. Pour mixture over bread pieces; sprinkle with remaining cheeses. Bake, uncovered, until cheeses are melted, 15-18 minutes.

1 serving: 417 cal., 28g fat (13g sat. fat), 59mg chol., 1243mg sod., 22g carb. (8g sugars, 3g fiber), 23g pro.

EAT SMART
GINGER SALMON WITH GREEN BEANS

I developed this flavor-packed dinner for a busy friend who wants to eat clean.
—Nicole Stevens, Mount Pleasant, SC

- -

Takes: 30 min. • **Makes:** 2 servings

- ¼ cup lemon juice
- 2 Tbsp. rice vinegar
- 3 garlic cloves, minced
- 2 tsp. minced fresh gingerroot
- 2 tsp. honey
- ⅛ tsp. salt
- ⅛ tsp. pepper
- 2 salmon fillets (4 oz. each)
- 1 medium lemon, thinly sliced

GREEN BEANS

- ¾ lb. fresh green beans, trimmed
- 2 Tbsp. water
- 2 tsp. olive oil
- ½ cup finely chopped onion
- 3 garlic cloves, minced
- ⅛ tsp. salt

1. Preheat oven to 325°. Mix first seven ingredients.

2. Place each salmon fillet on an 18x12-in. piece of heavy-duty foil; fold up edges of foil to create a rim around the fish. Spoon the lemon juice mixture over salmon; top with lemon slices. Carefully fold foil around fish, sealing tightly.

3. Place packets in a 15x10x1-in. pan. Bake until fish just begins to flake easily with a fork, 15-20 minutes. Open foil carefully to allow steam to escape.

4. Meanwhile, place green beans, water and oil in a large skillet; bring to a boil. Reduce heat; simmer, covered, 5 minutes. Stir in remaining ingredients; cook, uncovered, until beans are crisp-tender, stirring occasionally. Serve with salmon.

1 serving: 357 cal., 15g fat (3g sat. fat), 57mg chol., 607mg sod., 35g carb. (18g sugars, 8g fiber), 24g pro. **Diabetic exchanges:** 3 lean meat, 1 starch, 1 vegetable, 1 fat.

BEAN & RICE BURRITOS

These hearty, full-flavored burritos can be whipped up in a jiffy.

—Kimberly Hardison, Maitland, FL

- -

Takes: 25 min. • **Makes:** 8 servings

1½ cups water
1½ cups uncooked instant brown rice
 1 medium green pepper, diced
 ½ cup chopped onion
 1 Tbsp. olive oil
 1 tsp. minced garlic
 1 Tbsp. chili powder
 1 tsp. ground cumin
 ⅛ tsp. crushed red pepper flakes
 1 can (15 oz.) black beans,
    rinsed and drained
 8 flour tortillas (8 in.), warmed
 1 cup salsa
    Optional toppings: Reduced-fat
    shredded cheddar cheese and
    reduced-fat sour cream

1. In a small saucepan, bring water to a boil. Add rice. Return to a boil. Reduce heat; cover and simmer for 5 minutes. Remove from the heat. Let stand for 5 minutes or until water is absorbed.
2. Meanwhile, in a large skillet, saute the green pepper and onion in oil until tender, 3-4 minutes. Add garlic; cook 1 minute longer. Stir in the chili powder, cumin and pepper flakes until combined. Add beans and rice; cook and stir until heated through, 4-6 minutes.
3. Spoon about ½ cup of filling off-center on each tortilla; top with 2 Tbsp. salsa. Fold sides and ends over filling and roll up. Serve with cheese and sour cream if desired.
1 burrito: 290 cal., 6g fat (1g sat. fat), 0 chol., 504mg sod., 49g carb. (2g sugars, 4g fiber), 9g pro.

EAT SMART
WHAT'S IN THE FRIDGE FRITTATA

Great for a last-minute breakfast, brunch or lunch, this dish features a crab-Swiss combo guests rave about. I also like to use sausage and cheddar with asparagus or whatever is in season.

—Deborah Posey, Virginia Beach, VA

- -

Takes: 25 min. • **Makes:** 4 servings

 6 large eggs
 ⅓ cup chopped onion
 ⅓ cup chopped sweet red pepper
 ⅓ cup chopped fresh mushrooms
 1 Tbsp. olive oil
 1 can (6 oz.) lump crabmeat, drained
 ¼ cup shredded Swiss cheese
 1 Tbsp. minced fresh
    parsley, optional

1. In a small bowl, whisk eggs; set aside. In an 8-in. ovenproof skillet, saute the onion, pepper and mushrooms in oil until tender. Reduce heat; sprinkle with crab. Top with the eggs. Cover and cook until nearly set, 5-7 minutes.
2. Uncover skillet; sprinkle with cheese. Broil 3-4 in. from the heat until eggs are completely set, 2-3 minutes. Let stand for 5 minutes. Cut into wedges.
1 wedge: 215 cal., 13g fat (4g sat. fat), 361mg chol., 265mg sod., 3g carb. (2g sugars, 1g fiber), 21g pro. **Diabetic exchanges:** 3 lean meat, 1½ fat.

CHICKEN & VEGETABLE CURRY COUSCOUS

I find that a semi-homemade one-pot meal is often the best way to get dinner done in a hurry. Use your family's favorite blend of frozen veggies and serve with toasted pita bread for smiles all around.
—Elizabeth Hokanson, Arborg, MB

Takes: 25 min. • **Makes:** 6 servings

- 1 **Tbsp. butter**
- 1 **lb. boneless skinless chicken breasts, cut into strips**
- 1 **pkg. (16 oz.) frozen vegetable blend of your choice**
- 1¼ **cups water**
- 1 **pkg. (5.7 oz.) curry-flavored couscous mix**
- ½ **cup raisins**

1. In a large nonstick skillet, heat butter over medium-high heat. Add chicken; cook and stir until no longer pink.

2. Add vegetable blend, water and contents of couscous seasoning packet. Bring to a boil; stir in couscous and raisins. Remove from heat; let stand, covered, until water is absorbed, about 5 minutes. Fluff couscous with a fork.

1 cup: 273 cal., 4g fat (2g sat. fat), 47mg chol., 311mg sod., 39g carb. (9g sugars, 4g fiber), 21g pro. **Diabetic exchanges:** 2 starch, 2 lean meat, 1 vegetable, ½ fat.

MEATBALL FLATBREAD

As amazing as this flatbread is, you would never know how unbelievably effortless it is to make. Hidden veggies, unnoticed by the kids, are definitely a wonderful benefit. For a crispy crust, bake the flatbread in the oven until slightly crispy on top before applying tomato puree.
—Kimberly Berg, North Street, MI

Takes: 25 min. • **Makes:** 4 pizzas

- 1 **can (15 oz.) Italian tomato sauce**
- 1 **medium carrot, coarsely chopped**
- 3 **fresh basil leaves**
- 1 **garlic clove, halved**
- 4 **naan flatbreads**
- 2 **cups shredded mozzarella cheese**
- 14 **frozen fully cooked Italian meatballs, thawed and halved
  Dash each salt, pepper, dried parsley flakes and dried oregano**

1. Preheat oven to 400°. Place tomato sauce, carrot, basil and garlic in a food processor; cover and process until pureed. Place flatbreads on an ungreased baking sheet. Spread with tomato sauce mixture; top with cheese and meatballs. Sprinkle with seasonings.

2. Bake on a lower oven rack until cheese is melted, 12-15 minutes.

½ flatbread: 253 cal., 14g fat (7g sat. fat), 37mg chol., 911mg sod., 20g carb. (3g sugars, 2g fiber), 13g pro.

EAT SMART
PEPPERONI PIZZA BAKED POTATOES

These tasty taters became a spur-of-the-moment recipe borne of leftovers. It's a true mashup meal that combines two dinner favorites into one super fun dinner.
—Dawn E. Lowenstein, Huntingdon Valley, PA

- -

Takes: 30 min. • **Makes:** 4 servings

- 4 medium russet potatoes (about 8 oz. each)
- 1 Tbsp. olive oil
- 1 cup sliced fresh mushrooms
- 1 small green pepper, chopped
- 1 small onion, chopped
- 1 garlic clove, minced
- 1 can (8 oz.) pizza sauce
- ⅓ cup mini sliced turkey pepperoni
- ½ cup shredded Italian cheese blend
  Fresh oregano leaves or dried oregano, optional

1. Preheat oven to 400°. Scrub potatoes; place on a microwave-safe plate. Pierce several times with a fork. Microwave the potatoes, uncovered, on high until tender, 12-15 minutes.
2. In a large skillet, heat oil over medium-high heat; saute mushrooms, pepper and onion until tender, 6-8 minutes. Add garlic; cook and stir 1 minute. Stir in pizza sauce and pepperoni; heat through.
3. Place potatoes on a baking sheet; cut an "X" in the top of each. Fluff pulp with a fork. Top with the vegetable mixture; sprinkle with Italian cheese blend. Bake until the cheese is melted, 5-7 minutes. If desired, sprinkle with oregano.

1 baked potato with toppings: 311 cal., 9g fat (3g sat. fat), 23mg chol., 515mg sod., 46g carb. (5g sugars, 6g fiber), 13g pro. **Diabetic exchanges:** 3 starch, 1 medium-fat meat, ½ fat.

EAT SMART
EGG ROLL NOODLE BOWL

We love Asian egg rolls, but they can be challenging to make. Simplify everything with this deconstructed egg roll in a bowl made on the stovetop.
—Courtney Stultz, Weir, KS

- -

Takes: 30 min. • **Makes:** 4 servings

- 1 Tbsp. sesame oil
- ½ lb. ground pork
- 1 Tbsp. soy sauce
- 1 garlic clove, minced
- 1 tsp. ground ginger
- ½ tsp. salt
- ¼ tsp. ground turmeric
- ¼ tsp. pepper
- 6 cups shredded cabbage (about 1 small head)
- 2 large carrots, shredded (about 2 cups)
- 4 oz. rice noodles
- 3 green onions, thinly sliced
  Additional soy sauce, optional

1. In a large skillet, heat oil over medium-high heat; cook and crumble pork until browned, 4-6 minutes. Stir in soy sauce, garlic and seasonings. Add cabbage and carrots; cook until vegetables are tender, stirring occasionally, 4-6 minutes longer.
2. Cook rice noodles according to package directions; drain and immediately add to pork mixture, tossing to combine. Sprinkle with green onions. If desired, serve with additional soy sauce.

1½ cups: 302 cal., 12g fat (4g sat. fat), 38mg chol., 652mg sod., 33g carb. (2g sugars, 4g fiber), 14g pro. **Diabetic exchanges:** 2 medium-fat meat, 2 vegetable, 1½ starch, ½ fat.

QUICK PEPPERONI CALZONES

Take your calzones to the next level by adding Parmesan and herbs on top.
—Shannon Roum, Cudahy, WI

Takes: 30 min. • **Makes:** 4 servings

- 1 cup chopped pepperoni
- ½ cup pasta sauce with meat
- ¼ cup shredded part-skim mozzarella cheese
- 1 loaf (1 lb.) frozen bread dough, thawed
- 1 to 2 Tbsp. 2% milk
- 1 Tbsp. grated Parmesan cheese
- ½ tsp. Italian seasoning, optional

1. Preheat oven to 350°. In a small bowl, the mix the pepperoni, pasta sauce and mozzarella cheese.

2. On a lightly floured surface, divide dough into four portions. Roll each into a 6-in. circle; top each circle with a scant ⅓ cup pepperoni mixture. Fold dough over filling; pinch edges to seal. Place on a greased baking sheet.

3. Brush milk over tops; sprinkle with Parmesan cheese and, if desired, Italian seasoning. Bake until calzones are golden brown, 20-25 minutes.

1 calzone: 540 cal., 23g fat (8g sat. fat), 36mg chol., 1573mg sod., 59g carb. (7g sugars, 5g fiber), 21g pro.

EAT SMART
BLACKENED HALIBUT

Serve these spicy fillets with garlic mashed potatoes, crusty bread and a crisp salad to lure in your crew.
—Brenda Williams, Santa Maria, CA

Takes: 25 min. • **Makes:** 4 servings

- 2 Tbsp. garlic powder
- 1 Tbsp. salt
- 1 Tbsp. onion powder
- 1 Tbsp. dried oregano
- 1 Tbsp. dried thyme
- 1 Tbsp. cayenne pepper
- 1 Tbsp. pepper
- 2½ tsp. paprika
- 4 halibut fillets (4 oz. each)
- 2 Tbsp. butter

1. In a large shallow dish, combine the first eight ingredients. Add fillets, two at a time, and turn to coat.

2. In a large cast-iron skillet, cook fillets in butter over medium heat until fish flakes easily with a fork, 3-4 minutes on each side.

1 fillet: 189 cal., 8g fat (4g sat. fat), 51mg chol., 758mg sod., 3g carb. (1g sugars, 1g fiber), 24g pro. **Diabetic exchanges:** 3 lean meat, 1 fat.

SUN-DRIED TOMATO PASTA

At my house, this dish is known as Gus's Special Pasta. My oldest child claimed it as his own when he was 8, and I am always happy to oblige his desire for this cheesy, garlicky, pungent dish.
—Courtney Gaylord, Columbus, IN

Takes: 25 min. • **Makes:** 6 servings

- 1   pkg. (16 oz.) linguine
- 1   jar (7 oz.) julienned oil-packed sun-dried tomatoes
- 6   garlic cloves, minced
- 1   Tbsp. lemon juice
- ½   cup minced fresh parsley
- 1½ cups crumbled feta cheese
- 1½ cups grated Parmesan cheese

1. In a 6-qt. stockpot, cook linguine according to package directions for al dente. Drain, reserving ½ cup pasta water; return linguine to pot.
2. Meanwhile, drain tomatoes, reserving 2 Tbsp. oil. In a small microwave-safe bowl, combine garlic and reserved oil; microwave on high 45 seconds. Stir in the drained tomatoes and lemon juice.
3. Add tomato mixture to linguine. Toss with parsley, cheeses and enough pasta water to moisten.
1⅓ cups: 542 cal., 21g fat (8g sat. fat), 32mg chol., 726mg sod., 68g carb. (3g sugars, 6g fiber), 23g pro.

THAI PEANUT NAAN PIZZAS

I'm a huge fan of Thai food, but don't always have the time to make it at home. To get my fix, I top handy naan bread with a ginger-peanut sauce, fresh veggies, a sprinkle of cilantro and a drizzle of spicy Sriracha chili sauce.
—Rachel Bernard Seis, Milwaukee, WI

Takes: 25 min. • **Makes:** 4 servings

- ¼   cup creamy peanut butter
- 3   Tbsp. sesame ginger salad dressing
- 1   Tbsp. water
- 1   tsp. soy sauce
- 2   naan flatbreads
- 1   cup shredded part-skim mozzarella cheese
- 1   small sweet red pepper, julienned
- ½   cup julienned carrot
- ½   cup sliced baby portobello mushrooms
- ¼   cup chopped fresh cilantro Sriracha chili sauce, optional

1. Preheat oven to 425°. For sauce, mix first four ingredients until blended. Place naan on a baking sheet; spread with sauce. Top with cheese and vegetables.
2. Bake until cheese is melted and crust is golden brown, 8-10 minutes. Top with chopped cilantro and, if desired, drizzle with chili sauce.
½ pizza: 316 cal., 19g fat (6g sat. fat), 21mg chol., 698mg sod., 25g carb. (8g sugars, 2g fiber), 13g pro.

TEQUILA LIME SHRIMP ZOODLES

This tangy shrimp is a great way to cut carbs without sacrificing flavor. If you don't have a spiralizer, use thinly julienned zucchini to get a similar effect.
—Brigette Schroeder, Yorkville, IL

- -

Takes: 30 min. • **Makes:** 4 servings

- 3 Tbsp. butter, divided
- 1 shallot, minced
- 2 garlic cloves, minced
- ¼ cup tequila
- 1½ tsp. grated lime zest
- 2 Tbsp. lime juice
- 1 Tbsp. olive oil
- 1 lb. uncooked shrimp (31-40 per lb.), peeled and deveined
- 2 medium zucchini, spiralized (about 6 cups)
- ½ tsp. salt
- ¼ tsp. pepper
- ¼ cup minced fresh parsley
  Additional grated lime zest

1. In a large skillet, heat 2 Tbsp. butter over medium heat. Add shallot and garlic; cook 1-2 minutes. Remove from heat; stir in the tequila, lime zest and lime juice. Cook over medium heat until the liquid is almost evaporated, 2-3 minutes.
2. Add olive oil and remaining butter; stir in shrimp and zucchini. Sprinkle with salt and pepper. Cook and stir until shrimp begin to turn pink and zucchini is crisp-tender, 4-5 minutes. Sprinkle with parsley and additional lime zest.

1¼ cups: 246 cal., 14g fat (6g sat. fat), 161mg chol., 510mg sod., 7g carb. (3g sugars, 1g fiber), 20g pro. **Diabetic exchanges:** 3 lean meat, 3 fat, 1 vegetable.

CHICKEN & BROCCOLI WITH DILL SAUCE

I've had this chicken and broccoli recipe for so many years, I don't remember when I first made it. You can serve it with a side of couscous or rice for a complete meal, or add some sliced mushrooms or carrots for extra veggies.
—Kallee Krong-McCreery, Escondido, CA

- -

Takes: 30 min. • **Makes:** 4 servings

- 4 boneless skinless chicken breast halves (6 oz. each)
- ½ tsp. garlic salt
- ¼ tsp. pepper
- 1 Tbsp. olive oil
- 4 cups fresh broccoli florets
- 1 cup chicken broth
- 1 Tbsp. all-purpose flour
- 1 Tbsp. snipped fresh dill
- 1 cup 2% milk

1. Sprinkle the chicken with garlic salt and pepper. In a large skillet, heat the oil over medium heat; brown chicken on both sides. Remove from pan.
2. Add the broccoli and broth to same skillet; bring to a boil. Reduce heat; simmer, covered, until the broccoli is just tender, 3-5 minutes. Using a slotted spoon, remove broccoli from pan, reserving broth. Keep broccoli warm.
3. In a small bowl, mix flour, dill and milk until smooth; stir into broth in pan. Bring to a boil, stirring constantly; cook and stir until thickened, 1-2 minutes. Add the chicken; cook, covered, over medium heat until a thermometer inserted in chicken reads 165°, 10-12 minutes. Serve with broccoli.

1 serving: 274 cal., 9g fat (2g sat. fat), 100mg chol., 620mg sod., 8g carb. (4g sugars, 2g fiber), 39g pro. **Diabetic exchanges:** 5 lean meat, 1 vegetable, 1 fat.

PRETZEL-CRUSTED CATFISH

I'm not a big fish lover, so any concoction that has me enjoying fish is a keeper in my book. This combination of flavors works for me. It's awesome served with corn muffins, butter and honey!
—Kelly Williams, Forked River, NJ

- -

Takes: 30 min. • **Makes:** 4 servings

4 catfish fillets (6 oz. each)
½ tsp. salt
½ tsp. pepper
2 large eggs
⅓ cup Dijon mustard
2 Tbsp. 2% milk
½ cup all-purpose flour
4 cups honey mustard miniature pretzels, coarsely crushed
Oil for frying
Lemon slices, optional

1. Sprinkle catfish with salt and pepper. Whisk the eggs, mustard and milk in a shallow bowl. Place flour and pretzels in separate shallow bowls. Coat fillets with flour, then dip in egg mixture and coat with pretzels.
2. Heat ¼ in. of oil to 375° in an electric skillet. Fry fillets, a few at a time, until fish flakes easily with a fork, 3-4 minutes on each side. Drain on paper towels. Serve with lemon slices if desired.

1 fillet: 610 cal., 31g fat (4g sat. fat), 164mg chol., 1579mg sod., 44g carb. (2g sugars, 2g fiber), 33g pro.

EAT SMART
LEMON PORK WITH MUSHROOMS

This is my family's favorite go-to healthy dish because it tastes too good to be light. Lemon offers a bright flavor boost.
—Christine Datian, Las Vegas, NV

- -

Takes: 30 min. • **Makes:** 4 servings

1 large egg, lightly beaten
1 cup seasoned bread crumbs
8 boneless thin pork loin chops (2 oz. each)
¼ tsp. salt
⅛ tsp. pepper
1 Tbsp. olive oil
1 Tbsp. butter
½ lb. sliced fresh mushrooms
2 garlic cloves, minced
2 tsp. grated lemon zest
1 Tbsp. lemon juice
Lemon wedges, optional

1. Place egg and bread crumbs in separate shallow bowls. Sprinkle pork chops with salt and pepper; dip in egg, then coat with the crumbs, pressing to adhere.
2. In a large skillet, heat oil over medium heat. In batches, cook pork until golden brown, 2-3 minutes per side. Remove from pan; keep warm.
3. Wipe pan clean. In skillet, heat the butter over medium heat; saute mushrooms until tender, 2-3 minutes. Stir in the garlic, lemon zest and lemon juice; cook and stir 1 minute. Serve over pork. If desired, serve with lemon wedges.

1 serving: 331 cal., 15g fat (5g sat. fat), 109mg chol., 601mg sod., 19g carb. (2g sugars, 1g fiber), 28g pro. **Diabetic exchanges:** 3 lean meat, 1½ fat, 1 starch.

STOVETOP CHEESEBURGER PASTA

Cheeseburgers are delicious in any form, but I'm partial to this creamy pasta dish that seriously tastes just like the real thing. It's weeknight comfort in a bowl.
—Tracy Avis, Peterborough, ON

- -

Takes: 30 min. • **Makes:** 8 servings

1	pkg. (16 oz.) penne pasta
1	lb. ground beef
¼	cup butter, cubed
½	cup all-purpose flour
2	cups 2% milk
1¼	cups beef broth
1	Tbsp. Worcestershire sauce
3	tsp. ground mustard
2	cans (14½ oz. each) diced tomatoes, drained
4	green onions, chopped
3	cups shredded Colby-Monterey Jack cheese, divided
⅔	cup grated Parmesan cheese, divided

1. Cook pasta according to package directions; drain.

2. Meanwhile, in a Dutch oven, cook and crumble beef over medium heat until no longer pink, 5-7 minutes. Remove from pan with a slotted spoon; pour off drippings.

3. In same pan, melt butter over low heat; stir in flour until smooth. Cook and stir until lightly browned, 2-3 minutes (do not burn). Gradually whisk in the milk, beef broth, Worcestershire sauce and mustard. Bring to a boil, stirring constantly; cook and stir until thickened, 1-2 minutes. Stir in the tomatoes; return to a boil. Reduce heat; simmer, covered, 5 minutes.

4. Stir in green onions, pasta and beef; heat through. Stir in half of the cheeses until melted. Sprinkle with remaining cheese; remove from heat. Let stand, covered, until cheese is melted.

1½ cups: 616 cal., 29g fat (17g sat. fat), 98mg chol., 727mg sod., 56g carb. (7g sugars, 3g fiber), 33g pro.

VEGGIE FAJITAS

For scrumptious and super quick party fare, these colorful, hearty fajitas packed with crisp-tender veggies are perfect.
—Sarah Mercer, Wichita, KS

- -

Takes: 25 min. • **Makes:** 8 fajitas

1	small zucchini, thinly sliced
1	medium yellow summer squash, thinly sliced
½	lb. sliced fresh mushrooms
1	small onion, halved and sliced
1	medium carrot, julienned
1	tsp. salt
½	tsp. pepper
1	Tbsp. canola oil
8	flour tortillas (8 in.), warmed
2	cups shredded cheddar cheese
1	cup sour cream
1	cup salsa

In a large skillet, saute the vegetables, salt and pepper in oil until crisp-tender, 5-7 minutes. Using a slotted spoon, place about ½ cup vegetable mixture down the center of each tortilla. Sprinkle each with ¼ cup cheese; top with sour cream and salsa. Fold in sides.

1 fajita: 375 cal., 21g fat (10g sat. fat), 35mg chol., 853mg sod., 35g carb. (4g sugars, 3g fiber), 13g pro.

SPEEDY SURPRISE
"Really good veggie fajitas served with the shredded cheese, salsa and sour cream as recommended."
—KATLAYDEE3, TASTEOFHOME.COM

FIVE-SPICE GLAZED SMOKED CHOPS

I started fixing another recipe but didn't have all the ingredients, so I came up with this entree. The spice gives it a flavorful kick—you can make your own five-spice powder by combining cloves, cinnamon, anise and nutmeg. I love that you can make this on the stovetop or the grill.
—Jill Thomas, Washington, IN

Takes: 25 min. • **Makes:** 4 servings

- ¼ cup unsweetened apple juice
- ¼ cup grape jelly
- 2 Tbsp. cider vinegar
- ½ tsp. Chinese five-spice powder
- ½ tsp. minced fresh gingerroot
- ¼ tsp. crushed red pepper flakes
- 1 Tbsp. butter
- 4 smoked bone-in pork chops (7½ oz. each)

1. For glaze, place first six ingredients in a small saucepan; bring just to a boil. Reduce heat; simmer, uncovered, 10 minutes.
2. In a 12-in. skillet, heat the butter over medium-high heat. Add pork chops; cook until bottoms are browned, 4-5 minutes. Turn chops; spoon glaze over top. Cook, uncovered, until chops are glazed and heated through, 3-4 minutes.
1 pork chop: 363 cal., 22g fat (10g sat. fat), 77mg chol., 1345mg sod., 16g carb. (15g sugars, 0 fiber), 27g pro.

PRESSURE-COOKER RISOTTO WITH SHRIMP & ASPARAGUS

This speedy method of making risotto works every time!
—Kim Gray, Davie, FL

Takes: 30 min. • **Makes:** 8 servings

- 3 Tbsp. unsalted butter
- 1 small onion, finely diced
- 9 garlic cloves, minced, divided
- 1⅔ cups uncooked arborio rice
- 1 cup white wine
- 4 cups reduced-sodium chicken broth
- ½ cup shredded Parmesan cheese, divided
- 2 Tbsp. olive oil
- 2 lbs. uncooked shrimp (26-30 per lb.), peeled and deveined
- 1 Tbsp. unsalted butter
- ½ cup Italian salad dressing
- 1 lb. fresh asparagus, trimmed Salt and pepper to taste

1. Select saute setting on a 6-qt. electric pressure cooker and adjust for high heat; warm butter until melted. Add onion; cook 4-5 minutes. Add six minced garlic cloves; cook 1 minute. Add rice; cook and stir for 2 minutes. Stir in ½ cup wine; cook and stir until absorbed. Add remaining wine, broth and ¼ cup cheese. Lock lid; make sure vent is closed. Select manual setting; adjust pressure to high. Set the time for 8 minutes. When finished cooking, quick-release pressure according to manufacturer's directions; stir.
2. Meanwhile, heat oil in a large skillet over medium-high heat. Add remaining garlic; cook 1 minute. Add the shrimp; cook and stir until shrimp begin to turn pink, about 5 minutes. Add butter and dressing; stir until butter melts. Reduce heat. Add asparagus; cook until tender, 3-5 minutes. Serve over risotto. Season with salt and pepper. Sprinkle with remaining cheese.
1 serving: 424 cal., 15g fat (6g sat. fat), 157mg chol., 661mg sod., 39g carb. (3g sugars, 1g fiber), 26g pro.

COLA BBQ CHICKEN

My dad has been making a basic version of this family favorite for years. I've recently made it my own by spicing it up a bit with hoisin sauce and red pepper flakes. Sometimes I let the chicken and sauce simmer in my slow cooker.

—Brigette Schroeder, Yorkville, IL

Takes: 30 min. • **Makes:** 6 servings

- 1 cup cola
- ⅓ cup finely chopped onion
- ⅓ cup barbecue sauce
- 2 tsp. hoisin sauce
- 1 garlic clove, minced
- ⅛ tsp. salt
- ⅛ tsp. pepper
- ⅛ tsp. crushed red pepper flakes
- 6 boneless skinless chicken thighs (about 1½ lbs.)
  Hot cooked rice

1. In a small saucepan, combine the first eight ingredients; bring to a boil. Reduce heat; simmer, uncovered, until slightly thickened, 10-15 minutes, stirring occasionally. Reserve ¾ cup for serving.
2. Grill chicken, covered, over medium heat or broil 4 in. from heat until a thermometer reads 165°, 5-7 minutes on each side, basting occasionally with remaining sauce during the last 5 minutes of cooking. Serve chicken with rice and reserved sauce.
1 chicken thigh with 2 Tbsp. sauce: 213 cal., 8g fat (2g sat. fat), 76mg chol., 298mg sod., 12g carb. (10g sugars, 0 fiber), 21g pro.

5 INGREDIENT
COUNTRY HAM & POTATOES

The browned potatoes give simple ham a tasty touch. Not only do the potatoes pick up the flavor of the ham, but they look beautiful! Just add veggies or a salad and dinner's done.

—Helen Bridges, Washington, VA

Takes: 30 min. • **Makes:** 6 servings

- 2 lbs. fully cooked sliced ham (about ½ in. thick)
- 2 to 3 Tbsp. butter
- 1½ lbs. potatoes, peeled, quartered and cooked
  Snipped fresh parsley

In a large heavy skillet, brown ham over medium-high heat in butter on both sides until heated through. Move ham to one side of the skillet; brown potatoes in drippings until tender. Sprinkle potatoes with parsley.
1 serving: 261 cal., 9g fat (5g sat. fat), 64mg chol., 1337mg sod., 21g carb. (1g sugars, 1g fiber), 28g pro.

DILL PICKLE HAMBURGER PIZZA

My husband's favorite foods are pizza and cheeseburgers, so I combined the two into a weeknight dinner. People who try it start laughing because it's so silly yet so good.
—Angie Zimmerman, Eureka, IL

Takes: 30 min. • **Makes:** 6 servings

- ½ lb. ground beef
- 1 prebaked 12-in. pizza crust
- ½ cup ketchup
- ¼ cup prepared mustard
- 1½ cups shredded cheddar cheese
- 2 cups shredded lettuce
- ½ cup chopped dill pickle
- ¼ cup chopped onion
- ½ cup mayonnaise
- 2 to 3 Tbsp. dill pickle juice

1. Preheat oven to 425°. In a large skillet, cook and crumble beef over medium heat until no longer pink, 3-4 minutes; drain.
2. Meanwhile, place crust on an ungreased baking sheet or pizza pan. Mix ketchup and mustard; spread over crust. Add ground beef; bake 5 minutes. Sprinkle with cheese; bake until the cheese is bubbly and crust is lightly browned, 8-10 minutes longer.
3. Top with lettuce, pickle and onion. Whisk mayonnaise and enough pickle juice to reach desired consistency; pour over pizza.
1 slice: 521 cal., 32g fat (10g sat. fat), 59mg chol., 1192mg sod., 36g carb. (7g sugars, 2g fiber), 21g pro.

PO'BOY TACOS

I intended to make tostadas, but misread a couple of ingredients and had to use what I had available. I put my own tasty twist on a po'boy recipe and I think I ended up with something even better.
—Cynthia Nelson, Saskatoon, SK

Takes: 30 min. • **Makes:** 4 servings

- ¼ cup mayonnaise
- 2 Tbsp. seafood cocktail sauce
- ½ tsp. Buffalo wing sauce
- ½ medium ripe avocado, peeled
- 1 Tbsp. lime juice
- ½ cup all-purpose flour
- ½ cup cornmeal
- 2 Tbsp. Creole seasoning
- 1 lb. uncooked shrimp (26-30 per lb.), peeled and deveined
- 2 Tbsp. canola oil
- 8 flour tortillas (6 in.)
- 1 medium tomato, chopped
- 2 Tbsp. minced fresh cilantro

1. Combine mayonnaise, cocktail sauce and Buffalo wing sauce; set aside. In another bowl, mash avocado and lime juice until combined; set aside.
2. In a shallow bowl, mix flour, cornmeal and Creole seasoning. Add shrimp, a few pieces at a time, and turn to coat; shake off excess. In a large skillet, heat oil over medium-high heat. Add shrimp; cook and stir until shrimp turn pink, 4-6 minutes.
3. Spread reserved avocado mixture over tortillas. Top with the shrimp, reserved mayonnaise mixture, tomato and cilantro.
2 tacos: 551 cal., 29g fat (5g sat. fat), 139mg chol., 977mg sod., 47g carb. (3g sugars, 5g fiber), 25g pro.

EASY CHICKEN & DUMPLINGS

Perfect for fall nights, my simple version of comforting chicken and dumplings is speedy, low in fat and a delicious one-dish meal. Give it a try tonight!
—Nancy Tuck, Elk Falls, KS

- -

Takes: 30 min. • **Makes:** 6 servings

- 3 celery ribs, chopped
- 2 medium carrots, sliced
- 3 cans (14½ oz. each) reduced-sodium chicken broth
- 3 cups cubed cooked chicken breast
- ½ tsp. poultry seasoning
- ⅛ tsp. pepper
- 1⅔ cups reduced-fat biscuit/baking mix
- ⅔ cup fat-free milk

1. In a Dutch oven coated with cooking spray, cook and stir celery and carrots over medium heat until tender, about 5 minutes. Stir in broth, chicken and seasonings. Bring to a boil; reduce heat to a gentle simmer.
2. For dumplings, mix biscuit mix and milk until a soft dough forms. Carefully drop by tablespoonfuls on top of the simmering liquid. Reduce heat to low; cover and cook until a toothpick inserted in the dumplings comes out clean, 10-15 minutes (do not lift cover during the first 10 minutes).
1 cup: 260 cal., 4g fat (1g sat. fat), 54mg chol., 1039mg sod., 28g carb. (6g sugars, 2g fiber), 27g pro.

BEEF & BACON GNOCCHI SKILLET

Yum! This gnocchi dish tastes like bacon cheeseburgers. Go ahead and top servings it as you would a burger.
—Ashley Lecker, Green Bay, WI

- -

Takes: 30 min. • **Makes:** 6 servings

- 1 pkg. (16 oz.) potato gnocchi
- 1¼ lbs. lean ground beef (90% lean)
- 1 medium onion, chopped
- 8 cooked bacon strips, crumbled and divided
- 1 cup water
- ½ cup heavy whipping cream
- 1 Tbsp. ketchup
- ¼ tsp. salt
- ¼ tsp. pepper
- 1½ cups shredded cheddar cheese
- ½ cup chopped tomatoes
- 2 green onions, sliced

1. Preheat broiler. Cook gnocchi according to package directions; drain.
2. Meanwhile, in a large ovenproof skillet, cook beef and onion, crumbling beef, over medium heat until beef is no longer pink, 4-6 minutes. Drain.
3. Stir in half of the bacon; add gnocchi, water, cream and ketchup. Bring to a boil. Cook, stirring, over medium heat until sauce has thickened, 3-4 minutes. Add seasonings. Sprinkle with cheese.
4. Broil 3-4 in. from heat until cheese has melted, 1-2 minutes. Top with tomatoes, green onions and remaining bacon.
Note: Look for potato gnocchi in the pasta or frozen foods section.
1 cup: 573 cal., 31g fat (16g sat. fat), 136mg chol., 961mg sod., 35g carb. (7g sugars, 2g fiber), 36g pro.

MANGO SALSA CHICKEN WITH VEGGIE HASH

This hash has the fresh flavors of spring. Using precooked grilled chicken strips makes it come together quickly. And the veggies make the dish so pretty!
—Lori McLain, Denton, TX

- -

Takes: 30 min. • **Makes:** 4 servings

1   Tbsp. canola oil
2   cups chopped red potatoes
     (2-3 medium)
1   small sweet yellow
     pepper, chopped
½   cup chopped red onion
1½   cups cut fresh asparagus
     (1-in. pieces)
12   oz. frozen grilled chicken
     breast strips, partially
     thawed (about 2 cups)
1½   cups mango salsa, divided
1   Tbsp. chopped fresh cilantro
     Additional cilantro

1. In a large skillet, heat oil over medium-high heat; saute the potatoes, pepper and onion until potatoes are lightly browned, 6-8 minutes. Add asparagus; cook and stir until potatoes are tender, 2-3 minutes. Stir in chicken, ¾ cup salsa and 1 Tbsp. cilantro; heat through, stirring occasionally.
2. Sprinkle with additional cilantro. Serve with remaining salsa.
1½ cups: 237 cal., 6g fat (1g sat. fat), 51mg chol., 1025mg sod., 20g carb. (3g sugars, 2g fiber), 24g pro.

JALAPENO BURGERS WITH GORGONZOLA

On a whim, we mixed jalapeno pepper jelly into ground beef patties, then topped the burgers with caramelized onions and tangy Gorgonzola cheese. Fabulous!
—Becky Mollenkamp, St. Louis, MO

- -

Takes: 30 min. • **Makes:** 4 servings

1   Tbsp. canola oil
1   tsp. butter
1   medium onion, halved
     and thinly sliced
     Dash salt
     Dash sugar
BURGERS
⅓   cup jalapeno pepper jelly
½   tsp. salt
¼   tsp. pepper
1   lb. ground beef
4   hamburger buns, split and toasted
2   Tbsp. crumbled Gorgonzola cheese
     Thinly sliced jalapeno pepper,
     optional

1. In a small skillet, heat oil and butter over medium heat. Add onion, salt and sugar; cook and stir until the onion is softened, 3-4 minutes. Reduce heat to medium-low; cook until deep golden brown, stirring occasionally, 4-6 minutes longer.
2. In a large bowl, mix jelly, salt and pepper. Add beef; mix lightly but thoroughly. Shape into four ½-in. thick patties.
3. Grill burgers, covered, over medium heat or broil 4 in. from heat until a thermometer reads 160°, 4-5 minutes on each side. Serve on buns with the caramelized onion, cheese and, if desired, sliced jalapeno.
1 burger: 460 cal., 20g fat (7g sat. fat), 76mg chol., 669mg sod., 43g carb. (18g sugars, 2g fiber), 25g pro.

ZESTY CORKSCREWS

As a mother who works full time, I'm always looking for quick, easy meals to prepare. This is a timeless recipe.

—Lorie VanHorn, Waddell, AZ

Takes: 30 min. • **Makes:** 6 servings

- 1   lb. lean ground beef (90% lean)
- 1   small onion, chopped
- 1   pkg. (6 oz.) four-cheese corkscrew pasta mix
- 2   cups salsa
- 1   cup hot water
- 1   Tbsp. chili powder
- ½   tsp. salt
     Dash cayenne pepper
- 1   can (14½ oz.) diced tomatoes, undrained
- 1   can (2¼ oz.) sliced ripe olives, drained
- 1   cup shredded cheddar cheese
     Sour cream, optional

1. In a large skillet, cook beef and onion over medium heat until meat is no longer pink; drain. Stir the pasta, contents of seasoning packet, salsa, water, chili powder, salt and cayenne into the skillet.

2. Bring to a boil. Reduce heat; cover and simmer until pasta is tender, adding more water if necessary, about 15 minutes. Stir in tomatoes; sprinkle with olives and cheese. Cover and simmer until mixture is heated through, 3-4 minutes. If desired, serve with sour cream.

Note: This recipe was tested with Pasta Roni mix.

1¼ cups: 287 cal., 10g fat (3g sat. fat), 49mg chol., 1061mg sod., 29g carb. (7g sugars, 3g fiber), 19g pro.

QUICK CHICKEN & DUMPLINGS

Oh, the things you can make with frozen biscuit dough. I like to use the Pillsbury Buttermilk Biscuits to make this easy dumpling dish.

—Lakeya Astwood, Schenectady, NY

Takes: 30 min. • **Makes:** 6 servings

- 6   individually frozen biscuits
- ¼   cup chopped onion
- ¼   cup chopped green pepper
- 1   Tbsp. olive oil
- 4   cups shredded rotisserie chicken
- 3   cans (14½ oz. each) reduced-sodium chicken broth
- 1   can (4 oz.) mushroom stems and pieces, drained
- 1   tsp. chicken bouillon granules
- 1   tsp. minced fresh parsley
- ½   tsp. dried sage leaves
- ¼   tsp. dried rosemary, crushed
- ¼   tsp. pepper

1. Cut each biscuit into fourths; set aside. In a large saucepan, saute onion and green pepper in oil until tender. Stir in the chicken, broth, mushrooms, bouillon granules, fresh parsley, sage, rosemary and pepper.

2. Bring to a boil. Reduce heat; add biscuits for dumplings. Cover and simmer until a toothpick inserted in center of a dumpling comes out clean (do not lift cover while simmering), about 10 minutes.

1½ cups: 420 cal., 20g fat (5g sat. fat), 83mg chol., 1443mg sod., 26g carb. (6g sugars, 1g fiber), 34g pro.

SCALLOPS WITH SNOW PEAS

The crisp pea pods in this recipe are a nice contrast with the soft scallops. The main dish looks and tastes bright and fresh.
—Barb Carlucci, Orange Park, FL

Takes: 30 min. • **Makes:** 4 servings

- 2 Tbsp. cornstarch
- 2 Tbsp. reduced-sodium soy sauce
- ⅔ cup water
- 4 tsp. canola oil, divided
- 1 lb. bay scallops
- ½ lb. fresh snow peas, halved diagonally
- 2 medium leeks (white portion only), cut into 3x½-in. strips
- 1½ tsp. minced fresh gingerroot
- 3 cups hot cooked brown rice

1. Mix cornstarch, soy sauce and water. In a large nonstick skillet, heat 2 tsp. oil over medium-high heat; stir-fry scallops until firm and opaque, 1-2 minutes. Remove from the pan.
2. In same pan, heat remaining oil over medium-high heat; stir-fry snow peas, leeks and ginger until peas are just crisp-tender, 4-6 minutes. Stir cornstarch mixture; add to pan. Cook and stir until sauce is thickened, about 1 minute. Add scallops; heat through. Serve with rice.

1 cup stir-fry with ¾ cup rice: 378 cal., 7g fat (1g sat. fat), 27mg chol., 750mg sod., 57g carb. (4g sugars, 5g fiber), 21g pro.

EAT SMART
QUINOA-STUFFED SQUASH BOATS

My colorful boats with quinoa, chickpeas and pumpkin seeds use delicata squash, a winter squash that's cream-colored with green stripes. In a pinch, acorn squash will do just fine.
—Lauren Knoelke, Des Moines, IA

Takes: 30 min. • **Makes:** 8 servings

- 4 delicata squash (about 12 oz. each)
- 3 tsp. olive oil, divided
- ⅛ tsp. pepper
- 1 tsp. salt, divided
- 1½ cups vegetable broth
- 1 cup quinoa, rinsed
- 1 can (15 oz.) garbanzo beans or chickpeas, rinsed and drained
- ¼ cup dried cranberries
- 1 green onion, thinly sliced
- 1 tsp. minced fresh sage
- ½ tsp. grated lemon zest
- 1 tsp. lemon juice
- ½ cup crumbled goat cheese
- ¼ cup salted pumpkin seeds or pepitas, toasted

1. Preheat oven to 450°. Cut each squash lengthwise in half; remove and discard the seeds. Lightly brush cut sides with 1 tsp. oil; sprinkle with pepper and ½ tsp. salt. Place on a baking sheet, cut side down. Bake until tender, 15-20 minutes.
2. Meanwhile, in a large saucepan, combine broth and quinoa; bring to a boil. Reduce heat; simmer, covered, until the liquid is absorbed, 12-15 minutes.
3. Stir in garbanzo beans, cranberries, green onion, sage, lemon zest, lemon juice and the remaining oil and salt; spoon into squash. Sprinkle with cheese and pumpkin seeds.
1 stuffed squash half: 275 cal., 8g fat (2g sat. fat), 9mg chol., 591mg sod., 46g carb. (9g sugars, 10g fiber), 9g pro. **Diabetic exchanges:** 3 starch, 1 lean meat, ½ fat.

BISTRO TURKEY SANDWICH

As a turkey lover who can't get enough during fall and winter, I was inspired to come up with a restaurant-worthy sandwich. I especially enjoy it with a soft, rich cheese like Brie.
—Grace Voltolina, Westport, CT

- -

Takes: 30 min. • **Makes:** 4 servings

2 Tbsp. butter, divided
1 large Granny Smith or Honeycrisp apple, cut into ¼-in. slices
½ tsp. sugar
¼ tsp. ground cinnamon
½ medium sweet onion, sliced
¼ cup whole-berry or jellied cranberry sauce
4 ciabatta rolls, split
1 lb. cooked turkey, sliced
8 slices Camembert or Brie cheese (about 8 oz.)
3 cups arugula (about 2 oz.)

1. Preheat broiler. In a large skillet, heat 1 Tbsp. butter over medium heat; saute the apple slices with sugar and cinnamon until crisp-tender, 3-4 minutes. Remove from the pan.
2. In same pan, melt remaining butter over medium heat; saute the onion until lightly browned, 3-4 minutes. Remove from heat; stir in sauteed apple.
3. Spread cranberry sauce onto bottom of rolls; layer with turkey, apple mixture and cheese. Place on a baking sheet alongside roll tops, cut side up.
4. Broil 3-4 in. from heat until cheese begins to melt and roll tops are golden brown, 45-60 seconds. Add arugula; close sandwiches.
1 sandwich: 797 cal., 28g fat (14g sat. fat), 171mg chol., 1196mg sod., 87g carb. (16g sugars, 6g fiber), 55g pro.

LEMONY GREEK BEEF & VEGETABLES

I love the lemon in this recipe, which is the latest addition to my collection of quick, healthy dinners. I'm sensitive to cow's milk, so I use goat cheese crumbles on my portion instead of the Parmesan.
—Alice Neff, Lake Worth, FL

- -

Takes: 30 min. • **Makes:** 4 servings

1 bunch baby bok choy
1 lb. ground beef
1 Tbsp. olive oil
5 medium carrots, sliced
3 garlic cloves, minced
¼ cup plus 2 Tbsp. white wine, divided
1 can (15 to 16 oz.) navy beans, rinsed and drained
2 Tbsp. minced fresh oregano or 2 tsp. dried
¼ tsp. salt
2 Tbsp. lemon juice
½ cup shredded Parmesan cheese

1. Trim and discard root end of bok choy. Coarsely chop leaves. Cut stalks into 1-in. pieces. Set aside.
2. In a large skillet, cook beef over medium-high heat until no longer pink, breaking into crumbles, 5-7 minutes; drain. Remove from the skillet and set aside.
3. In same skillet, heat oil over medium-high heat. Add carrots and bok choy stalks; cook and stir until crisp-tender, 5-7 minutes. Stir in garlic, bok choy leaves and ¼ cup wine; increase heat to medium-high. Cook, stirring to loosen browned bits from pan, until the greens wilt, 3-5 minutes.
4. Stir in ground beef, beans, oregano, salt and enough remaining wine to keep the mixture moist. Reduce heat; simmer about 3 minutes. Stir in lemon juice; sprinkle with Parmesan cheese.
1½ cups: 478 cal., 21g fat (7g sat. fat), 77mg chol., 856mg sod., 36g carb. (7g sugars, 10g fiber), 36g pro.

TURKEY A LA KING

This is a smart way to use up leftover turkey. It's so tasty, you might want to make a double batch!

—Mary Gaylord, Balsam Lake, WI

- -

Takes: 25 min. • **Makes:** 6 servings

- 1 medium onion, chopped
- ¾ cup sliced celery
- ¼ cup diced green pepper
- ¼ cup butter, cubed
- ¼ cup all-purpose flour
- 1 tsp. sugar
- 1½ cups chicken broth
- ¼ cup half-and-half cream
- 3 cups cubed cooked turkey or chicken
- 1 can (4 oz.) sliced mushrooms, drained
- 6 slices bread, toasted

1. In a large skillet, saute the onion, celery and green pepper in butter until tender. Stir in flour and sugar until a paste forms.
2. Gradually stir in broth. Bring to a boil; boil until thickened, about 1 minute. Reduce heat. Add cream, turkey and mushrooms; heat through. Serve with toast.
1 serving: 297 cal., 13g fat (7g sat. fat), 98mg chol., 591mg sod., 21g carb. (4g sugars, 2g fiber), 24g pro.

TEST KITCHEN TIP

Don't have half-and-half? For cooked or baked dishes, swap in 4½ teaspoons melted butter plus enough whole milk to equal 1 cup half-and-half cream. One cup of evaporated milk may also be substituted for each cup of half-and-half.

DAD'S COLA BURGERS

Before you hand out the drinks, save a little soda to make these delectable burgers. Cola really sparks the flavor. Used in the meat mixture and brushed on during grilling, it takes burgers to a new level.

—Emily Nelson, Green Bay, WI

- -

Takes: 25 min. • **Makes:** 6 servings

- ½ cup crushed Saltines (about 15 crackers)
- ½ cup (nondiet) cola, divided
- 6 Tbsp. French salad dressing, divided
- 1 large egg
- 2 Tbsp. grated Parmesan cheese
- ½ tsp. salt, divided
- 1½ lbs. lean ground beef (90% lean)
- 6 hamburger buns, split

Optional toppings: Lettuce leaves and tomato and red onion slices

1. Combine the Saltine crumbs, ¼ cup cola, 3 Tbsp. salad dressing, egg, Parmesan cheese and ¼ tsp. salt. Add beef; mix well. Shape into six ¾-in.-thick patties (the mixture will be moist); sprinkle with the remaining salt. Combine the remaining cola and salad dressing.
2. Grill patties, covered, over medium heat 3 minutes per side. Brush with cola mixture. Grill, brushing and turning occasionally, until a thermometer reads 160°, 3-4 minutes longer. Serve on buns; if desired, top with lettuce, tomato and onion.
1 burger: 419 cal., 20g fat (6g sat. fat), 103mg chol., 698mg sod., 30g carb. (7g sugars, 1g fiber), 28g pro.

CHICKEN PASTA CAESAR SALAD

My colleagues and I made a pact to eat healthier, and we took turns sharing dishes. I'm happy to report that this crisp and tangy salad was a hit.

—Teresa Jordan, Springville, UT

- -

Takes: 30 min. • **Makes:** 6 servings

- 3 **cups uncooked whole wheat spiral pasta (about 8 oz.)**
- 6 **cups torn romaine**
- 3 **cups coarsely shredded rotisserie chicken**
- 2 **medium tomatoes, chopped**
- ½ **cup shredded Parmesan cheese**
- ½ **cup creamy Caesar salad dressing**
- ⅓ **cup slivered almonds, toasted**

Cook pasta according to the package directions. Drain; rinse with cold water and drain again. Toss with remaining ingredients; serve immediately.

Note: To toast nuts, bake in a shallow pan in a 350° oven for 5-10 minutes or cook in a skillet over low heat until lightly browned, stirring occasionally.

2 cups: 422 cal., 22g fat (5g sat. fat), 75mg chol., 416mg sod., 26g carb. (3g sugars, 5g fiber), 30g pro.

STEAK & MUSHROOM STROGANOFF

This homey recipe of steak and egg noodles in a creamy sauce is just like what we had at my gran's house when we'd visit. It's one of my favorite "memory meals," as I call them.
—Janelle Shank, Omaha, NE

Takes: 30 minutes • **Makes:** 6 servings

- 6 cups uncooked egg noodles (about 12 oz.)
- 1 beef top sirloin steak (1½ lbs.), cut into 2x½-in. strips
- 1 Tbsp. canola oil
- ½ tsp. salt
- ½ tsp. pepper
- 2 Tbsp. butter
- 1 lb. sliced fresh mushrooms
- 2 shallots, finely chopped
- ½ cup beef broth
- 1 Tbsp. snipped fresh dill
- 1 cup sour cream

1. Cook noodles according to package directions; drain.
2. Meanwhile, toss beef with oil, salt and pepper. Place a large skillet over medium-high heat; saute half of the beef until browned, 2-3 minutes. Remove from pan; repeat with remaining beef.
3. In same pan, heat butter over medium-high heat; saute mushrooms until lightly browned, 4-6 minutes. Add shallots; cook and stir until tender, 1-2 minutes. Stir in broth, dill and beef; heat through. Reduce heat to medium; stir in sour cream until blended. Serve with noodles.
1 serving: 455 cal., 19g fat (10g sat. fat), 115mg chol., 379mg sod., 34g carb. (4g sugars, 2g fiber), 34g pro.

SPINACH & GOUDA-STUFFED PORK CUTLETS

This started as a restaurant copycat dish at home. Cheese just oozes out of the center, and mustard lends a lot of flavor.
—Joan Oakland, Troy, MT

Takes: 30 min. • **Makes:** 2 servings

- 3 Tbsp. dry bread crumbs
- 2 Tbsp. grated Parmesan cheese
- 2 pork sirloin cutlets (3 oz. each)
- ¼ tsp. salt
- ⅛ tsp. pepper
- 2 slices smoked Gouda cheese (about 2 oz.)
- 2 cups fresh baby spinach
- 2 Tbsp. horseradish mustard

1. Preheat oven to 400°. In a shallow bowl, mix bread crumbs and Parmesan cheese.
2. Sprinkle tops of cutlets with salt and pepper. Layer one end of each with Gouda cheese and spinach. Fold cutlets in half, enclosing filling; secure with toothpicks. Brush mustard over outsides of pork; dip in bread crumb mixture, patting to help coating adhere.
3. Place on a greased foil-lined baking sheet. Bake until golden brown and pork is tender, 12-15 minutes. Discard the toothpicks before serving.
1 stuffed cutlet: 299 cal., 16g fat (7g sat. fat), 91mg chol., 898mg sod., 10g carb. (2g sugars, 2g fiber), 30g pro.

RAMONA'S CHILAQUILES

A dear neighbor shared this recipe, which she used to make from scratch. My version takes a few shortcuts.
—Marina Castle Kelley,
Canyon Country, CA

- -

Takes: 30 min. • **Makes:** 4 servings

- ½ lb. lean ground beef (90% lean)
- ½ lb. fresh chorizo or bulk spicy pork sausage
- 1 medium onion, finely chopped
- 1 garlic clove, minced
- 1 can (14½ oz.) diced tomatoes with mild green chiles, undrained
- 1 can (10 oz.) diced tomatoes and green chiles, undrained
- 4 cups tortilla chips (about 6 oz.)
- 1 cup shredded Monterey Jack cheese
   Chopped fresh cilantro
   Optional toppings: Sour cream, diced avocado and sliced red onion

1. Preheat oven to 350°. In a large skillet, cook and crumble beef and chorizo with onion and garlic over medium heat until beef is no longer pink, 5-7 minutes; drain. Stir in both tomatoes; bring to a boil. In a greased 1½-qt. or 8-in. square baking dish, layer 2 cups chips, half of the meat mixture and ½ cup cheese; repeat layers.
2. Bake, uncovered, until cheese is melted, 12-15 minutes. Sprinkle with cilantro. Serve with desired toppings.
1 serving: 573 cal., 35g fat (14g sat. fat), 110mg chol., 1509mg sod., 28g carb. (5g sugars, 4g fiber), 33g pro.

CHICKEN CORDON BLEU STROMBOLI

If chicken cordon bleu and stromboli had a baby, this would be it. Serve with jarred Alfredo sauce, homemade Alfredo sauce or classic Mornay sauce on the side if desired.
—Cyndi Gerken, Naples, FL

- -

Takes: 30 min. • **Makes:** 6 servings

- 1 tube (13.8 oz.) refrigerated pizza crust
- 4 pieces thinly sliced deli ham
- 1½ cups shredded cooked chicken
- 6 slices Swiss cheese
- 1 Tbsp. butter, melted
   Roasted garlic Alfredo sauce, optional

1. Preheat oven to 400°. Unroll pizza dough onto a baking sheet. Layer with the ham, chicken and cheese to within ½ in. of edges.

Roll up jelly-roll style, starting with a long side; pinch seam to seal and tuck ends under. Brush with melted butter.
2. Bake until crust is dark golden brown, 18-22 minutes. Let stand 5 minutes before slicing. If desired, serve with Alfredo sauce for dipping.
1 slice: 298 cal., 10g fat (4g sat. fat), 53mg chol., 580mg sod., 32g carb. (4g sugars, 1g fiber), 21g pro.

TEST KITCHEN TIP
Don't let this stand too long before slicing and eating, or the bottom of the stromboli will get too soggy.

30 MINUTE SWEETS

CRUNCHY CHOCOLATE CLUSTERS

This easy-to-make candy with cinnamon, chocolate and coffee has a south-of-the-border flavor. Sweet, salty and crunchy, it's a tasty no-bake treat.
—Roxanne Chan, Albany, CA

- -

Takes: 25 min. • **Makes:** ¾ lb. (12 pieces)

- ¾ cup coarsely crushed pretzels
- ¼ cup raisins
- 2 Tbsp. pine nuts, toasted
- 1⅓ cups semisweet chocolate chips
- ½ tsp. instant coffee granules
- ¼ tsp. ground cinnamon
- ¼ cup sour cream
- Coarse sea salt

1. Place pretzels, raisins and pine nuts in a bowl. In a microwave, melt chocolate chips; stir until smooth. Stir in coffee granules, cinnamon and sour cream. To rewarm, microwave in additional 5- to 10-second intervals. Add to the pretzel mixture; toss until combined.

2. Drop mixture by heaping tablespoonfuls onto a waxed paper-lined baking sheet. Sprinkle with salt.

3. Refrigerate until set, about 10 minutes. Store clusters in an airtight container in the refrigerator.

1 piece: 139 cal., 8g fat (4g sat. fat), 1mg chol., 86mg sod., 19g carb. (12g sugars, 1g fiber), 2g pro.

TEST KITCHEN TIP
To melt semisweet chocolate in the microwave, cook on high for 1 minute; stir. Microwave at additional 10- to 20-second intervals, stirring until smooth.

CRISPY NORWEGIAN BOWS

I've been making these cookies for so long, I don't recall where the recipe came from. They're a must at our house.
—Janie Norwood, Albany, GA

- -

Takes: 30 min. • **Makes:** about 4 dozen

- 3 large egg yolks, room temperature
- 3 Tbsp. sugar
- 3 Tbsp. heavy whipping cream
- ½ tsp. ground cardamom
- 1 to 1¼ cups all-purpose flour
- Oil for deep-fat frying
- Confectioners' sugar

1. Beat egg yolks and granulated sugar until pale yellow. Add cream and cardamom; mix well. Gradually add flour until the dough is firm enough to roll.

2. On a lightly floured surface, roll into a 15-in. square. Using a pastry wheel or knife, cut into 15x1½-in. strips; then cut diagonally at 2½-in. intervals to make diamond shapes. In the center of each diamond, make a 1-in. slit; pull one end through slit.

3. In an electric skillet or deep-fat fryer, heat oil to 375°. Fry the bows, a few at a time, until golden brown on both sides, 20-40 seconds. Drain on paper towels. Dust with confectioners' sugar.

1 cookie: 24 cal., 1g fat (0 sat. fat), 13mg chol., 1mg sod., 3g carb. (1g sugars, 0 fiber), 0 pro.

POT OF S'MORES

Mom's easy Dutch-oven version of the popular campout treat is so good and gooey. The hardest part is waiting for this to cool so you can devour it. Yum!
—June Dress, Meridian, ID

- -

Takes: 25 min. • **Makes:** 12 servings

1	pkg. (14½ oz.) whole graham crackers, crushed
½	cup butter, melted
1	can (14 oz.) sweetened condensed milk
2	cups semisweet chocolate chips
1	cup butterscotch chips
2	cups miniature marshmallows

1. Prepare grill or campfire for low heat, using 16-18 charcoal briquettes or large wood chips.

2. Line a Dutch oven with heavy-duty aluminum foil. Combine cracker crumbs and butter; press onto the bottom of the pot. Pour milk over the crust and sprinkle with chocolate and butterscotch chips. Top with marshmallows.

3. Cover the Dutch oven. When briquettes or wood chips are covered with white ash, place pot directly on top of six of them. Using long-handled tongs, place the remaining briquettes on pan cover.

4. Cook until marshmallows begin to melt, about 15 minutes. To check for doneness, use the tongs to carefully lift the cover.

1 serving: 584 cal., 28g fat (17g sat. fat), 31mg chol., 326mg sod., 83g carb. (47g sugars, 3g fiber), 8g pro.

HOLIDAY RUM BALLS

I use this recipe for special occasions with my wonderful family and friends. The sweet cookies are so easy to make and pack a festive rum punch.
—Diane Duschanek, Council Bluffs, IA

- -

Takes: 30 min. • **Makes:** About 2½ dozen

2	cups confectioners' sugar
¼	cup baking cocoa
1	pkg. (12 oz.) vanilla wafers, finely crushed
1	cup finely chopped walnuts
½	cup light corn syrup
¼	cup rum
	Additional confectioners' sugar

1. In a large bowl, mix confectioners' sugar and cocoa until blended. Add the crushed wafers and walnuts; toss to combine. In another bowl, mix corn syrup and rum; stir into the wafer mixture.

2. Shape into 1-in. balls. Roll in additional confectioners' sugar. Store rum balls in an airtight container.

1 ball: 125 cal., 4g fat (1g sat. fat), 2mg chol., 43mg sod., 21g carb. (16g sugars, 0 fiber), 1g pro.

CARAMELIZED PINEAPPLE SUNDAES

Whenever we get a craving for a tropical escape, this super simple recipe whisks us away to the islands in no time. Drizzling the sauce over salted caramel ice cream and taking a bite is just pure paradise.
—Elisabeth Larsen, Pleasant Grove, UT

- -

Takes: 30 min. • **Makes:** 6 servings

- ¼ cup butter, cubed
- ½ cup packed brown sugar
- 1 fresh pineapple, peeled and cut into ½-in. cubes
- 3 cups vanilla ice cream
- ½ cup flaked coconut, toasted
- ½ cup coarsely chopped macadamia nuts, toasted

1. In a large skillet, heat butter over medium heat; stir in brown sugar. Add the pineapple; cook and stir until tender, 8-10 minutes. Remove the pineapple with a slotted spoon; set aside.
2. Bring the remaining juices to a simmer; cook until thickened, 3-4 minutes. Remove from heat. Layer the pineapple and ice cream into six dessert dishes; sprinkle with toasted coconut and nuts. Drizzle with the reduced sauce.
Note: To toast coconut and nuts, bake separately in a shallow pan in a 350° oven for 5-10 minutes or cook in a skillet over low heat until golden brown, stirring occasionally.
1 sundae: 469 cal., 26g fat (13g sat. fat), 49mg chol., 180mg sod., 59g carb. (51g sugars, 4g fiber), 4g pro.

BLACK & BLUE BERRY GRUNT

If you're looking for something different from the usual cakes and fruit pies, try this old-fashioned dessert. It features a delicious combination of blackberries and blueberries topped with yummy homemade dumplings.
—Kelly Akin, Johnsonville, NY

- -

Takes: 30 min. • **Makes:** 8 servings

- 2½ cups fresh or frozen blackberries, thawed
- 2½ cups fresh or frozen blueberries, thawed
- ¾ cup sugar
- ¼ cup water
- 1 Tbsp. lemon juice
- ⅛ tsp. ground cinnamon
- ⅛ tsp. pepper

DUMPLINGS
- 1 cup all-purpose flour
- 2 Tbsp. sugar
- 1 tsp. baking powder
- ½ tsp. baking soda
- ⅛ tsp. salt
- 2 Tbsp. butter, melted
- ½ cup buttermilk
- 1 Tbsp. cinnamon-sugar
  Sweetened whipped cream, optional

1. In a large skillet, combine the first seven ingredients. Bring to a boil. Reduce heat; simmer, uncovered, for 5 minutes.
2. Meanwhile, in a large bowl, combine the first five dumpling ingredients. Add the melted butter and buttermilk; stir just until moistened. Drop by tablespoonfuls onto the berry mixture. Sprinkle with cinnamon-sugar.
3. Cover tightly; simmer until a toothpick inserted in a dumpling comes out clean, 10-15 minutes. Serve warm; if desired, top with sweetened whipped cream.
1 serving: 226 cal., 4g fat (2g sat. fat), 8mg chol., 229mg sod., 47g carb. (31g sugars, 4g fiber), 3g pro.

HAZELNUT DREAM COOKIES

I sampled these goodies at a Bible study and knew from the first bite that I had to have the recipe. To my surprise, the rich cookies require just four ingredients.
—Julie Peterson, Crofton, MD

Takes: 25 min. • **Makes:** 2 dozen

- 1 cup Nutella
- ⅔ cup all-purpose flour
- 1 large egg, room temperature
- ½ cup chopped hazelnuts

1. Preheat oven to 350°. In a large bowl, beat Nutella, flour and egg until blended. Stir in hazelnuts.

2. Drop by tablespoonfuls 2 in. apart onto ungreased baking sheets. Bake until set, 8-10 minutes. Remove from pans to wire racks to cool.

1 cookie: 92 cal., 5g fat (1g sat. fat), 8mg chol., 8mg sod., 11g carb. (7g sugars, 1g fiber), 2g pro.

BUTTERMILK BLUEBERRY SCOOKIES

The scookie idea came to me when I made cookie shapes out of scone dough. Light and crispy right from the oven, they're just sweet enough.
—Ally Phillips, Murrells Inlet, SC

Takes: 25 min. • **Makes:** 1 dozen

- 2 cups all-purpose flour
- ½ cup plus 1 Tbsp. sugar, divided
- 2 tsp. baking powder
- 1 tsp. baking soda
- ½ cup cold butter, cubed
- ½ cup buttermilk
- 1 large egg, room temperature, lightly beaten
- 1 cup fresh or frozen blueberries, thawed

1. Preheat oven to 375°. In a large bowl, whisk flour, ½ cup sugar, baking powder and baking soda. Cut in butter until the mixture resembles coarse crumbs. In another bowl, whisk buttermilk and egg until blended; stir into the crumb mixture just until moistened.

2. Drop dough by scant ¼ cupfuls 2 in. apart onto a parchment-lined baking sheet. Form a ½-in.-deep indentation in center of each with the back of a spoon coated with cooking spray. Gently press blueberries into the indentations; sprinkle with the remaining sugar.

3. Bake until golden brown, 11-14 minutes. Serve warm.

1 scookie: 197 cal., 8g fat (5g sat. fat), 36mg chol., 258mg sod., 28g carb. (11g sugars, 1g fiber), 3g pro.

CHOCOLATE CHIP DUTCH BABY

I modified a traditional Dutch baby recipe given to me by a friend to come up with this version my family thinks is terrific. You'll be surprised at how easy it is to make.
—Mary Thompson, La Crosse, WI

- -

Takes: 30 min. • **Makes:** 4 servings

¼ cup miniature semisweet chocolate chips
¼ cup packed brown sugar
DUTCH BABY
½ cup all-purpose flour
2 large eggs, room temperature
½ cup half-and-half cream
⅛ tsp. ground nutmeg
Dash ground cinnamon
3 Tbsp. butter
Maple syrup and additional butter, optional

1. In a small bowl, combine chocolate chips and brown sugar; set aside. In a small bowl, beat the flour, eggs, cream, nutmeg and cinnamon until smooth.
2. Place butter in a 9-in. pie plate or an 8-in. cast-iron skillet. Heat in a 425° oven until melted, about 4 minutes. Pour batter into hot pie plate or skillet. Sprinkle with the chocolate chip mixture. Bake until the top edges are golden brown, 13-15 minutes. Serve immediately, with syrup and butter if desired.

1 serving: 313 cal., 17g fat (10g sat. fat), 144mg chol., 140mg sod., 33g carb. (21g sugars, 1g fiber), 6g pro.

SIMPLE TURTLE CHEESECAKE

For an almost instant dessert, I spread homemade ganache and caramel sauce over pre-made cheesecake. It's a crowd-pleasing sweet that makes the holidays feel slightly less hectic.
—Laura McDowell, Lake Villa, IL

Takes: 25 min. • **Makes:** 8 servings

- 1 frozen New York-style cheesecake (30 oz.), thawed
- ½ cup semisweet chocolate chips
- ½ cup heavy whipping cream, divided
- 3 Tbsp. chopped pecans, toasted
- ¼ cup butter, cubed
- ½ cup plus 2 Tbsp. packed brown sugar
- 1 Tbsp. light corn syrup

1. Place cheesecake on a serving plate. Place chocolate chips in a small bowl. In a small saucepan, bring ¼ cup cream just to a boil. Pour over chocolate; stir with a whisk until smooth. Cool slightly, stirring occasionally. Pour over the cheesecake; sprinkle with pecans. Refrigerate until set.
2. In a small saucepan, melt butter; stir in brown sugar and corn syrup. Bring to a boil. Reduce heat; cook and stir until the sugar is dissolved. Stir in the remaining cream and return to a boil. Remove from heat. Serve warm with cheesecake or, if desired, cool completely and drizzle over the cheesecake.
Note: To toast nuts, bake in a shallow pan in a 350° oven for 5-10 minutes or cook in a skillet over low heat until lightly browned, stirring occasionally.
1 slice: 585 cal., 40g fat (20g sat. fat), 94mg chol., 276mg sod., 53g carb. (23g sugars, 1g fiber), 7g pro.

5 INGREDIENT

CAMPFIRE CINNAMON TWISTS

Cinnamon rolls get the toasty treatment when wrapped around skewers and warmed over a fire. Brush with butter, then sprinkle with sugar and spice.
—Lauren Knoelke, Des Moines, IA

Takes: 25 min. • **Makes:** 16 servings

- ¼ cup sugar
- 2 tsp. ground cinnamon
- 1 tube (12.4 oz.) refrigerated cinnamon rolls with icing
- 2 Tbsp. butter, melted

1. Mix sugar and cinnamon. Remove icing from the cinnamon rolls; transfer to a resealable plastic bag for drizzling.
2. Separate rolls; cut each in half. Roll each half into a 6-in. rope. Wrap each rope tightly around a long metal skewer, beginning ½ in. from pointed end; pinch each end to secure.
3. Cook rolls over a hot campfire until golden brown, about 5 minutes, turning occasionally. Brush with butter; sprinkle with sugar mixture. Cut a small hole in one corner of icing bag. Drizzle icing over twists.
1 twist: 98 cal., 4g fat (2g sat. fat), 4mg chol., 183mg sod., 15g carb. (8g sugars, 0 fiber), 1g pro.

CHOCOLATE BANANA BUNDLES

Banana and chocolate is such an irresistible combination! I make this dessert often—sometimes I sprinkle on a dash of sea salt. You can also top the bundles with any leftover butter and brown sugar mixture.
—Thomas Faglon, Somerset, NJ

- -

Takes: 30 min. • **Makes:** 4 servings

- 2   **Tbsp. butter**
- ¼   **cup packed brown sugar**
- 2   **medium ripe bananas, halved lengthwise**
- 1   **sheet frozen puff pastry, thawed**
- 4   **oz. semisweet chocolate, melted**
      Vanilla ice cream, optional

1. Preheat oven to 400°. In a large cast-iron or other heavy skillet, melt the butter over medium heat. Stir in the brown sugar until blended. Add bananas; stir to coat. Remove from heat; set aside.
2. Unfold the puff pastry. Cut into four rectangles. Place a halved banana in the center of each square. Overlap the two opposite corners of the pastry over the banana; pinch tightly to seal. Place on parchment-lined baking sheets.
3. Bake until golden brown, 20-25 minutes. Drizzle with chocolate. If desired, serve warm with ice cream.
1 bundle: 596 cal., 31g fat (12g sat. fat), 15mg chol., 249mg sod., 78g carb. (35g sugars, 8g fiber), 7g pro.
Caramel Banana Bundles: Omit chocolate. Drizzle with caramel ice cream topping.

HONEYDEW LIME COOLER

Serve up a frosty glass of this citrusy blend of lime sherbet and honeydew melon for a real thirst-quencher.
—Mitzi Sentiff, Annapolis, MD

- -

Takes: 30 min. • **Makes:** 5 servings

- 4½ **cups cubed honeydew (about 1 small melon)**
- 1½ **cups lime sherbet**
- 2   **Tbsp. lime juice**
- 5   **fresh strawberries**

1. Place melon cubes in a 15x10x1-in. baking pan; cover and freeze until firm, about 15 minutes. Set aside five melon cubes.
2. In a food processor, combine sherbet, lime juice and the remaining frozen melon; cover and process until smooth. Pour into glasses; garnish with strawberries and the reserved melon cubes.
¾ cup: 135 cal., 1g fat (0 sat. fat), 3mg chol., 34mg sod., 32g carb. (28g sugars, 1g fiber), 1g pro. **Diabetic exchanges:** 1 starch, 1 fruit.

DATE-WALNUT PINWHEELS

Every time someone drops in for coffee, I bake up a batch of these fruit and nut cookies—I always keep the ingredients in my pantry. The recipe's a cinch to double, too, so it's good for parties and potlucks.
—Lori McLain, Denton, TX

Takes: 25 min. • **Makes:** 1 dozen

- 3 Tbsp. sugar
- ½ tsp. ground cinnamon
- 1 sheet refrigerated pie crust
- 1 Tbsp. apricot preserves
- ⅔ cup finely chopped pitted dates
- ½ cup finely chopped walnuts

1. Preheat oven to 350°. Mix sugar and cinnamon. On a lightly floured surface, unroll crust; roll crust into a 12-in. square. Spread preserves over top; sprinkle with dates, walnuts and cinnamon-sugar.
2. Roll up jelly-roll style; pinch seam to seal. Cut crosswise into 12 slices, about 1 in. thick. Place 1 in. apart on an ungreased baking sheet. Bake until golden brown, 12-14 minutes. Remove from pan to a wire rack to cool.
1 pastry: 155 cal., 8g fat (2g sat. fat), 3mg chol., 68mg sod., 21g carb. (11g sugars, 1g fiber), 2g pro.

5 INGREDIENT
GRILLED HONEY BALSAMIC-GLAZED FRUIT

One summer my mother-in-law made us grilled peaches basted with a sweet and tangy sauce. These are so good I'm always tempted to eat the whole batch.
—Kristin Van Dyken, Kennewick, WA

Takes: 25 min.
Makes: 6 servings (½ cup glaze)

- ½ cup balsamic vinegar
- ½ cup honey
  Dash salt
- 6 medium peaches or nectarines, halved and pitted
  Vanilla ice cream, optional

1. In a small saucepan, combine vinegar, honey and salt; cook and stir over low heat until blended, 2-3 minutes. Reserve ⅓ cup of the mixture for brushing peaches.
2. Bring the remaining mixture to a boil over medium heat; cook and stir just until the mixture begins to thicken slightly (do not overcook), 4-6 minutes. Remove pan from the heat.
3. Brush peaches with some of the reserved balsamic mixture. Grill, covered, on an oiled rack over medium heat until caramelized, brushing occasionally with the remaining reserved balsamic mixture, 6-8 minutes on each side. Serve with glaze and, if desired, ice cream.
1 serving: 164 cal., 0 fat (0 sat. fat), 0 chol., 26mg sod., 43g carb. (40g sugars, 2g fiber), 1g pro.

MACAROON-TOPPED RHUBARB COBBLER

Crumbled macaroons are a surprising addition to this cobbler's topping. We love that you can make the sweet treat in a baking dish or a cast-iron skillet.
—*Taste of Home* Test Kitchen

- -

Takes: 30 min. • **Makes:** 4 servings

    4   cups sliced fresh or frozen
        rhubarb (1-in. pieces)
    1   large apple, peeled and sliced
    ½   cup packed brown sugar
    ½   tsp. ground cinnamon, divided
    1   Tbsp. cornstarch
    2   Tbsp. cold water
    8   macaroons, crumbled
    1   Tbsp. butter, melted
    2   Tbsp. sugar
        Vanilla ice cream, optional

1. In a large cast-iron or other ovenproof skillet, combine the rhubarb, apple, brown sugar and ¼ tsp. cinnamon; bring to a boil. Reduce heat; cover and simmer until the rhubarb is very tender, 10-13 minutes. Combine the cornstarch and water until smooth; gradually add to the fruit mixture. Bring to a boil; cook and stir until thickened, about 2 minutes.

2. In a small bowl, combine the crumbled cookies, butter, sugar and remaining cinnamon. Sprinkle over fruit mixture.

3. Broil 4 in. from the heat until lightly browned, 3-5 minutes. If desired, serve warm with ice cream.

Note: If using frozen rhubarb, measure rhubarb while still frozen, then thaw completely. Drain in a colander, but do not press liquid out.

1 serving: 368 cal., 12g fat (7g sat. fat), 8mg chol., 45mg sod., 62g carb. (55g sugars, 5g fiber), 3g pro.

GRILLED BANANAS FOSTER

Bananas Foster is my husband's favorite dessert, and this recipe is one of the easiest I have found. Not only is it delicious, it's a wonderful way to use bananas that are just a little too ripe to just peel and eat.
—Rebecca Clark, Warrior, AL

- -

Takes: 25 min. • **Makes:** 4 servings

- 4 small ripe bananas, unpeeled
  Disposable foil pie pan (9 in.), optional
- 3 Tbsp. butter
- 2 Tbsp. maple syrup
- 2 Tbsp. hot caramel ice cream topping
- 2 cups vanilla ice cream
- 8 vanilla wafers, crushed

1. Trim ends and cut unpeeled bananas in half lengthwise; place on oiled grill rack over medium heat. Grill, covered, until the peel is dark brown and the bananas are softened, 3-4 minutes on each side. Cool slightly.
2. Meanwhile, in a small cast-iron skillet or 9-in. disposable foil pie pan, combine butter, syrup and caramel topping; place on grill rack. Cook, uncovered, over medium heat until heated through, 4-5 minutes, stirring frequently. Remove from heat.
3. Remove peel from bananas; cut each in half crosswise. To serve, place ice cream in dessert dishes; top with bananas. Drizzle with sauce; sprinkle with crushed wafers.
1 serving: 386 cal., 18g fat (10g sat. fat), 53mg chol., 187mg sod., 56g carb. (41g sugars, 3g fiber), 4g pro.

CHOCOLATE MALT CRISPY BARS

This chunky, chewy square is a feast for your eyes. Malted milk flavor coats this bar from top to bottom.
—*Taste of Home* Test Kitchen

- -

Takes: 25 min. • **Makes:** 2 dozen

- 1 pkg. (10 oz.) large marshmallows
- 3 Tbsp. butter
- 5 cups crisp rice cereal
- 1 cup malted milk powder, divided
- 4 cups malted milk balls, chopped, divided
- 2 cups semisweet chocolate chips

1. In a Dutch oven, combine marshmallows and butter. Cook and stir over medium-low heat until melted. Remove from heat; stir in the cereal, ¾ cup of the malt powder and 2½ cups of the malted milk balls. Press into a greased 13x9-in. pan.
2. In a microwave-safe bowl, melt chocolate chips; stir until smooth. Stir in the remaining malt powder. Spread over the cereal bars. Sprinkle with the remaining malted milk balls; press into chocolate. Let stand until set. Using a serrated knife, cut into squares.
1 bar: 256 cal., 10g fat (6g sat. fat), 7mg chol., 118mg sod., 42g carb. (29g sugars, 1g fiber), 3g pro.

UPSIDE-DOWN PEAR PANCAKE

There's a pear tree in my yard that inspires me to bake with its fragrant fruit. My upside-down pancake works best with a pear that's firm and not yet fully ripe.
—Helen Nelander, Boulder Creek, CA

- -

Takes: 30 min. • **Makes:** 2 servings

½   cup all-purpose flour
½   tsp. baking powder
1   large egg, room temperature
¼   cup 2% milk
1   Tbsp. butter
1   tsp. sugar
1   medium pear, peeled and thinly sliced lengthwise
    Confectioners' sugar

1. Preheat oven to 375°. Whisk flour and baking powder. In a separate bowl, whisk egg and milk until blended. Add to the dry ingredients, stirring just until combined.
2. Meanwhile, in a small ovenproof skillet, melt butter over medium-low heat. Sprinkle with sugar. Add pear slices in a single layer; cook 5 minutes. Spread the prepared batter over the pears. Cover and cook until top is set, about 5 minutes.
3. Transfer pan to oven; bake until the edges are lightly brown, 8-10 minutes. Invert onto a serving plate. Sprinkle with confectioners' sugar. Serve warm.
½ pancake: 274 cal., 9g fat (5g sat. fat), 111mg chol., 197mg sod., 41g carb. (12g sugars, 4g fiber), 8g pro. **Diabetic exchanges:** 2 starch, 1½ fat, 1 medium-fat meat, ½ fruit.

PUMPKIN ICE CREAM

This recipe really captures the flavor of fall. It's good with or without the gingersnaps.
—Linda Young, Longmont, CO

- -

Takes: 30 min. • **Makes:** 5 servings

1   cup canned pumpkin
¼   tsp. pumpkin pie spice
1   qt. vanilla ice cream, softened
    Gingersnaps, optional

In a large bowl, combine the pumpkin and pumpkin pie spice until well blended. Stir in ice cream. Freeze until serving. Garnish with gingersnaps if desired.
1 cup: 190 cal., 10g fat (6g sat. fat), 39mg chol., 72mg sod., 24g carb. (17g sugars, 2g fiber), 4g pro.

45
MINUTES

45 MINUTE SNACKS

BAKED ONION DIP

Some people like this cheesy dip so much that they can't tear themselves away from the appetizer table to eat dinner!
—Mona Zignego, Hartford, WI

Prep: 5 min. • **Bake:** 40 min.
Makes: 16 servings (2 cups)

- 1 cup mayonnaise
- 1 cup chopped sweet onion
- 1 Tbsp. grated Parmesan cheese
- ¼ tsp. garlic salt
- 1 cup shredded Swiss cheese
   Minced fresh parsley, optional
   Assorted crackers

1. In a bowl, combine mayonnaise, onion, Parmesan cheese and garlic salt; stir in Swiss cheese. Spoon into a 1-qt. baking dish.
2. Bake, uncovered, at 325° until golden brown, about 40 minutes. If desired, sprinkle with parsley. Serve with crackers.
2 Tbsp.: 131 cal., 13g fat (3g sat. fat), 11mg chol., 127mg sod., 1g carb. (1g sugars, 0 fiber), 2g pro.

TEST KITCHEN TIP

While you are chopping the sweet onion, why not cut extra for future dishes? Chop onions and place in a 15x10x1-in. pan in the freezer. When they're frozen, place in freezer bags or containers and freeze for up to 1 year. Frozen chopped onions are best used in recipes such as soups, sauces and casseroles.

5 INGREDIENT
BACON-WRAPPED APRICOT BITES

These sweet and slightly smoky snacks are easy to eat, so be prepared with an extra batch. For a change, sprinkle them with a bit of blue cheese or toasted almonds.
—Tammie Floyd, Plano, TX

Prep: 20 min. • **Bake:** 20 min.
Makes: about 2 dozen (⅔ cup sauce)

- 8 maple-flavored bacon strips
- 1 pkg. (6 oz.) dried apricots
- ½ cup honey barbecue sauce
- 1 Tbsp. honey
- 1½ tsp. prepared mustard

1. Cut bacon strips widthwise into thirds. In a large skillet, cook bacon over medium heat until partially cooked but not crisp. Remove to paper towels to drain.
2. Wrap a bacon piece around each apricot; secure with a toothpick. Place in an ungreased 15x10x1-in. baking pan.
3. Bake at 350° until the bacon is crisp, 18-22 minutes. Meanwhile, in a small bowl, combine the barbecue sauce, honey and mustard. Serve with warm apricot bites.
1 serving: 47 cal., 1g fat (0 sat. fat), 3mg chol., 105mg sod., 8g carb. (6g sugars, 1g fiber), 1g pro.

HOT SAUSAGE & BEAN DIP

This is a spin-off of a Mexican dip I once had. The original was wicked good, but I began going through an "I'm-so-over-Mexican-dip" phase and decided to switch it up. Take this version to a party—I'll bet you no one else will bring anything like it!
—Mandy Rivers, Lexington, SC

- -

Prep: 25 min. • **Bake:** 20 min.
Makes: 16 servings

- 1 lb. bulk hot Italian sausage
- 1 medium onion, finely chopped
- 4 garlic cloves, minced
- ½ cup dry white wine or chicken broth
- ½ tsp. dried oregano
- ¼ tsp. salt
- ¼ tsp. dried thyme
- 1 pkg. (8 oz.) cream cheese, softened
- 1 pkg. (6 oz.) fresh baby spinach, coarsely chopped
- 1 can (15 oz.) cannellini beans, rinsed and drained
- 1 cup chopped seeded tomatoes
- 1 cup shredded part-skim mozzarella cheese
- ½ cup shredded Parmesan cheese Assorted crackers or toasted French bread baguette slices

1. Preheat oven to 375°. In a skillet, cook the sausage, onion and garlic over medium heat until sausage is no longer pink, breaking up sausage into crumbles; drain. Stir in wine, oregano, salt and thyme. Bring to a boil; cook until liquid is almost evaporated.
2. Add cream cheese; stir until melted. Stir in spinach, beans and tomatoes; cook and stir until spinach is wilted. Transfer to a greased 8-in. square baking dish; if using an ovenproof skillet, leave in skillet. Sprinkle with cheeses.
3. Bake until bubbly, 20-25 minutes. Serve with crackers.
¼ cup: 200 cal., 14g fat (7g sat. fat), 41mg chol., 434mg sod., 7g carb. (2g sugars, 2g fiber), 10g pro.

ALMOND-BACON CHEESE CROSTINI

For a change from the usual toasted tomato appetizer, try these baked bites. If you'd like, slice the baguette at an angle instead of making a straight cut.
—Leondre Hermann, Stuart, FL

- -

Prep: 30 min. • **Bake:** 15 min.
Makes: 3 dozen

- 1 French bread baguette (1 lb.), cut into 36 slices
- 2 cups shredded Monterey Jack cheese
- ⅔ cup mayonnaise
- ½ cup sliced almonds, toasted
- 6 bacon strips, cooked and crumbled
- 1 green onion, chopped Dash salt Additional toasted almonds, optional

1. Place bread slices on an ungreased baking sheet. Bake at 400° until lightly browned, 8-9 minutes.
2. Meanwhile, in a large bowl, combine the cheese, mayonnaise, almonds, bacon, onion and salt. Spread over bread. Bake until cheese is melted, 7-8 minutes. Sprinkle with additional almonds if desired. Serve warm.
1 piece: 120 cal., 8g fat (2g sat. fat), 8mg chol., 160mg sod., 10g carb. (0 sugars, 1g fiber), 3g pro.

SPEEDY SURPRISE
"Such a tasty, easy appetizer. I change the cheese variety and they are still gobbled up! I cut back on the mayo to make the cheese flavor come out more."
—RENA 55,
TASTEOFHOME.COM

CHEESY PIZZA ROLLS

The cast-iron skillet browns these delicious rolls to perfection. My family can't get enough. Use whatever pizza toppings your gang likes best.
—Dorothy Smith, El Dorado, AR

- -

Prep: 15 min. • **Bake:** 25 min.
Makes: 8 appetizers

 1   loaf (1 lb.) frozen pizza
     dough, thawed
 ½   cup pasta sauce
 1   cup shredded part-skim
     mozzarella cheese, divided
 1   cup coarsely chopped
     pepperoni (about 64 slices)
 ½   lb. bulk Italian sausage,
     cooked and crumbled
 ¼   cup grated Parmesan cheese
     Minced fresh basil, optional
     Crushed red pepper flakes,
     optional

1. Preheat oven to 400°. On a lightly floured surface, roll the dough into a 16x10-in. rectangle. Brush with pasta sauce to within ½ in. of edges.
2. Sprinkle with ½ cup mozzarella cheese, pepperoni, sausage and Parmesan. Gently roll up jelly-roll style, starting with a long side; pinch seam to seal. Cut into eight slices. Place in a greased 9-in. cast-iron skillet or greased 9-in. round baking pan, cut side down.
3. Bake 20 minutes; sprinkle with remaining mozzarella cheese. Bake until golden brown, 5-10 minutes longer. If desired, serve with minced basil and crushed red pepper flakes.
1 pizza roll: 355 cal., 19g fat (7g sat. fat), 42mg chol., 978mg sod., 29g carb. (3g sugars, 1g fiber), 14g pro.

CHEESE LOVER'S FONDUE

French bread cubes and apples are the perfect dippers for this classic fondue, made with white wine and Swiss and Gruyere cheeses. It's a crowd-pleaser.
—Linda Vogel, Elgin, IL

- -

Prep: 15 min. • **Cook:** 20 min.
Makes: 2 cups

 4   tsp. cornstarch, divided
 1   Tbsp. plus 1 cup dry
      white wine, divided
 1½   cups shredded Gruyere cheese
 1½   cups shredded Swiss cheese
 1   garlic clove, peeled and halved
 1½   tsp. lemon juice
 ⅛   tsp. garlic powder
 ⅛   tsp. dried oregano
 ⅛   tsp. Worcestershire sauce
 3   drops hot pepper sauce
      Miniature smoked sausages,
      dill pickles and pretzels

1. In a bowl, combine 2 tsp. cornstarch with 1 Tbsp. wine; set aside. Combine cheeses and remaining cornstarch; set aside.
2. Rub sides of a large saucepan with cut sides of garlic; discard garlic. Add remaining wine to the pan and heat over medium heat until bubbles form around sides of pan. Stir in lemon juice.
3. Reduce heat to medium-low; add a handful of cheese mixture. Stir constantly, using a figure-eight motion, until almost completely melted. Continue adding the cheese, one handful at a time, allowing cheese to almost completely melt between additions. Stir in the garlic powder, oregano, Worcestershire sauce and pepper sauce. Stir cornstarch mixture; gradually add to the pan. Cook and stir until mixture is thickened and smooth. Keep warm. Serve with miniature smoked sausages, dill pickles and pretzels.
¼ cup: 196 cal., 12g fat (8g sat. fat), 42mg chol., 127mg sod., 3g carb. (1g sugars, 0 fiber), 12g pro.

BARBECUED MEATBALLS

Grape jelly and chili sauce are the secrets that make these meatballs so fantastic. If I'm serving them at a party, I make the meatballs and sauce in advance and reheat them right before everyone arrives.
—Irma Schnuelle, Manitowoc, WI

Prep: 20 min. • **Cook:** 15 min.
Makes: about 3 dozen

- ½ cup dry bread crumbs
- ⅓ cup finely chopped onion
- ¼ cup whole milk
- 1 large egg, lightly beaten
- 1 Tbsp. minced fresh parsley
- 1 tsp. salt
- 1 tsp. Worcestershire sauce
- ½ tsp. pepper
- 1 lb. lean ground beef (90% lean)
- ¼ cup canola oil
- 1 bottle (12 oz.) chili sauce
- 1 jar (10 oz.) grape jelly

1. In a large bowl, combine the first eight ingredients. Crumble beef over mixture and mix well. Shape into 1-in. balls. In a large skillet, brown meatballs in oil on all sides.
2. Remove meatballs and drain. In the same skillet, combine chili sauce and jelly; cook and stir over medium heat until the jelly has melted. Return the meatballs to pan; heat through.
3 meatballs: 124 cal., 5g fat (1g sat. fat), 22mg chol., 394mg sod., 16g carb., trace fiber, 5g pro.

JALAPENO POPPER SPREAD

I've been told by guests that this recipe tastes exactly like a jalapeno popper. I like that it can be mixed up without much fuss and simply set in the oven.
—Ariane McAlpine, Penticton, BC

Prep: 10 min. • **Bake:** 25 min.
Makes: 16 servings

- 2 pkg. (8 oz. each) cream cheese, softened
- 1 cup mayonnaise
- ½ cup shredded Monterey Jack cheese
- ¼ cup canned chopped green chiles
- ¼ cup canned diced jalapeno peppers
- 1 cup shredded Parmesan cheese
- ½ cup panko (Japanese) bread crumbs
  Sweet red and yellow pepper pieces and corn chips

In a large bowl, beat the first five ingredients until blended; spread into an ungreased 9-in. pie plate. Sprinkle with Parmesan cheese; top with bread crumbs. Bake at 400° until lightly browned, 25-30 minutes. Serve with peppers and chips.
¼ cup: 239 cal., 23g fat (9g sat. fat), 43mg chol., 304mg sod., 3g carb. (1g sugars, 0 fiber), 5g pro.

ARTICHOKE CRESCENT APPETIZERS

This fun, colorful appetizer is sure to please guests at any affair. My family loves it both warm and cold.
—Mary Ann Dell, Phoenixville, PA

Prep: 20 min. • **Bake:** 15 min.
Makes: about 2 dozen

- 1 tube (8 oz.) refrigerated crescent rolls
- 2 Tbsp. grated Parmesan cheese
- 6 oz. cream cheese, softened
- ½ cup sour cream
- 1 large egg, room temperature
- ½ tsp. dill weed
- ¼ tsp. seasoned salt
- 1 can (14 oz.) water-packed artichoke hearts, rinsed, drained and chopped
- ⅓ cup thinly chopped green onions
- 1 jar (2 oz.) diced pimientos, drained

1. Unroll crescent dough and press onto the bottom and ½ in. up the sides of an ungreased 13x9-in. baking dish; seal seams and perforations. Sprinkle with Parmesan cheese. Bake at 375° until lightly browned, 8-10 minutes.

2. Meanwhile, in a small bowl, beat the cream cheese, sour cream and egg until smooth. Stir in the dill and seasoned salt. Spread over crust. Sprinkle with artichokes, green onions and pimientos.

3. Bake until edges are golden brown, 15-20 minutes. Cut into squares.

1 appetizer: 77 cal., 5g fat (3g sat. fat), 19mg chol., 151mg sod., 5g carb. (1g sugars, 0 fiber), 2g pro.

QUESO FUNDIDO

Dig in to this hot one-skillet dip and enjoy the gooey cheese and the spicy kick from chorizo and pepper jack.
—Julie Merriman, Seattle, WA

Prep: 20 min. • **Bake:** 15 min.
Makes: 6 cups

- 1 lb. uncooked chorizo
- 2 cups fresh or frozen corn, thawed
- 1 large red onion, chopped
- 1 poblano pepper, chopped
- 8 oz. fresh goat cheese, crumbled
- 2 cups cubed Monterey Jack cheese
- 1 cup cubed pepper jack cheese
- 1 large tomato, seeded and chopped
- 3 green onions, thinly sliced
  Blue corn tortilla chips

1. Preheat oven to 350°. Crumble chorizo into a 10-in. cast-iron or other ovenproof skillet; add corn, red onion and pepper. Cook over medium heat until meat is fully cooked, 6-8 minutes; drain. Stir in cheeses.

2. Bake until bubbly, 14-16 minutes. Sprinkle with the tomato and green onions. Serve with chips.

¼ cup: 161 cal., 12g fat (6g sat. fat), 38mg chol., 365mg sod., 4g carb. (1g sugars, 1g fiber), 9g pro.

45 MINUTE SIDES

ROSEMARY ROOT VEGETABLES

This heartwarming side dish from our Test Kitchen is sure to get rave reviews! The ingredient list may look longer, but you'll soon see, this colorful fall medley is a snap to prepare.
—*Taste of Home* Test Kitchen

- -

Prep: 20 min. • **Bake:** 20 min.
Makes: 10 servings

- 1 small rutabaga, peeled and chopped
- 1 medium sweet potato, peeled and chopped
- 2 medium parsnips, peeled and chopped
- 1 medium turnip, peeled and chopped
- ¼ lb. fresh Brussels sprouts, halved
- 2 Tbsp. olive oil
- 2 Tbsp. minced fresh rosemary or 2 tsp. dried rosemary, crushed
- 1 tsp. minced garlic
- ½ tsp. salt
- ½ tsp. pepper

Preheat oven to 425°. Place vegetables in a large bowl. In a small bowl, combine oil, rosemary, garlic, salt and pepper. Pour over vegetables; toss to coat. Arrange vegetables in a single layer in two 15x10x1-in. baking pans coated with cooking spray. Bake, uncovered, stirring once, until tender, 20-25 minutes.

¾ cup: 78 cal., 3g fat (0 sat. fat), 0 chol., 137mg sod., 13g carb. (5g sugars, 3g fiber), 1g pro. **Diabetic exchanges:** 1 starch, ½ fat.

RED PEPPER CORNBREAD MUFFINS

The name of this recipe says it all—except how perfect they are for scooping up that last drop of soups and stews!
—Katherine Thompson, Tybee Island, GA

- -

Prep: 20 min. • **Bake:** 25 min.
Makes: 9 servings

- 1 cup all-purpose flour
- 1 cup cornmeal
- ¼ cup ground flaxseed
- 1 Tbsp. sugar
- 2½ tsp. baking powder
- 1 tsp. salt
- 2 large eggs, room temperature
- 1½ cups fat-free milk
- 1 Tbsp. olive oil
- 1½ cups frozen corn, thawed
- 1½ cups shredded reduced-fat Colby-Monterey Jack cheese, divided
- ½ cup finely chopped sweet red pepper

1. In a large bowl, combine the flour, cornmeal, flax, sugar, baking powder and salt. In a small bowl, whisk the eggs, milk and oil. Stir into dry ingredients just until moistened. Fold in the corn, 1 cup cheese and pepper.

2. Transfer to an 11x7-in. baking pan coated with cooking spray. Sprinkle with remaining cheese. Bake at 350° until a toothpick inserted in the center comes out clean, 25-30 minutes. Serve warm.

1 piece: 251 cal., 8g fat (3g sat. fat), 58mg chol., 563mg sod., 34g carb. (5g sugars, 3g fiber), 12g pro.

Note: For regular-sized muffins, drop ¼ cup batter into each greased muffin cup and bake at 350° until a toothpick inserted in center comes out clean, 12-15 minutes. Makes about 1 ½ dozen.

EAT SMART
CREAMY GRILLED POTATO SALAD

To avoid turning on my oven in the summer, I grill just about everything—including this creamy potato salad. My friends have dubbed this "The Best Potato Salad You'll Ever Put in Your Mouth!"
—Gayle Robinson, Carrollton, GA

- -

Prep: 15 min. • **Grill:** 25 min.
Makes: 6 servings

- 8 medium red potatoes (about 2 lbs.), cut into 1-in. slices
- 2 Tbsp. olive oil
- ½ tsp. garlic salt
- ¼ tsp. paprika
- ¼ tsp. pepper
- 1 cup fat-free mayonnaise
- 2 hard-boiled large eggs, chopped
- 1 dill pickle spear, chopped
- 3 Tbsp. dill pickle juice
- 1 Tbsp. spicy brown mustard

1. Place the first five ingredients in a large bowl; toss to coat. Moisten a paper towel with cooking oil; using long-handled tongs, lightly coat the grill rack. Grill potatoes, covered, over medium heat until tender, turning once, 25-30 minutes. Cool. Cut into quarters and place in a large bowl.
2. In a small bowl, combine remaining ingredients. Pour over potatoes; toss to coat. Serve potato salad immediately. Refrigerate leftovers.
¾ cup: 209 cal., 8g fat (1g sat. fat), 75mg chol., 651mg sod., 30g carb. (5g sugars, 4g fiber), 5g pro. **Diabetic exchanges:** 2 starch, 1 fat.

BUTTERY SWEET POTATO CASSEROLE

When we get together for major holidays or family reunions, my kids, nieces and nephews beg me to make this side dish. It goes together in minutes with canned sweet potatoes, which is ideal for the busy holiday season.
—Sue Miller, Mars, PA

- -

Prep: 15 min. • **Bake:** 20 min.
Makes: 8 servings

- 2 cans (15¾ oz. each) sweet potatoes, drained and mashed
- ½ cup sugar
- 1 large egg
- ¼ cup butter, melted
- ½ tsp. ground cinnamon
  Dash salt

TOPPING
- 1 cup coarsely crushed butter-flavored crackers (about 25 crackers)
- ½ cup packed brown sugar
- ¼ cup butter, melted

1. Preheat oven to 350°. In a large bowl, combine first six ingredients. Transfer to a greased 8-in. square baking dish. Combine topping ingredients; sprinkle over sweet potato mixture.
2. Bake, uncovered, until a thermometer reads 160°, 20-25 minutes.
½ cup: 369 cal., 15g fat (8g sat. fat), 57mg chol., 255mg sod., 57g carb. (42g sugars, 3g fiber), 3g pro.

LEMON POUND CAKE MUFFINS

I make these lemony muffins for all kinds of occasions, but they're great as a side on a brunch buffet. My family is always asking for them. They have a cakelike texture and a sweet, tangy flavor. All I can say is: They're so unbelievably good!
—Lola Baxter, Winnebago, MN

Prep: 15 min. • **Bake:** 20 min.
Makes: 1 dozen

- ½ cup butter, softened
- 1 cup sugar
- 2 large eggs, room temperature
- ½ cup sour cream
- 1 tsp. vanilla extract
- ½ tsp. lemon extract
- 1¾ cups all-purpose flour
- ½ tsp. salt
- ¼ tsp. baking soda

GLAZE
- 2 cups confectioners' sugar
- 3 Tbsp. lemon juice

1. In a large bowl, cream the butter and sugar until light and fluffy. Add eggs, one at a time, beating well after each addition. Beat in the sour cream and extracts. Combine the flour, salt and baking soda; add to creamed mixture just until moistened.
2. Fill greased or paper-lined muffin cups three-fourths full. Bake at 400° until a toothpick inserted in the center comes out clean, 18-20 minutes. Cool for 5 minutes before removing from pan to a wire rack.
3. Combine the glaze ingredients; drizzle over muffins. Serve warm.
1 muffin: 311 cal., 10g fat (6g sat. fat), 63mg chol., 218mg sod., 51g carb. (36g sugars, 1g fiber), 3g pro.

EAT SMART
ROASTED VEGGIE ORZO

My sister inspired this recipe. I added a few more spices, but the concept is hers. It's easy to vary, and it's a simple way to add veggies to your diet.
—Jackie Termont, Ruther Glen, VA

Prep: 25 min. • **Bake:** 20 min.
Makes: 8 servings

- 1½ cups fresh mushrooms, halved
- 1 medium zucchini, chopped
- 1 medium sweet yellow pepper, chopped
- 1 medium sweet red pepper, chopped
- 1 small red onion, cut into wedges
- 1 cup cut fresh asparagus (1-in. pieces)
- 1 Tbsp. olive oil
- 1 tsp. each dried oregano, thyme and rosemary, crushed
- ½ tsp. salt
- 1¼ cups uncooked orzo pasta
- ¼ cup crumbled feta cheese

1. Place vegetables in a 15x10x1-in. baking pan coated with cooking spray. Drizzle with the oil and sprinkle with seasonings; toss to coat. Bake at 400° until tender, stirring occasionally, 20-25 minutes.
2. Meanwhile, cook orzo according to package directions. Drain; transfer to a serving bowl. Stir in roasted vegetables. Sprinkle with cheese.
¾ cup: 164 cal., 3g fat (1g sat. fat), 2mg chol., 188mg sod., 28g carb. (3g sugars, 3g fiber), 6g pro. **Diabetic exchanges:** 1½ starch, 1 vegetable, ½ fat.

SOUTHERN GREEN BEANS WITH APRICOTS

Green beans and apricots have become a family tradition. Enhanced with balsamic vinegar, the flavors will make your taste buds pop.
—Ashley Davis, Easley, SC

- -

Prep: 15 min. • **Cook:** 20 min.
Makes: 8 servings

  2 lbs. fresh green beans, trimmed
  1 can (14½ oz.) chicken broth
  ½ lb. bacon strips, chopped
  1 cup dried apricots, chopped
  ¼ cup balsamic vinegar
  ¾ tsp. salt
  ¾ tsp. garlic powder
  ¾ tsp. pepper

1. Place the beans and broth in a large saucepan. Bring to a boil. Cook, covered, until the green beans are crisp-tender, 4-7 minutes; drain.
2. In a large skillet, cook bacon over medium heat until crisp, stirring occasionally. Remove with a slotted spoon; drain on paper towels. Discard drippings, reserving 1 Tbsp. drippings in pan.
3. Add apricots to drippings; cook and stir over medium heat until softened. Stir in vinegar, salt, garlic powder, pepper and beans; cook and stir until beans are coated, 2-3 minutes longer. Sprinkle with bacon.
¾ cup: 149 cal., 6g fat (2g sat. fat), 12mg chol., 464mg sod., 21g carb. (14g sugars, 5g fiber), 6g pro.

BROCCOLI-MUSHROOM BUBBLE BAKE

I got bored with the same old side-dish casseroles served at our monthly moms' meeting, so I decided to create something new. Judging by the reactions of the other moms, this one's a keeper.
—Shannon Koene, Blacksburg, VA

- -

Prep: 20 min. • **Bake:** 25 min.
Makes: 12 servings

  1 tsp. canola oil
  ½ lb. fresh mushrooms, finely chopped
  1 medium onion, finely chopped
  1 tube (16.3 oz.) large refrigerated flaky biscuits
  1 pkg. (10 oz.) frozen broccoli with cheese sauce
  3 large eggs
  1 can (5 oz.) evaporated milk
  1 tsp. Italian seasoning
  ½ tsp. garlic powder
  ½ tsp. salt
  ¼ tsp. pepper
  1½ cups shredded Colby-Monterey Jack cheese

1. Preheat oven to 350°. In a large skillet, heat oil over medium-high heat. Add the mushrooms and onion; cook and stir until tender, 4-6 minutes.
2. Cut each biscuit into eight pieces; place in a greased 13x9-in. baking dish. Top with mushroom mixture.
3. Cook broccoli with cheese sauce according to package directions. Spoon over mushroom mixture.
4. In a large bowl, whisk the eggs, milk and seasonings; pour over top. Sprinkle with cheese. Bake until golden brown, 25-30 minutes.
1 serving: 233 cal., 13g fat (6g sat. fat), 64mg chol., 648mg sod., 21g carb. (6g sugars, 1g fiber), 9g pro.

CAULIFLOWER CASSEROLE

To dress up cauliflower, Mom used a delightful mixture of a cheesy sauce, bright red and green pepper pieces and crushed cornflakes. We enjoyed this casserole so much that leftovers were rare.
—Linda McGinty, Parma, OH

Prep: 15 min. • **Bake:** 30 min.
Makes: 8 servings

- 1 medium head cauliflower, broken into florets
- 1 cup sour cream
- 1 cup shredded cheddar cheese
- ½ cup crushed cornflakes
- ¼ cup chopped green pepper
- ¼ cup chopped sweet red pepper
- 1 tsp. salt
- ¼ cup grated Parmesan cheese
  Paprika

1. Place 1 in. of water in a saucepan; add the cauliflower. Bring to a boil. Reduce heat; cover and simmer until crisp-tender, 5-10 minutes. Drain.
2. In a large bowl, combine the cauliflower, sour cream, cheddar cheese, cornflakes, peppers and salt; transfer to a greased 2-qt. baking dish. Sprinkle with Parmesan cheese and paprika.
3. Bake, uncovered, at 325° until heated through, 30-35 minutes.
1 serving: 162 cal., 10g fat (7g sat. fat), 37mg chol., 503mg sod., 10g carb. (4g sugars, 2g fiber), 7g pro.

EAT SMART
WATERMELON & TOMATO SALAD

You cannot beat this light and refreshing salad on hot summer days! The combo of watermelon, cilantro, lime and heirloom tomatoes is just unusual enough to keep folks commenting on the great flavor—and coming back for more!
—Bev Jones, Brunswick, MO

Prep: 40 min. • **Makes:** 12 servings

- 3 Tbsp. lime juice
- 2 Tbsp. white balsamic vinegar
- 2 Tbsp. olive oil
- 2 Tbsp. honey
- 1 medium mango, peeled and chopped
- 1 tsp. grated lime zest
- 1 tsp. kosher salt
- ¼ tsp. white pepper
- 8 cups cubed seedless watermelon
- 1½ lbs. yellow tomatoes, coarsely chopped (about 5 medium)
- 1½ lbs. red tomatoes, coarsely chopped (about 5 medium)
- 2 sweet onions, thinly sliced and separated into rings
- ⅔ cup minced fresh cilantro

1. For the dressing, place the first eight ingredients in a blender; cover and process until pureed.
2. In a large bowl, combine the watermelon, tomatoes, onions and cilantro. Just before serving, add dressing and toss to coat. Serve with a slotted spoon.
1 cup: 102 cal., 3g fat (0 sat. fat), 0 chol., 181mg sod., 22g carb. (17g sugars, 3g fiber), 2g pro. **Diabetic exchanges:** 1 vegetable, 1 fruit, ½ fat.

PARMESAN RISOTTO

Risotto is a creamy Italian rice dish. In this version, the rice is briefly sauteed, then slowly cooked in wine and seasonings.
—*Taste of Home* Test Kitchen

- -

Prep: 15 min. • **Cook:** 30 min.
Makes: 12 servings

  8   cups chicken broth
  ½   cup finely chopped onion
  ¼   cup olive oil
  3   cups arborio rice
  2   garlic cloves, minced
  1   cup dry white wine or water
  ½   cup shredded Parmesan cheese
  ¼   tsp. salt
  ¼   tsp. pepper
  3   Tbsp. minced fresh parsley

1. In a large saucepan, heat broth and keep warm. In a Dutch oven, saute onion in oil until tender. Add rice and garlic; cook and stir for 2-3 minutes. Reduce heat; stir in wine. Cook and stir until all of the liquid is absorbed.

2. Add heated broth, ½ cup at a time, stirring constantly and allowing the liquid to absorb between additions. Cook just until risotto is creamy and rice is almost tender, about 20 minutes. Add the remaining ingredients; cook and stir until heated through. Serve immediately.

¾ cup: 260 cal., 6g fat (1g sat. fat), 2mg chol., 728mg sod., 41g carb. (1g sugars, 1g fiber), 6g pro.

TEST KITCHEN TIP

Feel free to experiment with this risotto, adding a dash or two of your favorite dried herb when you add the Parmesan.

APPALACHIAN CORNBREAD

On this westernmost ridge of the Appalachians, we get abundant rain and sunshine, which allows our children to grow a super-sweet corn crop. With staggered plantings, there is enough to eat from mid-July through August, plus plenty to freeze for the long winter. This cornbread is just one way we use some of the bounty!
—Anne Wiehler, Farmington, PA

- -

Prep: 15 min. • **Bake:** 20 min.
Makes: 9 servings

  2   Tbsp. chopped onion
  4   Tbsp. canola oil, divided
  1   cup all-purpose flour
  1   cup cornmeal
  2   Tbsp. sugar
  4   tsp. baking powder
  ½   tsp. salt
  2   large eggs, room temperature
  1   cup whole milk
  ½   cup fresh or frozen corn, thawed
  ⅓   cup shredded cheddar cheese
  ¼   cup salsa
  2   Tbsp. minced chives

1. Preheat oven to 425°. In a saucepan, saute the onion in 1 Tbsp. oil until tender; set aside.

2. In a large bowl, combine flour, cornmeal, sugar, baking powder and salt. In another bowl, whisk eggs, milk and remaining oil. Stir in corn, cheese, salsa, chives and reserved onion. Stir into the dry ingredients just until combined.

3. Transfer to a greased 9-in. square baking pan. Bake until a toothpick inserted in the center comes out clean and top is lightly browned, 20-25 minutes. Cut into squares; serve warm.

1 piece: 229 cal., 10g fat (3g sat. fat), 55mg chol., 395mg sod., 29g carb. (5g sugars, 2g fiber), 6g pro.

45 MINUTE **MAINS**

CHICKEN CHILI WITH BLACK BEANS

Because it looks a little different than traditional chili, my family was hesitant to try this dish at first. But thanks to full, hearty flavor, it's become a real favorite.
—Jeanette Urbom, Louisburg, KS

- -

Prep: 10 min. • **Cook:** 25 min.
Makes: 10 servings (3 qt.)

- 3 whole boneless skinless chicken breasts (1¾ lbs.), cubed
- 2 medium sweet red peppers, chopped
- 1 large onion, chopped
- 3 Tbsp. olive oil
- 1 can (4 oz.) chopped green chiles
- 4 garlic cloves, minced
- 2 Tbsp. chili powder
- 2 tsp. ground cumin
- 1 tsp. ground coriander
- 2 cans (15 oz. each) black beans, rinsed and drained
- 1 can (28 oz.) Italian stewed tomatoes, cut up
- 1 cup chicken broth or beer
- ½ to 1 cup water

In a Dutch oven, saute the chicken, red peppers and onion in oil until the chicken is no longer pink, about 5 minutes. Add the green chiles, garlic, chili powder, cumin and coriander; cook 1 minute longer. Stir in the beans, tomatoes, broth and ½ cup water; bring to a boil. Reduce heat and simmer, uncovered, for 15 minutes, stirring often and adding water as necessary.

1¼ cups: 236 cal., 6g fat (1g sat. fat), 44mg chol., 561mg sod., 21g carb. (5g sugars, 6g fiber), 22g pro. **Diabetic exchanges:** 2 lean meat, 1½ starch, 1 fat.

SMOKIN' HOT CHICKEN BREASTS

Combine cream cheese filling, crunchy coating and smoky heat from chipotle peppers in adobo sauce to seriously kick up your dinner game a few notches.
—Carolyn Kumpe, El Dorado, CA

- -

Prep: 30 min. • **Bake:** 15 min.
Makes: 4 servings

- 1 pkg. (8 oz.) cream cheese, softened
- ½ cup finely chopped fully cooked smoked ham
- 2 green onions, chopped
- 1 Tbsp. minced chipotle pepper in adobo sauce
- ½ tsp. salt
- ½ tsp. smoked paprika
- 4 boneless skinless chicken breast halves (6 oz. each)
- ⅓ cup all-purpose flour
- 1 large egg, beaten
- 1 cup panko (Japanese) bread crumbs
- ¼ cup canola oil

1. Preheat oven to 400°. In a small bowl, combine the first six ingredients; set aside. Cut a pocket in the thickest part of each chicken breast; fill with the cream cheese mixture. Secure with toothpicks.
2. Place the flour, egg and bread crumbs in three separate shallow bowls. Coat chicken with flour, then dip in egg mixture and coat with crumbs.
3. In a cast-iron or other ovenproof skillet, brown chicken in oil over medium heat; transfer skillet to oven. Bake, uncovered, for 15-20 minutes or until a thermometer reads 170°. Discard toothpicks before serving.
1 serving: 578 cal., 40g fat (15g sat. fat), 182mg chol., 821mg sod., 9g carb. (1g sugars, 1g fiber), 44g pro.

PRESSURE-COOKER BEEF TIPS

These beef tips remind me of a childhood favorite—made easy.
—Amy Lents, Grand Forks, ND

Prep: 20 min. • Cook: 15 min.
Makes: 4 servings

- 3 tsp. olive oil
- 1 beef top sirloin steak (1 lb.), cubed
- ½ tsp. salt
- ¼ tsp. pepper
- ⅓ cup dry red wine or beef broth
- ½ lb. sliced baby portobello mushrooms
- 1 small onion, halved and sliced
- 2 cups beef broth
- 1 Tbsp. Worcestershire sauce
- 3 to 4 Tbsp. cornstarch
- ¼ cup cold water
    Hot cooked mashed potatoes

1. Select saute setting on a 6-qt. electric pressure cooker and adjust for high heat. Add 2 tsp. oil. Sprinkle beef with salt and pepper. Brown meat in batches, adding oil as needed. Transfer meat to a bowl. Add wine to cooker, stirring to loosen browned bits. Return the beef to cooker; carefully add the mushrooms, onion, broth and the Worcestershire sauce. Lock lid; make sure vent is closed. Select manual setting; adjust the pressure to high and set the time for 15 minutes. When finished cooking, quick-release pressure according to the manufacturer's directions.
2. Select saute setting and adjust for high heat; bring liquid to a boil. In a small bowl, mix cornstarch and water until smooth; gradually stir into beef mixture. Cook and stir until sauce is thickened, 1-2 minutes. Serve with mashed potatoes.
1 cup: 212 cal., 7g fat (2g sat. fat), 46mg chol., 836mg sod., 8g carb. (2g sugars, 1g fiber), 27g pro.

PEAR SAUSAGE SALAD WITH CINNAMON VINAIGRETTE

Making croutons with cinnamon-raisin bread is genius. Toss together the rest of the salad while they toast.
—Kim Van Dunk, Caldwell, NJ

Prep: 25 min. • Bake: 10 min.
Makes: 6 servings

- 4 slices cinnamon-raisin bread
- ⅓ cup olive oil
- 3 Tbsp. cider vinegar
- 2 tsp. honey
- ½ tsp. ground cinnamon
- ⅛ tsp. sea salt
    Dash pepper
- 1 pkg. (12 oz.) fully cooked apple chicken sausage links, cut diagonally in ½-in.-thick slices
- 2 pkg. (5 oz. each) spring mix salad greens
- 2 cups sliced fresh Bartlett pears
- ½ cup chopped walnuts, toasted
- ½ cup dried sweet cherries

1. Preheat oven to 375°. Cut each slice of cinnamon-raisin bread into 12 cubes; scatter over a 15x10x1-in. pan. Bake until toasted, 8-10 minutes, stirring halfway. Cool for 5 minutes.
2. Meanwhile, combine next six ingredients in a jar with a tight-fitting lid. Shake until blended. In a large nonstick skillet, cook sausage over medium heat until browned and heated through, 2-3 minutes per side.
3. Divide salad greens among six dinner-size plates; add sausage to each plate. Top with pear slices, walnuts, cherries and croutons. Shake dressing again; spoon over salad and serve immediately.
1 serving: 404 cal., 23g fat (4g sat. fat), 40mg chol., 441mg sod., 39g carb. (23g sugars, 5g fiber), 14g pro.

RED CURRY CARROT SOUP

With its mix of delicious colors, textures and tastes, this easy soup is something special. The meatballs make it substantial enough to serve as a light entree.
—Dilnaz Heckman, Buckley, WA

Prep: 20 min. • **Cook:** 15 min.
Makes: 8 servings (2½ qt.)

- 5   pkg. (3 oz. each) ramen noodles
- 3   garlic cloves, minced
- 2   Tbsp. peanut oil
- 1   can (13.66 oz.) coconut milk, divided
- 2   Tbsp. red curry paste
- 1½ tsp. curry powder
- ½   tsp. ground turmeric
- 32   frozen fully cooked homestyle meatballs (½ oz. each)
- 4   cups chicken broth
- 1   medium zucchini, finely chopped
- 1   medium carrot, halved and sliced
- ¼   cup shredded cabbage
- 2   tsp. fish sauce or soy sauce
       Optional garnishes: Bean sprouts, chow mein noodles, chopped fresh basil, green onions and micro greens

1. Cook noodles according to the package directions (discard seasoning packets or save for another use).

2. Meanwhile, in a Dutch oven, saute garlic in oil for 1 minute. Spoon ½ cup cream from top of coconut milk and place in the pan. Add the curry paste, curry powder and turmeric; cook and stir until the oil separates from the coconut milk mixture, about 5 minutes.

3. Stir in the meatballs, broth, zucchini, carrot, cabbage, fish sauce and remaining coconut milk. Bring to a boil. Reduce heat; simmer, uncovered, until carrot is tender and the meatballs are heated through, 15-20 minutes. Drain noodles; carefully stir into soup.

4. Garnish with the optional ingredients as desired.

Note: This recipe was tested with regular (full-fat) coconut milk. Light coconut milk contains less cream.

1¼ cups: 572 cal., 38g fat (22g sat. fat), 26mg chol., 1204mg sod., 43g carb. (2g sugars, 3g fiber), 15g pro.

1. Unroll pizza crust into a lightly greased 15x10x1-in. baking pan; flatten dough and build up edges slightly. Bake at 400° for 7 minutes. Brush dough with 3 Tbsp. Buffalo wing sauce. Combine cheddar and mozzarella cheeses; sprinkle a third over the crust. Set aside.

2. In a large skillet, cook the chicken, garlic salt, pepper and chili powder in butter until chicken is no longer pink. Add the remaining wing sauce; cook and stir over medium heat 5 minutes longer.

3. Spoon over pizza. Sprinkle with oregano and remaining cheese.

4. Bake until crust is golden brown and cheese is melted, 18-20 minutes. Serve with celery and blue cheese dressing.

Freeze option: Bake pizza crust as directed; cool. Top with all the ingredients as directed and securely wrap and freeze unbaked pizza. To use, unwrap pizza; bake as directed, increasing time as necessary.

Note: This recipe was tested with Frank's Red Hot Buffalo Wing Sauce.

2 pieces: 958 cal., 38 g fat (20 g sat. fat), 218 mg chol., 3,563 mg sod., 74 g carb., 3 g fiber, 76 g pro.

SPEEDY SURPRISE

"Home run! My guys loved this recipe. It's perfect for watching a football game with ice cold beer or soda. The spices on the chicken were perfect. I can't wait to make it again."

—CWHICH,
TASTEOFHOME.COM

FREEZE IT
BUFFALO CHICKEN PIZZA

Fans of spicy chicken wings will love this change-of-pace pizza. Serve slices with blue cheese dressing and crisp celery, just like the tasty original.
—Shari DiGirolamo, Newton, PA

- -

Prep: 20 min. • **Bake:** 20 min.
Makes: 4 servings

- 1 tube (13.8 oz.) refrigerated pizza crust
- 1 cup Buffalo wing sauce, divided
- 1½ cups shredded cheddar cheese
- 1½ cups part-skim shredded mozzarella cheese
- 2 lbs. boneless skinless chicken breasts, cubed
- ½ tsp. each garlic salt, pepper and chili powder
- 2 Tbsp. butter
- ½ tsp. dried oregano
    Celery sticks and blue cheese salad dressing

GREEK TILAPIA

While on a trip through the Greek islands, my husband and I had a dish that we loved. I tried to duplicate it by combining several different recipes and came up with this tasty seafood entree.
—Sally Jean Burrell, Idaho Falls, ID

- -

Prep: 30 min. • **Bake:** 10 min.
Makes: 4 servings

- 4   tilapia fillets (4 oz. each)
- 4   tsp. butter
- 1   large egg
- ¾   cup crumbled tomato and basil feta cheese
- ¼   cup fat-free milk
- ¼   tsp. cayenne pepper
- 1   large tomato, seeded and chopped
- ¼   cup chopped ripe olives
- ¼   cup pine nuts, toasted
- 1   Tbsp. minced fresh parsley
- 1   Tbsp. lemon juice
- ⅛   tsp. pepper

1. In a large cast-iron or other ovenproof skillet, brown fish in butter.
2. In a small bowl, combine the egg, cheese, milk and cayenne; spoon over fish. Sprinkle with tomato, olives and pine nuts. Bake, uncovered, at 425° until fish just begins to flake easily with a fork, 10-15 minutes.
3. In a small bowl, combine the parsley, lemon juice and pepper; drizzle over fish.
1 fillet: 279 cal., 16g fat (6g sat. fat), 123mg chol., 362mg sod., 5g carb. (2g sugars, 2g fiber), 29g pro.

DECONSTRUCTED WONTON SOUP

Wonton is one of my favorite types of soup. When I wanted to whip up a homemade version, I decided to take a shortcut and combined pork meatballs with wide egg noodles. If I have them on hand, I'll add sliced water chestnuts, barbecued pork or sesame seeds. This is an easy way to switch it up a bit.
—Joanne Neidhamer, Tuolumne, CA

- -

Prep: 20 min. • **Cook:** 20 min.
Makes: 4 servings (1 qt.)

- 6   oz. bulk pork sausage
- ⅓   cup panko (Japanese) bread crumbs
- 1   large egg, lightly beaten
- 2   Tbsp. plus ⅓ cup thinly sliced green onions, divided
- 1   carton (32 oz.) reduced-sodium chicken broth
- 1   Tbsp. reduced-sodium soy sauce
- 1   bunch baby bok choy, coarsely chopped, or 2 cups fresh spinach
- 2   celery ribs, thinly sliced
- 1   cup uncooked extra-wide egg noodles
- ½   cup coarsely chopped fresh basil

1. Combine sausage, bread crumbs, egg and 2 Tbsp. green onion; mix lightly but thoroughly. Shape into ¾-in. balls.
2. In a large saucepan, bring broth and soy sauce to a boil. Carefully drop meatballs into soup. Stir in bok choy, celery and noodles; return to a boil. Cook, uncovered, until meatballs are cooked through and noodles are tender, 10-12 minutes. Stir in basil and remaining green onions; remove from heat.
1 cup: 234 cal., 13g fat (4g sat. fat), 83mg chol., 1193mg sod., 15g carb. (2g sugars, 1g fiber), 14g pro.

COWBOY CASSEROLE

This quick and creamy Tater Tot bake makes a comforting dinner, especially on a cold night. It is ideal for small households. You can't say that about many casseroles, can you?

—Donna Donhauser, Remsen, NY

Prep: 15 min. • **Bake:** 20 min.
Makes: 2 servings

- ½ lb. lean ground beef (90% lean)
- 1 can (8¾ oz.) whole kernel corn, drained
- ⅔ cup condensed cream of chicken soup, undiluted
- ½ cup shredded cheddar cheese, divided
- ⅓ cup 2% milk
- 2 Tbsp. sour cream
- ¾ tsp. onion powder
- ¼ tsp. pepper
- 2 cups frozen Tater Tots

1. Preheat oven to 375°. In a large skillet, cook the ground beef over medium heat until no longer pink. Stir in the corn, soup, ¼ cup cheese, milk, sour cream, onion powder and pepper.

2. Place 1 cup Tater Tots in a greased 3-cup baking dish. Layer with the beef mixture and remaining Tater Tots; sprinkle with remaining cheese. Bake, uncovered, until bubbly, 20-25 minutes.

1 serving: 714 cal., 38g fat (15g sat. fat), 120mg chol., 1675mg sod., 56g carb. (9g sugars, 6g fiber), 37g pro.

SAUSAGE & PEPPER SANDWICHES

It's easy to make a delicious summer meal. Pick a dark, malty lager for simmering the sausages. Grill 'em, split 'em and load 'em on toasted buns with garlicky peppers and onions. They're easy, fast and fun!
—Jeanne Horn, Duluth, MN

- -

Prep: 30 min. • **Grill:** 5 min.
Makes: 8 servings

- 2 bottles (12 oz. each) beer or nonalcoholic beer
- 2 Tbsp. prepared mustard
- 1 Tbsp. ketchup
- 8 fresh Italian sausage, bratwurst or Polish sausage links
- 1 large onion, thinly sliced
- 1 Tbsp. olive oil
- 1 medium sweet red pepper, coarsely chopped
- 1 medium green pepper, coarsely chopped
- 1 medium onion, chopped
- 1 garlic clove, minced
- 1 tsp. Italian seasoning
- ½ tsp. salt
- ¼ tsp. pepper
- 8 hot dog buns, split
  Spicy brown mustard

1. In a 6-qt. stockpot, combine the beer, prepared mustard and ketchup. Add the sausages, sliced onion and, if necessary, water to cover. Bring to a simmer and cook, uncovered, until a thermometer inserted in sausage reads 160°, 10-12 minutes.
2. Meanwhile, in a large skillet, heat oil over medium heat. Add peppers and chopped onion; cook and stir 6-8 minutes or until tender. Stir in garlic and seasonings; cook 30 seconds longer. Remove from heat.
3. Remove sausages from beer mixture. Grill sausages, covered, over medium heat or broil 4 in. from heat until lightly browned, 1-2 minutes on each side. Cut each sausage lengthwise in half. Serve in buns with pepper mixture and brown mustard.
1 sandwich with ¼ cup pepper mixture: 442 cal., 26g fat (10g sat. fat), 60mg chol., 1137mg sod., 31g carb. (9g sugars, 2g fiber), 20g pro.

SPEEDY SURPRISE
"I passed this recipe along to my granddaughter, who is recently married. When I asked her how the party went, she raved about how easy it was to make such a 'delish' meal."
—BEEMA, TASTEOFHOME.COM

BACON CHEESEBURGER SLIDER BAKE

I created this dish to fill two pans because these sliders disappear fast. Simply cut the recipe in half if you're only interested in making one batch.
—Nick Iverson, Denver, CO

Prep: 20 min. • **Bake:** 25 min.
Makes: 2 dozen

- 2 pkg. (17 oz. each) Hawaiian sweet rolls
- 4 cups shredded cheddar cheese, divided
- 2 lbs. ground beef
- 1 cup chopped onion
- 1 can (14½ oz.) diced tomatoes with garlic and onion, drained
- 1 Tbsp. Dijon mustard
- 1 Tbsp. Worcestershire sauce
- ¾ tsp. salt
- ¾ tsp. pepper
- 24 bacon strips, cooked and crumbled

GLAZE
- 1 cup butter, cubed
- ¼ cup packed brown sugar
- 4 tsp. Worcestershire sauce
- 2 Tbsp. Dijon mustard
- 2 Tbsp. sesame seeds

1. Preheat oven to 350°. Without separating the rolls, cut each package of rolls horizontally in half; arrange bottom halves in two greased 13x9-in. baking pans. Sprinkle each pan of rolls with 1 cup cheese. Bake until cheese is melted, 3-5 minutes.

2. In a large skillet, cook beef and onion over medium heat until beef is no longer pink and onion is tender, breaking up beef into crumbles, 6-8 minutes; drain. Stir in the tomatoes, mustard, Worcestershire sauce, salt and pepper. Cook and stir mixture until combined, 1-2 minutes.

3. Spoon beef mixture evenly over rolls; sprinkle with remaining cheese. Top with the bacon. Replace tops. For glaze, in a microwave-safe bowl combine the butter, brown sugar, Worcestershire sauce and mustard. Microwave, covered, on high until butter is melted, stirring occasionally. Pour over rolls; sprinkle with sesame seeds. Bake, uncovered, until golden brown and heated through, 20-25 minutes.

Freeze option: Cover and freeze unbaked sandwiches; prepare and freeze glaze. To use, partially thaw in refrigerator overnight. Remove from refrigerator 30 minutes before baking. Preheat oven to 350°. Pour the glaze over buns and sprinkle with sesame seeds. Bake the sandwiches as directed, increasing baking time by 10-15 minutes or until cheese is melted and a thermometer inserted in the center reads 165°.

1 slider: 380 cal., 24g fat (13g sat. fat), 86mg chol., 628mg sod., 21g carb. (9g sugars, 2g fiber), 18g pro.

SHEET-PAN CHICKEN PARMESAN

Saucy chicken, melty mozzarella and crisp-tender broccoli, all in one pan. What could be better?
—Becky Hardin, St. Peters, MO

- -

Prep: 15 min. • **Bake:** 25 min.
Makes: 4 servings

- 1 large egg
- ½ cup panko (Japanese) bread crumbs
- ½ cup grated Parmesan cheese
- ½ tsp. salt
- 1 tsp. pepper
- 1 tsp. garlic powder
- 4 boneless skinless chicken breast halves (6 oz. each)
  Olive oil-flavored cooking spray
- 4 cups fresh or frozen broccoli florets (about 10 oz.)
- 1 cup marinara sauce
- 1 cup shredded mozzarella cheese
- ¼ cup minced fresh basil, optional

1. Preheat oven to 400°. Lightly coat a 15x10x1-in. baking pan with cooking spray.
2. In a shallow bowl, whisk egg. In a separate shallow bowl, stir together the next five ingredients. Dip chicken breast in egg; allow excess to drip off. Then dip in the crumb mixture, patting to help coating adhere. Repeat with remaining chicken. Place chicken breasts in center third of baking pan. Spritz with cooking spray.
3. Bake 10 minutes. Remove from oven. Spread broccoli in a single layer along both sides of sheet pan (if broccoli is frozen, break pieces apart). Return to oven; bake 10 minutes longer. Remove from oven.
4. Preheat broiler. Spread marinara sauce over chicken; top with shredded cheese. Broil chicken and broccoli 3-4 in. from heat until cheese is golden brown and vegetables are tender, 3-5 minutes. If desired, sprinkle with basil.

1 serving: 504 cal., 17g fat (7g sat. fat), 147mg chol., 1151mg sod., 27g carb. (10g sugars, 8g fiber), 52g pro.

TEST KITCHEN TIP
Like most Italian-inspired dishes, this would pair nicely with a thick slice of garlic bread. Or serve the chicken and broccoli on a bed of riced cauliflower. A number of brands are available in the vegetable section of the freezer case.

SAUCY BEEF & CABBAGE SUPPER

My beef and cabbage supper began as a Reuben sandwich idea without the gluten. We also make it with smoked sausage. It's comforting on cooler days.
—Courtney Stultz, Weir, KS

- -

Prep: 15 min. • **Cook:** 20 min.
Makes: 6 servings

- 1 lb. lean ground beef (90% lean)
- 1 medium onion, chopped
- 2 large garlic cloves, minced
- 1 small head cabbage, chopped (about 8 cups)
- 5 medium carrots, peeled and diced
- 3 Tbsp. olive oil, divided
- 1 tsp. salt
- 1 tsp. pepper
- ½ tsp. caraway seeds
- ¼ tsp. ground allspice
- ⅛ tsp. ground cloves
- ½ cup ketchup
- 2 tsp. cider vinegar

1. In a 6-qt. stockpot, cook and crumble beef with onion and garlic over medium-high heat until no longer pink, 5-7 minutes. Stir in cabbage, carrots, 2 Tbsp. oil and seasonings; cook and stir until vegetables are slightly softened, 7-11 minutes.
2. Stir in ketchup, vinegar and remaining oil. Cook, uncovered, 5 minutes, stirring occasionally.
1¼ cups: 260 cal., 13g fat (3g sat. fat), 47mg chol., 671mg sod., 20g carb. (12g sugars, 5g fiber), 17g pro. **Diabetic exchanges:** 2 lean meat, 2 vegetable, 1½ fat, ½ starch.

BARBECUED STRAWBERRY CHICKEN

When it's time to impress family and friends, we serve barbecued chicken garnished with strawberries. It's easier than anyone would ever guess.
—Bonnie Hawkins, Elkhorn, WI

- -

Prep: 25 min. • **Bake:** 15 min.
Makes: 4 servings

- 2 Tbsp. canola oil
- 4 boneless skinless chicken breast halves (6 oz. each)
- 2 Tbsp. butter
- ¼ cup finely chopped red onion
- 1 cup barbecue sauce
- 2 Tbsp. brown sugar
- 2 Tbsp. balsamic vinegar
- 2 Tbsp. honey
- 1 cup sliced fresh strawberries

1. Preheat the oven to 350°. In a large ovenproof skillet, heat oil over medium-high heat. Brown chicken on both sides. Remove from pan. In same pan, heat butter over medium-high heat. Add onion; cook and stir until tender, about 1 minute.
2. Stir in barbecue sauce, brown sugar, vinegar and honey. Bring to a boil. Reduce heat; simmer, uncovered, until thickened, 4-6 minutes. Return the chicken to pan. Bake until a thermometer reads 165°, 12-15 minutes. Stir in strawberries.
1 chicken breast half with ⅓ cup sauce: 495 cal., 17g fat (5g sat. fat), 109mg chol., 829mg sod., 49g carb. (42g sugars, 2g fiber), 35g pro.

OPEN-FACED CHICKEN AVOCADO BURGERS

A creamy avocado spread and thick slices of fresh mozzarella and tomato dress up these chicken patties. I serve the burgers with boiled potatoes and a bit of butter.
—Lisa Kennedy, Aberdeen, NC

Prep: 30 min. • **Cook:** 15 min.
Makes: 4 servings plus ¼ cup leftover spread

- 1 Tbsp. lemon juice
- ¼ tsp. Worcestershire sauce
- ½ medium ripe avocado, peeled
- ½ cup mayonnaise
- ¼ cup sour cream
- 4 green onions, coarsely chopped
- ½ tsp. salt
- ½ tsp. cayenne pepper

BURGERS
- ¼ cup shredded Parmesan cheese
- 2 Tbsp. prepared pesto
- 3 garlic cloves, minced
- ¼ tsp. salt
- 1 lb. ground chicken
- 4 Tbsp. olive oil, divided
- ½ lb. fresh mozzarella cheese, cut into 4 slices
- 4 slices Italian bread (¾ in. thick)
- 2 cups fresh arugula or baby spinach
- 8 slices tomato
- ¼ tsp. dried basil
- ¼ tsp. pepper

1. In a blender, combine the first eight ingredients; cover and process until smooth. Chill until serving. For burgers, in a small bowl, combine the Parmesan cheese, pesto, garlic and salt. Crumble chicken over mixture and mix well. Shape into four patties.
2. In a large skillet over medium heat, cook burgers in 2 Tbsp. oil until a thermometer reads 165° and juices run clear, 5-7 minutes on each side. Top with cheese; cover and cook 1 minute longer.
3. Meanwhile, brush bread with remaining oil; place on a baking sheet. Broil 3-4 in. from the heat until toasted, 1-2 minutes on each side.
4. Spread each slice of toast with 2 Tbsp. avocado spread (refrigerate remaining spread for another use). Top with arugula, a burger and sliced tomato. Sprinkle with basil and pepper.
1 burger: 723 cal., 55g fat (17g sat. fat), 136mg chol., 849mg sod., 22g carb. (3g sugars, 3g fiber), 35g pro.

EAT SMART
TUNA-FILLED SHELLS

Hot tuna's a hit when you mix it with sizable pasta shells and a cheesy sauce. Dill also complements the fish nicely in this creamy comfort food. It's a great change of pace from the traditional tuna casserole.
—Connie Staal, Greenbrier, AR

Prep: 20 min. • **Bake:** 25 min.
Makes: 6 servings

- 12 jumbo pasta shells
- 5 tsp. all-purpose flour
- 2 cups 2% milk
- 1 tsp. dill weed
- ½ tsp. salt
- 1 celery rib, diced
- 1 small onion, diced
- 1 Tbsp. canola oil
- 2 slices white bread, crumbled
- 1 can (12 oz.) light water-packed tuna, drained and flaked
- ½ cup reduced-fat ranch salad dressing
- ½ cup shredded part-skim mozzarella cheese

1. Cook pasta shells according to package directions. Meanwhile in a saucepan, combine the flour, milk, dill and salt until smooth. Bring to a boil; cook and stir until thickened, about 2 minutes. Pour 1¼ cups sauce into a 2-qt. baking dish; set aside.
2. In a nonstick skillet, saute celery and onion in oil until tender. Add bread. Stir in the tuna, salad dressing and cheese; mix well. Drain shells; stuff with tuna mixture. Place over sauce. Drizzle with remaining sauce. Cover and bake at 350° until bubbly and heated through, 25-30 minutes.
2 shells: 291 cal., 9g fat (3g sat. fat), 34mg chol., 733mg sod., 27g carb. (0 sugars, 1g fiber), 24g pro. **Diabetic exchanges:** 2 starch, 2 lean meat, ½ fat.

MUFFIN-TIN PIZZAS

I just baked these mini pizzas and the kids are already demanding more. The no-cook pizza sauce and refrigerated dough make this meal a snap.
—Melissa Haines, Valparaiso, IN

- -

Prep: 25 min. • **Bake:** 10 min.
Makes: 16 pizzas

- 1 can (15 oz.) tomato sauce
- 1 can (6 oz.) tomato paste
- 1 tsp. dried basil
- ½ tsp. garlic salt
- ¼ tsp. onion powder
- ¼ tsp. sugar
- 1 tube (11 oz.) refrigerated thin pizza crust
- 1½ cups shredded part-skim mozzarella cheese
- ½ cup finely chopped fresh mushrooms
- ½ cup finely chopped fresh broccoli
- 16 slices pepperoni, halved

1. Preheat oven to 425°. In a small bowl, mix the first six ingredients.

2. Unroll pizza crust; cut into 16 squares. Press squares onto bottoms and up sides of 16 ungreased muffin cups, allowing corners to hang over the edges.

3. Spoon 1 Tbsp. sauce mixture into each cup. Top with cheese, mushrooms, broccoli and pepperoni. Bake until crusts are golden brown, 10-12 minutes. Serve the remaining sauce mixture, warmed if desired, with the pizzas.

Freeze option: Freeze cooled baked pizzas in an airtight container. To use, reheat pizzas on a baking sheet in a preheated 425° oven until heated through.

2 pizzas with 2 Tbsp. sauce: 233 cal., 9g fat (4g sat. fat), 16mg chol., 755mg sod., 26g carb. (5g sugars, 2g fiber), 12g pro.

PRESSURE-COOKER CHICKEN BOG

Traditional South Carolina chicken bog has lots of variations in herbs, spices and fresh veggies, but the standard ingredients remain: sausage, chicken and rice. This pressure-cooked rendition is a simple take on the classic.
—Anna Hanson, Spanish Fork, UT

- -

Prep: 20 min. • **Cook:** 10 min. + releasing
Makes: 8 servings

- 1 Tbsp. canola oil
- 1 medium onion, chopped
- 8 oz. smoked sausage, halved and sliced ½-in. thick
- 3 garlic cloves, minced
- 5 cups chicken broth, divided
- 2 cups uncooked converted rice
- 1 tsp. salt
- 1 tsp. pepper
- 1 rotisserie chicken (about 3 lbs.), meat removed and shredded
  Thinly sliced green onions, optional
  Hot sauce

1. Select saute setting and adjust for high heat on a 6-qt. electric pressure cooker. Heat oil. Add onion and sausage; cook until sausage is lightly browned. Add garlic and cook 1 minute longer.

2. Stir in 4 cups broth, rice, salt and pepper. Lock lid; make sure vent is closed. Select manual setting; adjust pressure to low and set time for 3 minutes. When finished cooking, allow pressure to naturally release for 10 minutes, then quick-release any remaining pressure according to the manufacturer's directions. Rice should be tender.

3. Select saute setting; adjust for high heat. Stir in chicken and remaining broth. Cook until chicken is heated through, about 5 minutes. If desired, sprinkle with green onions. Serve with hot sauce.

1¼ cups: 409 cal., 14g fat (5g sat. fat), 77mg chol., 1275mg sod., 40g carb. (2g sugars, 0 fiber), 27g pro.

PRESSURE-COOKER SWEET & SOUR PORK

Even though a co-worker gave me this recipe a while ago, my family still enjoys it today. It's ready in no time!
—Martha Nickerson, Hancock, ME

- -

Prep: 20 min. • **Cook:** 15 min.
Makes: 6 servings

2	Tbsp. plus 1½ tsp. paprika
1½	lbs. boneless pork loin roast, cut into 1-in. strips
1	Tbsp. canola oil
1	can (20 oz.) unsweetened pineapple chunks
1	medium onion, chopped
1	medium green pepper, chopped
¼	cup cider vinegar
3	Tbsp. packed brown sugar
3	Tbsp. reduced-sodium soy sauce
1	Tbsp. Worcestershire sauce
½	tsp. salt
2	Tbsp. cornstarch
¼	cup cold water
	Thinly sliced / chopped green onions, optional
	Hot cooked rice, optional

1. Place paprika in a large shallow dish. Add pork, a few pieces at a time, and turn to coat. Select saute setting on a 6-qt. electric pressure cooker and adjust for medium heat; add oil. Brown pork in batches. Return all pork to pressure cooker.

2. Drain the pineapple, reserving juice; refrigerate the pineapple. Add pineapple juice, onion, green pepper, vinegar, brown sugar, soy sauce, Worcestershire sauce and salt to pressure cooker. Lock lid; make sure vent is closed. Select the manual setting; adjust pressure to high and set the time for 10 minutes. When finished cooking, quick-release pressure according to the manufacturer's instructions.

3. Select saute setting and adjust for high heat; bring liquid to a boil. In a small bowl, mix cornstarch and water until smooth; gradually stir into pork mixture. Add the pineapple. Cook and stir until sauce is thickened, 1-2 minutes. If desired, sprinkle with green onions and serve over rice.

1 serving: 312 cal., 10g fat (3g sat. fat), 73mg chol., 592mg sod., 28g carb. (21g sugars, 2g fiber), 27g pro.

LENTIL, BACON & BEAN SOUP

This soup feels extra cozy with lots of lentils and a touch of bacony goodness. I think it's even better the next day.
—Janie Zirbser, Mullica Hill, NJ

Prep: 15 min. • **Cook:** 30 min.
Makes: 8 servings (2 qt.)

- 4 bacon strips, chopped
- 6 medium carrots, chopped
- 2 small onions, diced
   Olive oil, optional
- 2 Tbsp. tomato paste
- 2 garlic cloves, minced
- 1 tsp. minced fresh thyme
- ½ tsp. pepper
- 5 cups chicken stock
- 1 cup dry white wine or additional chicken stock
- 2 cans (15 to 16 oz. each) butter beans, rinsed and drained
- 2 cans (15 oz. each) cooked lentils, rinsed and drained
- 6 fresh thyme sprigs

1. In a Dutch oven, cook bacon over medium heat until crisp, stirring occasionally. Remove with a slotted spoon; drain on paper towels. Cook and stir carrots and onions in bacon drippings, adding olive oil if necessary, 3-4 minutes or until crisp-tender. Add tomato paste, garlic, thyme and pepper; cook 1 minute longer.
2. Add stock and wine; increase heat to medium-high. Cook 2 minutes, stirring to loosen any browned bits from pan. Stir in butter beans, lentils and bacon. Bring to a boil. Reduce heat; simmer, covered, 5 minutes. Uncover; continue simmering until vegetables are tender, 15-20 minutes. Serve with thyme sprigs.

1 cup: 271 cal., 6g fat (2g sat. fat), 9mg chol., 672mg sod., 41g carb. (7g sugars, 13g fiber), 18g pro. **Diabetic exchanges:** 3 starch, 1 medium-fat meat.

TEST KITCHEN TIP
Lighten up this dish even further by replacing the bacon with a little shredded chicken or turkey. For a low-fat garnish, top with a dollop of light sour cream. It offers a refreshing flavor contrast.

BAKED MUSHROOM CHICKEN

Here's a way to dress up chicken breasts for a weeknight meal or weekend dinner party. Fresh mushrooms, green onions and two kinds of cheese make it a recipe I can count on to yield impressive results every time I serve it.
—Barbara McCalley, Allison Park, PA

Prep: 20 min. • **Bake:** 20 min.
Makes: 4 servings

- 4 boneless skinless chicken breast halves (1 lb.)
- ¼ cup all-purpose flour
- 3 Tbsp. butter, divided
- 1 cup sliced fresh mushrooms
- ½ cup chicken broth
- ¼ tsp. salt
- ⅛ tsp. pepper
- ⅓ cup shredded part-skim mozzarella cheese
- ⅓ cup grated Parmesan cheese
- ¼ cup sliced green onions

1. Flatten each chicken breast half to ¼-in. thickness. Place flour in a shallow bowl. Dip chicken in flour to coat both sides; shake off any excess.
2. In a large skillet, brown chicken in 2 Tbsp. butter on both sides. Transfer to a greased 11x7-in. baking dish. In the same skillet, saute mushrooms in the remaining butter until tender. Add the broth, salt and pepper. Bring to a boil; cook until liquid is reduced to ½ cup, about 5 minutes. Spoon mixture over the chicken.
3. Bake, uncovered, at 375° until chicken is no longer pink, about 15 minutes. Sprinkle with cheeses and green onions. Bake until cheese is melted, about 5 minutes longer.
1 chicken breast half : 311 cal., 16g fat (9g sat. fat), 109mg chol., 575mg sod., 8g carb. (1g sugars, 1g fiber), 33g pro.

EAT SMART
LIGHT & LEMONY SCAMPI

A touch of lemon helped me easily trim the calories from our favorite shrimp scampi dish. For those who want to indulge, simply pass the Parmesan cheese!
—Ann Sheehy, Lawrence, MA

Prep: 20 min. • **Cook:** 15 min.
Makes: 4 servings

- 1 lb. uncooked shrimp (26-30 per lb.)
- 8 oz. uncooked multigrain angel hair pasta
- 1 Tbsp. butter
- 1 Tbsp. olive oil
- 2 green onions, thinly sliced
- 4 garlic cloves, minced
- ½ cup reduced-sodium chicken broth
- 2 tsp. grated lemon zest
- 3 Tbsp. lemon juice
- ½ tsp. freshly ground pepper
- ¼ tsp. salt
- ¼ tsp. crushed red pepper flakes
- ¼ cup minced fresh parsley
  Grated Parmesan cheese, optional

1. Peel and devein shrimp, removing tails. Cut each shrimp lengthwise in half. Cook pasta according to package directions.
2. In a large nonstick skillet, heat butter and oil over medium-high heat. Add the shrimp, green onions and garlic; cook and stir until shrimp turn pink, 2-3 minutes. Remove from pan with a slotted spoon.
3. Add broth, lemon zest, lemon juice, pepper, salt and pepper flakes to same pan. Bring to a boil; cook until liquid is slightly reduced, about 1 minute. Return shrimp to pan; heat through. Remove from heat.
4. Drain pasta; divide among four bowls. Top with shrimp mixture; sprinkle with parsley. If desired, serve with cheese.
1 serving: 378 cal., 10g fat (3g sat. fat), 146mg chol., 405mg sod., 42g carb. (3g sugars, 5g fiber), 29g pro. **Diabetic exchanges:** 3 very lean meat, 2½ starch, 1½ fat.

ONE-SKILLET PORK CHOP SUPPER

My husband, Clark, and I reserve this recipe for Sundays after the grandkids have gone home and we're too tired to prepare a big meal. It's comforting and quick.
—Kathy Thompson, Port Orange, FL

- -

Prep: 10 min. • **Cook:** 30 min.
Makes: 4 servings

- 1 Tbsp. butter
- 4 pork loin chops (½ in. thick and 7 oz. each)
- 3 medium red potatoes, cut into small wedges
- 3 medium carrots, cut into ½-in. slices, or 2 cups fresh baby carrots
- 1 medium onion, cut into wedges
- 1 can (10¾ oz.) condensed cream of mushroom soup, undiluted
- ¼ cup water
  Optional: Cracked black pepper and chopped fresh parsley

1. In a large cast-iron or other heavy skillet, heat butter over medium heat. Brown the pork chops on both sides; remove from the pan, reserving drippings.
2. In same pan, saute the vegetables in drippings until lightly browned. Whisk together the soup and water; stir into vegetables. Bring to a boil. Reduce heat; simmer, covered, just until vegetables are tender, 15-20 minutes.
3. Add chops; cook, covered, until a thermometer inserted in pork reads 145°. Remove from heat; let stand 5 minutes. If desired, sprinkle with pepper and parsley.
1 serving: 390 cal., 15g fat (6g sat. fat), 97mg chol., 700mg sod., 28g carb. (6g sugars, 4g fiber), 33g pro.

CHILI COTTAGE PIE

This filling cottage pie is super simple and loaded with flavor. The kids love to help layer the ingredients in the baking dish.
—Jacob Miller, Ledyard, CT

- -

Prep: 25 min. • **Bake:** 15 min.
Makes: 8 servings

- 1 lb. ground beef
- ¼ tsp. salt
- ¼ tsp. pepper
- 1 Tbsp. olive oil
- 1 medium red onion, diced
- 6 garlic cloves, minced
- 1 pkg. (16 oz.) frozen mixed vegetables
- 1 can (16 oz.) kidney beans, rinsed and drained
- 1 can (14½ oz.) diced tomatoes
- 1 cup beef stock
- 1 envelope chili seasoning mix
- 1 pkg. (24 oz.) refrigerated mashed potatoes
- 1 cup shredded cheddar-Monterey Jack cheese
- 4 green onions, thinly sliced
  Grated Parmesan cheese

1. Preheat oven to 350°. In a large skillet, cook and crumble beef, salt and pepper until beef is no longer pink; drain and remove from skillet.
2. In same skillet, heat oil over medium heat. Add the onion; cook and stir until the onion is tender, 2-3 minutes. Add the garlic, cook 1 minute longer.
3. Add the beef, mixed vegetables, kidney beans, tomatoes, beef stock and chili seasoning; bring to a boil. Cook and stir until thickened, about 5 minutes. Transfer to a greased 13x9-in. baking dish. Heat mashed potatoes according to microwave package directions; spread over top of beef mixture.
4. Sprinkle with cheese; bake until bubbly and cheese is melted, 15-20 minutes. Cool for 5 minutes; sprinkle with green onions and Parmesan cheese.
1 serving: 390 cal., 16g fat (8g sat. fat), 58mg chol., 992mg sod., 33g carb. (7g sugars, 7g fiber), 21g pro.

BEEF & NOODLE CASSEROLE

When life calls for a potluck dish or family event, we stir up a batch of beef and noodles. It's truly our cheesy, bubbly comfort food.
—Susan Lavery, McKinney, TX

Prep: 20 min. • **Bake:** 15 min. + standing
Makes: 6 servings

- 2 cups uncooked elbow macaroni
- 1 lb. ground beef
- 1 can (14½ oz.) diced tomatoes, drained
- 1 can (8 oz.) tomato sauce
- 1 Tbsp. sugar
- ½ tsp. salt
- ¼ tsp. garlic salt
- ¼ tsp. pepper
- 1 cup sour cream
- 3 oz. cream cheese, softened
- 3 green onions, chopped
- 1 cup shredded cheddar cheese

1. Preheat oven to 350°. In a 6-qt. stockpot, cook macaroni according to package directions for al dente; drain and return pasta to pot.
2. Meanwhile, in a large skillet, cook beef over medium heat until no longer pink, breaking into crumbles, 6-8 minutes; drain. Stir in tomatoes, tomato sauce, sugar and seasonings. Carefully transfer to a greased 11x7-in. baking dish.
3. Stir sour cream, cream cheese and green onions into macaroni. Spoon over the beef mixture, spreading evenly. Sprinkle with the cheese.
4. Bake casserole, covered, until bubbly, 15-20 minutes. Let stand for 10 minutes before serving.

1 cup: 506 cal., 27g fat (15g sat. fat), 107mg chol., 745mg sod., 37g carb. (8g sugars, 3g fiber), 27g pro.

EAT SMART
SPANISH RICE WITH CHICKEN & PEAS

This dish reminds me of my wonderful family dinners growing up. My mom made juicy chicken and rice for us every week, and now I make the same dish for my very own family.
—Josee Lanzi, New Port Richey, FL

Prep: 15 min. • **Cook:** 30 min.
Makes: 6 servings

- 1 lb. boneless skinless chicken breasts, cut into 1½-in. pieces
- 1 Tbsp. all-purpose flour
- ½ tsp. pepper
- ½ tsp. salt, divided
- 4 tsp. plus 1 Tbsp. olive oil, divided
- 1 small sweet red pepper, chopped
- 1 small onion, chopped
- 1 celery rib, chopped
- 1½ cups uncooked long grain rice
- 1 tsp. ground cumin
- 1 tsp. chili powder
- 2¼ cups chicken broth
- 1 can (14½ oz.) diced tomatoes, undrained
- 1 cup frozen peas, thawed

1. In a small bowl, toss chicken with flour, pepper and ¼ tsp. salt. In a Dutch oven, heat 4 tsp. oil over medium-high heat. Brown chicken, stirring occasionally; remove from pan.
2. In same pan, heat remaining oil over medium heat. Add the pepper, onion and celery; cook and stir until onion is tender, 2-4 minutes. Add rice, cumin, chili powder and remaining salt; stir to coat rice. Stir in remaining ingredients; bring to a boil. Reduce heat; simmer, covered, 10 minutes.
3. Place browned chicken over rice (do not stir in). Cook, covered until rice is tender and the chicken is cooked through, about 5 minutes longer.

1½ cups: 367 cal., 8g fat (1g sat. fat), 44mg chol., 755mg sod., 50g carb. (5g sugars, 4g fiber), 22g pro. **Diabetic exchanges:** 3 starch, 2 lean meat, 1 vegetable, 1 fat.

PEANUT BUTTER PORK CURRY

For an anniversary with my boyfriend, I cooked pork Asian style with peanut, coconut and curry flavors.
—Angela Robinson, Findlay, OH

- -

Prep: 15 min. • **Cook:** 20 min.
Makes: 6 servings

- 2 pork tenderloins (¾ lb. each), cubed
- 1 tsp. salt, divided
- ½ tsp. pepper
- 1 Tbsp. olive oil
- 1 cup sliced fresh carrots
- 1 medium onion, chopped
- 2 garlic cloves, minced
- 1 can (14½ oz.) diced tomatoes, drained
- 1 cup chicken broth
- 1 cup cream of coconut or coconut milk
- ½ cup creamy peanut butter
- 3 tsp. curry powder
- ¼ tsp. cayenne pepper
   Cooked brown rice

1. Sprinkle pork with ½ tsp. salt and pepper. In a large nonstick skillet, heat the oil over medium-high heat. Add pork; cook and stir until no longer pink, 4-6 minutes. Remove.
2. In same skillet, cook carrots and onion until softened, 4-6 minutes. Add the garlic; cook 2 minutes. Return pork to skillet. Add tomatoes and broth. Reduce heat; simmer, covered, 6-8 minutes.
3. Stir in cream of coconut, peanut butter, curry and cayenne and the remaining salt until smooth. Simmer, uncovered, until thickened slightly, about 2 minutes. Serve with brown rice.
1 cup: 463 cal., 24g fat (9g sat. fat), 64mg chol., 837mg sod., 36g carb. (29g sugars, 4g fiber), 29g pro.

EGG-TOPPED WILTED SALAD

Tossed with a bright champagne vinegar dressing and topped with maple-chipotle bacon and sunny eggs, this is the ultimate brunch salad. But it's so delicious I'd gladly enjoy it any time of day!
—Courtney Gaylord, Columbus, IN

- -

Prep: 20 min. • **Bake:** 25 min.
Makes: 4 servings

- 8 bacon strips
- 1 tsp. packed brown sugar
- ¼ tsp. ground chipotle pepper
- 1 small red onion, halved and thinly sliced
- 2 Tbsp. champagne vinegar
- 1 tsp. sugar
- ½ tsp. pepper
- 4 large eggs
- ¼ tsp. salt
- 8 cups spring mix salad greens (about 5 oz.)
- ½ cup crumbled feta cheese

1. Preheat oven to 350°. Place bacon on one half of a foil-lined 15x10x1-in. pan. Mix brown sugar and chipotle pepper; sprinkle evenly over bacon. Bake until bacon begins to shrink, about 10 minutes.
2. Using tongs, move bacon to other half of pan. Add onion to bacon drippings, stirring to coat. Return to oven; bake until the bacon is crisp, about 15 minutes. Drain on paper towels, reserving 2 Tbsp. drippings.
3. In a small bowl, whisk together vinegar, sugar, pepper and reserved drippings. Coarsely chop bacon.
4. Place a large skillet coated with cooking spray over medium-high heat. Break eggs, one at a time, into pan. Reduce heat to low; cook eggs until desired doneness, turning after the whites are set if desired. Sprinkle with salt.
5. Toss greens with dressing; divide among four dishes. Top with bacon, onion, cheese and eggs. Serve immediately.
1 serving: 279 cal., 20g fat (8g sat. fat), 216mg chol., 730mg sod., 10g carb. (3g sugars, 3g fiber), 17g pro.

EAT SMART
CHILI MAC CASSEROLE

This entree uses several of my family's favorite ingredients, including macaroni, kidney beans, tomatoes and cheese.
—Marlene Wilson, Rolla, ND

- -

Prep: 15 min. • **Bake:** 30 min.
Makes: 10 servings

- 1 cup uncooked elbow macaroni
- 2 lbs. lean ground beef (90% lean)
- 1 medium onion, chopped
- 2 garlic cloves, minced
- 1 can (28 oz.) diced tomatoes, undrained
- 1 can (16 oz.) kidney beans, rinsed and drained
- 1 can (6 oz.) tomato paste
- 1 can (4 oz.) chopped green chiles
- 1¼ tsp. salt
- 1 tsp. chili powder
- ½ tsp. ground cumin
- ½ tsp. pepper
- 2 cups shredded reduced-fat Mexican cheese blend
  Thinly sliced green onions, optional

1. Cook macaroni according to package directions. Meanwhile, in a large nonstick skillet, cook the beef, onion and garlic over medium heat until meat is no longer pink; drain. Stir in the tomatoes, beans, tomato paste, chiles and seasonings. Drain the macaroni; add to the beef mixture.
2. Transfer to a 13x9-in. baking dish coated with cooking spray. Cover and bake at 375° until bubbly, 25-30 minutes. Uncover; sprinkle with cheese. Bake until cheese is melted, 5-8 minutes longer. If desired, top with sliced green onions.

1 cup: 313 cal., 13g fat (6g sat. fat), 69mg chol., 758mg sod., 22g carb. (6g sugars, 5g fiber), 30g pro. **Diabetic exchanges:** 3 lean meat, 1½ starch, 1 fat.

FREEZE IT
CREAMY BUFFALO CHICKEN ENCHILADAS

I love spicy food, but I think the creaminess of the topping on these enchiladas makes them more friendly to a variety of palates.
—Crystal Schlueter, Babbitt, MN

- -

Prep: 15 min. • **Bake:** 25 min.
Makes: 6 servings

- 3 cups shredded rotisserie chicken
- 1 can (10 oz.) enchilada sauce
- ¼ cup Buffalo wing sauce
- 1¼ cups shredded Monterey Jack or cheddar cheese, divided
- 12 corn tortillas (6 in.), warmed
- 1 can (10¾ oz.) condensed cream of celery soup, undiluted
- ½ cup blue cheese salad dressing
- ¼ cup 2% milk
- ¼ tsp. chili powder
  Optional toppings: sour cream, thinly sliced green onions and additional Buffalo wing sauce

1. Preheat oven to 350°. In a large bowl, mix chicken, enchilada sauce and wing sauce. Stir in ¾ cup cheese.
2. Place ¼ cup chicken mixture off center on each tortilla. Carefully roll up and place in a greased 13x9-in. baking dish, seam side down.
3. In a bowl, mix soup, salad dressing and milk; pour over enchiladas. Sprinkle with remaining cheese; top with chili powder.
4. Bake, uncovered, until heated through and cheese is melted, 25-30 minutes. Add toppings as desired.
Freeze option: Cover and freeze unbaked enchiladas. To use, partially thaw in the refrigerator overnight. Remove from refrigerator 30 minutes before baking. Preheat oven to 350°. Bake enchiladas as directed, increasing time as necessary to heat through and for a thermometer inserted in center to read 165°.

2 enchiladas: 477 cal., 27g fat (8g sat. fat), 92mg chol., 1195mg sod., 31g carb. (3g sugars, 5g fiber), 31g pro.

PRESSURE-COOKER WHITE BEAN CHICKEN CHILI

My sister shared this chili recipe with me. The jalapeno adds just enough heat to notice but not too much for my children.
—Kristine Bowles, Rio Rancho, NM

- -

Prep: 25 min. • **Cook:** 20 min.
Makes: 6 servings (1½ qt.)

- ¾ lb. boneless skinless chicken breasts, cut into 1¼-in. pieces
- ¼ tsp. salt
- ¼ tsp. pepper
- 2 Tbsp. olive oil, divided
- 1 medium onion, chopped
- 1 jalapeno pepper, seeded and chopped
- 4 garlic cloves, minced
- 2 tsp. dried oregano
- 1 tsp. ground cumin
- 2 cans (15 oz. each) cannellini beans, rinsed and drained, divided
- 2½ cups chicken broth, divided
- 1½ cups shredded cheddar cheese
  Optional toppings: Sliced avocado, quartered cherry tomatoes and chopped fresh cilantro

1. Toss chicken with salt and pepper. Select saute setting and adjust for high heat on a 6-qt. electric pressure cooker. Heat 1 Tbsp. olive oil. Add chicken; brown on all sides. Remove chicken.

2. Add remaining oil to pressure cooker. Saute onion until tender. Add jalapeno, garlic, oregano and cumin; cook and stir for 2 minutes. Return the chicken to the pressure cooker.

3. In a bowl, mash 1 cup cannellini beans; stir in ½ cup broth. Stir bean mixture and remaining whole beans and broth into chicken mixture.

4. Lock lid; make sure vent is closed. Select manual setting; adjust pressure to high, and set time for 10 minutes. When finished cooking, quick-release pressure according to manufacturer's directions. Stir before serving. Sprinkle with cheese; add toppings as desired.

1 cup: 344 cal., 16 fat (6g sat. fat), 62mg chol., 894mg sod., 23g carb. (1g sugars, 6g fiber), 25g pro.

1. Pulse croutons and pistachios in a food processor until finely chopped. Whisk egg white with water. Pat salmon fillets dry; dip in egg white, then roll in crouton-pistachio mixture. Refrigerate 30 minutes. Meanwhile, combine cream cheese, lemon juice, dill and capers until well blended.

2. Preheat the oven to 350°. In a large ovenproof skillet, heat 1 Tbsp. oil over medium-high heat. Add carrots, squash, pepper and salt; cook and stir until tender and lightly caramelized, 6-8 minutes. Remove from skillet.

3. In same skillet, heat remaining oil over medium heat. Add salmon; cook 1 minute on each side until golden brown. Place skillet in oven; bake until fish just begins to flake easily with a fork, 8-10 minutes. Serve vegetables with salmon; top with sauce. Sprinkle with radishes. If desired, serve with lemon wedges.

1 fillet with 3 Tbsp. sauce and ¾ cup vegetables: 550 cal., 37g fat (9g sat. fat), 106mg chol., 722mg sod., 18g carb. (8g sugars, 4g fiber), 38g pro.

SPEEDY SURPRISE

"This was such a delicious, easy meal. The cream cheese sauce really gives the salmon a nice flavor, and I will make another batch of it with the remaining 4 oz. to spread on my bagel in the morning."

—SMADDEN85,
TASTEOFHOME.COM

PISTACHIO-CRUSTED SALMON WITH RAINBOW VEGETABLE CREAM

I make salmon often, so I like to experiment with it. I use pistachios in this version for crunch and a sauce inspired by the cream cheese I spread on bagels.
—Devon Delaney, Westport, CT

- -

Prep: 35 min. • **Bake:** 10 min.
Makes: 4 servings

½	cup onion and garlic salad croutons
½	cup pistachios
1	large egg white, beaten
2	Tbsp. water
4	salmon fillets (6 oz. each), about 1 in. thick
4	oz. reduced-fat cream cheese
2	Tbsp. lemon juice
2	Tbsp. snipped fresh dill
1	Tbsp. capers, drained
2	Tbsp. olive oil, divided
1½	cups julienned fresh carrots
1½	cups julienned yellow summer squash
1½	cups julienned sweet red pepper
½	tsp. salt
¼	cup radishes, halved and finely sliced
	Lemon wedges, optional

BAKED MONTEREY CHICKEN WITH ROASTED VEGGIES

Everyone asks me for this baked chicken. Roasting the veggies brings out their sweetness. They're delicious with fettuccine, rice or mashed potatoes.
—Gloria Bradley, Naperville, IL

- -

Prep: 15 min. • **Bake:** 25 min.
Makes: 6 servings

- 1   lb. fresh asparagus, trimmed and cut into 2-in. pieces
- 2   large sweet red peppers, cut into strips
- 1   Tbsp. olive oil
- 1½ tsp. salt, divided
- ¾   tsp. coarsely ground pepper, divided
- 6   boneless skinless chicken breast halves (6 oz. each)
- 5   Tbsp. butter, divided
- ¼   cup all-purpose flour
- 1   cup chicken broth
- 1   cup heavy whipping cream
- ¼   cup white wine or additional chicken broth
- 1½ cups shredded Monterey Jack cheese, divided

1. Preheat oven to 400°. Place asparagus and red peppers in a greased 13x9-in. baking dish; toss with oil, ½ tsp. salt and ¼ tsp. pepper. Roast until crisp-tender, 5-8 minutes. Remove vegetables from dish.
2. Season chicken with the remaining salt and pepper. In a large skillet, heat 1 Tbsp. butter over medium heat; brown 3 chicken breasts on both sides. Transfer to the same baking dish. Repeat with an additional 1 Tbsp. butter and remaining chicken. Top chicken with roasted vegetables.
3. In same skillet, melt remaining butter over medium heat. Stir in flour until smooth; gradually whisk in broth, cream and wine. Bring to a boil over medium heat, stirring constantly; cook and stir until thickened, 2-3 minutes. Stir in 1 cup cheese until melted. Pour over chicken.
4. Bake, uncovered, 25-30 minutes or until a thermometer inserted in chicken reads 165°. Sprinkle with remaining cheese.
1 serving: 581 cal., 40g fat (22g sat. fat), 200mg chol., 1093mg sod., 11g carb. (3g sugars, 2g fiber), 44g pro.

FOIL-PACKET SHRIMP & SAUSAGE JAMBALAYA

This hearty, satisfying dinner has all the flavors of an authentic jambalaya but is ready in minutes. The foil packets can be prepared a day ahead, stored in the refrigerator and cooked right before serving. These are also good on the grill!
—Allison Stroud, Oklahoma City, OK

- -

Prep: 20 min. • **Bake:** 20 min.
Makes: 6 servings

- 12 oz. fully cooked andouille sausage links, cut into ½-in. slices
- 12 oz. uncooked shrimp (31-40 per lb.), peeled and deveined
- 1   medium green pepper, chopped
- 1   medium onion, chopped
- 2   celery ribs, chopped
- 3   garlic cloves, minced
- 2   tsp. Creole seasoning
- 1   can (14½ oz.) fire-roasted diced tomatoes, drained
- 1   cup uncooked instant rice
- 1   can (8 oz.) tomato sauce
- ½   cup chicken broth

Preheat oven to 425°. In a large bowl, combine all ingredients. Divide mixture among six greased 18x12-in. pieces of heavy-duty foil. Fold foil around mixture and crimp edges to seal, forming packets; place on a baking sheet. Bake until shrimp turn pink and rice is tender, 20-25 minutes.
1 packet: 287 cal., 12g fat (4g sat. fat), 143mg chol., 1068mg sod., 23g carb. (3g sugars, 2g fiber), 23g pro.

TACO SALAD CASSEROLE

This casserole tastes like a taco salad and is a breeze to assemble. I crush tortilla chips to form a bottom layer, then spread on refried beans, a spicy meat mixture and cheddar cheese.

—Rhonda McKee, Greensburg, KS

- -

Prep: 25 min. • **Bake:** 15 min.
Makes: 4 servings

- 1 lb. ground beef
- ¼ cup chopped onion
- ¼ cup chopped green pepper
- 1 envelope taco seasoning
- ½ cup water
- 1 cup crushed tortilla chips
- 1 can (16 oz.) refried beans
- 1 cup shredded cheddar cheese
  Toppings: Chopped lettuce and tomatoes, sliced ripe olives, sour cream and picante sauce

1. In a large skillet, cook beef, onion and green pepper over medium heat until the meat is no longer pink; drain. Stir in taco seasoning and water. Cook and stir until thickened, about 3 minutes; set aside.
2. Place chips in a greased 8-in. square baking dish. In a small bowl, stir refried beans; spread over chips. Top with beef mixture and cheese.
3. Bake, uncovered, at 375° until heated through, 15-20 minutes. Top with lettuce, tomatoes and olives. Serve with sour cream and picante sauce.
1 cup: 405 cal., 12g fat (0 sat. fat), 47mg chol., 1181mg sod., 31g carb. (0 sugars, 6g fiber), 37g pro.

CHICKEN FRANCESE

I grew up on this tender, lemony chicken Francese dish that's a classic in Italian cooking. It's delicious as is, but we often add sauteed mushrooms. Serve it with pasta or crusty bread to mop up all that delicious sauce.

—Joe Losardo, New York, NY

- -

Prep: 20 min. • **Cook:** 20 min.
Makes: 4 servings

- 1 lb. boneless skinless chicken breasts
- 1 large egg, beaten
- ¾ cup dry bread crumbs
- 3 Tbsp. grated Parmesan cheese
- 1 tsp. dried parsley flakes
- ½ tsp. garlic powder
- ½ tsp. salt
- ½ tsp. pepper
- ¼ cup olive oil

LEMON SAUCE
- 1 cup water
- ⅓ cup lemon juice
- 2 chicken bouillon cubes
  Lemon slices

1. Pound chicken breasts with a meat mallet to ¼-in. thickness; slice into cutlets 1½ in. wide. Place beaten eggs in a shallow bowl; in a separate shallow bowl, combine the next six ingredients. Dip chicken in the egg, then in the crumb mixture, patting to help coating adhere.
2. In a large skillet, heat 2 Tbsp. oil over medium heat. Brown chicken in batches, adding oil as needed, until golden brown, 2-3 minutes per side. Remove; drain on paper towels.
3. For lemon sauce, add water, lemon juice and bouillon to skillet, stirring to loosen browned bits from pan. Bring to a boil over medium-high heat. Reduce heat; simmer, uncovered, until liquid is reduced by half, 8-10 minutes. Return the chicken to pan; toss to coat. Cook until heated through, 4-6 minutes. Serve with lemon slices.
1 serving: 318 cal., 19g fat (3g sat. fat), 111mg chol., 806mg sod., 10g carb. (2g sugars, 1g fiber), 27g pro.

45 MINUTE SWEETS

5 INGREDIENT
MOM'S FRIED APPLES

Mom often made these rich, cinnamon-sugar apples when I was growing up. It's a trip down memory lane when I make the dessert. The recipe is very dear to me.
—Margie Tappe, Prague, OK

- -

Prep: 15 min. • **Cook:** 30 min.
Makes: 8 servings

½	cup butter, cubed
6	medium unpeeled tart red apples, sliced
¾	cup sugar, divided
¾	tsp. ground cinnamon

1. Melt butter in a large cast-iron or other ovenproof skillet. Add apples and ½ cup sugar; stir to mix well. Cover and cook over low heat for 20 minutes or until apples are tender, stirring frequently.
2. Add cinnamon and remaining sugar. Cook and stir over medium-high heat 5-10 minutes longer.

1 serving: 235 cal., 12g fat (7g sat. fat), 31mg chol., 116mg sod., 35g carb. (31g sugars, 3g fiber), 0 pro.

SPEEDY SURPRISE
"Made these as our dessert for supper tonight, so I thought. The guys used them over their cornbread. It was a huge success either way! Thanks for sharing it."
—CHOCOLATEMUDCAKE, TASTEOFHOME.COM

5 INGREDIENT
ANGEL FOOD CANDY

It was my dad who inspired me to first try making this candy. He remembered it from when he was a boy. He gave the ultimate compliment was when he told me my version tasted even better!
—Shelly Matthys, New Richmond, WI

- -

Prep: 20 min. • **Cook:** 25 min.
Makes: 1½ lbs. (12 servings)

1	cup sugar
1	cup dark corn syrup
1	Tbsp. white vinegar
1	Tbsp. baking soda
1	lb. milk chocolate candy coating, melted

1. In a heavy saucepan, combine the sugar, corn syrup and vinegar. Cook over medium heat, stirring constantly, until the sugar dissolves. Cook without stirring until the temperature reaches 300° (hard-crack stage) on a candy thermometer. Do not overcook.
2. Remove from the heat and quickly stir in baking soda. Pour into a buttered 13x9-in. pan. Do not spread candy; mixture will not fill pan.
3. When cool, break into bite-size pieces. Dip into melted chocolate; place on waxed paper until the chocolate is firm. Store candy tightly covered.

2 oz.: 337 cal., 11g fat (10g sat. fat), 0 chol., 356mg sod., 63g carb. (61g sugars, 1g fiber), 1g pro.

5 INGREDIENT
CAKE & BERRY CAMPFIRE COBBLER

This warm cobbler is one of our favorite ways to end a busy day of fishing, hiking, swimming or rafting. It's yummy with ice cream—and so easy to make!
—June Dress, Meridian, ID

Prep: 10 min. • **Grill:** 30 min.
Makes: 12 servings

- 2 cans (21 oz. each) raspberry pie filling
- 1 pkg. yellow cake mix (regular size)
- 1¼ cups water
- ½ cup canola oil
  Vanilla ice cream, optional

1. Prepare grill or campfire for low heat, using 16-20 charcoal briquettes or large wood chips.
2. Line an ovenproof Dutch oven with heavy-duty aluminum foil; add pie filling. In a large bowl, combine the cake mix, water and oil. Spread over pie filling.
3. Cover Dutch oven. When briquettes or wood chips are covered with white ash, place Dutch oven directly on top of 8-10 of them. Using long-handled tongs, place remaining briquettes on pan cover.
4. Cook until filling is bubbly and a toothpick inserted in the topping comes out clean, 30-40 minutes. To check for doneness, use the tongs to carefully lift the cover. Serve with ice cream if desired.
Note: This recipe does not use eggs.
1 serving: 342 cal., 12g fat (2g sat. fat), 0 chol., 322mg sod., 57g carb. (34g sugars, 2g fiber), 1g pro.

SKILLET CHOCOLATE DUMPLINGS

Why bake when you can make an entire dessert on the stovetop? These dumplings are often requested by my family for special events like birthdays.
—Becky Magee, Chandler, AZ

Prep: 20 min. • **Cook:** 20 min.
Makes: 8 servings

- ¾ cup packed brown sugar
- ¼ cup baking cocoa
- 1 Tbsp. cornstarch
  Dash salt
- 2 cups water
- 2 Tbsp. butter

DUMPLINGS

- 1¼ cups all-purpose flour
- 2 tsp. baking powder
- ½ tsp. salt
- ½ cup sugar
- 2 Tbsp. baking cocoa
- 3 Tbsp. butter
- 1 large egg, lightly beaten
- ⅓ cup whole milk
- 1 tsp. vanilla extract
  Whipped cream or ice cream

1. For sauce, combine the brown sugar, cocoa, cornstarch and salt in a large, heavy cast-iron or other ovenproof skillet. Stir in water; cook, stirring constantly, until mixture begins to boil and thicken slightly. Add butter; mix well. Remove sauce from the heat.
2. For dumplings, sift together flour, baking powder, salt, sugar and cocoa. Cut in butter until mixture resembles a fine meal. Combine the egg, milk and vanilla; blend gradually into flour mixture.
3. Return skillet to heat; bring the chocolate sauce to a boil. Drop dumplings by Tbsp. into hot sauce. Reduce heat to low; cover and simmer until just set, about 20 minutes. Serve warm dumplings with whipped cream or ice cream.
1 serving: 294 cal., 9g fat (5g sat. fat), 43mg chol., 527mg sod., 52g carb. (33g sugars, 1g fiber), 4g pro.

MACAROON APPLE COBBLER

When time is short, use apple pie filling instead of the fresh apples.
—Phyllis Hinck, Lake City, MN

Prep: 15 min. • **Bake:** 25 min.
Makes: 8 servings

- 4 cups thinly sliced peeled tart apples
- ⅓ cup sugar
- ½ tsp. ground cinnamon
- ½ cup sweetened shredded coconut
- ¼ cup chopped pecans

TOPPING
- ½ cup butter, softened
- ½ cup sugar
- 1 large egg, room temperature
- ½ tsp. vanilla extract
- ¾ cup all-purpose flour
- ¼ tsp. baking powder

1. Place the apples in an ungreased 9-in. pie plate. Combine sugar and cinnamon; sprinkle over apples. Top with coconut and pecans; set aside.
2. To make topping, cream butter and sugar until light and fluffy. Beat in egg and vanilla extract. Combine the flour and the baking powder; gradually add to the creamed mixture until blended.
3. Drop small spoonfuls over apples. Bake at 350° until top is golden brown and fruit is tender, 25-35 minutes. Serve warm.
1 serving: 320 cal., 17g fat (9g sat. fat), 57mg chol., 152mg sod., 41g carb. (29g sugars, 2g fiber), 3g pro.

FUDGE BROWNIE PIE

Here's a fun and festive way to serve brownies. Family and friends will love topping their own slices with whipped cream and strawberries.
—Johnnie McLeod, Bastrop, LA

Prep: 15 min. • **Bake:** 25 min.
Makes: 6 servings

- 1 cup sugar
- ½ cup butter, melted
- 2 large eggs, room temperature
- 1 tsp. vanilla extract
- ½ cup all-purpose flour
- ⅓ cup baking cocoa
- ¼ tsp. salt
- ½ cup chopped pecans
  Optional toppings: Whipped cream and strawberries

1. In a large bowl, beat sugar and butter. Add eggs and vanilla; mix well. Add flour, cocoa and salt. Stir in nuts.
2. Pour into a greased 9-in. pie pan or ovenproof skillet. Bake at 350° until almost set, 25-30 minutes. If desired, serve with whipped cream and strawberries.
1 slice: 409 cal., 24g fat (11g sat. fat), 112mg chol., 274mg sod., 46g carb. (33g sugars, 2g fiber), 5g pro.

CHERRY-PEACH DUMPLINGS

You can make this fruity dessert on your stovetop, but to really impress your guests, simmer it in an electric skillet right at the dinner table. There's no more convenient way to enjoy the fruits of the season.
—Patricia Frerk, Syracuse, NY

Prep: 15 min. • **Cook:** 20 min.
Makes: 6 servings

- 1 can (21 oz.) cherry pie filling
- ½ cup water
- 2 Tbsp. lemon juice
- ½ tsp. ground cinnamon
- ¼ tsp. ground cloves
- 1 can (15¼ oz.) sliced peaches, drained
- 1 large egg, room temperature
   Whole milk
- 1½ cups biscuit/baking mix
   Optional: Additional cinnamon and whipped cream

In a 10-in. skillet, combine the first five ingredients. Add peaches; bring to a boil. Place egg in a 1-cup measuring cup; add enough milk to measure ½ cup and stir until combined. Place the biscuit mix in a bowl; stir in milk mixture with a fork just until moistened. Drop by six spoonfuls over top of boiling fruit. Simmer, uncovered, for 10 minutes; cover and simmer until a toothpick inserted in a dumpling comes out clean, about 10 minutes longer. Sprinkle with cinnamon if desired. Serve warm, with whipped cream if desired.

1 serving: 286 cal., 4g fat (1g sat. fat), 32mg chol., 349mg sod., 58g carb. (10g sugars, 2g fiber), 4g pro.

ORANGE CRISPIES

Add a little sunshine to your cookie jar with this recipe. When I want to spread a little cheer, I'll bake up a double batch to share.
—Ruth Gladstone, Brunswick, MD

Prep: 15 min. • **Bake:** 10 min./batch
Makes: 3½ dozen

- 1 cup shortening
- 1 cup sugar
- 1 large egg, room temperature
- 1½ tsp. orange extract
- ½ tsp. salt
- 1½ cups all-purpose flour
   Sugar or orange-colored sugar

1. In a small bowl, cream shortening and sugar until light and fluffy. Beat in the egg, extract and salt. Add flour; mix well. Drop rounded tablespoonfuls of dough 2 in. apart onto ungreased baking sheets.
2. Bake at 375° until edges begin to brown, about 10 minutes. Cool for 1-2 minutes; remove from pans to wire racks. Sprinkle warm cookies with sugar.

2 cookies: 158 cal., 9g fat (2g sat. fat), 10mg chol., 59mg sod., 16g carb. (9g sugars, 0 fiber), 1g pro.

CARAMEL DUMPLINGS

My family just loves these tender dumplings in a sweet, rich sauce. I enjoy them because they turn out wonderful every time I make them...which is a lot!

—Faye Johnson, Connersville, IN

Prep: 10 min. • **Cook:** 30 min.
Makes: 8 servings

2	Tbsp. butter
1½	cups packed brown sugar
1½	cups water

DUMPLINGS

1¼	cups all-purpose flour
½	cup sugar
2	tsp. baking powder
½	tsp. salt
½	cup whole milk
2	Tbsp. butter, softened
2	tsp. vanilla extract
½	cup coarsely chopped peeled apple, optional

1. In a large skillet, heat the butter, brown sugar and water to boiling. Reduce heat to simmer.

2. Meanwhile, combine the dumpling ingredients. Drop by tablespoonfuls into the simmering sauce. Cover tightly and simmer for 20 minutes. Do not lift lid. If desired, serve warm with cream or ice cream.

½ cup: 336 cal., 6g fat (4g sat. fat), 17mg chol., 329mg sod., 68g carb. (53g sugars, 1g fiber), 3g pro.

SPEEDY SURPRISE

"Very quick and easy and so tasty! I served this at a dinner party and it was a big hit!"
DMOEHRING, TASTEOFHOME.COM

CHEWY PEANUT BUTTER PAN SQUARES

With seven in our family, including two teenage boys, these peanut butter cookie bars never last long! It's hard to believe how simple they are to prepare.

—Deb DeChant, Milan, OH

Prep: 10 min. • **Bake:** 30 min.
Makes: 2 dozen

½	cup butter, cubed
½	cup creamy peanut butter
1½	cups sugar
1	cup all-purpose flour
2	large eggs, room temperature, lightly beaten
1	tsp. vanilla extract

1. In a microwave-safe bowl, melt butter and peanut butter; stir until smooth. Combine sugar and flour; gradually add to butter mixture and mix well. Beat in eggs and vanilla.

2. Spread into a greased 13x9-in. baking pan. Bake at 350° until lightly browned and edges start to pull away from sides of pan, 28-32 minutes. Cool on a wire rack.

Note: Reduced-fat peanut butter is not recommended for this recipe.

1 square: 139 cal., 7g fat (3g sat. fat), 28mg chol., 69mg sod., 18g carb. (13g sugars, 0 fiber), 2g pro.

DATE PUDDING COBBLER

There were eight children in my family when I was a girl, and all of us enjoyed this cobbler. I now serve it for weeknights and special occasions alike.
—Carolyn Miller, Guys Mills, PA

- -

Prep: 15 min. • **Bake:** 25 min.
Makes: 8 servings

- 1 cup all-purpose flour
- 1½ cups packed brown sugar, divided
- 2 tsp. baking powder
- 1 Tbsp. cold butter
- ½ cup whole milk
- ¾ cup chopped dates
- ¾ cup chopped walnuts
- 1 cup water
  Whipped cream and ground cinnamon, optional

1. In a large bowl, combine the flour, ½ cup brown sugar and baking powder. Cut in the butter until crumbly. Gradually add the milk, dates and walnuts.
2. In a large saucepan, combine water and remaining brown sugar; bring to a boil. Remove from the heat; add the date mixture and mix well.
3. Transfer to a greased 10-in. cast-iron skillet or 8-in. square baking pan. Bake at 350° until top is golden brown and fruit is tender, 25-30 minutes. Serve warm.
1 serving: 347 cal., 9g fat (2g sat. fat), 5mg chol., 150mg sod., 65g carb. (50g sugars, 2g fiber), 4g pro.

CHOCOLATE PEANUT COOKIES

When I want chocolate chip cookies, I bake this variation, which is full of other goodies, such as candy and peanuts. The cookies are crisp on the outside and moist and tender in the middle.
—Clara Coulson Minney, Washington Court House, OH

- -

Prep: 20 min. • **Bake:** 10 min./batch
Makes: about 2 dozen

- ¼ cup butter, softened
- ¼ cup peanut butter
- ¼ cup packed brown sugar
- 2 Tbsp. sugar
- 2 Tbsp. beaten egg, room temperature
- 2 Tbsp. 2% milk
- ½ tsp. vanilla extract
- 1 cup all-purpose flour
- ½ tsp. baking soda
- ⅛ tsp. salt
- ⅓ cup honey-roasted peanuts
- ⅓ cup semisweet chocolate chips
- ⅓ cup coarsely chopped miniature peanut butter cups

1. In a large bowl, cream the butter, peanut butter and sugars until light and fluffy. Beat in the egg, milk and vanilla. Combine the flour, baking soda and salt; gradually add to creamed mixture and mix well. Stir in the peanuts, chocolate chips and chopped peanut butter cups.
2. Drop by tablespoonfuls 2 in. apart onto ungreased baking sheets. Bake at 350° until golden brown, 10-12 minutes. Remove to wire racks. Store in an airtight container.
1 cookie: 82 cal., 5g fat (2g sat. fat), 9mg chol., 68mg sod., 9g carb. (5g sugars, 1g fiber), 2g pro.

60 MINUTES

ROASTED PUMPKIN NACHOS

Previously, I had made this dish with black beans and corn off the cob in the summer. Wanting to try it with fresh fall ingredients, I replaced the corn with roasted pumpkin— yum! It's also good with butternut squash.
—Lesle Harwood, Douglassville, PA

- -

Prep: 40 min. • **Bake:** 10 min.
Makes: 12 servings

- 4   cups cubed fresh pumpkin or butternut squash (about 1 lb.)
- 2   Tbsp. olive oil
- ¼   tsp. salt
- ⅛   tsp. pepper
- 1   pkg. (13 oz.) tortilla chips
- 1   can (15 oz.) black beans, rinsed and drained
- 1   jar (16 oz.) salsa
- 3   cups shredded Mexican cheese blend
     Optional toppings: Minced fresh cilantro, sliced green onions and hot pepper sauce

1. Preheat oven to 400°. Place pumpkin in a greased 15x10x1-in. baking pan. Drizzle with oil; sprinkle with salt and pepper. Toss to coat. Roast until tender, 25-30 minutes, stirring occasionally.
2. Reduce the oven setting to 350°. On a greased 15x10x1-in. baking pan, layer half of the chips, beans, pumpkin, salsa and cheese. Repeat layers. Bake until cheese is melted, 8-10 minutes. Add toppings of your choice; serve immediately.
1 serving: 347 cal., 18g fat (6g sat. fat), 25mg chol., 559mg sod., 36g carb. (3g sugars, 4g fiber), 10g pro.

5 INGREDIENT
SMOKY BACON WRAPS

These cute little sausage and bacon bites are finger-licking good. They have a sweet and salty taste that's fun for breakfast or as an appetizer.
—Cara Flora, Kokomo, IN

- -

Prep: 20 min. • **Bake:** 30 min.
Makes: about 3½ dozen

- 1   lb. sliced bacon
- 1   pkg. (16 oz.) miniature smoked sausage links
- ⅓   cup packed brown sugar

1. Cut each bacon strip in half widthwise. Wrap one piece of bacon around each sausage link.
2. Place in a foil-lined 15x10x1-in. baking pan. Sprinkle with the brown sugar. Bake, uncovered, at 400° until bacon is crisp and sausage is heated through, 30-40 minutes.
1 piece: 90 cal., 7g fat (2g sat. fat), 18mg chol., 293mg sod., 2g carb. (2g sugars, 0 fiber), 5g pro.

SPICY PUMPKIN SEEDS

We look forward to fall in anticipation of making these spicy pumpkin seeds. I often put some in a decorated jar to give as a gift.
—Carolyn Hayes, Johnston City, IL

- -

Prep: 10 min. • **Bake:** 45 min. + cooling
Makes: 2 cups

- 2 cups fresh pumpkin seeds
- 2 Tbsp. canola oil
- 1 tsp. Worcestershire sauce
- ⅛ to ¼ tsp. hot pepper sauce
- ½ tsp. salt
- ½ tsp. paprika
- ¼ tsp. ground cumin
- ¼ tsp. cayenne pepper

1. In a small bowl, toss pumpkin seeds with oil, Worcestershire sauce and hot pepper sauce. Combine the salt, paprika, cumin and cayenne pepper; sprinkle over seeds and toss to coat.
2. Line a 15x10x1-in. baking pan with foil; grease the foil. Spread pumpkin seeds in pan. Bake, uncovered, at 250° until lightly browned and dry, 45-50 minutes, stirring occasionally. Cool completely. Store in an airtight container.
¼ cup: 103 cal., 7g fat (1g sat. fat), 0 chol., 158mg sod., 9g carb. (0 sugars, 1g fiber), 3g pro.

SPEEDY SURPRISE

"I've made these for the past 3 years now! Friends and family will bring pumpkins to our home so we will make them some more! We are addicted."
—OOH!, TASTEOFHOME.COM

POPPY SEED SQUARES

When I came across this unusual appetizer, I just knew I had to try it. Although I prepare these squares every Christmas, no one tires of them.
—Jo Baden, Independence, KS

- -

Prep: 35 min. • **Bake:** 25 min.
Makes: about 10 dozen

- 1 lb. ground beef
- 1½ cups finely chopped fresh mushrooms
- 1 medium onion, finely chopped
- 1 can (10¾ oz.) condensed cream of celery or mushroom soup, undiluted
- 1 Tbsp. prepared horseradish
- 1 tsp. salt
- ½ tsp. pepper

CRUST

- 3 cups all-purpose flour
- 2 Tbsp. poppy seeds
- ¾ tsp. baking powder
- ¾ tsp. salt
- 1 cup shortening
- ½ cup cold water

1. In a large skillet, cook the ground beef, mushrooms and onion over medium heat until meat is no longer pink. Add the soup, horseradish, salt and pepper. Remove from the heat; set aside.
2. In a large bowl, combine the flour, poppy seeds, baking powder and salt. Cut in the shortening until the mixture resembles coarse crumbs. Gradually add water, tossing with a fork until a ball forms. Divide dough in half. Roll out one portion into a 15x10-in. rectangle; transfer to an ungreased 15x10x1-in. baking pan.
3. Spoon meat mixture over dough. Roll out the remaining dough into 15x10-in. rectangle; place over filling. Bake at 425° until golden brown, about 25 minutes. Cut into small squares.
3 pieces: 100 cal., 6g fat (2g sat. fat), 6mg chol., 120mg sod., 8g carb. (0 sugars, 0 fiber), 3g pro.

5 INGREDIENT | EAT SMART
APPLE SAUSAGE APPETIZERS

Bake sausage slices in this sweet glaze for a tasty, no-fuss appetizer. The recipe yields a big batch, so it's great for holiday parties and other large gatherings.
—Dolores M. Barnas, Blasdell, NY

- -

Prep: 10 min. • **Bake:** 40 min.
Makes: 20 servings

2 jars (23 oz. each) unsweetened chunky applesauce

½ cup packed brown sugar
2 lbs. fully cooked kielbasa or Polish sausage, cut into ½-in. slices
1 medium onion, chopped

In a bowl, combine applesauce and brown sugar. Stir in sausage and onion. Transfer mixture to a greased 13x9-in. baking dish. Bake, uncovered, at 350° until bubbly, 40-50 minutes.

½ cup: 117 cal., 4g fat (0 sat. fat), 30mg chol., 404mg sod., 14g carb. (0 sugars, 1g fiber), 7g pro. **Diabetic exchanges:** 1 lean meat, 1 fruit.

SWISS MUSHROOM LOAF

I'm always prepared for recipe requests whenever I serve this outstanding loaf stuffed with Swiss cheese and mushrooms. It's excellent as an appetizer or served with pasta, chili or spaghetti.
—Heidi Mellon, Waukesha, WI

- -

Prep: 15 min. • **Bake:** 40 min.
Makes: 12 servings

1 loaf (1 lb.) Italian bread, unsliced
1 block (8 oz.) Swiss cheese, cut into cubes
1 cup sliced fresh mushrooms
¼ cup softened butter, cubed
1 small onion, finely chopped
1½ tsp. poppy seeds
2 garlic cloves, minced
½ tsp. seasoned salt
½ tsp. ground mustard
½ tsp. lemon juice

1. Preheat oven to 350°. Cut bread diagonally into 1-in. slices to within 1 in. of bottom of loaf. Repeat cuts in opposite direction. Place the cheese cubes and mushrooms in cuts.
2. In a microwave-safe bowl, combine the remaining ingredients; microwave, covered, on high until the butter is melted, 30-60 seconds. Stir until blended. Spoon over bread.
3. Wrap the loaf in foil; place on a baking sheet. Bake until cheese is melted, about 40 minutes.
1 serving: 214 cal., 11g fat (6g sat. fat), 28mg chol., 372mg sod., 21g carb. (2g sugars, 1g fiber), 9g pro.

GREEK-STYLE PIZZA

Save yourself a trip to Greece and serve this appetizer pizza at your next party. To ensure a crisp and flaky crust, before assembling the pizza, drain the tomato slices on a paper towel to soak up any extra moisture.
—Claire Torrice, Oswego, NY

- -

Prep: 25 min. • **Bake:** 25 min.
Makes: 18 servings

¼ cup butter, cubed
¼ cup olive oil
½ lb. sliced fresh mushrooms
1 medium onion, sliced
3 garlic cloves, minced
1 pkg. (10 oz.) fresh spinach, trimmed and coarsely chopped
1 Tbsp. lemon juice
1 tsp. dried basil
1 tsp. dried oregano
1 pkg. (16 oz., 14x9-in. sheet size) frozen phyllo dough, thawed
2 cups shredded part-skim mozzarella cheese
1 cup crumbled feta cheese
3 medium ripe tomatoes, sliced
½ cup seasoned bread crumbs

1. In a large skillet, melt butter. Transfer to a small bowl; add oil and set aside. In the same skillet, saute the mushrooms, onion and garlic until tender. Add spinach; saute until wilted. Add the lemon juice, basil and oregano; set aside.

2. Brush a 13x9-in. baking dish with the reserved butter mixture. Place one sheet of phyllo dough in baking dish; brush lightly with butter mixture. (Keep remaining phyllo covered with a damp towel to prevent it from drying out.) Repeat the layers with remaining phyllo, brushing each layer.

3. Top with the spinach mixture; sprinkle with cheeses. Coat both sides of tomato slices with bread crumbs; arrange over top. Bake at 375° until the cheese is melted and crust is golden brown, 25-30 minutes.

1 piece: 198 cal., 9g fat (4g sat. fat), 17mg chol., 310mg sod., 21g carb. (3g sugars, 2g fiber), 8g pro.

TEST KITCHEN TIP
Salty, crumbly Greek feta cheese is traditionally made with sheep's or goat's milk, but most American brands are made with cow's milk instead.

GINGER-ORANGE WINGS

The sweet-and-sour sauce in this recipe was originally for pork spareribs, but my family has always enjoyed it on chicken wings. The longer the wings sit in the ketchup, ginger and orange marmalade sauce, the better they taste. They're delicious served warm or cold.

—Lora Fletcher, Lyons, OR

- -

Prep: 45 min. • **Cook:** 10 min.
Makes: 50 pieces

- 25 whole chicken wings (about 5 lbs.)
- 2 cups all-purpose flour
- 3 tsp. seasoned salt
- 2 tsp. garlic salt
- ⅓ cup vegetable oil
- 2 cups orange marmalade
- 1 cup ketchup
- ½ cup soy sauce
- ¾ tsp. ground ginger

1. Cut chicken wings into three sections; discard wing tip section. In a large bowl, combine the flour, seasoned salt and garlic salt. Add chicken wings, in batches, and toss to coat. In a large cast-iron or other heavy skillet, fry wings in oil, in batches, until golden and crispy, 3-4 minutes.
2. Drain pan drippings; return all chicken to the skillet. Combine the marmalade, ketchup, soy sauce and ginger; pour over chicken and stir to coat. Cover and cook over medium-low heat for 10-15 minutes.
Note: Uncooked chicken wing sections (wingettes) may be substituted for whole chicken wings.
1 piece: 119 cal., 5g fat (1g sat. fat), 14mg chol., 399mg sod., 14g carb. (9g sugars, 0 fiber), 6g pro.

PARTY FRANKS

These tiny, tangy appetizers have such broad appeal. I prepare them often for gatherings, weddings and reunions. They're convenient to serve at parties since the sauce can be made ahead, then reheated with the franks right before serving to guests.
—Lucille Howell, Portland, OR

- -

Prep: 30 min. • **Bake:** 20 min.
Makes: 16 servings

- ¾ cup chopped onion
- 2 Tbsp. canola oil
- 1 cup ketchup
- ½ cup water
- ½ cup cider vinegar
- 2 Tbsp. sugar
- 2 Tbsp. Worcestershire sauce
- 2 Tbsp. honey
- 2 tsp. ground mustard
- 2 tsp. paprika
- ¾ tsp. salt
- ¼ tsp. pepper
- ⅛ tsp. hot pepper sauce
- 1 large lemon, sliced
- 2½ to 3 lbs. miniature hot dogs or smoked sausage links

In a saucepan, saute onion in oil until tender. Stir in the next 11 ingredients. Add lemon. Bring to a boil. Reduce heat; simmer, uncovered, until slightly thickened, stirring occasionally, 20-25 minutes. Discard lemon slices. Place hot dogs in a 13x9-in. baking dish. Top with sauce. Bake, uncovered, at 350° until heated through, 18-20 minutes. Keep warm; serve with toothpicks.
⅓ cup: 268 cal., 21g fat (7g sat. fat), 45mg chol., 1047mg sod., 11g carb. (9g sugars, 0 fiber), 9g pro.

SPICY-GOOD CHICKEN WINGS

My family enjoys eating these chicken wings while watching football on TV, but they make a great dish to pass for any occasion! They have just the right amount of spice.
—Della Clutts, New Tazewell, TN

- -

Prep: 30 min. • **Bake:** 20 min.
Makes: about 1½ dozen

- 1 cup self-rising flour
- 1 tsp. celery salt
- 1 tsp. garlic powder
- 1 tsp. onion salt
- 1 tsp. barbecue seasoning
- ½ tsp. salt
- 2 lbs. chicken wingettes
  Oil for frying
- ½ cup butter, melted
- 1 bottle (2 oz.) hot pepper sauce
  Blue cheese salad dressing

1. In a large shallow dish, mix the first six ingredients. Add chicken, a few pieces at a time; turn chicken to coat.
2. In an electric skillet, heat 1 in. of oil to 375°. Fry wingettes, a few at a time, until browned, 4-5 minutes on each side. Drain on paper towels. Preheat oven to 350°.
3. In a 13x9-in. baking dish, mix melted butter and pepper sauce. Add wings and turn to coat. Bake, uncovered, 10 minutes. Turn; bake until chicken juices run clear, 10-15 minutes longer. Serve with dressing.
Note: As a substitute for 1 cup of self-rising flour, place 1½ tsp. baking powder and ½ tsp. salt in a measuring cup. Add all-purpose flour to measure 1 cup.
1 appetizer: 225 cal., 18g fat (6g sat. fat), 51mg chol., 473mg sod., 5g carb. (0 sugars, 0 fiber), 10g pro.

SOUTHWEST SPANAKOPITA BITES

I'm a big fan of the southwest-style egg rolls served at restaurants and wanted to recreate them without the fat of deep frying. Phyllo dough was the perfect solution! For a main dish, I fill small flour tortillas and bake them.
—Marianne Shira, Osceola, WI

Prep: 40 min. • **Bake:** 10 min.
Makes: 2 dozen (½ cup sauce)

- 2   Tbsp. finely chopped sweet red pepper
- 1   green onion, finely chopped
- 1   tsp. canola oil
- 1   pkg. (10 oz.) frozen chopped spinach, thawed and squeezed dry
- ¾   cup shredded reduced-fat Monterey Jack cheese or Mexican cheese blend
- ½   cup frozen corn, thawed
- ½   cup canned black beans, rinsed and drained
- 1   Tbsp. chopped seeded jalapeno pepper
- ½   tsp. ground cumin
- ½   tsp. chili powder
- ¼   tsp. salt
- 8   sheets phyllo dough (14x9 in.) Butter-flavored cooking spray

SAUCE
- ⅓   cup cubed avocado
- ¼   cup reduced-fat mayonnaise
- ¼   cup reduced-fat sour cream
- 1½ tsp. white vinegar

1. In a small skillet, saute red pepper and onion in oil until tender. Transfer to a large bowl; stir in ½ cup spinach (save the rest for another use). Stir in the cheese, corn, black beans, jalapeno, cumin, chili powder and salt.

2. Place one sheet of phyllo dough on a work surface with a short end facing you. (Keep remaining phyllo covered with a damp cloth to prevent it from drying out.) Spray sheet with butter-flavored spray; cut into three 14x3-in. strips.

3. Place a scant tablespoon of the filling on lower corner of each strip. Fold dough over filling, forming a triangle. Fold the triangle up, then over, forming another triangle. Continue folding, like a flag, until you come to the end of the strip.

4. Spritz end of dough with spray and press onto triangle to seal. Turn triangle and spritz top with spray. Repeat with remaining phyllo and filling.

5. Place triangles on baking sheets coated with cooking spray. Bake at 375° until golden brown, 10-12 minutes. Mash the avocado with the mayonnaise, sour cream and vinegar. Serve with warm appetizers.

Note: Wear disposable gloves when cutting hot peppers; the oils can burn skin. Avoid touching your face.

1 serving: 50 cal., 3g fat (1g sat. fat), 4mg chol., 103mg sod., 5g carb. (1g sugars, 1g fiber), 2g pro. **Diabetic exchanges:** ½ starch, ½ fat.

1. In a large cast-iron or other heavy skillet, saute green peppers and onion in 1 Tbsp. butter and 1 Tbsp. oil for 10 minutes or until golden brown.
2. Add half of the mushrooms and remaining butter and oil; saute until tender. Remove onion mixture and set aside. Saute the remaining mushrooms until tender. Return all to the pan. Cover and simmer over medium-high heat for 2 minutes.
3. Add the olives, vinegar, tomato paste, sugar, oregano, salt and pepper. Reduce heat; simmer, uncovered, until thickened, about 10 minutes.
4. Serve warm or at room temperature with bagel chips or baguette slices..

¼ cup: 53 cal., 3g fat (1g sat. fat), 3mg chol., 107mg sod., 6g carb. (3g sugars, 1g fiber), 2g pro. **Diabetic exchanges:** ½ starch, ½ fat.

TEST KITCHEN TIP
You can prepare this caponata up to 2 days in advance. Reheat the mixture over low heat, stirring occasionally, when ready to serve.

EAT SMART
MUSHROOM CAPONATA

This is a lovely appetizer when served with crostini, pita bread, bagel chips or crackers. I've also used it as a topping over a salad of mixed greens. This mushroom version of a caponata is more nutritious than the eggplant one.
—Julia Cotton, Chalfont, PA

- -

Prep: 40 min. • **Cook:** 10 min.
Makes: 6 cups

- 2 large green peppers, chopped
- 1 large onion, chopped
- 2 Tbsp. butter, divided
- 2 Tbsp. olive oil, divided
- 2 lbs. fresh mushrooms, coarsely chopped
- ½ cup pitted Greek olives, chopped
- ¼ cup balsamic vinegar
- ¼ cup tomato paste
- 1 Tbsp. sugar
- 1 tsp. dried oregano
- ½ tsp. salt
- ¼ tsp. coarsely ground pepper
  Bagel chips or lightly toasted French bread baguette slices

AUSSIE SAUSAGE ROLLS

I was born and raised in Australia but moved to the U.S. when I married my husband. When I long for a taste of my homeland, I bake up a batch of these cute little sausage rolls and share them with my neighbors or co-workers.
—Melissa Landon, Port Charlotte, FL

Prep: 30 min. • **Bake:** 20 min.
Makes: 3 dozen

- 1 medium onion, finely chopped
- 2 Tbsp. minced fresh chives or 2 tsp. dried chives
- 2 tsp. minced fresh basil or ½ tsp. dried basil
- 2 garlic cloves, minced
- ½ tsp. salt
- ¼ tsp. pepper
- 1 tsp. paprika, divided
- 1¼ lbs. bulk pork sausage
- 1 pkg. (17.3 oz.) frozen puff pastry, thawed

1. Preheat oven to 350°. Combine the first six ingredients and ¾ tsp. paprika. Add the sausage; mix lightly but thoroughly.
2. On a lightly floured surface, roll each pastry sheet into an 11x10½-in. rectangle. Cut lengthwise into three strips. Spread ½ cup sausage mixture lengthwise down the center of each strip. Fold over sides, pinching edges to seal. Cut each log into six pieces.
3. Place on a rack in a 15x10x1-in. pan, seam side down. Sprinkle with remaining paprika. Bake until golden brown and sausage is no longer pink, 20-25 minutes.

1 appetizer: 116 cal., 8g fat (2g sat. fat), 11mg chol., 198mg sod., 8g carb. (0 sugars, 1g fiber), 3g pro

PARTY APPETIZER MEATBALLS

These are a favorite snack at parties and gatherings. The recipe is easy, and the meatballs can be made well ahead of time and frozen until needed. I think what makes them taste so good is the sauce.
—Nathalie Guest, Caledon, ON

Prep: 20 min. • **Bake:** 40 min.
Makes: 8 dozen

- 2 lbs. lean ground beef
- 2 large eggs, lightly beaten
- 1 cup shredded part-skim mozzarella cheese
- ½ cup dry bread crumbs
- ¼ cup finely chopped onion
- 2 Tbsp. grated Parmesan cheese
- 1 Tbsp. ketchup
- 2 tsp. Worcestershire sauce
- 1 tsp. Italian seasoning
- 1 tsp. dried basil
- 1 tsp. salt
- ¼ tsp. pepper

SAUCE
- 1 bottle (14 oz.) hot or regular ketchup
- 2 Tbsp. cornstarch
- 1 jar (12 oz.) apple jelly
- 1 jar (12 oz.) currant jelly

1. In a large bowl, combine the first 12 ingredients. Shape into 1-in. balls. Place meatballs on a greased rack in a shallow baking pan.
2. Bake at 350° for 10-15 minutes; drain. Combine ketchup and cornstarch in roasting pan. Stir in jellies; add the meatballs. Cover and bake for 30 minutes.

1 meatball: 50 cal., 1g fat (1g sat. fat), 13mg chol., 94mg sod., 6g carb. (5g sugars, 0 fiber), 3g pro.

SOUTHWESTERN BEAN DIP

Just by using different types of beans, you can make this dip as spicy as you like it. My family could eat this as a complete meal.
—Jeanne Shear, Sabetha, KS

Prep: 20 min. • **Bake:** 30 min.
Makes: about 9 cups

- 2 lbs. ground beef
- 1 Tbsp. dried minced onion
- 1 can (8 oz.) tomato sauce
- 1 can (16 oz.) kidney beans, rinsed and drained
- 1 can (16 oz.) chili beans, undrained
- 4 cups shredded cheddar cheese
  Sliced jalapeno pepper
  Tortilla chips

1. Preheat oven to 350°. In a large skillet, cook ground beef over medium heat until no longer pink; drain. Transfer to a bowl; add onion. Mash with a fork until crumbly; set aside.
2. In a blender, process tomato sauce and beans until chunky. Add to beef mixture and mix well. Spoon half into a greased 13x9-in. baking dish; top with half of the cheese. Repeat layers.
3. Bake, uncovered, until cheese is melted, about 30 minutes. Top with sliced jalapeno. Serve warm with chips.
2 Tbsp.: 53 cal., 3g fat (2g sat. fat), 13mg chol., 88mg sod., 3g carb. (0 sugars, 1g fiber), 4g pro.

MOROCCAN STUFFED MUSHROOMS

Coriander and cumin are zesty updates to the familiar stuffed mushrooms. The addition of couscous makes them very filling and delicious.
—Raymonde Bourgeois, Swastika, ON

Prep: 45 min. • **Bake:** 10 min.
Makes: 2 dozen

- 24 medium fresh mushrooms
- ½ cup chopped onion
- ⅓ cup finely shredded carrot
- 1 tsp. canola oil
- 1 garlic clove, minced
- ½ tsp. salt
- ½ tsp. ground cumin
- ¼ tsp. ground coriander
- ¾ cup vegetable broth
- 2 Tbsp. dried currants
- ½ cup uncooked couscous
- 2 Tbsp. minced fresh parsley
- 2 Tbsp. minced fresh mint

1. Remove stems from mushrooms and finely chop stems; set caps aside. In a large nonstick skillet, saute the onion, carrot and chopped stems in oil until crisp-tender.
2. Add the garlic, salt, cumin and coriander. Cook and stir for 1 minute. Add broth and currants; bring to a boil. Stir in couscous. Remove from the heat; cover and let stand for 5-10 minutes or until broth is absorbed. Fluff with a fork. Stir in parsley and mint. Stuff into mushroom caps.
3. Place on a baking sheet. Bake at 400° until mushrooms are tender, 10-15 minutes.
1 stuffed mushroom: 25 cal., 0 fat (0 sat. fat), 0 chol., 81mg sod., 5g carb. (1g sugars, 1g fiber), 1g pro.

CHICKEN POT STICKERS

Chicken and mushrooms make up the filling in these pot stickers, a traditional Chinese dumpling. Greasing the steamer rack makes it easy to remove them once they're steamed.
—Jacquelynne Stine, Las Vegas, NV

- -

Prep: 50 min. • **Cook:** 5 min./batch
Makes: 4 dozen

- 1 lb. boneless skinless chicken thighs, cut into chunks
- 1½ cups sliced fresh mushrooms
- 1 small onion, cut into wedges
- 2 Tbsp. hoisin sauce
- 2 Tbsp. prepared mustard
- 2 Tbsp. Sriracha chili sauce or 1 Tbsp. hot pepper sauce
- 1 pkg. (10 oz.) pot sticker or gyoza wrappers
- 1 large egg, lightly beaten

SAUCE
- 1 cup reduced-sodium soy sauce
- 1 green onion, chopped
- 1 tsp. ground ginger

1. In a food processor, combine the uncooked chicken, mushrooms, onion, hoisin sauce, mustard and chili sauce; cover and process until blended.
2. Place 1 Tbsp. chicken mixture in the center of one wrapper. (Until ready to use, keep remaining wrappers covered with a damp towel to prevent them from drying out.) Moisten entire edge with egg. Fold wrapper over filling to form a semicircle. Press edges firmly to seal, pleating the front side to form several folds.
3. Holding sealed edges, stand each dumpling on an even surface; press to flatten bottom. Curve ends to form a crescent shape. Repeat with remaining wrappers and filling.
4. Working in batches, arrange pot stickers in a single layer on a large greased steamer basket rack; place in a Dutch oven over 1 in. of water. Bring to a boil; cover and steam until the filling juices run clear, 5-7 minutes. Repeat with the remaining pot stickers.
5. Meanwhile, in a small bowl, combine sauce ingredients. Serve with pot stickers. Refrigerate leftovers.

Freeze option: Cover and freeze uncooked pot stickers in a single layer on waxed paper-lined sheets until firm. Transfer to freezer containers; return to freezer. To use, steam as directed until heated through and juices run clear.

1 pot sticker with 1 tsp. sauce: 43 cal., 1g fat (0 sat. fat), 11mg chol., 374mg sod., 5g carb. (0 sugars, 0 fiber), 3g pro.

TEST KITCHEN TIP
No steamer basket? Then place a batch of the pot stickers in a Dutch oven or large skillet, using a little cooking oil, over medium-high heat (don't overcrowd). Cook until bottoms are lightly browned, then add a few tablespoons water, cover and steam the dumplings a few minutes until dumplings are fully cooked. Repeat.

5 INGREDIENT

BREAKFAST SAUSAGE BACON BITES

These tasty morsels are perfect with almost any egg dish or as finger foods that party guests can just pop into their mouths while mingling.
—Pat Waymire, Yellow Springs, OH

Prep: 20 min. • **Bake:** 35 min.
Makes: about 3½ dozen

- ¾ **lb. sliced bacon**
- 2 **pkg. (8 oz. each) frozen fully cooked breakfast sausage links, thawed**
- ½ **cup plus 2 Tbsp. packed brown sugar, divided**

1. Preheat oven to 350°. Cut bacon strips widthwise in half; cut sausage links in half. Wrap a piece of bacon around each piece of sausage. Place ½ cup brown sugar in a shallow bowl; roll sausages in sugar. Secure each with a toothpick. Place in a foil-lined 15x10x1-in. baking pan.
2. Sprinkle with 1 Tbsp. brown sugar. Bake until bacon is crisp, 35-40 minutes, turning once. Sprinkle with remaining brown sugar.
1 piece: 51 cal., 4g fat (1g sat. fat), 6mg chol., 100mg sod., 4g carb. (4g sugars, 0 fiber), 2g pro.

CANDIED ACORN SQUASH RINGS

This acorn squash recipe was given to me by my grandma, who always served it at Thanksgiving. Now I make it whenever I'm feeling nostalgic.
—Rita Addicks, Weimar, TX

- -

Prep: 15 min. • **Bake:** 40 min.
Makes: 6 servings

2 medium acorn squash
⅔ cup packed brown sugar
½ cup butter, softened

1. Preheat oven to 350°; cut squash in half lengthwise; remove and discard seeds. Cut each half crosswise into ½-in. slices; discard ends. Arrange squash in a shallow baking pan; cover with foil. Bake until just tender, 25-30 minutes.
2. Combine sugar and butter; spread over squash. Bake, uncovered, 15-20 minutes longer, basting occasionally.
1 serving: 287 cal., 15g fat (9g sat. fat), 41mg chol., 168mg sod., 40g carb. (27g sugars, 2g fiber), 1g pro.

TEST KITCHEN TIP
You can use either light or dark brown sugar for the squash—it's a matter of personal taste. Light brown sugar has less molasses flavor and is more delicate. Dark brown tastes more "old-fashioned" and has a stronger molasses flavor.

BACON-GOUDA STUFFED ONIONS

Serve these tender, sweet and savory onions as a side with steak. For an added splash, drizzle everything with any leftover buttery pan juices from baking the onions.
—Barb Templin, Norwood, MN

- -

Prep: 10 min. • **Bake:** 45 min.
Makes: 4 servings

4 large sweet onions
¼ tsp. salt
¼ tsp. pepper
5 bacon strips, cooked and crumbled
½ cup shredded smoked Gouda cheese
¼ cup butter, softened
Minced chives

1. Preheat oven to 400°. Cut a ¼-in. slice from top and bottom of each onion. Peel onions. Carefully cut and remove the center of each onion, leaving a ½-in. shell; discard removed onion or save for another use.
2. Place onion shells in a greased 13x9-in. baking dish. Sprinkle with salt and pepper. Cover and bake for 40-45 minutes or until tender. Combine the bacon, cheese and butter; spoon into onions. Bake, uncovered, 5-10 minutes longer or until the cheese is melted. Sprinkle with chives.
1 stuffed onion: 308 cal., 19g fat (11g sat. fat), 57mg chol., 553mg sod., 26g carb. (17g sugars, 3g fiber), 10g pro.

CREOLE CORNBREAD

Cornbread is a staple of Cajun and Creole cuisine. This is an old favorite that I found in the bottom of my recipe drawer, and it really tastes wonderful.
—Enid Hebert, Lafayette, LA

- -

Prep: 15 min. • **Bake:** 45 min.
Makes: 12 servings

- 2 cups cooked rice
- 1 cup yellow cornmeal
- ½ cup chopped onion
- 1 to 2 Tbsp. seeded chopped jalapeno peppers
- 1 tsp. salt
- ½ tsp. baking soda
- 2 large eggs
- 1 cup whole milk
- ¼ cup canola oil
- 1 can (16½ oz.) cream-style corn
- 3 cups shredded cheddar cheese
  Additional cornmeal

1. Preheat oven to 350°. In a large bowl, combine rice, cornmeal, onion, peppers, salt and baking soda.
2. In another bowl, beat eggs, milk and oil. Add corn; mix well. Stir into the rice mixture until blended. Fold in cheese. Sprinkle a well-greased 10-in. ovenproof skillet with cornmeal. Pour the batter into the skillet.
3. Bake for 45-50 minutes or until bread tests done. Cut into wedges and serve cornbread warm.
Note: Wear disposable gloves when cutting hot peppers; the oils can burn skin. Avoid touching your face.
1 wedge: 293 cal., 16g fat (6g sat. fat), 61mg chol., 557mg sod., 27g carb. (3g sugars, 1g fiber), 11g pro.

EAT SMART
BUTTERNUT SQUASH APPLE BAKE

Sweet slices of butternut squash topped with sliced tart apples are covered in cinnamon-sugar glaze for a quick, easy dinner accompaniment.
—Ellie Klopping, Toledo, OH

- -

Prep: 15 min. • **Bake:** 45 min.
Makes: 8 servings

- 1 butternut squash (2 lbs.), peeled and cut into ½-in. slices
- 3 medium tart apples, peeled and thinly sliced
- ⅓ cup packed brown sugar
- 1½ tsp. all-purpose flour
- ¼ tsp. ground cinnamon
- 2 Tbsp. butter, melted

1. Preheat oven to 350°. Layer squash and apples in a 13x9-in. baking dish coated with cooking spray. Mix brown sugar, flour and cinnamon; sprinkle over top. Drizzle with melted butter.
2. Bake, covered, until squash and apples are tender, 45-55 minutes.
1 serving: 120 cal., 3g fat (2g sat. fat), 8mg chol., 36mg sod., 25g carb. (15g sugars, 4g fiber), 1g pro. **Diabetic exchanges:** 1 starch, ½ fruit, ½ fat.

GREEN ONION ROLLS

The classic combination of cheese and onions is wrapped in tender dough in these delicious rolls that are best served warm. Better double the batch—these savory, elegant mouthfuls will disappear fast.
—Jane Kroeger, Key Largo, FL

- -

Prep: 30 min. + rising • **Bake:** 20 min.
Makes: 1 dozen

1	Tbsp. butter
1½	cups chopped green onions
½	tsp. pepper
¾	tsp. garlic salt, optional
1	loaf (1 lb.) frozen bread dough, thawed
½	cup shredded part-skim mozzarella cheese
⅓	cup grated Parmesan cheese

1. Preheat oven to 375°. In a large skillet, heat butter over medium-high heat; saute green onions until tender. Stir in pepper and, if desired, garlic salt. Remove mixture from heat.

2. On a lightly floured surface, roll the dough into a 12x8-in. rectangle. Spread with the onion mixture. Sprinkle with mozzarella and Parmesan cheese.

3. Roll up jelly-roll style, starting with a long side; pinch seam to seal. Cut into 12 slices; place in greased muffin cups. Cover with greased plastic wrap; let rise in a warm place until doubled, about 30 minutes. Preheat oven to 375°.

4. Bake until golden brown, 18-20 minutes. Remove rolls from pan to a wire rack to cool slightly. Serve warm.

1 roll: 142 cal., 4g fat (1g sat. fat), 7mg chol., 415mg sod., 20g carb. (2g sugars, 2g fiber), 6g pro.

FIVE-CHEESE RIGATONI

Who can resist cheesy pasta hot from the oven? This ooey-gooey rigatoni boasts a homemade creamy Swiss sauce that comes together in just a few minutes.
—Shirley Foltz, Dexter, KS

- -

Prep: 25 min. • **Bake:** 25 min.
Makes: 9 servings

- 1 pkg. (16 oz.) rigatoni or large tube pasta
- 2 Tbsp. butter
- 3 Tbsp. all-purpose flour
- 1 tsp. salt
- ½ tsp. pepper
- 2½ cups whole milk
- ½ cup shredded Swiss cheese
- ½ cup shredded fontina cheese
- ½ cup shredded part-skim mozzarella cheese
- ½ cup grated Parmesan cheese, divided
- ½ cup grated Romano cheese, divided

1. Cook rigatoni according to package directions.
2. Preheat oven to 375°. In a large saucepan, melt the butter. Stir in the flour, salt and pepper until smooth. Gradually stir in milk; bring to a boil. Cook and stir 1-2 minutes or until thickened. Stir in the Swiss, fontina, and mozzarella cheeses, ¼ cup of the Parmesan cheese and ¼ cup of the Romano cheese until all are melted.
3. Drain rigatoni; stir in the cheese sauce. Transfer to a greased 13x9-in. baking dish. Sprinkle with the remaining Parmesan and Romano cheeses. Cover and bake for 20 minutes. Uncover; bake 5-10 minutes longer or until bubbly.
¾ cup: 362 cal., 14g fat (8g sat. fat), 40mg chol., 586mg sod., 42g carb. (5g sugars, 2g fiber), 18g pro.

CARAMEL SWEET POTATOES

The sauce is the star of this recipe. It really does taste like butterscotch. It makes a lovely side dish for poultry or ham.
—Mary Jo Patrick, Napoleon, OH

- -

Prep: 35 min. • **Bake:** 25 min.
Makes: 10 servings

- 6 medium sweet potatoes, peeled and cut into 1-in. chunks
- ½ cup packed brown sugar
- ½ cup corn syrup
- ¼ cup whole milk
- 2 Tbsp. butter
- ½ to 1 tsp. salt
- ½ tsp. ground cinnamon

1. Preheat oven to 325°. Place the sweet potatoes in a Dutch oven; cover with water. Bring to a boil. Reduce heat; cover and simmer for 20 minutes.
2. Drain and transfer to a greased 13x9-in. baking dish. Bake, uncovered, at 325° for 15 minutes.
3. Meanwhile, in a small saucepan, combine the remaining ingredients. Bring to a boil; pour over the sweet potatoes. Bake for 10-15 minutes longer or until glazed, basting frequently.
¾ cup: 182 cal., 3g fat (2g sat. fat), 7mg chol., 158mg sod., 40g carb. (22g sugars, 2g fiber), 1g pro.

BAKED CORN PUDDING

Here's a comforting side dish that can turn even ordinary meals into something to celebrate. A yuletide favorite with our entire family, it spoons up as sweet and creamy as custard. Our guests love it just as much as we do.
—Peggy West, Georgetown, DE

- -

Prep: 10 min. • **Bake:** 45 min.
Makes: 10 servings

½ cup sugar
3 Tbsp. all-purpose flour
3 large eggs
1 cup whole milk
¼ cup butter, melted
½ tsp. salt
½ tsp. pepper
1 can (15¼ oz.) whole kernel corn, drained
1 can (14¾ oz.) cream-style corn

1. Preheat oven to 350°. In a large bowl, combine the sugar and flour. Whisk in the eggs, milk, butter, salt and pepper. Stir in the corn and cream-style corn.
2. Pour into a greased 1½-qt. baking dish. Bake, uncovered, for 45-50 minutes or until a knife inserted in the center comes out clean.
½ cup: 186 cal., 7g fat (4g sat. fat), 79mg chol., 432mg sod., 26g carb. (14g sugars, 1g fiber), 4g pro.

TEST KITCHEN TIP
Cream-style corn is a great pantry staple. Add it to a beef soup for added flavor and thicker broth, or stir it into pancakes for a sweet-savory breakfast treat.

SWEET POTATO ORANGE CUPS

Serve this refreshingly sweet side dish to your guests in separate cups you craft from oranges! All you have to do is cut oranges in half, scoop out the fruit and fill the peel with the sweet potato mixture. It's a hit among our family and friends.
—Melonie Bowers, Sugarcreek, OH

- -

Prep: 30 min. • **Bake:** 20 min.
Makes: 8 servings

3 large sweet potatoes (2 to 2½ lbs.), peeled and cubed
1 can (6 oz.) orange juice concentrate, thawed
¼ cup packed brown sugar
¼ cup half-and-half cream
2 Tbsp. butter
¾ cup miniature marshmallows
¼ cup chopped pecans
4 large oranges, halved
32 additional miniature marshmallows
Chopped pecans, toasted, optional

1. Place sweet potatoes in a large saucepan or Dutch oven; cover with water. Bring to a boil. Reduce heat; cover and cook just until tender, 25-30 minutes. Drain.
2. In a large bowl, beat sweet potatoes, concentrate, sugar, cream and butter on low speed until smooth. Stir in ¾ cup of marshmallows and the pecans; set aside.
3. Remove pulp from oranges, leaving a shell. (Discard pulp or save for another use.) Spoon sweet potato mixture into shells. Top each with four marshmallows.
4. Place in a greased 15x10x1-in. baking pan. Bake, uncovered, at 350° for 20 minutes or until heated through. If desired, top with toasted pecans.
1 serving: 401 cal., 7g fat (3g sat. fat), 11mg chol., 51mg sod., 83g carb. (48g sugars, 9g fiber), 6g pro.

5 INGREDIENT | EAT SMART
ROASTED ROOT VEGETABLES

Pleasantly seasoned with rosemary and garlic, this appealing side dish showcases good-for-you turnips, carrots and even potatoes. It's a nice homey addition to Sunday dinner, and the mix of vegetables makes it great for holidays, too.
—Kerry Sullivan, Longwood, FL

- -

Prep: 15 min. • **Bake:** 45 min.
Makes: 12 servings

- 5 medium red potatoes, cubed
- 4 medium carrots, cut into ½-in. slices
- 2 small turnips, peeled and cubed
- 1 garlic clove, minced
- 2 to 4 Tbsp. olive oil
- 1 Tbsp. minced fresh rosemary or 1 tsp. dried rosemary, crushed
- ½ tsp. salt
- ¼ tsp. pepper

1. Preheat oven to 350°. Place the potatoes, carrots, turnips and garlic in a greased 13x9-in. baking dish. Drizzle with oil; sprinkle with rosemary, salt and pepper. Stir to coat.
2. Bake, uncovered, 35 minutes. Increase temperature to 450°; bake 10-15 minutes longer or until the vegetables are tender.
¾ cup: 55 cal., 3g fat (0 sat. fat), 0 chol., 144mg sod., 7g carb. (0 sugars, 2g fiber), 1g pro. **Diabetic exchanges:** 1 vegetable, ½ fat.

SPINACH SOUFFLE

You just can't make an easier, more delicious side dish than this. It's great with beef, pork and lamb. I especially like serving it for a festive occasion such as New Year's Eve.
—Bette Duffy, Kenmore, WA

- -

Prep: 20 min. • **Bake:** 35 min.
Makes: 6 servings

- 2 pkg. (10 oz. each) frozen chopped spinach, thawed and squeezed dry
- 1 pkg. (8 oz.) cream cheese, cubed
- 1½ cups shredded Monterey Jack cheese
- 4 large eggs, lightly beaten
- ¼ cup butter, melted
- 1 garlic clove, minced
- ½ tsp. salt

Preheat oven to 350°. In a large bowl, combine all the ingredients. Transfer to a greased 1½-qt. baking dish. Bake until edges are lightly browned, 35-40 minutes.
½ cup: 375 cal., 33g fat (20g sat. fat), 228mg chol., 630mg sod., 5g carb. (0 sugars, 3g fiber), 17g pro.

CORNBREAD DRESSING WITH OYSTERS

My father's dressing bakes separately from our Thanksgiving turkey and is simply delicious. The secret is to prepare the cornbread first, let it cool and then crumble it to form the base for the rest of the ingredients. My father always added oysters to give the dressing a special flavor.
—Nell Bass, Macon, GA

- -

Prep: 10 min. • **Bake:** 45 min.
Makes: 15 servings

- 8 to 10 cups coarsely crumbled cornbread
- 2 slices white bread, toasted and torn into small pieces
- 2 large hard-boiled eggs, chopped
- 2 cups chopped celery
- 1 cup chopped onion
- 1 pint shucked oysters, drained and chopped, or 2 cans (8 oz. each) whole oysters, drained and chopped
- ½ cup egg substitute
- 1 tsp. poultry seasoning
- 5 to 6 cups turkey or chicken broth

Preheat oven to 400°. Combine the first eight ingredients in a large bowl. Stir in enough broth to make the mixture very wet. Pour into a greased 13x9-in. baking dish or shallow 3-qt. baking dish. Bake, uncovered, for 45 minutes or until lightly browned.

1 cup: 171 cal., 3g fat (0 sat. fat), 42mg chol., 753mg sod., 28g carb. (3g sugars, 2g fiber), 7g pro.

ENGLISH MUFFIN BREAD LOAF

Many years ago, a good friend gave me her mother's recipe for this delightful bread, and I've made it ever since. It's perfect smothered with your favorite jam.
—Jane Zielinski, Rotterdam Junction, NY

- -

Prep: 15 min. + rising • **Bake:** 35 min.
Makes: 2 loaves (32 slices)

- 5 cups all-purpose flour, divided
- 2 pkg. (¼ oz. each) active dry yeast
- 1 Tbsp. sugar
- 2 tsp. salt
- ¼ tsp. baking soda
- 2 cups warm whole milk (120° to 130°)
- ½ cup warm water (120° to 130°) Cornmeal

1. In a large bowl, combine 2 cups flour, yeast, sugar, salt and baking soda. Add warm milk and water; beat on low speed for 30 seconds, scraping bowl occasionally. Beat on high for 3 minutes.
2. Stir in the remaining flour (batter will be stiff). Do not knead. Grease two 8x4-in. loaf pans. Sprinkle pans with cornmeal. Spoon batter into the pans and sprinkle cornmeal on top. Cover and let rise in a warm place until doubled, about 45 minutes.
3. Bake at 375° for 35 minutes or until golden brown. Remove loaves from pans immediately and cool on wire racks. Slice and toast.

1 slice: 83 cal., 1g fat (trace sat. fat), 2mg chol., 165mg sod., 16g carb. (1g sugars, 1g fiber), 3g pro.

60 MINUTE MAINS

PEASANT SKILLET

I prepare this entree frequently throughout the year, substituting whatever vegetables are in season. No matter how often I make it, I'm always asked for the recipe.
—Lisbeth Whitehead, Watertown, SD

Prep: 20 min. • **Cook:** 40 min.
Makes: 8 servings

6   bacon strips
4   medium potatoes, thinly sliced
3   cups broccoli florets
3   medium carrots, thinly sliced
1   medium onion, chopped
½   cup thinly sliced celery
¼   tsp. salt
⅛   tsp. pepper
1   lb. fully cooked Polish sausage

In a large skillet over medium-high heat, cook the bacon until crisp. Drain on paper towels, reserving 2 Tbsp. drippings in skillet. Add the next five ingredients to drippings. Reduce heat to medium; cook, covered, stirring frequently, until vegetables are crisp-tender, 10-15 minutes. Sprinkle with salt and pepper. Cut sausage diagonally into ½-in. slices; place on top of the vegetables. Reduce heat; simmer, covered, stirring frequently, about 10 minutes. Crumble bacon; sprinkle on top.
1 cup: 382 cal., 25g fat (10g sat. fat), 52mg chol., 707mg sod., 26g carb. (5g sugars, 4g fiber), 12g pro.

CHILES RELLENOS QUICHE

I keep the ingredients for this recipe on hand so I can whip up a tasty meal on demand. It's great any time of day.
—Linda Miritello, Mesa, AZ

Prep: 25 min. • **Bake:** 35 min.
Makes: 6 servings

      Pastry for single-crust pie (9 in.)
2   Tbsp. cornmeal
1½ cups shredded Monterey Jack cheese
1   cup shredded cheddar cheese
1   can (4 oz.) chopped green chiles
3   large eggs
¾   cup sour cream
1   Tbsp. minced fresh cilantro
2   to 4 drops hot pepper sauce, optional

1. In a pie plate, line the unpricked crust with a double thickness of heavy-duty foil. Bake at 450° for 8 minutes. Remove foil; bake 5 minutes longer. Cool on a wire rack. Reduce heat to 350°.
2. Sprinkle cornmeal over bottom of crust. In a small bowl, combine cheeses; set aside ½ cup for topping. Add the chiles to the remaining cheese mixture; sprinkle into the crust.
3. In a small bowl, whisk the eggs, sour cream, cilantro and hot pepper sauce if desired. Pour into crust; sprinkle with reserved cheese mixture.
4. Bake until a knife inserted in the center comes out clean, 35-40 minutes. Let stand for 5 minutes before cutting.
1 slice: 444 cal., 31g fat (18g sat. fat), 178mg chol., 520mg sod., 23g carb. (3g sugars, 1g fiber), 17g pro.

SLOPPY JOE PIE

I don't hear many compliments on this dish...folks are always too busy eating it! I developed the recipe by grabbing a few ingredients from my refrigerator and cupboards one night when I needed an easy, fast dinner.
—Kathy McCreary, Goddard, KS

- -

Prep: 30 min. • **Bake:** 20 min.
Makes: 7 servings

- 1 lb. ground beef
- ½ cup chopped onion
- 1 can (8 oz.) tomato sauce
- 1 can (8¾ oz.) whole kernel corn, drained
- ¼ cup water
- 1 envelope sloppy joe mix
- 2 tubes (6 oz. each) refrigerated buttermilk biscuits
- 2 Tbsp. whole milk
- ⅓ cup cornmeal
- 1 cup shredded cheddar cheese, divided
  Minced fresh parsley, optional

1. Preheat oven to 375°. In a large skillet, cook beef and onion over medium heat until meat is no longer pink; drain. Stir in tomato sauce, corn, water and sloppy joe seasoning; cook over medium heat until bubbly. Reduce heat and simmer 5 minutes; remove from heat and set aside.

2. Separate biscuits; flatten each to a 3½-in. circle. Place milk and cornmeal in separate shallow bowls; dip both sides into milk and then into cornmeal. Place seven biscuits around the sides and three on the bottom of an ungreased 9-in. pie plate.

3. Press the biscuits together to form a crust, leaving a scalloped edge around rim. Sprinkle with ½ cup cheese. Spoon meat mixture over cheese.

4. Bake until crust is deep golden brown, 20-25 minutes. Sprinkle with remaining cheese and, if desired, fresh parsley. Let stand 5 minutes before serving.

1 piece: 401 cal., 20g fat (8g sat. fat), 56mg chol., 1197 sod., 38g carb. (6g sugars, 2g fiber), 20g pro.

TEST KITCHEN TIP
Craving barbecue? This recipe is even easier using premade (or leftover) barbecued pork or beef instead of the sloppy joe mix, beef and onion. Just add 12-16 oz. of precooked barbecue meat to the drained corn.

CHEESEBURGER & FRIES CASSEROLE

Kids love this meal because it combines two of their favorite foods. I like the fact that I can whip it up with just a few items, and in almost no prep time.
—Karen Owen, Rising Sun, IN

Prep: 10 min. • **Bake:** 50 min.
Makes: 8 servings

2 lbs. lean ground beef (90% lean)
1 can (10¾ oz.) condensed golden mushroom soup, undiluted
1 can (10¾ oz.) condensed cheddar cheese soup, undiluted
1 pkg. (20 oz.) frozen crinkle-cut french fries

1. Preheat oven to 350°. In a large skillet, cook beef over medium heat until no longer pink; drain. Stir in the soups. Pour into a greased 13x9-in. baking dish.
2. Arrange the french fries on top. Bake, uncovered, until fries are golden brown, 50-55 minutes.
1½ cups: 352 cal., 17g fat (5g sat. fat), 62mg chol., 668mg sod., 25g carb. (1g sugars, 2g fiber), 25g pro.

OVEN-BARBECUED PORK CHOPS

I grew up on this tasty main course, and now I prepare it for my family. The chops are delicious with scalloped potatoes and home-baked bread.
—Teresa King, Whittier, CA

- -

Prep: 10 min. • **Bake:** 40 min.
Makes: 6 servings

6 bone-in pork loin chops (¾ in. thick)
1 Tbsp. Worcestershire sauce
2 Tbsp. vinegar
2 tsp. brown sugar
½ tsp. pepper
½ tsp. chili powder
½ tsp. paprika
¾ cup ketchup
⅓ cup hot water

Place the chops, overlapping slightly if necessary, in a large cast-iron or other ovenproof skillet. Combine remaining ingredients; pour over meat. Bake, uncovered, at 375° for 40 minutes, turning chops halfway through cooking.
1 pork chop: 359 cal., 18g fat (7g sat. fat), 111mg chol., 491mg sod., 10g carb. (10g sugars, 0 fiber), 36g pro.

FREEZE IT
ITALIAN SAUSAGE RIGATONI BAKE

This dish combines all of our favorite Italian flavors, but the fresh mozzarella really sets it apart!
—Blair Lonergan, Rochelle, VA

- -

Prep: 30 min. • **Bake:** 25 min.
Makes: 2 casseroles (4 servings each)

1 pkg. (16 oz.) rigatoni
1 lb. bulk Italian sausage
½ lb. sliced fresh mushrooms
1 medium sweet red pepper, chopped
5 cups marinara sauce
¼ cup grated Parmesan cheese
2 Tbsp. half-and-half cream
1 lb. sliced part-skim mozzarella cheese

1. Preheat oven to 375°. Cook the rigatoni according to package directions; drain.

2. In a large skillet, cook sausage, mushrooms and pepper over medium-high heat until the sausage is no longer pink and vegetables are tender, breaking up sausage into crumbles, 8-10 minutes; drain. Stir in the marinara sauce, Parmesan cheese and cream. Add rigatoni and toss to coat.
3. In each of two greased 8-in. square baking dishes, layer one-fourth of the rigatoni mixture and one-fourth of the mozzarella cheese. Repeat layers. Bake, uncovered, until heated through and the cheese is melted, 25-35 minutes. (Cover loosely with foil if tops brown too quickly.)
Freeze option: Cool unbaked casseroles; cover and freeze. To use, partially thaw in refrigerator overnight. Remove from refrigerator 30 minutes before baking. Preheat oven to 375°. Bake casseroles as directed, increasing time as necessary to heat through and for a thermometer inserted in center to read 165°.
1 serving: 535 cal., 26g fat (11g sat. fat), 71mg chol., 774mg sod., 48g carb. (4g sugars, 3g fiber), 29g pro.

SPINACH SKILLET BAKE

Over the years, I've tried to instill a love of cooking in our children. We've enjoyed a variety of delicious recipes, including this savory, comforting stovetop entree.
—Nancy Robaidek, Krakow, WI

- -

Prep: 30 min. • **Bake:** 20 min.
Makes: 6 servings

- 1 lb. ground beef
- 1 medium onion, chopped
- 1 pkg. (10 oz.) frozen chopped spinach, thawed and squeezed dry
- 1 can (4 oz.) mushroom stems and pieces, drained
- 1 tsp. garlic salt
- 1 tsp. dried basil
- ¼ cup butter
- ¼ cup all-purpose flour
- ½ tsp. salt
- 2 cups whole milk
- 1 cup shredded Monterey Jack cheese or part-skim mozzarella cheese
  Biscuits, optional

1. In a 10-in. cast-iron or other ovenproof skillet, cook beef and onion over medium heat until the meat is no longer pink; drain. Add the spinach, mushrooms, garlic salt and basil. Cover and cook for 5 minutes.
2. In a saucepan, melt butter over medium heat. Stir in the flour and salt until smooth. Gradually add milk. bring to a boil; cook and stir until thickened, about 2 minutes. Stir in cheese. Pour over meat mixture; mix well. Reduce heat; cook, covered, until heated through. If desired, serve with biscuits.
Note: To avoid ending up with lumps in the white sauce, stir with a whisk while it cooks.
1 serving: 351 cal., 23g fat (13g sat. fat), 85mg chol., 872mg sod., 13g carb. (6g sugars, 2g fiber), 23g pro.

CHEDDAR-HAM OVEN OMELET

We had a family reunion for 50 relatives from the U.S. and Canada, and it took four pans of this hearty, five-ingredient omelet to feed the crowd. Bowls of fresh fruit and an assortment of muffins helped round out our menu.
—Betty Abrey, Imperial, SK

- -

Prep: 15 min. • **Bake:** 40 min. + standing
Makes: 12 servings

- 16 large eggs
- 2 cups whole milk
- 2 cups shredded cheddar cheese
- ¾ cup cubed fully cooked ham
- 6 green onions, chopped

1. Preheat the oven to 350°. In a large bowl, whisk eggs and milk. Stir in cheese, ham and onions. Pour mixture into a greased 13x9-in. baking dish.
2. Bake, uncovered, until a knife inserted in the center comes out clean, 40-45 minutes. Let stand 10 minutes before cutting.
1 serving: 208 cal., 14g fat (7g sat. fat), 314mg chol., 330mg sod., 4g carb. (3g sugars, 0 fiber), 15g pro.

TEST KITCHEN TIP
Check the freshness of an uncooked egg by placing it in a glass of cold water. If the egg is fresh, it will remain on the bottom of the glass. If the egg floats to the surface of the water, it is not fresh and should not be used. If it stands upright and bobs on the bottom, it is less than fresh but fine to use.

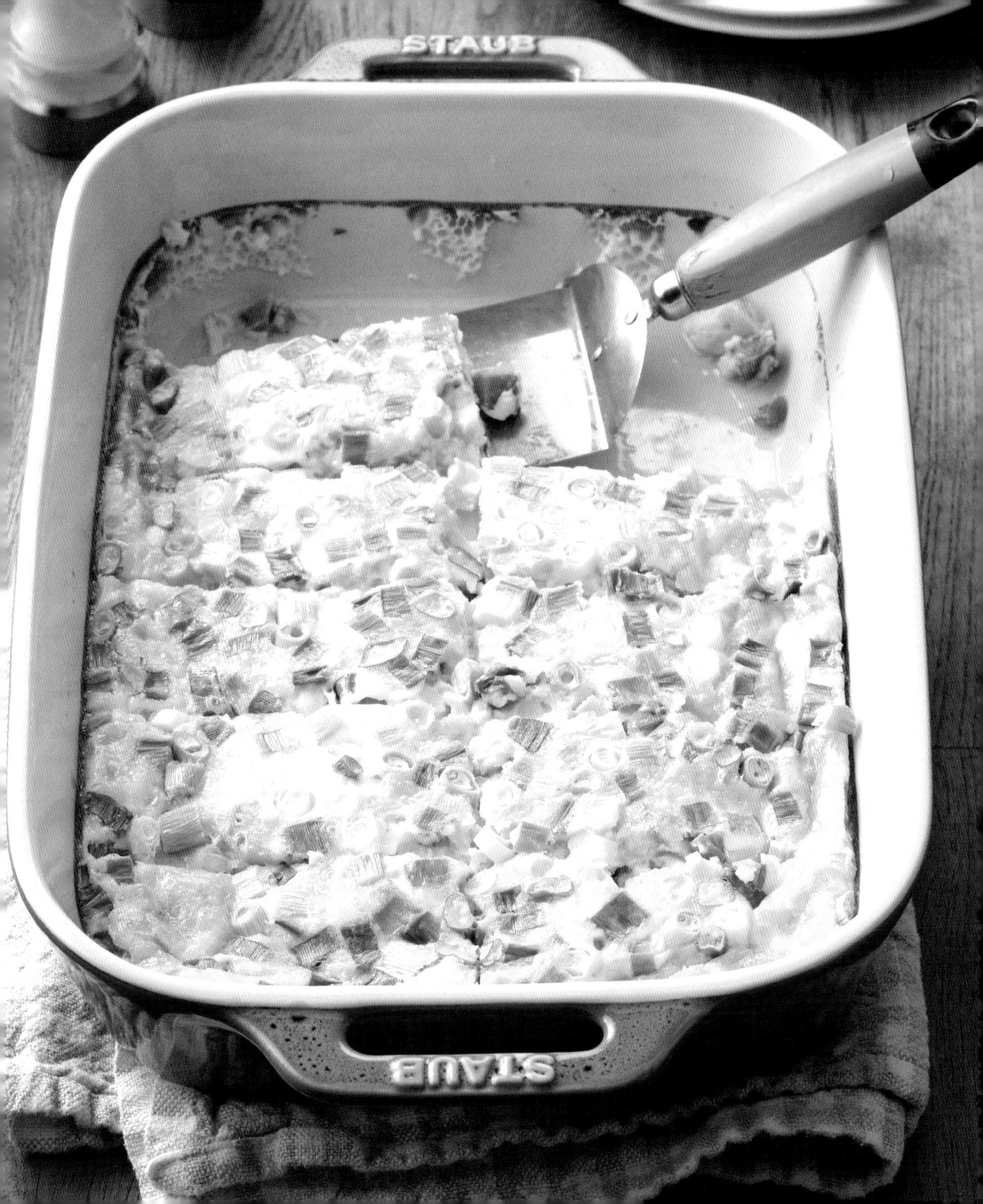
STAUB
STAUB

RHUBARB-APRICOT BARBECUED CHICKEN

Springtime brings back memories of the rhubarb that grew beside my childhood home. When I found ruby red stalks in the store, I created this recipe for them. My family gives it a big thumbs up.
—Laurie Hudson, Westville, FL

- -

Prep: 30 min. • **Grill:** 30 min.
Makes: 6 servings

1	Tbsp. olive oil
1	cup finely chopped sweet onion
1	garlic clove, minced
2	cups chopped fresh or frozen rhubarb
¾	cup ketchup
⅔	cup water
⅓	cup apricot preserves
¼	cup cider vinegar
¼	cup molasses
1	Tbsp. honey Dijon mustard
2	tsp. finely chopped chipotle pepper in adobo sauce
5	tsp. barbecue seasoning, divided
1¼	tsp. salt, divided
¾	tsp. pepper, divided
12	chicken drumsticks (about 4 lbs.)

1. In a large saucepan, heat oil over medium heat. Add onion; cook and stir until tender, 4-6 minutes. Add garlic; cook 1 minute longer. Stir in rhubarb, ketchup, water, preserves, vinegar, molasses, mustard, chipotle pepper, 1 tsp. barbecue seasoning, ¼ tsp. salt and ¼ tsp. pepper. Bring to a boil. Reduce heat; simmer, uncovered, until rhubarb is tender, 8-10 minutes. Puree the rhubarb mixture using an immersion blender, or cool slightly and puree in a blender. Reserve 2 cups sauce for serving.
2. Meanwhile, in a small bowl, mix the remaining barbecue seasoning, salt and pepper; sprinkle over chicken. On a lightly oiled grill rack, grill chicken, covered, over indirect medium heat 15 minutes. Turn; grill 15-20 minutes longer, brushing occasionally with remaining sauce, until a thermometer reads 170°-175°. Serve with reserved sauce.
2 chicken drumsticks with ⅓ cup sauce: 469 cal., 19g fat (5g sat. fat), 126mg chol., 1801mg sod., 35g carb. (28g sugars, 1g fiber), 39g pro.

SPEEDY SURPRISE
"This sauce did not disappoint! It was a little tangy, yet slightly sweet. Next time we will try it over grilled pork chops."
—LPHJKITCHEN, TASTEOFHOME.COM

ROASTED KIELBASA & VEGETABLES

The first reason I like this dish, featuring kielbasa and veggies, is because it's so hearty. Second, it's a one-pan meal. That's a win-win dinner to me!
—Marietta Slater, Justin, TX

- -

Prep: 20 min. • **Bake:** 40 min.
Makes: 6 servings

3   medium sweet potatoes, peeled and cut into 1-in. pieces
1   large sweet onion, cut into 1-in. pieces
4   medium carrots, cut into 1-in. pieces
2   Tbsp. olive oil
1   lb. smoked kielbasa or Polish sausage, halved and cut into 1-in. pieces
1   medium yellow summer squash, cut into 1-in. pieces
1   medium zucchini, cut into 1-in. pieces
¼   tsp. salt
¼   tsp. pepper
     Dijon mustard, optional

1. Preheat oven to 400°. Divide sweet potatoes, onion and carrots between two greased 15x10x1-in. baking pans. Drizzle with oil; toss to coat. Roast 25 minutes, stirring occasionally.

2. Add the kielbasa, squash and zucchini to pans; sprinkle with salt and pepper. Roast until vegetables are tender, 15-20 minutes longer. Transfer to a serving bowl; toss to combine. If desired, serve with mustard.

1⅔ cups: 378 cal., 25g fat (8g sat. fat), 51mg chol., 954mg sod., 26g carb. (12g sugars, 4g fiber), 13g pro.

CHILI CHEESE DOG CASSEROLE

Big and little kids alike dive into this filling, comforting dish. With its warm cornbread crust, this recipe is a keeper.
—*Taste of Home* Test Kitchen

Prep: 20 min. • **Bake:** 30 min.
Makes: 6 servings

- 1 pkg. (8½ oz.) cornbread/muffin mix
- 1 cup chopped green pepper
- ½ cup chopped onion
- ½ cup chopped celery
- 1 Tbsp. olive oil
- 1 pkg. (1 lb.) hot dogs, halved lengthwise and cut into bite-sized pieces
- 1 can (15 oz.) chili with beans
- 2 Tbsp. brown sugar
- ½ tsp. garlic powder
- ½ tsp. chili powder
- 1 cup shredded cheddar cheese, divided

1. Prepare the cornbread batter according to the package directions. Spread half the batter into a greased 8-in. square baking dish; set aside.
2. In a large skillet, saute the green pepper, onion and celery in oil until crisp-tender. Stir in hot dogs; saute until lightly browned, 3-4 minutes longer. Stir in the chili, brown sugar, garlic powder and chili powder; heat through. Stir in ¾ cup cheese.
3. Spoon over cornbread batter; top with remaining cornbread batter. Sprinkle remaining cheese over the top.
4. Bake the casserole, uncovered, at 350° until a toothpick inserted in the center comes out clean, 28-32 minutes. Let stand for 5 minutes before serving.
1 piece: 615 cal., 37g fat (16g sat. fat), 115mg chol., 1585mg sod., 49g carb. (18g sugars, 4g fiber), 22g pro.

FREEZE IT
CHICKEN SPAGHETTI CASSEROLE

This creamy, cheesy casserole is so homey, second helpings are a must!
—Lynne German, Woodland Hills, CA

Prep: 25 min. • **Bake:** 25 min.
Makes: 6 servings

- 8 oz. uncooked spaghetti, broken into 3-in. pieces
- 3 cups cubed cooked chicken
- 1 can (10¾ oz.) condensed cream of chicken soup, undiluted
- 1 medium onion, chopped
- 1 cup 2% milk
- 1 cup shredded sharp cheddar cheese, divided
- 1 cup shredded Swiss cheese, divided
- 1 can (4 oz.) mushroom stems and pieces, drained
- ½ cup chopped roasted sweet red peppers
- 3 Tbsp. mayonnaise
- 1½ tsp. steak seasoning
- ½ tsp. dried basil

1. Cook spaghetti according to package directions. Meanwhile, in a large bowl, combine the chicken, soup, onion, milk, ½ cup cheddar cheese, ½ cup Swiss cheese, mushrooms, peppers, mayonnaise, steak seasoning and basil.
2. Drain spaghetti. Add to chicken mixture; toss to coat. Transfer to a greased 13x9-in. baking dish. Cover and bake at 350° for 20 minutes. Uncover; sprinkle with the remaining cheeses. Bake until the casserole is heated through and the cheese is melted, 5-10 minutes longer. Serve immediately or, before baking, cover and freeze casserole for up to 3 months.
To use frozen casserole: Thaw in the refrigerator overnight. Remove from the refrigerator 30 minutes before baking. Bake according to directions.
1⅓ cups: 549 cal., 25g fat (11g sat. fat), 109mg chol., 957mg sod., 40g carb. (6g sugars, 2g fiber), 38g pro.

CHILES RELLENOS CASSEROLE

I love green chiles and cook with them often when I entertain. This easy version of the classic Mexican dish gives you big pepper taste in every meaty bite.
—Nadine Estes, Alto, NM

Prep: 15 min. • **Bake:** 45 min.
Makes: 6 servings

- 1 can (7 oz.) whole green chiles
- 1½ cups shredded Colby-Monterey Jack cheese
- ¾ lb. ground beef
- ¼ cup chopped onion
- 1 cup whole milk
- 4 large eggs
- ¼ cup all-purpose flour
- ¼ tsp. salt
- ⅛ tsp. pepper

1. Split chiles and remove seeds; dry on paper towels. Arrange chiles on the bottom of a greased 2-qt. baking dish. Top with cheese. In a skillet, cook beef and onion over medium heat until meat is no longer pink; drain. Spoon over the cheese.
2. In a bowl, beat milk, eggs, flour, salt and pepper until smooth; pour over beef mixture. Bake, uncovered, at 350° until a knife inserted in the center comes out clean, 45-50 minutes. Let casserole stand for 5 minutes before serving.
1 piece: 321 cal., 20g fat (11g sat. fat), 212mg chol., 406mg sod., 9g carb. (3g sugars, 0 fiber), 24g pro.

GAME DAY GUMBO

Tailgating brings our friends together to share great food. Gumbo is a southern tradition that feeds our hungry crowd.
—Heidi Jobe, Carrollton, GA

Prep: 20 min. • **Cook:** 40 min.
Makes: 10 servings (3¾ qt.)

- 6 Tbsp. butter, divided
- 1 lb. boneless skinless chicken thighs, cut into 1-in. pieces
- 1 pkg. (13½ oz.) smoked beef sausage, halved lengthwise and sliced
- 2 medium carrots, chopped
- 2 celery ribs, chopped
- 1 small sweet red pepper, chopped
- 3 garlic cloves, minced
- ¼ cup all-purpose flour
- 4 cups chicken stock
- 4 cups water
- 1 can (14½ oz.) no-salt-added diced tomatoes, undrained
- 1 pkg. (8 oz.) jambalaya mix
- 1 pkg. (8 oz.) dirty rice mix

1. In a Dutch oven, heat 2 Tbsp. butter over medium-high heat. Add chicken; cook and stir until browned. Remove from pan.
2. In same pan, brown the sausage over medium heat; remove from pan and drain on paper towels.
3. Heat remaining butter in same pan over medium heat. Add the carrots, celery and pepper; cook and stir until tender. Add the garlic; cook 1 minute longer.
4. Stir in flour until blended; gradually stir in the stock, water, tomatoes and rice mixes. Return chicken and sausage to pan. Bring to a boil. Reduce heat; simmer, covered, until rice is tender, 20-25 minutes.
1½ cups: 433 cal., 20g fat (9g sat. fat), 69mg chol., 1385mg sod., 44g carb. (4g sugars, 1g fiber), 19g pro.

5 INGREDIENT
BEEF & RICE ENCHILADAS

When there are young children in the house, you want foods that are a snap to prepare. Loaded with beef, cheese and a flavorful rice mix, these enchiladas fit the bill. But they're so good that I make them for company, too.
—Jennifer Smith, Colona, IL

- -

Prep: 30 min. • **Bake:** 20 min.
Makes: 10 enchiladas

- 1 pkg. (6.8 oz.) Spanish rice and pasta mix
- 1 lb. ground beef
- 2 cans (10 oz. each) enchilada sauce, divided
- 10 flour tortillas (8 in.), warmed
- 1⅔ cups shredded cheddar cheese, divided

1. Prepare rice mix according to package directions. Meanwhile, in a large skillet, cook beef over medium heat until no longer pink; drain. Stir in the Spanish rice and 1¼ cups enchilada sauce.

2. Spoon about ⅔ cup beef mixture down the center of each tortilla. Top each with 1 Tbsp. cheese; roll up.

3. Place in an ungreased 13x9-in. baking dish. Top with the remaining enchilada sauce and cheese. Bake, uncovered, at 350° until cheese is melted, 20-25 minutes.

1 enchilada: 415 cal., 17g fat (8g sat. fat), 47mg chol., 1141mg sod., 46g carb. (3g sugars, 3g fiber), 20g pro.

FRENCH ONION SOUP

Our daughter and I enjoy spending time together cooking, but our days are busy, so we appreciate quick and tasty recipes like this one. Hot and delicious, this soup hits the spot for lunch or dinner.
—Sandra Chambers, Carthage, MS

- -

Prep: 30 min. • **Cook:** 30 min.
Makes: 6 servings

- 4 cups thinly sliced onions
- 1 garlic clove, minced
- ¼ cup butter
- 6 cups water
- 8 beef bouillon cubes
- 1 tsp. Worcestershire sauce
- 6 slices French bread (¾ in. thick), buttered and toasted
- 6 slices Swiss cheese

1. In a large covered saucepan, cook onions and garlic in butter over medium-low heat for 8-10 minutes or until tender and golden, stirring occasionally. Add water, bouillon and Worcestershire sauce; bring to a boil. Reduce the heat; cover and simmer for 30 minutes.

2. Ladle hot soup into six ovenproof bowls. Top each with a piece of French bread. Cut each slice of cheese in half and place over the bread. Broil until cheese melts. Serve soup immediately.

1 serving: 244 cal., 15g fat (10g sat. fat), 46mg chol., 1387mg sod., 17g carb. (5g sugars, 2g fiber), 9g pro.

REUBEN BREAD PUDDING

Our Aunt Renee always brought this casserole to family picnics in Chicago. It became so popular that she started bringing two or three. I have also used dark rye bread or marbled rye and ham instead of corned beef.
—Johnna Johnson, Scottsdale, AZ

Prep: 20 min. • **Bake:** 35 min.
Makes: 6 servings

- 4 cups cubed rye bread (about 6 slices)
- 2 Tbsp. butter, melted
- 2 cups cubed or shredded cooked corned beef (about ½ lb.)
- 1 can (14 oz.) sauerkraut, rinsed and well drained
- 1 cup shredded Swiss cheese, divided
- 3 large eggs
- 1 cup 2% milk
- ⅓ cup prepared Thousand Island salad dressing
- 1½ tsp. prepared mustard
- ¼ tsp. pepper

1. Preheat oven to 350°. In a large bowl, toss bread cubes with butter. Stir in corned beef, sauerkraut and ½ cup cheese; transfer to a greased 11x7-in. baking dish.

2. In same bowl, whisk eggs, milk, salad dressing, mustard and pepper; pour over top. Bake, uncovered, 30 minutes. Sprinkle with remaining cheese. Bake until golden and a knife inserted in the center comes out clean, 5-7 minutes longer.

1 serving: 390 cal., 25g fat (10g sat. fat), 165mg chol., 1295mg sod., 21g carb. (7g sugars, 3g fiber), 19g pro.

NEW ENGLAND BEAN & BOG CASSOULET

When I moved to New England, I embraced the local cuisine. My cassoulet with baked beans pays tribute to a French classic and to New England.
—Devon Delaney, Westport, CT

- -

Prep: 15 min. • **Cook:** 35 min.
Makes: 8 servings (3½ qt.)

    5   Tbsp. olive oil, divided
    8   boneless skinless chicken
        thighs (about 2 lbs.)
    1   pkg. (12 oz.) fully cooked
        Italian chicken sausage links,
        cut into ½-in. slices
    4   shallots, finely chopped
    2   tsp. minced fresh rosemary or
        ½ tsp. dried rosemary, crushed
    2   tsp. minced fresh thyme
        or ½ tsp. dried thyme
    1   can (28 oz.) fire-roasted
        diced tomatoes, undrained
    1   can (16 oz.) baked beans
    1   cup chicken broth
    ½   cup fresh or frozen cranberries
    3   day-old croissants, cubed
        (about 6 cups)
    ½   tsp. lemon-pepper seasoning
    2   Tbsp. minced fresh parsley

1. Preheat oven to 400°. In a Dutch oven, heat 2 Tbsp. oil over medium heat. In batches, brown chicken thighs on both sides; remove from the pan, reserving drippings. Add sausage; cook and stir until lightly browned. Remove from pan.
2. In same pan, heat 1 Tbsp. oil over medium heat. Add shallots, rosemary and thyme; cook and stir until the shallots are tender, 1-2 minutes. Stir in tomatoes, beans, broth and cranberries. Return the chicken and sausage to pan; bring to a boil. Bake, covered, until the chicken is tender, 20-25 minutes.
3. Toss croissant pieces with remaining oil; sprinkle with lemon pepper. Arrange over chicken mixture. Bake the cassoulet, uncovered, until the croissants are golden brown, 12-15 minutes. Sprinkle with parsley.
1¾ cups: 500 cal., 26g fat (7g sat. fat), 127mg chol., 1050mg sod., 32g carb. (6g sugars, 5g fiber), 35g pro.

SPEEDY SURPRISE

"This was amazing. The flavors were complex, sweet, savory and all-around wonderful. I was surprised how easy it was to prepare. It's now in our regular rotation of dishes!"
—CBRIDENBECKER,
TASTEOFHOME.COM

MAKEOVER
MAC & CHEESE

Macaroni and cheese just may be king of the comfort foods. This sensational version is bubbling with creamy, cheesy goodness—but is a little lighter on calories.
—April Taylor, Holcomb, KS

Prep: 30 min. • **Bake:** 25 min.
Makes: 10 servings

- 1   pkg. (16 oz.) elbow macaroni
- ⅓   cup all-purpose flour
- ½   tsp. garlic powder
- ½   tsp. pepper
- ¼   tsp. salt
- 2   cups fat-free half-and-half
- 2   Tbsp. butter
- 2   cups fat-free milk
- 3   cups shredded reduced-fat sharp cheddar cheese

OPTIONAL TOPPING
- 2   Tbsp. butter
- 1   medium onion, chopped
- 3   cups soft bread crumbs
- ½   cup shredded reduced-fat cheddar cheese

OPTIONAL GARNISH
- Sliced cherry tomatoes and minced chives

1. Preheat oven to 350°. Cook macaroni according to package directions; drain.
2. Meanwhile, in small bowl, whisk flour, seasonings and half-and-half until smooth. In a large saucepan, melt butter over medium heat. Stir in half-and-half mixture. Add milk. Bring to a gentle boil, stirring constantly; remove from heat. Add cheese; stir until melted. Stir in macaroni. Transfer to a 13x9-in. baking dish coated with cooking spray.

3. For optional topping, in a large skillet, heat butter over medium-high heat. Add onion; cook and stir until tender. Add bread crumbs; cook and stir 2 minutes longer. Sprinkle over macaroni mixture; top with the cheese.

4. Bake, uncovered, until heated through, 25-30 minutes. Garnish as desired.
1 cup: 343 cal., 11g fat (6g sat. fat), 31mg chol., 354mg sod., 45g carb. (8g sugars, 2g fiber), 18g pro.

2. In a small bowl, mix paprika and the remaining salt, rosemary and pepper. Sprinkle chicken with paprika mixture; arrange over vegetables. Roast until a thermometer inserted in chicken reads 170°-175° and vegetables are just tender, 35-40 minutes.

3. Remove chicken to a serving platter; keep warm. Top vegetables with spinach. Roast until vegetables are tender and spinach is wilted, 8-10 minutes longer. Stir vegetables to combine; serve with chicken.

1 chicken thigh with 1 cup vegetables: 357 cal., 14g fat (3g sat. fat), 87mg chol., 597mg sod., 28g carb. (3g sugars, 4g fiber), 28g pro. **Diabetic exchanges:** 4 lean meat, 1½ starch, 1 vegetable, 1 fat.

TEST KITCHEN TIP
Prepare your sheet pan the night before and just pop it in the preheated oven to bake it. This actually helps to deeply flavor the chicken. A win-win! If you want an even richer dish, you can use skin-on chicken, and if you want a lighter dish, use bone-in chicken breasts. Be sure to cook bone-in breasts just to 165-170 degrees, since leaner meat can become dry at higher temperatures.

EAT SMART
PAN-ROASTED CHICKEN & VEGETABLES

This sheet-pan supper tastes like it took hours of hands-on time, but it actually takes just minutes to prep the ingredients for hands-off baking. The rosemary gives it a very rich flavor, and the meat juices cook the veggies to perfection. So easy!
—Sherri Melotik, Oak Creek, WI

- -

Prep: 15 min. • **Bake:** 45 min.
Makes: 6 servings

2 lbs. red potatoes (about 6 medium), cut into ¾-in. pieces
1 large onion, coarsely chopped
2 Tbsp. olive oil
3 garlic cloves, minced
1¼ tsp. salt, divided
1 tsp. dried rosemary, crushed, divided
¾ tsp. pepper, divided
½ tsp. paprika
6 bone-in chicken thighs (about 2¼ lbs.), skin removed
6 cups fresh baby spinach (about 6 oz.)

1. Preheat oven to 425°. In a large bowl, combine potatoes, onion, oil, garlic, ¾ tsp. salt, ½ tsp. rosemary and ½ tsp. pepper; toss to coat. Transfer to a 15x10x1-in. baking pan coated with cooking spray.

CAMPFIRE HASH

In our area we are able to camp almost all year-round. My family invented this recipe using ingredients we all love so we could enjoy them on the campfire. This hearty meal tastes so good after a full day of outdoor activities.
—Janet Danilow, Winkleman, AZ

Prep: 15 min. • **Cook:** 40 min.
Makes: 6 servings

- 1 large onion, chopped
- 2 Tbsp. canola oil
- 2 garlic cloves, minced
- 4 large potatoes, peeled and cubed (about 2 lbs.)
- 1 lb. smoked kielbasa or Polish sausage, halved and sliced
- 1 can (4 oz.) chopped green chiles
- 1 can (15¼ oz.) whole kernel corn, drained

1. In a large ovenproof skillet over medium heat, cook and stir onion in oil under tender. Add garlic; cook 1 minute longer. Add potatoes. Cook, uncovered, for 20 minutes, stirring occasionally.
2. Add kielbasa; cook and stir until the meat and potatoes are tender and browned, 10-15 minutes. Stir in chiles and corn; heat through.
1 serving: 535 cal., 26g fat (8g sat. fat), 51mg chol., 1097mg sod., 57g carb. (10g sugars, 6g fiber), 17g pro.

FREEZE IT
CHICKEN TATER BAKE

You'll please everyone in the family with this inviting dish. It tastes like chicken potpie with a crispy Tater Tot crust.
—Fran Allen, St. Louis, MO

Prep: 20 min. • **Bake:** 35 min.
Makes: 2 casseroles (6 servings each)

- 2 cans (10¾ oz. each) condensed cream of chicken soup, undiluted
- ½ cup 2% milk
- ¼ cup butter, cubed
- 3 cups cubed cooked chicken
- 1 pkg. (16 oz.) frozen peas and carrots, thawed
- 1½ cups shredded cheddar cheese, divided
- 1 pkg. (32 oz.) frozen Tater Tots

1. In a large saucepan, combine the soup, milk and butter. Cook and stir over medium heat until heated through. Remove from the heat; stir in the chicken, peas and carrots, and 1 cup cheese.
2. Transfer to two greased 8-in. square baking dishes. Top with Tater Tots.
3. Cover and freeze one casserole for up to 3 months. Bake the remaining casserole at 400° until bubbling, 25-30 minutes. Sprinkle with ¼ cup cheese; bake until the cheese is melted, about 5 minutes longer.

To use frozen casserole: Remove from the freezer 30 minutes before baking (do not thaw). Sprinkle with ¼ cup cheese. Cover and bake at 350° until heated through, 1½-1¾ hours.
1 serving: 356 cal., 21g fat (9g sat. fat), 61mg chol., 844mg sod., 29g carb. (3g sugars, 4g fiber), 18g pro.

5 INGREDIENT
SAUSAGE & PEPPER SHEET-PAN SANDWICHES

Sausage with peppers was always on the table when I was growing up. Here's how I do it the easy way. Just grab a sheet pan and the ingredients, then let your oven do all the work.

—Debbie Glasscock, Conway, AR

- -

Prep: 20 min. • **Bake:** 35 min.
Makes: 6 servings

1   **lb. uncooked sweet Italian turkey sausage links, roughly chopped**
3   **medium sweet red peppers, seeded and sliced**
1   **large onion, halved and sliced**
1   **Tbsp. olive oil**
6   **hot dog buns, split**
6   **slices provolone cheese**

1. Preheat oven to 375°. Place the sausage pieces in a 15x10x1-in. sheet pan, arranging peppers and onions around sausage. Drizzle olive oil over sausage and vegetables; bake, stirring the mixture after 15 minutes, until sausage is no longer pink and vegetables are tender, 30-35 minutes.
2. During last 5 minutes of baking, arrange buns cut side up in a second sheet pan; top each bun bottom with a cheese slice. Bake until buns are golden brown and cheese is melted. Spoon sausage and pepper mixture onto bun bottoms. Replace tops.

1 sandwich: 315 cal., 15g fat (5g sat. fat), 43mg chol., 672mg sod., 28g carb. (7g sugars, 2g fiber), 18g pro.

EAT SMART | FREEZE IT

CREAMLESS CREAMY SQUASH SOUP

Here's my go-to recipe for get-togethers with family and friends. Everyone asks for seconds, and they can't believe they are eating something so healthy and meat-free. It's also a smart option for many with food allergy issues.
—Sharon Verea, Thomasville, GA

- -

Prep: 20 min. • **Cook:** 35 min.
Makes: 8 servings (2 qt.)

2	Tbsp. olive oil
2	small onions, chopped
2	celery ribs, chopped
2	medium carrots, chopped
1	medium butternut squash (3 lbs.), peeled, seeded and cut into 1-in. cubes
1	medium sweet potato (about 8 oz.), peeled and cut into 1-in. cubes
1	yellow summer squash, halved lengthwise and sliced
4	garlic cloves, minced
4	cups vegetable broth
2	tsp. dried savory or herbes de Provence
¼	tsp. pepper
	Grated Parmesan cheese, optional

1. In a Dutch oven, heat oil over medium heat. Add onions, celery and carrots; cook and stir until onion is tender, 6-8 minutes. Stir in butternut squash, sweet potato and summer squash. Cook and stir until the squash and potato are lightly browned, 5-7 minutes. Add minced garlic; cook for 1 minute longer.

2. Add broth, savory and pepper; bring to a boil. Reduce heat; simmer, uncovered, until vegetables are tender, 20-25 minutes.

3. Puree soup using an immersion blender, or cool slightly and, in batches, puree in a blender and return to pan; heat through. If desired, serve with cheese.

Freeze option: Freeze cooled soup in freezer containers. To use, partially thaw in refrigerator overnight. Heat through in a saucepan, stirring occasionally and adding a little broth if necessary.

1 cup: 138 cal., 4g fat (1g sat. fat), 0 chol., 497mg sod., 27g carb. (8g sugars, 7g fiber), 2g pro. **Diabetic exchanges:** 1½ starch, 1 vegetable, ½ fat.

SPEEDY SURPRISE

"This soup is wonderful. It has a rich flavor. I will make this many times."
—AWAYOFLIFE,
TASTEOFHOME.COM

CORN DOG CASSEROLE

Reminiscent of traditional corn dogs, this fun main dish really hits the spot. It tastes especially good hot from the oven.
—Marcy Suzanne Olipane, Belleville, IL

- -

Prep: 25 min. • **Bake:** 30 min.
Makes: 12 servings

- 2 cups thinly sliced celery
- 2 Tbsp. butter
- 1½ cups sliced green onions
- 1½ lbs. hot dogs
- 2 large eggs
- 1½ cups 2% milk
- 2 tsp. rubbed sage
- ¼ tsp. pepper
- 2 pkg. (8½ oz. each) cornbread/muffin mix
- 2 cups shredded sharp cheddar cheese, divided

1. In a small skillet, saute celery in butter for 5 minutes. Add the onions; saute 5 minutes longer or until vegetables are tender. Place in a large bowl; set aside.
2. Preheat oven to 400°. Cut hot dogs into ½-in. slices. In the same skillet, saute the hot dogs until lightly browned; add to the vegetables, about 5 minutes. Set aside 1 cup.
3. In a large bowl, whisk eggs, milk, sage and pepper. Add remaining hot dog mixture. Stir in cornbread mixes. Add 1½ cups cheese. Spread into a shallow 3-qt. baking dish. Top with reserved hot dog mixture and the remaining cheese.
4. Bake, uncovered, until golden brown, about 30 minutes.

1 piece: 389 cal., 28g fat (14g sat. fat), 101mg chol., 925mg sod., 20g carb. (7g sugars, 1g fiber), 14g pro.

BUFFALO BLUE CHEESE MEAT LOAF

I made meat loaf with wing sauce for my guy, who prefers food with bold flavors. He went crazy for it, and now likes it even more than traditional Buffalo wings!
—Latesha Harris, Beaverton, OR

- -

Prep: 20 min. • **Bake:** 40 min.
Makes: 4 servings

- 1 large egg, lightly beaten
- 1 small onion, finely chopped
- ¼ cup panko (Japanese) bread crumbs
- ¼ cup Buffalo wing sauce
- 1 tsp. dried oregano
- ½ tsp. pepper
- 1 lb. ground beef

TOPPING

- ¼ cup Buffalo wing sauce
- ¼ cup crumbled blue cheese

1. Preheat oven to 350°. In a large bowl, combine the first six ingredients. Add beef; mix lightly but thoroughly. Shape into an 8x4-in. loaf in a greased 11x7-in. baking dish.
2. Bake 20 minutes. Spread the wing sauce over top; sprinkle with cheese. Bake until a thermometer reads 160°, 20-30 minutes longer. Let meat loaf stand for 5 minutes before slicing.

1 slice: 286 cal., 17g fat (7g sat. fat), 123mg chol., 1093mg sod., 7g carb. (1g sugars, 1g fiber), 24g pro.

ROASTED CHICKEN THIGHS WITH PEPPERS & POTATOES

My family loves this easy-to-make dish! Peppers and herbs from the garden make the chicken and potatoes special.
—Patricia Prescott, Manchester, NH

- -

Prep: 20 min. • **Bake:** 35 min.
Makes: 8 servings

- 2 lbs. red potatoes (about 6 medium)
- 2 large sweet red peppers
- 2 large green peppers
- 2 medium onions
- 2 Tbsp. olive oil, divided
- 4 tsp. minced fresh thyme or 1½ tsp. dried thyme, divided
- 3 tsp. minced fresh rosemary or 1 tsp. dried rosemary, crushed, divided
- 8 boneless skinless chicken thighs (about 2 lbs.)
- ½ tsp. salt
- ¼ tsp. pepper

1. Preheat oven to 450°. Cut the potatoes, peppers and onions into 1-in. pieces. Place vegetables in a roasting pan. Drizzle with 1 Tbsp. oil; sprinkle with 2 tsp. each thyme and rosemary and toss to coat. Place the chicken over vegetables. Brush chicken with remaining oil; sprinkle with remaining thyme and rosemary. Sprinkle the vegetables and chicken with salt and pepper.

2. Roast until a thermometer inserted in the chicken reads 170° and vegetables are tender, 35-40 minutes.

1 chicken thigh with 1 cup vegetables: 308 cal., 12g fat (3g sat. fat), 76mg chol., 221mg sod., 25g carb. (5g sugars, 4g fiber), 24g pro.
Diabetic exchanges: 3 lean meat, 1 starch, 1 vegetable, ½ fat.

SEAFOOD CASSEROLE

A family favorite, this hot rice dish is filled with plenty of seafood and veggies. It's hearty, homey and so simple!
—Nancy Billups, Princeton, IA

- -

Prep: 20 min. • **Bake:** 40 min.
Makes: 6 servings

- 1 pkg. (6 oz.) long grain and wild rice
- 1 lb. frozen crabmeat, thawed or 2½ cups canned lump crabmeat, drained
- 1 lb. cooked shrimp, peeled, deveined and cut into ½-in. pieces
- 2 celery ribs, chopped
- 1 medium onion, finely chopped
- ½ cup finely chopped green pepper
- 1 can (4 oz.) mushroom stems and pieces, drained
- 1 jar (2 oz.) diced pimientos, drained
- 1 cup mayonnaise
- 1 cup 2% milk
- ½ tsp. pepper
  Dash Worcestershire sauce
- ¼ cup dry bread crumbs

1. Cook rice according to the package directions. Meanwhile, preheat the oven to 375°.

2. In a large bowl, combine crab, shrimp, celery, onion, green pepper, mushrooms and pimientos. In a bowl, whisk mayonnaise, milk, pepper and Worcestershire sauce; stir into seafood mixture. Stir in rice.

3. Transfer to a greased 13x9-in. baking dish. Sprinkle with bread crumbs. Bake, uncovered, until bubbly, 40-50 minutes.

1½ cups: 585 cal., 34g fat (5g sat. fat), 209mg chol., 1045mg sod., 31g carb. (5g sugars, 2g fiber), 37g pro.

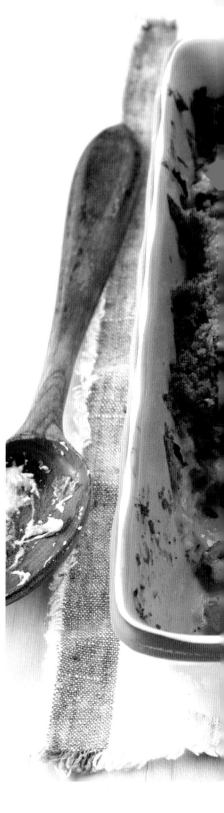

CHICKEN FLORENTINE CASSEROLE

Creamy and comforting, this chicken and spinach bake is sure to be a hit at dinnertime. The toasty bread crumb topping delivers a bit of a crunch.
—Dori Jackson, Gulf Breeze, FL

Prep: 20 min. • **Bake:** 40 min.
Makes: 6 servings

- 2 cups uncooked elbow macaroni
- 3 cups shredded cooked chicken
- 1 can (10¾ oz.) condensed cream of mushroom soup, undiluted
- 2 cups shredded Swiss cheese
- 1 pkg. (10 oz.) frozen creamed spinach, thawed
- ½ cup mayonnaise
- ¼ cup loosely packed minced fresh basil
- 1 tsp. garlic powder
- ½ tsp. dried thyme
- ½ tsp. pepper
- ½ cup seasoned bread crumbs
- 2 Tbsp. butter, melted

1. Preheat oven to 350°. Cook macaroni according to package directions.
2. Meanwhile, in a large bowl, combine the chicken, soup, cheese, spinach, mayonnaise, basil, garlic powder, thyme and pepper.
3. Drain macaroni; gently stir into chicken mixture. Transfer to an ungreased 2½-qt. baking dish. Toss the bread crumbs and butter; sprinkle over casserole.
4. Bake casserole, uncovered, until bubbly, 40-45 minutes.

1½ cups: 539 cal., 36g fat (13g sat. fat), 111mg chol., 1006mg sod., 17g carb. (4g sugars, 2g fiber), 36g pro.

RHUBARB PORK CHOP CASSEROLE

The usual reaction to this casserole is that it's a nice mix of sweet and tart—and an unusual use of rhubarb! I like rhubarb, but I'm not a dessert person. I always thought pies and cobblers shouldn't be the only ways to enjoy it.
—Jeanie Castor, Decatur, IL

- -

Prep: 20 min. • **Bake:** 40 min.
Makes: 4 servings

- 4 boneless pork loin chops (¾ in. thick and 4 oz. each)
- 1 Tbsp. canola oil
   Salt and pepper to taste
- 2 Tbsp. butter
- 3 cups soft bread crumbs
- 3 cups sliced fresh or frozen rhubarb (1-in. pieces)
- ½ cup packed brown sugar
- ¼ cup all-purpose flour
- 1 tsp. ground cinnamon

1. In a large skillet, brown pork chops in oil; sprinkle with salt and pepper. Remove and keep warm. Add butter to the drippings to melt; mix with bread crumbs. Remove from the heat.
2. In a large bowl, combine the rhubarb, sugar, flour and cinnamon; spoon into a greased 11x7-in. baking dish. Sprinkle the crumbs over top.
3. Cover with foil and bake at 350° for 25-30 minutes. Remove foil. Arrange pork chops on top. Bake, uncovered, until heated through, 10-15 minutes.
1 serving: 477 cal., 17g fat (7g sat. fat), 70mg chol., 254mg sod., 54g carb. (30g sugars, 3g fiber), 26g pro.

CREAM OF LENTIL SOUP

Lentil lovers will want a second bowl of this nourishing soup with a subtle touch of curry. It looks particularly appealing thanks to the color the fresh spinach adds.
—Kim Russell, North Wales, PA

- -

Prep: 20 min. • **Cook:** 35 min.
Makes: 10 servings (2½ qt.)

- 6 cups reduced-sodium chicken broth or vegetable broth, divided
- 2 cups dried lentils, rinsed
- 1 bay leaf
- 1 whole clove
- 1 medium red onion, chopped
- 2 celery ribs, chopped
- 2 Tbsp. butter
- 2 medium carrots, chopped
- 1 tsp. salt
- 1 tsp. sugar
- ½ tsp. curry powder
- ⅛ tsp. pepper
- 2 garlic cloves, minced
- 3 cups coarsely chopped fresh spinach
- 2 cups heavy whipping cream
- 1 Tbsp. lemon juice
- ⅓ cup minced fresh parsley

1. In a large saucepan, combine 4 cups of broth, lentils, bay leaf and clove. Bring to a boil. Reduce heat; cover and simmer until lentils are tender, 25-30 minutes.
2. Meanwhile, in a Dutch oven, saute onion and celery in butter until crisp-tender. Add the carrots, salt, sugar, curry powder and pepper; saute until vegetables are tender, 2-3 minutes longer. Add garlic; cook for 1 minute.
3. Drain lentils; discard bay leaf and clove. Add lentils to vegetable mixture. Stir in the spinach, remaining broth, cream, lemon juice and parsley; cook over low heat until heated through and spinach is wilted.
1 cup: 344 cal., 20g fat (13g sat. fat), 60mg chol., 635mg sod., 30g carb. (4g sugars, 5g fiber), 13g pro.

EAT SMART | FREEZE IT
CHICKEN BUTTERNUT CHILI

At our house, we just love a hearty comforting tomato-based chili with bold flavors! This version is loaded with veggies. You can also prepare the recipe in the slow cooker. Simply add the ingredients to the crock and cook over high heat for about 4 hours.
—Courtney Stultz, Weir, KS

- -

Prep: 20 min. • **Cook:** 35 min.
Makes: 4 servings

- 1 Tbsp. canola oil
- 2 medium carrots, chopped
- 2 celery ribs, chopped
- 1 medium onion, chopped
- 2 cups cubed peeled butternut squash
- 1 medium tomato, chopped
- 2 Tbsp. tomato paste
- 1 envelope reduced-sodium chili seasoning mix
- 2 cups chicken stock
- 1 cup cubed cooked chicken breast
   Chopped fresh cilantro

1. In a large saucepan, heat oil over medium heat; saute carrots, celery and onion until tender, 6-8 minutes.
2. Stir in squash, tomato, tomato paste, seasoning mix and stock; bring to a boil. Reduce heat; simmer, covered, until squash is tender, 20-25 minutes. Stir in chicken; heat through. Sprinkle with cilantro.
Freeze option: Freeze cooled chili in freezer containers. To use, partially thaw in the refrigerator overnight. Heat through in a saucepan, stirring occasionally.
1¼ cups: 201 cal., 5g fat (1g sat. fat), 27mg chol., 591mg sod., 25g carb. (8g sugars, 4g fiber), 15g pro. **Diabetic exchanges:** 2 lean meat, 1 starch, 1 vegetable, ½ fat.

5 INGREDIENT
BREADED RANCH CHICKEN

A coating of cornflakes, Parmesan and ranch dressing mix adds delectable flavor to the chicken pieces in this recipe and bakes to a pretty golden color. It's a mainstay main dish for us.
—Launa Shoemaker, Landrum, SC

- -

Prep: 10 min. • **Bake:** 45 min
Makes: 8 servings

- ¼ cup unsalted butter, melted
- ¾ cup crushed cornflakes
- ¾ cup grated Parmesan cheese
- 1 envelope ranch salad dressing mix
- 8 boneless skinless chicken breast halves (4 oz. each)

1. Place butter in a shallow bowl. In another shallow bowl, combine the cornflakes, cheese and salad dressing mix. Dip chicken in butter, then roll in the cornflake mixture to coat.
2. Place in a greased 13x9-in. baking dish. Bake, uncovered, at 350° for 45 minutes or until a thermometer reads 170°.
4 oz.: 200 cal., 14g fat (9g sat. fat), 44mg chol., 1031mg sod., 12g carb. (1g sugars, 0 fiber), 7g pro.

EASY & ELEGANT TENDERLOIN ROAST

I love the simplicity of the recipe. Just season the tenderloin and pop it in the oven. In an hour or so you have a great main dish to feed a crowd. This leaves you with more time to enjoy yourself and less time fussing in the kitchen.
—Mary Kandell, Huron, OH

- -

Prep: 10 min. • **Bake:** 45 min. + standing
Makes: 12 servings

- 1 beef tenderloin (5 lbs.)
- 2 Tbsp. olive oil
- 4 garlic cloves, minced
- 2 tsp. sea salt
- 1½ tsp. coarsely ground pepper

1. Preheat oven to 425°. Place roast on a rack in a shallow roasting pan. In a small bowl, mix the oil, garlic, salt and pepper; rub over roast.

2. Roast until the tenderloin reaches desired doneness (for medium-rare, a thermometer should read 135°; medium, 140°; medium-well, 145°), 45-65 minutes. Remove from oven; tent with foil. Let stand 15 minutes before slicing.

5 oz. cooked beef: 294 cal., 13g fat (5g sat. fat), 82mg chol., 394mg sod., 1g carb. (0 sugars, 0 fiber), 40g pro. **Diabetic exchanges:** 5 lean meat, ½ fat.

> ### TEST KITCHEN TIP
> Have some leftover roast? Turn to the beef section of the "Planned Overs" chapter starting on page 420. There you'll find tasty, time-saving ways to use it up!

SPINACH & SAUSAGE LENTIL SOUP

During the cooler months of the year, this soup makes regular appearances on our dinner table. It is approved by all, including my picky 6-year-old.
—Kalyn Gensic, Ardmore, OK

- -

Prep: 5 min. • **Cook:** 45 min.
Makes: 6 servings (2 qt.)

- 1 lb. bulk spicy pork sausage
- 1 cup dried brown lentils, rinsed
- 1 can (15 oz.) cannellini beans, rinsed and drained
- 1 carton (32 oz.) reduced-sodium chicken broth
- 1 cup water
- 1 can (14½ oz.) fire-roasted diced tomatoes, undrained
- 6 cups fresh spinach (about 4 oz.)
    Crumbled goat cheese, optional

1. In a Dutch oven, cook and crumble the sausage over medium heat until no longer pink, 5-7 minutes; drain.

2. Stir in lentils, beans, broth and water; bring to a boil. Reduce the heat; simmer, covered, until the lentils are tender, about 30 minutes. Stir in tomatoes; heat through.

3. Remove from heat; stir in spinach until wilted. If desired, serve with goat cheese.

Freeze option: Freeze cooled soup in freezer containers. To use, partially thaw in refrigerator overnight. Heat through in a saucepan, stirring occasionally.

1⅓ cups: 390 cal., 17g fat (5g sat. fat), 41mg chol., 1242mg sod., 37g carb. (3g sugars, 8g fiber), 22g pro.

GREAT PORK CHOP BAKE

A friend brought this hearty meat-and-potatoes bake to our home when I returned from the hospital with our youngest child. Since then, we have enjoyed it many times. It's a snap to throw together on a busy day, then pop in the oven to bake. The tender chops, potato wedges and golden gravy are both simple and satisfying.

—Rosie Glenn, Los Alamos, NM

- -

Prep: 10 min. • **Bake:** 50 min.
Makes: 6 servings

- 1 can (10¾ oz.) condensed cream of chicken soup, undiluted
- 3 Tbsp. ketchup
- 2 Tbsp. Worcestershire sauce
- ½ tsp. salt
- ¼ tsp. pepper
- 4 medium potatoes, cut into ½-in. wedges
- 1 medium onion, sliced into rings
- 6 bone-in pork loin chops (¾ in. thick and 8 oz. each)
- 1 Tbsp. canola oil

1. In a bowl, combine the soup, ketchup, Worcestershire sauce, salt and pepper. Add potatoes and onion; toss to coat. Transfer to a greased 13x9-in. baking dish. Cover and bake at 350° for 40 minutes.
2. Meanwhile, in a skillet, brown pork chops in oil. Place chops on top of potatoes and onions. Bake, covered, until a thermometer reads 145° and the potatoes are tender, 10-15 minutes longer.

1 serving: 520 cal., 24g fat (8g sat. fat), 115mg chol., 801mg sod., 34g carb. (5g sugars, 4g fiber), 40g pro.

HAM & RICE HOT DISH

One of my best friends shared this recipe with me. My family loves it since it includes one of our favorite vegetables, broccoli. It's a delicious and colorful way to use up leftover ham.

—Margaret Allen, Abingdon, VA

- -

Prep: 20 min. • **Bake:** 30 min.
Makes: 8 servings

- 2 pkg. (10 oz. each) frozen cut broccoli
- 2 cups cooked rice
- 6 Tbsp. butter, cubed
- 2 cups fresh bread crumbs (about 2½ slices)
- 1 medium onion, chopped
- 3 Tbsp. all-purpose flour
- 1 tsp. salt
- ¼ tsp. pepper
- 3 cups milk
- 1½ lbs. fully cooked ham, cubed
   Shredded cheddar or Swiss cheese

1. Preheat oven to 350°. Cook broccoli according to package directions; drain. Spoon rice into a 13x9-in. baking pan. Place broccoli over rice.
2. Melt butter in a large skillet. Sprinkle 2 Tbsp. of melted butter over the bread crumbs and set aside. In remaining butter, saute onion until soft. Add flour, salt and pepper, stirring constantly until blended; stir in milk. Bring to a boil; cook and stir until thickened, about 2 minutes. Add ham.
3. Pour over rice and broccoli. Sprinkle with crumbs. Bake until heated through, about 30 minutes. Sprinkle with cheese; let stand 5 minutes before serving.

1 cup: 379 cal., 19g fat (10g sat. fat), 81mg chol., 1583mg sod., 29g carb. (6g sugars, 2g fiber), 22g pro.

HEARTY CHICKPEA POTPIE

You won't miss the meat in this savory veggie potpie! The spring veggies, easy prep and impressive presentation make it a perfect addition to family dinners.
—Deanna McDonald, Muskegon, MI

- -

Prep: 35 min. • **Cook:** 25 min.
Makes: 6 servings

- 1 pkg. (14.1 oz.) Refrigerated pie crust
- 3 Tbsp. butter
- 1 cup diced onions
- 1 cup diced celery
- 1 cup diced carrots
- 1 cup diced potatoes
- 1 cup (4 oz.) frozen peas, thawed
- ¼ cup all-purpose flour
- 1 tsp. poultry seasoning
- ½ tsp. ground turmeric
- ¼ tsp. salt
- ¼ tsp. pepper
- 2 cups vegetable broth
- 1 can (15 oz.) chickpeas or garbanzo beans, rinsed and drained

1. Preheat oven to 400°. Unroll one crust into a 9-in. pie plate; trim even with rim. Line unpricked crust with parchment. Fill with pie weights or dried beans. Bake on a lower oven rack until edges are light golden brown, 15-20 minutes. Remove parchment and weights; bake until the bottom is golden brown, 3-6 minutes longer. Cool crust on a wire rack.

2. Meanwhile, in a large skillet, melt butter over medium heat. Add onions, celery and carrots; cook and stir until onions are translucent, about 5 minutes. Stir in the potatoes and peas, cooking until vegetables are tender, 5-7 minutes. Whisk in next five ingredients. Increase heat to medium-high; gradually whisk in vegetable broth. Bring to a boil; cook, stirring constantly, until thickened, 4-6 minutes. Stir in chickpeas. Remove from heat.

3. Spoon vegetable filling over bottom crust. Unroll remaining crust; place over filling. Trim; cut slits in top.

4. Bake until top crust is golden, about 15 minutes. Cool 5 minutes before serving.

1 piece: 496 cal., 25g fat (11g sat. fat), 28mg chol., 760mg sod., 61g carb. (8g sugars, 6g fiber), 8g pro.

THAI PEANUT CHICKEN CASSEROLE

I used traditional pizza sauce and toppings in this recipe for years. After becoming a fan of Thai peanut chicken pizza, I decided to use those flavors instead. Serve with stir-fried vegetables or a salad with sesame dressing for an easy, delicious meal.
—Katherine Wollgast, Troy, MO

- -

Prep: 30 min. • **Bake:** 30 min.
Makes: 10 servings

- 2 tubes (12 oz. each) refrigerated buttermilk biscuits
- 3 cups shredded cooked chicken
- 1 cup sliced fresh mushrooms
- 1 bottle (11½ oz.) Thai peanut sauce, divided
- 2 cups shredded mozzarella cheese, divided
- ½ cup chopped sweet red pepper
- ½ cup shredded carrot
- 4 green onions, sliced
- ¼ cup honey-roasted peanuts, coarsely chopped

1. Preheat oven to 350°. Cut each biscuit into four pieces. Place in a greased 13x9-in. baking pan.

2. In a large bowl, combine the chicken, mushrooms and 1 cup peanut sauce; spread over biscuits. Top with 1 cup cheese, red pepper, carrot and green onions. Sprinkle with remaining cheese.

3. Bake until the topping is set, cheese is melted and biscuits have cooked all the way through, about 40 minutes. Sprinkle with the peanuts and serve with remaining peanut sauce.

1 serving: 490 cal., 25g fat (8g sat. fat), 55mg chol., 1013mg sod., 43g carb. (13g sugars, 1g fiber), 26g pro.

FRENCH MEAT & VEGETABLE PIE

Some time ago, a co-worker brought a meat pie to lunch. The aroma was so familiar—and after one taste, I was just amazed to discover it was the pie my grandmother used to serve when I was a youngster! My friend shared the recipe, and I have been enjoying it ever since.
—Rita Winterberger, Huson, MT

Prep: 20 min. • **Bake:** 30 min.
Makes: 8 servings

- 2 Tbsp. canola oil
- 1 large onion, thinly sliced
- 1 lb. ground beef
- 1 lb. ground pork
- 1 cup mashed potatoes (with added milk and butter)
- 1 can (8 oz.) mixed vegetables, drained
- 2 tsp. ground allspice
- 1 tsp. salt
- ¼ tsp. pepper
  Pastry for double-crust pie (9 in.)
- 1 large egg, lightly beaten, optional

1. In a skillet, heat oil over medium heat. Saute onion until tender. Remove and set aside. Brown beef and pork together; drain. Combine onion, meat, potatoes, vegetables and seasonings.

2. Line pie plate with crust; fill with meat mixture. Top with crust; seal and flute edges. Make slits in top crust. Brush with egg if desired.

3. Bake at 375° until top crust is golden brown, 30-35 minutes.

1 piece: 531 cal., 32g fat (12g sat. fat), 103mg chol., 724mg sod., 35g carb. (4g sugars, 1g fiber), 25g pro.

CORDON BLEU CASSEROLE

I often roast a turkey just to have leftovers for this creamy casserole. It makes for a pretty presentation at potlucks.
—Joyce Paul, Qu'Appelle, SK

Prep: 25 min. • **Bake:** 25 min.
Makes: 6 servings

- 2 cups cubed fully cooked ham
- 4 cups cubed cooked turkey
- 1 cup shredded Swiss cheese
- 1 large onion, chopped
- ⅓ cup butter, cubed
- ⅓ cup all-purpose flour
- ⅛ tsp. ground mustard
- ⅛ tsp. ground nutmeg
- 1¾ cups whole milk

TOPPING

- 1½ cups soft bread crumbs
- ½ cup shredded Swiss cheese
- ¼ cup butter, melted

1. In a large nonstick skillet, cook ham until browned, 4-5 minutes; drain and pat dry. In a greased 2-qt. baking dish, layer the turkey, cheese and ham; set aside.

2. In a large saucepan, saute onion in butter until tender. Stir in the flour, mustard and nutmeg until blended. Gradually stir in milk. Bring to a boil; cook and stir until thickened, about 2 minutes. Pour over ham.

3. Combine the topping ingredients; sprinkle over the top. Bake, uncovered, at 350° until golden brown and bubbly, 25-30 minutes.

1 cup: 601 cal., 37g fat (20g sat. fat), 178mg chol., 1008mg sod., 18g carb. (6g sugars, 1g fiber), 48g pro.

60 MINUTE SWEETS

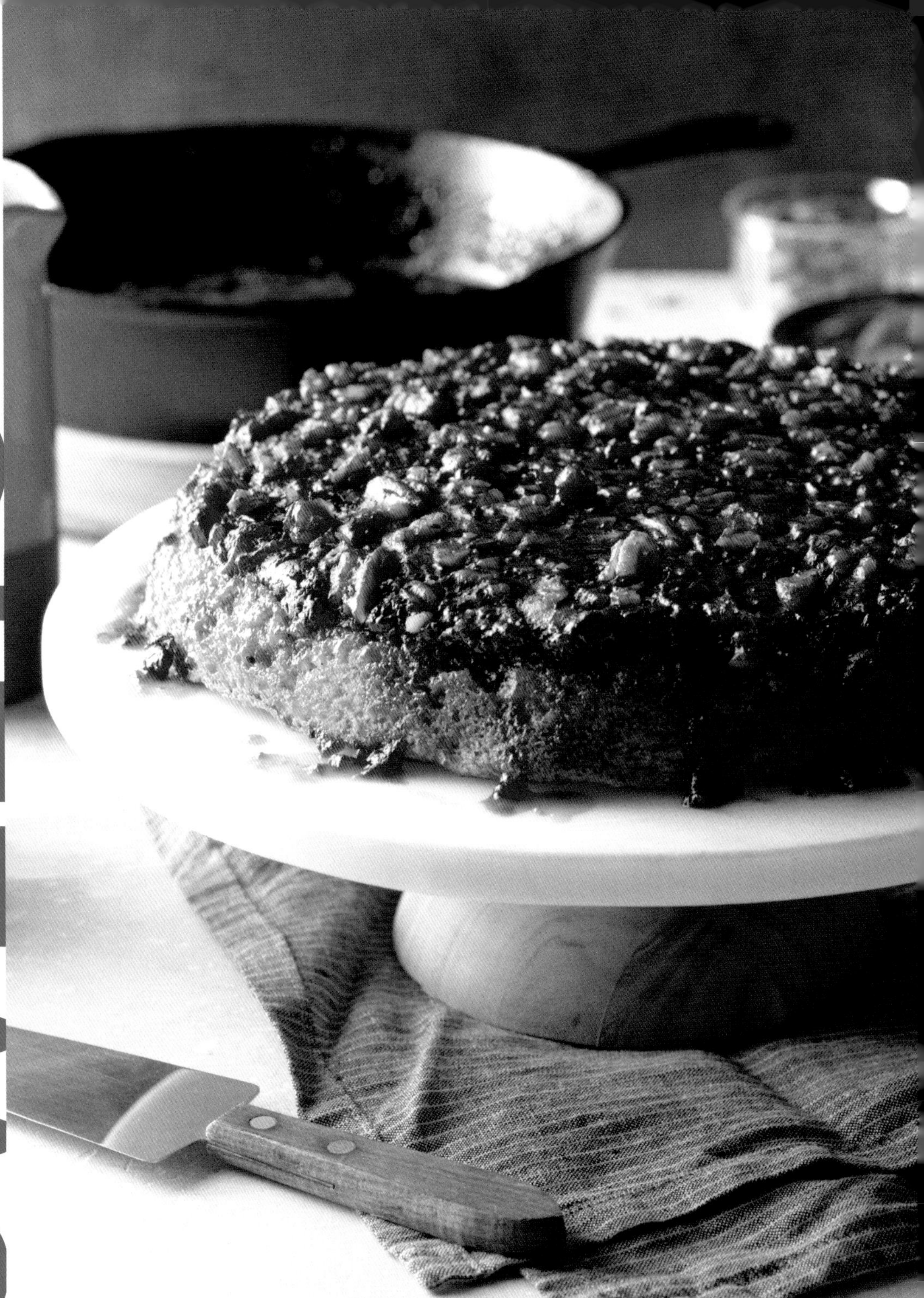

CRANBERRY PECAN UPSIDE-DOWN CAKE

Cranberries are a favorite in our house. I made this dessert for the first time in the 1990s. It started out as a basic pineapple upside-down cake—I just changed a few of the ingredients! It keeps and travels well, so it's perfect for taking to parties and potlucks. And we love to share it with our son and grandchildren.
—Doris Heath, Franklin, NC

- -

Prep: 20 min. • **Bake:** 30 min.
Makes: 10 servings

½ cup butter, cubed
2 cups sugar, divided
1 can (14 oz.) whole-berry cranberry sauce
½ cup coarsely chopped pecans
3 large eggs, separated, room temperature
⅓ cup orange juice
1 cup all-purpose flour
1 tsp. baking powder
¼ tsp. salt

1. Melt butter in a 10-in. iron skillet. Add 1 cup sugar; cook and stir 3 minutes over medium heat. Remove from heat. Spoon cranberry sauce over the butter mixture; sprinkle pecans over all. Set aside.
2. In a bowl, beat the egg yolks until foamy. Gradually add remaining sugar; beat well. Blend in orange juice. Combine flour, baking powder and salt; add to egg mixture. Beat the egg whites until stiff; fold into batter. Carefully spoon batter over the cranberry mixture in the skillet. Bake at 375° until a toothpick inserted in center comes out clean, 30 minutes. Cool 5 minutes in skillet; invert onto serving plate. Serve warm.
1 piece: 413 cal., 15g fat (7g sat. fat), 88mg chol., 221mg sod., 68g carb. (51g sugars, 2g fiber), 4g pro.

CHOCOLATE COBBLER

Talk about comfort food! This ultra moist cobbler makes a decadent ending to any meal. Best of all, it comes together in no time with just a few ingredients.
—Margaret McNeil, Germantown, TN

- -

Prep: 10 min. • **Bake:** 40 min.
Makes: 8 servings

1 cup self-rising flour
½ cup sugar
2 Tbsp. plus ¼ cup baking cocoa, divided
½ cup whole milk
3 Tbsp. vegetable oil
1 cup packed brown sugar
1¾ cups hot water
    Vanilla ice cream, optional

In a bowl, combine the flour, sugar and 2 Tbsp. cocoa. Stir in the milk and oil until smooth. Pour into a greased 8-in. square baking pan. Combine the brown sugar and remaining cocoa; sprinkle over batter. Pour hot water over top (do not stir). Bake at 350° until top of cake springs back when lightly touched, for 40-45 minutes. Serve warm, with ice cream if desired.
Note: As a substitute for 1 cup of self-rising flour, place 1½ tsp. baking powder and ½ tsp. salt in a measuring cup. Add all-purpose flour to measure 1 cup.
1 serving: 267 cal., 6g fat (1g sat. fat), 2mg chol., 198mg sod., 53g carb. (40g sugars, 1g fiber), 3g pro.

APPLE SNICKERDOODLE DUMP CAKE

We live down the road from an apple farm, and I'm always looking for creative ways to use up the bushels we pick. We love this cozy cake with caramel drizzle and a scoop of vanilla or cinnamon ice cream.
—Rachel Garcia, Honolulu, HI

Prep: 15 min. • **Bake:** 35 min.
Makes: 10 servings

- 6 cups sliced, peeled tart apple (about 8 medium)
- ⅓ cup packed brown sugar
- ¼ cup sugar
- ¼ cup orange juice
- 1 Tbsp. lemon juice
- 1 pkg. (17.9 oz.) snickerdoodle cookie mix
- ½ cup butter, melted
- 1 cup coarsely chopped pecans or walnuts

1. Preheat oven to 350°. Toss apples with sugars and fruit juices; spread into a greased 11x7-in. baking dish.
2. Place cookie mix in a bowl; stir in the contents of the cinnamon-sugar packet. Sprinkle over apples. Drizzle with butter. Top with pecans.
3. Bake until golden brown and apples are tender, 35-40 minutes. Serve warm.

1 serving: 475 cal., 23g fat (7g sat. fat), 24mg chol., 193mg sod., 67g carb. (48g sugars, 3g fiber), 3g pro.

SPEEDY SURPRISE
"While I wouldn't call this a cake, I will call it delicious!"
—MS11145, TASTEOFHOME.COM

RHUBARB-BLUEBERRY CRUMBLE

Rhubarb is often paired with strawberries, and while that's a winning combo, rhubarb and blueberries are a fresh and colorful match. This crumble is especially good in summer when both fruits are in season.
—Mike Schulz, Tawas City, MI

Prep: 15 min. • **Bake:** 40 min.
Makes: 8 servings

- ⅔ cup sugar
- 2 Tbsp. cornstarch
- ¼ tsp. salt
- 3 cups fresh blueberries
- 3 cups sliced fresh or frozen rhubarb, thawed

TOPPING
- ¾ cup biscuit/baking mix
- ⅓ cup sugar
- ⅛ tsp. salt
- ⅓ cup cold unsalted butter, cubed
- ½ cup old-fashioned oats
- ½ cup chopped almonds

1. Preheat oven to 375°. In a bowl, mix the sugar, cornstarch and salt. Add blueberries and rhubarb; toss to coat. Transfer mixture to a greased 8-in. square baking dish.
2. For topping, in a small bowl, mix baking mix, sugar and salt. Cut in the butter until crumbly; stir in oats and almonds. Sprinkle over filling. Bake until filling is bubbly and topping is golden brown, 40-45 minutes.
Note: If using frozen rhubarb, measure rhubarb while still frozen, then let it thaw completely. Drain in a colander, but do not press liquid out.

1 serving: 324 cal., 14g fat (6g sat. fat), 20mg chol., 255mg sod., 49g carb. (32g sugars, 4g fiber), 4g pro.

CHERRY PUDDING CAKE

A cross between a cake and a cobbler, this cherry dessert is one to add to your keeper files of trusty potluck recipes, because it's sure to go fast.
—Brenda Parker, Kalamazoo, MI

- -

Prep: 10 min. • **Bake:** 40 min.
Makes: 12 servings

2 cups all-purpose flour
2½ cups sugar, divided
4 tsp. baking powder
1 cup whole milk
2 Tbsp. canola oil
2 cans (14½ oz. each) water-packed pitted tart red cherries, well drained
2 to 3 drops red food coloring, optional
⅛ tsp. almond extract
Optional: Whipped cream, ice cream

1. In a bowl, combine flour, 1 cup of sugar, baking powder, milk and oil; pour into a greased shallow 3-qt. baking dish. In a bowl, combine cherries, food coloring if desired, extract and remaining sugar; spoon mixture over the batter.
2. Bake at 375° for 40-45 minutes or until a toothpick inserted in the cake portion comes out clean. Serve warm, if desired with whipped cream or ice cream.

1 serving: 296 cal., 3g fat (1g sat. fat), 3mg chol., 147mg sod., 65g carb. (48g sugars, 1g fiber), 3g pro.

PLUM UPSIDE-DOWN CAKE

The delicate flavor of plums is a pleasing change of pace in this upside-down cake.
—Bobbie Talbott, Veneta, OR

- -

Prep: 15 min. • **Bake:** 40 min.
Makes: 10 servings

- ⅓ **cup butter**
- ½ **cup packed brown sugar**
- 1¾ **to 2 lbs. medium plums, pitted and halved**
- 2 **large eggs, room temperature**
- ⅔ **cup sugar**
- 1 **cup all-purpose flour**
- 1 **tsp. baking powder**
- ¼ **tsp. salt**
- ⅓ **cup hot water**
- ½ **tsp. lemon extract**
  Whipped cream, optional

1. Melt the butter in a 10-in. cast-iron or ovenproof skillet. Sprinkle brown sugar over butter. Arrange plum halves, cut side down, in a single layer over sugar; set aside.

2. In a large bowl, beat eggs until thick and lemon-colored; gradually beat in the sugar. Combine the flour, baking powder and salt; add to egg mixture and mix well. Blend the water and lemon extract; beat into batter. Pour over plums.

3. Bake at 350° until a toothpick inserted in the center comes out clean, 40-45 minutes. Immediately invert onto a serving plate. Serve warm, with whipped cream if desired.

1 piece: 245 cal., 7g fat (4g sat. fat), 53mg chol., 173mg sod., 43g carb. (32g sugars, 1g fiber), 3g pro.

MAPLE PECAN PIE

Pecan pie is one of my favorite desserts. I use our delicious Vermont maple syrup to make it even more amazing.
—Mildred Wescom, Belvidere, VT

- -

Prep: 10 min. • **Bake:** 40 min. + cooling
Makes: 8 servings

- **Pastry for single-crust pie (9 in.)**
- 3 **large eggs, room temperature**
- ½ **cup sugar**
- 1 **cup maple syrup**
- 3 **Tbsp. butter, melted**
- ½ **tsp. vanilla extract**
- ¼ **tsp. salt**
- 2 **cups pecan halves**
  Whipped cream, optional

1. Preheat oven to 375°. Roll out dough to fit a 9-in. pie plate. Transfer crust to pie plate. Trim to 1-in. beyond edge of plate; flute edges.

2. In a bowl, the whisk eggs and sugar until smooth. Add maple syrup, butter, vanilla, salt and pecans. Pour into prepared crust.

3. Bake until a knife inserted in the center comes out clean, 30-40 minutes. Cool on a wire rack for 1 hour. If desired, top with whipped cream to serve. Store any unused portion in refrigerator.

1 piece: 561 cal., 35g fat (12g sat. fat), 111mg chol., 294mg sod., 58g carb. (38g sugars, 3g fiber), 7g pro.

HOLIDAY LACE COOKIES

It's hard to stop eating these crisp, buttery cookies dotted with pecans and dried red cranberries. This is one of the recipes from my mother that I cherish the most.
—Mildred Sherrer, Fort Worth, TX

- -

Prep: 45 min. + chilling
Bake: 15 min./batch
Makes: 4 dozen

- 1 cup butter, softened
- 2¼ cups confectioners' sugar
- ¼ cup light corn syrup
- 1¼ cups all-purpose flour
- 1 cup chopped pecans
- ¼ cup dried cranberries

1. In a large bowl, cream the butter and confectioners' sugar until light and fluffy. Beat in corn syrup. Gradually beat in flour; mix well. Fold in pecans and cranberries. Shape dough into two 6-in. logs; wrap each and chill until firm, 2 hours.
2. Unwrap and cut into ¼-in. slices. Place 3 in. apart on ungreased foil-lined baking sheets. Bake at 350° until the center and edges are browned and lacy, 11-12 minutes. Allow cookies to cool completely before carefully removing from foil.
1 cookie: 121 cal., 7g fat (3g sat. fat), 14mg chol., 54mg sod., 14g carb. (9g sugars, 0 fiber), 1g pro.

> **TEST KITCHEN TIP**
> Use a thin sharp knife to slice through the cookie dough. Cut one roll at a time, keeping the additional roll refrigerated until ready to use.

GRANDMA PIETZ'S CRANBERRY CAKE PUDDING

The recipe for this cranberry-studded cake has been passed down through several generations in our family. It's simple and unique, and it remains a favorite for parties and gatherings.
—Lisa Potter, Camp Douglas, WI

- -

Prep: 30 min. • **Bake:** 20 min.
Makes: 15 servings (2 cups sauce)

- 3 Tbsp. butter, softened
- 1 cup sugar
- 1 large egg, room temperature
- 2 cups all-purpose flour
- 2 tsp. baking powder
  Dash salt
- 1 cup 2% milk
- 2 cups fresh or frozen cranberries, thawed

SAUCE
- 2 cups packed brown sugar
- 1 cup water
- ½ cup sugar
- 3 Tbsp. butter
- ¼ tsp. vanilla extract

1. Preheat oven to 350°. Grease a 13x9-in. baking pan.
2. In a large bowl, beat butter and sugar until crumbly. Beat in egg. In another bowl, whisk flour, baking powder and salt; add to butter mixture alternately with milk, beating well after each addition. If desired, coarsely chop cranberries; fold into batter.
3. Transfer to prepared pan. Bake until a toothpick inserted in center comes out clean, 20-25 minutes.
4. In a large saucepan, combine the brown sugar, water, sugar and butter; bring to a boil over medium heat, stirring constantly to dissolve sugar. Cook and stir until slightly thickened; stir in vanilla. Serve sauce warm with the cake.
1 piece with 2 Tbsp. sauce: 311 cal., 5g fat (3g sat. fat), 26mg chol., 125mg sod., 64g carb. (50g sugars, 1g fiber), 3g pro.

CHOCOLATE MINT TRUFFLE TART

Eating a slice of this decadent dessert is like biting into a smooth truffle candy. You can vary the flavor by using different baking chips, like raspberry-chocolate instead of mint-chocolate chips.
—Sally Sibthorpe, Shelby Township, MI

- -

Prep: 25 min. • **Bake:** 25 min.
Makes: 16 servings

  2 **cups Oreo cookie crumbs**
  ¾ **cup softened butter, divided**
  1 **pkg. (10 oz.) mint chocolate chips**
  ½ **cup sugar**
  2 **tsp. vanilla extract**
  1 **cup heavy whipping cream**
  3 **large eggs, room temperature, lightly beaten**
     Optional: Chopped dark chocolate, chocolate curls, whipped cream

1. Preheat oven to 350°. Combine cookie crumbs and ¼ cup butter; press onto the bottom and up sides of an ungreased 10-in. tart pan. Place tart pan on a baking sheet; bake until crust is set, 12-15 minutes.
2. In a small heavy saucepan, heat cream and remaining butter over medium heat until bubbles form around sides of pan. Place the mint chocolate chips, sugar and vanilla in a bowl; pour cream mixture over chocolate and stir until chocolate is melted and sugar has dissolved. Slowly pour ⅓ of the warm chocolate mixture into eggs while stirring continuously; return egg mixture to chocolate and stir until smooth.
3. Pour into prepared tart shell. Bake until center is just set (mixture will jiggle), 25-30 minutes. Cool completely on a wire rack. If desired, top with whipped cream, chopped chocolate and chocolate curls. Refrigerate.
1 slice: 343 cal., 24g fat (13g sat. fat), 83mg chol., 174mg sod., 31g carb. (23g sugars, 2g fiber), 4g pro.

CARAMEL PEAR PUDDING

Don't expect this old-fashioned dessert to last long. The delicate pears and irresistible caramel topping make it a winner whenever I serve it. It's nice to have a tempting fall cake that puts the season's best pears to excellent use.
—Sharon Mensing, Greenfield, IA

- -

Prep: 15 min. • **Bake:** 45 min.
Makes: 8 servings

  1   **cup all-purpose flour**
  ⅔   **cup sugar**
  1½   **tsp. baking powder**
  ½   **tsp. ground cinnamon**
  ¼   **tsp. salt**
       Pinch ground cloves
  ½   **cup whole milk**
  4   **medium pears, peeled and cut into ½-in. cubes**
  ½   **cup chopped pecans**
  ¾   **cup packed brown sugar**
  ¼   **cup butter**
  ¾   **cup boiling water**
       Vanilla ice cream or whipped cream, optional

1. Preheat oven to at 375°. In a large bowl, combine the first six ingredients; beat in milk until smooth. Stir in pears and pecans. Spoon into an ungreased 2-qt. baking dish.
2. In another bowl, combine the brown sugar, butter and water; pour over batter. Bake, uncovered, for 45-50 minutes. Serve pudding warm, with ice cream or whipped cream if desired.
1 serving: 359 cal., 12g fat (4g sat. fat), 17mg chol., 223mg sod., 63g carb. (46g sugars, 3g fiber), 3g pro.

ALMOND RHUBARB COBBLER

I make this tangy biscuit-topped treat when warm weather rolls in. The bright color looks pretty on a spring or summer table.
—Pat Habiger, Spearville, KS

- -

Prep: 35 min. • **Bake:** 20 min.
Makes: 6 servings

- 1   cup sugar, divided
- ½   cup water
- 6   cups chopped fresh or frozen rhubarb
- 2   Tbsp. all-purpose flour
- 2   Tbsp. butter
- ½   cup slivered almonds, toasted

TOPPING
- 1   cup all-purpose flour
- 2   Tbsp. sugar
- 1½ tsp. baking powder
- ¼   tsp. salt
- ¼   cup cold butter
- 1   large egg, room temperature
- ¼   cup whole milk
    Toasted slivered almonds, optional

1. In a large saucepan, bring ½ cup sugar and water to a boil. Add rhubarb. Reduce heat; cover and simmer until tender, about 5 minutes. Combine flour and remaining sugar; stir into rhubarb mixture. Return to a boil; cook and stir until the mixture is thickened and bubbly, 2 minutes. Stir in butter and almonds. Reduce heat to low; stir occasionally until butter is melted.
2. In a large bowl, combine dry ingredients; cut in butter until crumbly. Whisk egg and milk; stir into the crumb mixture just until moistened. Pour hot rhubarb mixture into a 2-qt. shallow baking dish. Drop topping into six mounds over the rhubarb mixture.
3. Bake, uncovered, at 400° until golden brown, 20-25 minutes. If desired, sprinkle cobbler with almonds after removing from oven. Serve warm.
Note: If using frozen rhubarb, measure the rhubarb while still frozen, then thaw completely. Drain in a colander, but do not press liquid out.
1 serving: 427 cal., 18g fat (8g sat. fat), 67mg chol., 335mg sod., 63g carb. (41g sugars, 4g fiber), 7g pro.

CITRUS CORNMEAL CAKE

Cornmeal adds a rustic quality to this tart-shaped cake flavored with citrus and almond. It is sure to become a staple in your recipe collection, and it also makes a great hostess gift.
—Roxanne Chan, Albany, CA

- -

Prep: 25 min. • **Bake:** 25 min.
Makes: 8 servings

- ½   cup lemon yogurt
- ⅓   cup honey
- ¼   cup olive oil
- 1   large egg, room temperature
- 2   large egg whites, room temperature
- ¼   tsp. almond extract
- ¾   cup all-purpose flour
- ½   cup cornmeal
- 1   tsp. baking powder
- ½   tsp. grated orange zest
- 1   can (15 oz.) mandarin oranges, drained
- 3   Tbsp. sliced almonds

1. Coat 9-in. fluted tart pan with removable bottom with cooking spray. In a large bowl, beat the yogurt, honey, oil, egg, egg whites and extract until well blended. Combine the flour, cornmeal and baking powder; gradually beat dry ingredients into yogurt mixture until blended. Stir in orange zest.
2. Pour into prepared pan. Arrange oranges over batter; sprinkle with almonds. Bake at 350° until a toothpick inserted in the center comes out clean, 25-30 minutes. Cool on a wire rack 10 minutes before cutting. Serve warm or at room temperature.
1 slice: 240 cal., 9g fat (1g sat. fat), 27mg chol., 85mg sod., 36g carb. (20g sugars, 2g fiber), 5g pro.

PLANNED OVERS

USING LEFTOVER BEEF

ITALIAN POT ROAST

This delicious pot roast is a favorite of my husband's. He just loves the tender beef seasoned with Italian herbs. Use the leftovers in any recipe that calls for cooked roast beef.

—Debbie Daly, Buckingham, IL

Prep: 20 min. • **Cook:** 5 hours
Makes: 8 servings

- 1 boneless beef chuck roast (3 to 4 lbs.)
- 1 can (28 oz.) diced tomatoes, drained
- ¾ cup chopped onion
- ¾ cup Burgundy wine or beef broth
- 1½ tsp. salt
- 1 tsp. dried basil
- ½ tsp. dried oregano
- 1 garlic clove, minced
- ¼ tsp. pepper
- ¼ cup cornstarch
- ½ cup cold water

1. Cut roast in half. Place in a 5-qt. slow cooker. Add the tomatoes, onion, wine, salt, basil, oregano, garlic and pepper. Cover and cook on low for 5-6 hours or until the meat is tender.

2. Remove meat to a serving platter; keep warm. Skim the fat from cooking juices; transfer to a small saucepan. Combine the cornstarch and water until smooth. Gradually stir into pan. Bring to a boil; cook and stir until thickened, about 2 minutes. Serve with meat.

5 oz. cooked beef: 345 cal., 16g fat (6g sat. fat), 111mg chol., 641mg sod., 10g carb. (4g sugars, 2g fiber), 34g pro.

ROAST BEEF WITH CHIVE ROASTED POTATOES

It's hard to believe that last night's beef roast could get any better, but it shines in this heartwarming dish.

—*Taste of Home* Test Kitchen

Prep: 20 min. • **Bake:** 25 min.
Makes: 6 servings

- 2 lbs. red potatoes, cut into 1-in. cubes
- 2 Tbsp. olive oil
- 2 tsp. minced chives
- ¾ tsp. salt, divided
- 2 medium onions, halved and thinly sliced
- 1 lb. sliced fresh mushrooms
- ¼ cup butter, cubed
- 1 garlic clove, minced
- 1 tsp. dried rosemary, crushed
- ¼ tsp. pepper
- ⅓ cup dry red wine or beef broth
- 2 cups cubed cooked roast beef
- 1 cup beef gravy

1. Place potatoes in a greased 15x10x1-in. baking pan. Drizzle with oil and sprinkle with chives and ¼ tsp. salt; toss to coat. Bake, uncovered, at 425° for 25-30 minutes or until tender, stirring occasionally.

2. Meanwhile, in a large skillet, saute onions and mushrooms in butter until tender. Add the garlic, rosemary, pepper and remaining salt; cook 1 minute longer. Stir in the wine. Add beef and gravy; heat through. Serve with the potatoes.

1 serving: 379 cal., 15g fat (6g sat. fat), 66mg chol., 591mg sod., 35g carb. (6g sugars, 5g fiber), 24g pro.

ROAST BEEF PASTA SKILLET

Leftover beef is the star in a skillet dinner that's perfect for two. Chopped tomato adds a burst of fresh flavor.
—Bill Hilbrich, St. Cloud, MN

Takes: 20 min. • **Makes:** 2 servings

- 1 cup uncooked spiral pasta
- ½ cup chopped onion
- 1 tsp. olive oil
- 1 tsp. butter
- 1 cup cubed cooked roast beef
- 1 tsp. pepper
- ½ cup chopped tomato
- ½ cup grated Parmesan cheese

Cook the pasta according to package directions. Meanwhile, in a large skillet, saute onion in oil and butter until tender. Add roast beef and pepper; heat through. Drain pasta; add to beef mixture. Stir in tomato and cheese.

2 cups: 448 cal., 14g fat (6g sat. fat), 87mg chol., 358mg sod., 38g carb. (4g sugars, 3g fiber), 40g pro.

BEEFY MUSHROOM SOUP

This is a quick and tasty way to use up extra roast or steak. It's a delicious supper for small households. The warm, rich taste of this mushroom soup is sure to please.
—Ginger Ellsworth, Caldwell, ID

Takes: 30 min. • **Makes:** 3 cups

- 1 medium onion, chopped
- ½ cup sliced fresh mushrooms
- 2 Tbsp. butter
- 2 Tbsp. all-purpose flour
- 2 cups reduced-sodium beef broth
- ⅔ cup cubed cooked roast beef
- ½ tsp. garlic powder
- ¼ tsp. paprika
- ¼ tsp. pepper
- ⅛ tsp. salt

   Dash hot pepper sauce
- ¼ cup shredded part-skim mozzarella cheese, optional

1. In a large saucepan, saute onion and mushrooms in butter until onion is tender; remove with a slotted spoon and set aside. In a small bowl, whisk flour and broth until smooth; gradually add to the pan. Bring to a boil; cook and stir for 1-2 minutes or until thickened.

2. Add the roast beef, garlic powder, paprika, pepper, salt, pepper sauce and onion mixture; cook and stir until heated through. Garnish with cheese if desired.

1 cup: 151 cal., 6g fat (3g sat. fat), 42mg chol., 472mg sod., 11g carb. (4g sugars, 1g fiber), 14g pro.

ASPARAGUS BEEF STIR-FRY

A local restaurant once handed out asparagus recipes, including this one that makes great use of any extra roast you might have on hand.

—Joyce Huebner, Marinette, WI

- -

Prep: 20 min. • **Cook:** 25 min.
Makes: 6 servings

  2 Tbsp. cornstarch
  1 cup beef broth
  3 Tbsp. soy sauce
  ½ tsp. sugar
  2 Tbsp. canola oil
  2 whole garlic cloves
  2 lbs. fresh asparagus, trimmed
     and cut into 2½-in. pieces
  2 medium onions, halved
     and thinly sliced
  1 medium sweet red pepper,
     julienned 1 large carrot,
     cut into 2½-in. strips
 2½ cups sliced cooked roast
     beef (2½-in. strips)
  1 cup salted cashew halves
     Hot cooked rice

1. In a small bowl, combine cornstarch and broth until smooth. Stir in soy sauce and sugar; set aside. In a wok or large skillet, heat oil; add garlic. Cook and stir until lightly browned, about 1 minute; discard garlic.
2. Stir-fry the asparagus, onions, red pepper and carrot until crisp-tender, 15-20 minutes. Add roast beef heat through. Stir reserved sauce; add to the span. Bring to a boil; cook and stir until thickened, about 2 minutes. Sprinkle with cashews. Serve with rice.

¾ cup: 382 cal., 21g fat (4g sat. fat), 54mg chol., 815mg sod., 18g carb. (7g sugars, 4g fiber), 30g pro.

USING LEFTOVER CHICKEN

GRILLED BUTTERMILK CHICKEN

I created this recipe years ago, after one of our farmers market customers, a chef, shared the idea of marinating chicken in buttermilk. The chicken is easy to prepare and always turns out moist and delicious! It makes a lot of chicken, so you can always refrigerate or freeze the extra and use it in dishes calling for cooked chicken. What a timesaver on busy weeknights!
—Sue Gronholz, Beaver Dam, WI

- -

Prep: 10 min. + marinating • **Grill:** 10 min.
Makes: 12 servings

- 1½ cups buttermilk
- 4 fresh thyme sprigs
- 4 garlic cloves, halved
- ½ tsp. salt
- 12 boneless skinless chicken breast halves (about 4.5 lbs.)

1. Place the buttermilk, thyme, garlic and salt in a large bowl or shallow dish. Add chicken and turn to coat. Refrigerate for 8 hours or overnight, turning occasionally.
2. Drain chicken breasts, discarding the marinade. Grill chicken, covered, over medium heat until a thermometer reads 165°, 5-7 minutes per side.
1 chicken breast half: 189 cal., 4g fat (1g sat. fat), 95mg chol., 168mg sod., 1g carb. (1g sugars, 0 fiber), 35g pro. **Diabetic exchanges:** 5 lean meat.

CHICKEN BISCUIT POTPIE

Because it relies on cooked chicken, this hearty meal-in-one takes just 10 minutes to assemble before popping it in the oven.
—Dorothy Smith, El Dorado, AR

- -

Prep: 10 min. • **Bake:** 25 min.
Makes: 4 servings

- 1⅔ cups frozen mixed vegetables, thawed
- 1½ cups cubed cooked chicken
- 1 can (10¾ oz.) condensed cream of chicken soup, undiluted
- ¼ tsp. dried thyme
- 1 cup biscuit/baking mix
- ½ cup milk
- 1 large egg

1. In a large bowl, combine the vegetables, chicken, soup and thyme. Pour into an ungreased deep-dish 9-in. pie plate. Combine the biscuit mix, milk and egg; spoon over chicken mixture.
2. Bake at 400° until golden brown, 25-30 minutes.
1 serving: 376 cal., 14g fat (4g sat. fat), 103mg chol., 966mg sod., 38g carb. (5g sugars, 5g fiber), 23g pro.

FLAKY CHICKEN WELLINGTON

I rely on cooked chicken and tubes of refrigerated crescent rolls to make this impressive dinner in a snap. The buttery pastry and savory filling are sensational with the cool, creamy dipping sauce.
—Kerry Dingwall, Wilmington, NC

- -

Prep: 30 min. • **Bake:** 15 min.
Makes: 6 servings

2   cups cubed cooked chicken
1   pkg. (10 oz.) frozen chopped spinach, thawed and squeezed dry
3   large hard-boiled eggs, chopped
½   cup finely chopped dill pickles
⅓   cup finely chopped celery
2   tubes (8 oz. each) refrigerated crescent rolls
2   tsp. prepared mustard, divided
1   cup sour cream
2   Tbsp. dill pickle juice

1. Preheat oven to 350°. In a large bowl, combine the first five ingredients. Unroll one tube of crescent dough into one long rectangle; press perforations to seal.
2. Spread half the mustard over dough; top with half the chicken mixture to within ¼ in. of edges. Roll up jelly-roll style, starting with a long side; pinch seam to seal. Place on a parchment-lined baking sheet, cut side down. Cut slits in top. Repeat with the remaining crescent dough, mustard and chicken mixture.
3. Bake until golden brown, 15-20 minutes. Meanwhile, combine sour cream and pickle juice; serve with pastries

⅓ pastry with about 3 Tbsp. sauce:
495 cal., 28g fat (6g sat. fat), 144mg chol., 830mg sod., 37g carb. (10g sugars, 2g fiber), 25g pro.

CHICKEN, NECTARINE & AVOCADO SALAD

This salad is really summery and comes together very quickly. Using granola adds crunch and makes it different. I like using granola that isn't terribly sweet but has a lot of nuts. What a tasty way to finish up that extra chicken from last night.
—Elisabeth Larsen, Pleasant Grove, UT

- -

Takes: 15 min. • **Makes:** 4 servings

- 6 oz. fresh baby spinach (about 8 cups)
- 2 medium nectarines, thinly sliced
- 2 cups cubed cooked chicken
- 1 cup crumbled feta cheese
- ½ cup poppy seed salad dressing
- 1 medium ripe avocado, peeled and sliced
- 1 cup granola with fruit and nuts

In a large bowl, combine the spinach, nectarines, chicken and feta. Drizzle with dressing; toss to coat. Top with the avocado and granola. Serve immediately.

1½ cups: 561 cal., 32g fat (7g sat. fat), 87mg chol., 539mg sod., 38g carb. (18g sugars, 7g fiber), 30g pro.

5 INGREDIENT
CREAMY CHICKEN SOUP

Kids won't think twice about eating vegetables once they're incorporated into this creamy and cheesy soup.
—LaVonne Lundgren, Sioux City, IA

- -

Takes: 30 min. • **Makes:** 7 servings

- 4 cups cubed cooked chicken breast
- 3½ cups water
- 2 cans (10¾ oz. each) condensed cream of chicken soup, undiluted
- 1 pkg. (16 oz.) frozen mixed vegetables, thawed
- 1 can (14½ oz.) diced potatoes, drained
- 1 pkg. (16 oz.) process cheese (Velveeta), cubed

In a Dutch oven, combine the first five ingredients. Bring to a boil. Reduce heat; cover and simmer for 8-10 minutes or until vegetables are tender. Stir in cheese just until melted (do not boil).

1½ cups: 481 cal., 24g fat (12g sat. fat), 121mg chol., 1650mg sod., 26g carb. (8g sugars, 4g fiber), 39g pro.

USING LEFTOVER HAM

SLOW-COOKED HAM

Entertaining doesn't get much easier than with this five-ingredient ham from the slow cooker. And the leftovers are delicious in casseroles, soups and all sorts of dishes.
—Heather Spring
Sheppard Air Force Base, TX

Prep: 5 min. • **Cook:** 6 hours
Makes: 20 servings

- ½ cup packed brown sugar
- 1 tsp. ground mustard
- 1 tsp. prepared horseradish
- 2 Tbsp. plus ¼ cup cola, divided
- 1 fully cooked boneless ham (5 to 6 lbs.), cut in half

In a small bowl, combine the brown sugar, mustard, horseradish and 2 Tbsp. cola. Rub over ham. Transfer to a 5-qt. slow cooker; add remaining cola to slow cooker. Cover and cook on low for 6-8 hours or until a thermometer reads 140°.

3 oz. cooked ham: 143 cal., 4g fat (1g sat. fat), 58mg chol., 1180mg sod., 6g carb. (6g sugars, 0 fiber), 21g pro.

SPEEDY SURPRISE

"Made this for the family at Easter, and it got rave reviews, so I made again this week just for us! It's so simple and tasty, it's the only way I'll make a ham going forward."
—GDUBMOM, TASTEOFHOME.COM

CREAMY NOODLE CASSEROLE

My husband works long hours and often doesn't get home until well past 7 p.m. This casserole is great for those nights—it's just as tasty after reheating in the microwave.
—Barb Marshall, Pickerington, OH

Takes: 25 min. • **Makes:** 8 servings

- 1 pkg. (12 oz.) egg noodles
- 1 pkg. (16 oz.) frozen broccoli cuts
- 3 cups cubed fully cooked ham
- 1 cup shredded part-skim mozzarella cheese
- 1 cup shredded Parmesan cheese
- ⅓ cup butter, cubed
- ½ cup half-and-half cream
- ¼ tsp. each garlic powder, salt and pepper

1. In a Dutch oven, cook noodles in boiling water for 5 minutes. Add broccoli and ham; cook 5-10 minutes longer or until noodles are tender.

2. Drain; return to pan. Stir in the remaining ingredients. Cook and stir over low heat until the butter is melted and mixture is heated through.

Freeze option: Freeze cooled noodle mixture in freezer containers. To use, partially thaw in refrigerator overnight. Microwave, covered, on high in a microwave-safe dish until heated through, gently stirring and adding a little broth or milk if necessary.

1 serving: 428 cal., 20g fat (11g sat. fat), 112mg chol., 1087mg sod., 35g carb. (3g sugars, 3g fiber), 25g pro.

QUICK ANTIPASTO SALAD

I used to work in a pizza shop, where this salad was the most popular item on the menu. It's great for nights when it's just too hot to cook.
—Webbie Carvajal, Alpine, TX

- -

Takes: 25 min. • **Makes:** 8 servings

1½ cups cubed fully cooked ham
1 jar (10 oz.) pimiento-stuffed olives, drained and sliced
1 can (3.8 oz.) sliced ripe olives, drained
1 pkg. (3½ oz.) sliced pepperoni, quartered
8 cups shredded lettuce
10 to 12 cherry tomatoes, quartered
1 cup Italian salad dressing
1½ cups shredded part-skim mozzarella cheese

In a large bowl, combine the ham, olives and pepperoni. On a platter or individual salad plates, arrange the lettuce, olive mixture and tomatoes. Drizzle with dressing; sprinkle with cheese.

1⅔ cups: 342 cal., 29g fat (7g sat. fat), 41mg chol., 1830mg sod., 9g carb. (3g sugars, 2g fiber), 13g pro.

5 INGREDIENT
SPINACH-HAM CASSEROLE

Ham and veggies join forces with a savory sauce and a pretty lattice topping to create a hearty meal-in-one. This is down-home cooking at its best!
—*Taste of Home* Test Kitchen

- -

Prep: 25 min. • **Bake:** 20 min.
Makes: 4 servings

3 cups cubed fully cooked ham
1 pkg. (16 oz.) frozen sliced carrots, thawed
1 can (10¾ oz.) condensed cream of potato soup, undiluted
1 pkg. (10 oz.) frozen creamed spinach, thawed
¼ cup water
¼ tsp. pepper
⅛ tsp. salt
1 tube (4 oz.) refrigerated crescent rolls

1. In a large skillet coated with cooking spray, cook ham over medium heat until lightly browned. Stir in the carrots, soup, spinach, water, pepper and salt; heat through. Pour into a greased 8-in. square baking dish.
2. Unroll crescent dough; carefully separate into two rectangles. Seal perforations. Cut each rectangle lengthwise into four strips; make a lattice crust. Bake at 375° until the filling is bubbly and crust is golden brown, 18-22 minutes.

1 serving: 438 cal., 19g fat (7g sat. fat), 62mg chol., 2593mg sod., 38g carb. (11g sugars, 6g fiber), 26g pro.

CHEDDAR HAM SOUP

I knew this recipe was a keeper when my mother-in-law asked for it! The filling soup, loaded with extra ham, veggies and cheese, is creamy and comforting. Although the recipe makes enough to feed a crowd, don't expect leftovers!
—Marty Matthews, Clarksville, TN

- -

Takes: 30 min. • **Makes:** 7 servings

- 2 cups diced peeled potatoes
- 2 cups water
- ½ cup sliced carrot
- ¼ cup chopped onion
- ¼ cup butter, cubed
- ¼ cup all-purpose flour
- 2 cups 2% milk
- ¼ to ½ tsp. salt
- ¼ tsp. pepper
- 2 cups shredded cheddar cheese
- 1½ cups cubed fully cooked ham
- 1 cup frozen peas

1. In a large saucepan, combine potatoes, water, carrot and onion. Bring to a boil. Reduce heat; cover and cook until tender, 10-15 minutes.

2. Meanwhile, in another saucepan, melt butter. Stir in flour until smooth. Gradually add the milk, salt and pepper. Bring to a boil; cook and stir until soup is thickened, about 2 minutes. Stir in cheese until melted. Stir into undrained potato mixture. Add ham and peas; heat through.

1 cup: 303 cal., 17g fat (11g sat. fat), 64mg chol., 763mg sod., 20g carb. (6g sugars, 2g fiber), 17g pro.

USING LEFTOVER PORK

GARLIC-APPLE PORK ROAST

This is the meal I have become famous for, and it is so simple to prepare in the slow cooker. The garlic and apple flavors really complement the pork. It's great with steamed fresh asparagus and roasted red potatoes. Plus, the extras are great in all sorts of dishes.
—Jennifer Loos, WA Boro, PA

- -

Prep: 10 min. • **Cook:** 8 hours + standing
Makes: 12 servings

- 1 boneless pork loin roast (3½ to 4 lbs.)
- 1 jar (12 oz.) apple jelly
- ½ cup water
- 2½ tsp. minced garlic
- 1 Tbsp. dried parsley flakes
- 1 to 1½ tsp. seasoned salt
- 1 to 1½ tsp. pepper

1. Cut the roast in half; place in a 5-qt. slow cooker. In a small bowl, combine the jelly, water and garlic; pour over roast. Sprinkle with parsley, salt and pepper.
2. Cover and cook on low for 8-10 hours or until meat is tender. Let stand 15 minutes before slicing. Serve pork with cooking juices if desired.
4 oz. cooked pork: 236 cal., 6g fat (2g sat. fat), 66mg chol., 165mg sod., 19g carb. (0 sugars, 0 fiber), 26g pro. **Diabetic exchanges:** 3 lean meat, 1 fruit.

CHINESE SPINACH-ALMOND SALAD

My favorite salad combines power-packed spinach, a good source of vitamins A and K, with other veggies, lean meat and crunchy heart-healthy almonds. The flavors work well with a light Asian dressing.
—Mary Ann Kieffer, Lawrence, KS

- -

Takes: 10 min. • **Makes:** 4 servings

- 1 pkg. (6 oz.) fresh baby spinach
- 2 cups cubed cooked pork
- 1 cup bean sprouts
- 2 medium carrots, thinly sliced
- ½ cup sliced fresh mushrooms
- ¼ cup sliced almonds, toasted
- ½ cup reduced-fat sesame ginger salad dressing

In a bowl, combine the first six ingredients. Divide among four salad plates; drizzle each serving with 2 Tbsp. dressing. Serve salads immediately.
1 serving: 244 cal., 11g fat (3g sat. fat), 63mg chol., 500mg sod., 12g carb. (6g sugars, 3g fiber), 24g pro. **Diabetic exchanges:** 3 lean meat, 1 vegetable, 1 fat, ½ starch.

HOMEMADE BARBECUES

Growing up, we were happy when there was pork roast on the menu because we were sure that, within the next few days, we'd be feasting on leftover pork in these tasty sandwiches.

—George Hascher, Phoenicia, NY

- -

Takes: 30 min. • **Makes:** 3 servings

- 2 **celery ribs, finely chopped**
- 1 **medium onion, finely chopped**
- 1 **tsp. canola oil**
- 1 **cup ketchup**
- 1 **to 1½ tsp. salt**
- 1 **tsp. ground mustard**
- 2 **cups shredded cooked pork**
- 3 **kaiser rolls or hamburger buns, split**

In a large saucepan, saute celery and onion in oil until tender. Stir in the ketchup, salt and mustard. Add pork. Bring to a boil. Reduce heat; cover. Simmer 20-30 minutes to allow flavors to blend. Serve on rolls.

1 serving: 427 cal., 12g fat (3g sat. fat), 85mg chol., 2025mg sod., 48g carb. (14g sugars, 3g fiber), 33g pro.

TEST KITCHEN TIP
Think outside the bun! This tasty barbecue is great wrapped in a flour tortilla, used as a pizza topping or even served over fresh salad greens.

ROAST PORK SOUP

This well-seasoned, satisfying soup has a rich full-bodied broth brimming with tender chunks of cooked pork, potatoes and navy beans. It 's a family favorite.
—Sue Gulledge, Springville, AL

Prep: 15 min. • **Cook:** 55 min.
Makes: 9 servings

3 cups cubed cooked pork roast
2 medium potatoes, peeled and chopped
1 large onion, chopped
1 can (15 oz.) navy beans, rinsed and drained
1 can (14½ oz.) Italian diced tomatoes, undrained
4 cups water
½ cup unsweetened apple juice
½ tsp. salt, optional
½ tsp. pepper
Minced fresh basil

In a soup kettle or Dutch oven, combine the first nine ingredients. Bring to a boil. Reduce heat; cover and simmer for 45 minutes or until vegetables are crisp-tender. Sprinkle with basil.

1 cup: 192 cal., 5g fat (0 sat. fat), 29mg chol., 236mg sod., 22g carb. (0 sugars, 4g fiber), 16g pro. **Diabetic exchanges:** 1 starch, 1 meat, 1 vegetable.

PORK SPANISH RICE

My family wasn't fond of pork roast until I used some leftovers in this dish.
—Betty Unrau, MacGregor, MB

Prep: 20 min. • **Bake:** 20 min.
Makes: 4 servings

1 medium green pepper, chopped
1 small onion, chopped
2 Tbsp. butter
1 can (14½ oz.) diced tomatoes, drained
1 cup chicken broth
½ tsp. salt
¼ tsp. pepper
1¾ cups cubed cooked pork
1 cup uncooked instant rice

1. In a large skillet, saute green pepper and onion in butter until tender. Stir in the tomatoes, broth, salt and pepper. Bring to a boil; stir in pork and rice.
2. Transfer to a greased 2-qt. baking dish. Cover and bake at 350° for 20-25 minutes or until rice is tender and liquid is absorbed. Stir before serving.

1 cup: 304 cal., 12g fat (6g sat. fat), 71mg chol., 756mg sod., 29g carb. (5g sugars, 3g fiber), 21g pro.

USING LEFTOVER TACO MEAT

SEASONED TACO MEAT

I got this recipe from the restaurant where I work. Everyone in town loves the blend of seasonings. Try this beef blend in all your favorite southwestern dishes.
—Denise Mumm, Dixon, IA

Prep: 10 min. • **Cook:** 35 min.
Makes: 2½ cups

- 3 lbs. ground beef
- 2 large onions, chopped
- 2 cups water
- 5 Tbsp. chili powder
- 2 tsp. salt
- 1 tsp. ground cumin
- ¾ tsp. garlic powder
- ¼ to ½ tsp. crushed red pepper flakes

In a large skillet or Dutch oven, cook beef and onion over medium heat until meat is no longer pink; drain. Add water and seasonings. Bring to a boil. Reduce heat; simmer, uncovered, until water is absorbed, about 15 minutes.

¼ cup: 272 cal., 17g fat (6g sat. fat), 84mg chol., 665mg sod., 5g carb. (2g sugars, 2g fiber), 25g pro.

TEST KITCHEN TIP
Use Seasoned Taco Meat for tacos, enchiladas and burritos, or beat the clock when you use it in the recipes that follow.

SPICY EGG BAKE

This family favorite makes a wonderful morning meal served with muffins and fresh fruit. It's also a great way to use up extra taco meat. Adjust the heat by choosing a hotter or milder salsa.
—Michelle Jibben, Springfield, MN

Takes: 30 min. • **Makes:** 8 servings

- 1 tube (8 oz.) refrigerated crescent rolls
- 10 large eggs
- ⅓ cup water
- 3 Tbsp. butter
- 1½ cups prepared taco meat
- 1 cup shredded cheddar cheese
- 1 cup shredded Monterey Jack cheese
- 1 cup salsa

1. Unroll crescent roll dough into a greased 13x9-in. baking dish. Seal seams and perforations; set aside.

2. In a small bowl, whisk eggs and water. In a large skillet, heat butter until hot. Add egg mixture; cook and stir over medium heat until eggs are almost set. Remove from the heat.

3. Sprinkle taco meat over dough. Layer with the eggs, cheeses and salsa. Bake, uncovered, at 375° for 14-16 minutes or until bubbly and cheese is melted.

1 piece: 481 cal., 32g fat (14g sat. fat), 327mg chol., 981mg sod., 19g carb. (4g sugars, 3g fiber), 30g pro.

5 INGREDIENT
TACO PIZZA SQUARES

This dish is always popular at our house. I top convenient refrigerated pizza dough with leftover taco meat, tomatoes and cheese, bringing a full-flavored fiesta to the table in under half an hour—even on busy weeknights.
—Sarah Vovos, Middleton, WI

- -

Takes: 25 min. • **Makes:** 10 servings

1 tube (13.8 oz. each) refrigerated pizza crust
1 can (8 oz.) pizza sauce
2 cups prepared taco meat
2 medium tomatoes, seeded and chopped
2 cups shredded mozzarella cheese Shredded lettuce or sour cream, optional

Unroll pizza dough and place in a 15x10x1-in. baking pan. Spread dough with pizza sauce; sprinkle with the taco meat, tomatoes and cheese. Bake at 400° for 15-20 minutes or until crust is golden brown. Top with the shredded lettuce and sour cream if desired.
1 piece: 259 cal., 11g fat (5g sat. fat), 40mg chol., 660mg sod., 23g carb. (4g sugars, 2g fiber), 17g pro.

MEAT-AND-POTATO QUICHE

This hearty dish is perfect anytime, of course, but our family especially enjoys it at breakfast! It just seems to get the day off to an extra-good start.
—Esther Beachy, Hutchinson, KS

- -

Prep: 20 min. • **Bake:** 30 min.
Makes: 6 servings

3 Tbsp. canola oil
3 cups shredded peeled potatoes, well drained
1 cup shredded part-skim mozzarella cheese
¾ cup prepared taco meat
¼ cup chopped onion
1 cup heavy whipping cream
5 large eggs
½ tsp. salt
⅛ tsp. pepper
1 Tbsp. minced fresh parsley

1. Combine oil and potatoes in a 10-in. pie plate. Press mixture down evenly to form a crust. Bake at 425° for 10 minutes or until lightly browned.
2. Layer with the mozzarella, taco meat and onion. Whisk together the cream, eggs, salt and pepper; pour over the beef mixture. Sprinkle with parsley. Bake for 30 minutes or until a knife inserted in the center comes out clean.
1 slice: 377 cal., 29g fat (13g sat. fat), 242mg chol., 356mg sod., 18g carb. (3g sugars, 2g fiber), 12g pro.

TACO PINWHEELS

Extra taco meat makes these appealing appetizers easy to assemble. Just add the seasoned meat to a simple cream cheese mixture and roll up in tortillas. They're a welcome addition to any party.
—Cindy Reams, Philipsburg, PA

- -

Prep: 15 min. + chilling
Makes: about 3 dozen appetizers

- 4 oz. cream cheese, softened
- ¾ cup prepared taco meat
- ¼ cup finely shredded cheddar cheese
- ¼ cup salsa
- 2 Tbsp. mayonnaise
- 2 Tbsp. chopped ripe olives
- 2 Tbsp. finely chopped onion
- 5 flour tortillas (8 in.), room temperature
- ½ cup shredded lettuce
  Additional salsa

1. In a small bowl, beat the cream cheese until smooth. Stir in the taco meat, cheese, salsa, mayonnaise, olives and onion. Spread over tortillas. Sprinkle with lettuce; roll up tightly. Wrap in plastic and refrigerate for at least 1 hour.

2. Unwrap and cut into 1-in. pieces. Serve with additional salsa.

1 pinwheel: 51 cal., 3g fat (1g sat. fat), 6mg chol., 84mg sod., 4g carb. (0 sugars, 0 fiber), 2g pro.

10 MINUTES

10 MINUTE SNACKS

HERB MIX FOR DIPPING OIL

Combine a blend of herbs to create this mouthwatering mix. Plumping the herbs in water before stirring into olive oil enhances the flavor.
—*Taste of Home* Test Kitchen

Takes: 5 min. • **Makes:** ½ cup per batch

- 1 Tbsp. dried minced garlic
- 1 Tbsp. dried rosemary, crushed
- 1 Tbsp. dried oregano
- 2 tsp. dried basil
- 1 tsp. crushed red pepper flakes
- ½ tsp. salt
- ½ tsp. coarsely ground pepper

ADDITIONAL INGREDIENTS (FOR EACH BATCH)
- 1 Tbsp. water
- ½ cup olive oil
- 1 French bread baguette (10½ oz.)

1. In a small bowl, combine the first seven ingredients. Store in an airtight container in a cool, dry place for up to 6 months.
2. To prepare the dipping oil: In a small microwave-safe bowl, combine 4 tsp. herb mix with water. Microwave, uncovered, on high for 10-15 seconds. Drain excess water. Transfer to a shallow serving plate; add oil and stir. Serve with bread.

1 Tbsp.: 122 cal., 14g fat (2g sat. fat), 0 chol., 50mg sod., 1g carb. (0 sugars, 0 fiber), 0 pro.

5 INGREDIENT
CREAMY GREEN ONION SPREAD

You need only a few basic ingredients to make this guaranteed hit.
—Sue Seymour, Valatie, NY

Takes: 5 min. • **Makes:** 1 cup (8 servings)

- 1 pkg. (8 oz.) cream cheese, softened
- 2 Tbsp. whole milk
- 2 green onions with tops, chopped
- ¼ cup crushed pineapple, drained, optional
  Crackers

In a small bowl, beat cream cheese and milk until smooth. Stir in onions and, if desired, pineapple. Serve with crackers.

2 Tbsp.: 102 cal., 10g fat (6g sat. fat), 32mg chol., 86mg sod., 1g carb. (1g sugars, 0 fiber), 2g pro.

5 INGREDIENT
FLUFFY
ORANGE SPREAD

With its pleasant orange flavor, this simple spread perfectly tops a variety of breads. Each bit has just the right amount of sweetness for a fast snack.
—Ruth Hastings, Louisville, IL

Takes: 5 min. • **Makes:** 1 cup (8 servings)

- 6 oz. cream cheese, softened
- ¼ cup orange juice
- 1 Tbsp. sugar
- 1 Tbsp. grated orange zest
  Bagels, bread or toast

In a small bowl, beat cream cheese and orange juice until smooth and creamy. Add the sugar and orange zest; mix well. Refrigerate until serving. Serve with bread of your choice.

2 Tbsp.: 47 cal., 4g fat (2g sat. fat), 12mg chol., 32mg sod., 3g carb. (2g sugars, 0 fiber), 1g pro.

PANTRY SALSA

Canned tomatoes simplify this no-fuss salsa. Combine them with a handful of seasonings, and you'll have a treat that begs to be paired with tortilla chips. Use it in all of your recipes that call for salsa.
—Lois Wyant, Manassas, VA

Takes: 5 min. • **Makes:** 3 cups (12 servings)

- 1 can (14½ oz.) diced tomatoes with onion, drained
- 1 can (14½ oz.) diced tomatoes with green chiles, undrained
- ¾ tsp. ground cumin
- ½ tsp. onion powder
- ½ tsp. garlic powder
- ½ tsp. sugar
- ½ tsp. seasoned salt
- ¼ tsp. garlic salt
  Tortilla chips

Combine the first eight ingredients in a large bowl. Serve with tortilla chips.
¼ cup: 18 cal., 0 fat (0 sat. fat), 0 chol., 323mg sod., 4g carb. (0 sugars, 1g fiber), 1g pro.

SPEEDY SURPRISE
"This was very good and took only 5 minutes to prepare."
—KATLAYDEE3, TASTEOFHOME.COM

ODDS & ENDS

RECIPE MEAL PLANNER

BURRITO NIGHT

Amp up your dinner game by giving Taco Tuesday a quick, easy makeover.

SIDE
Sauteed Squash with Tomatoes & Onions, p. 83

MAIN
Black Bean Burritos, p. 38

SWEET
Chocolate Peanut Cookies, p. 342

FAST FAMILY FAVORITES

Pizza night was never so memorable as when no-fuss flatbreads take center stage.

SIDE
Spring Pea & Radish Salad, p. 73

MAIN
Meatball Flatbread, p. 221

SWEET
Grilled Banana Brownie Sundaes, p. 129

GRILLED GREATS

Fire up the coals for a flame-broiled meal, followed by a fast, frosty treat.

SIDE
Creamy Grilled Potato Salad, p. 286

MAIN
Spinach Dip Burgers, p. 109

SWEET
Lemon Meringue Floats, p. 48

EASY ITALIAN MENU

This stovetop entree and golden breadsticks each take just 20 minutes. The dessert? Only 10!

SIDE
Savory Biscuit-Breadsticks, p. 77

MAIN
Gnocchi Chicken Skillet, p. 87

SWEET
Cannoli Dip, p. 47

SUNNY-SALMON LINEUP

Easily impress with this citrus-kissed meal starring salmon fillets seasoned to perfection.

SIDE
Lemon-Roasted Asparagus, p. 80

MAIN
Ginger-Glazed Grilled Salmon, p. 118

SWEET
Mango Sorbet Dessert, p. 51

CASUAL COMFORT

Invite the gang over to get cozy with a combo of hearty classics. This menu warms up chilly days.

SIDE
Appalachian Cornbread, p. 294

MAIN
Chicken Chili with Black Beans, p. 297

SWEET
Maple Pecan Pie, p. 413

TAKEOUT AT HOME

Surprise your family with an Asian-inspired dinner you whipped up in no time flat.

SIDE
Spicy Edamame, p. 60

MAIN
Asian Pork Linguine, p. 213

SWEET
Orange Crispies, p. 338

SMART SUNDAY DINNER

Making memories over a weekend meal doesn't require a lot of work. Let this menu show you how.

SIDE
Parmesan Risotto, p. 294

MAIN
Easy & Elegant Tenderloin Roast, p. 402

SWEET
Simple Turtle Cheesecake, p. 262

TABLE TALK!

Make your time at the table as memorable as possible. Consider the following conversation starters, and liven up family meals at your home. Give them a try and see just how fun dinnertime can be!

Who is your all-time favorite athlete?
Why is that person your favorite? What makes them stand out from the crowd? Share a highlight you love from that athlete's career and why it's so memorable.

What's the meal you enjoyed most?
We're talking best of the best here! Was it a meal prepared by Mom, Grandma or someone else? Why did it strike a chord with you? Have you tried to re-create it yourself?

Do you have a favorite vacation?
Whether they're a delightful getaway or perhaps a comedy of errors, vacations have a way of creating the best moments. Discuss everyone's favorite and why that particular trip stands out.

MAIN COURSES BY TIME

10-MINUTE MAINS

Apricot Ham Steak, 44
Bart's Black Bean Soup, 31
Black Bean Burritos, 38
Caesar Chicken with Feta, 40
Chinese Spinach-Almond Salad, 433
Curried Chicken & Peach Salad, 37
Jazzed-Up Clam Chowder, 32
Lemon-Butter Tilapia with Almonds, 34
Mexicali Pork Chops, 39
Peanut Butter, Honey & Pear Open-Faced
  Sandwiches, 41
Sesame Cilantro Shrimp, 37
Sesame Shrimp & Rice, 44
Sesame Tuna Steaks, 35
Smoked Salmon Bagel Sandwiches, 34
Sourdough Turkey Melts, 42
Split-Second Shrimp, 41
Tilapia with Corn Salsa, 42
Tomato & Avocado Sandwiches, 33
Tuna Ciabatta Melts, 40
Tuna Dill Spread, 39
Turkey-Cranberry Bagels, 45
Turkey Pitas with Creamy Slaw, 32
Yellow Squash Turkey Salad, 31
Zippy Egg Salad, 35

20-MINUTE MAINS

Asian Chicken Rice Bowl, 110
Asian Ramen Shrimp Soup, 117
Asian Salmon Tacos, 94
Avocado Crab Boats, 92
Basil-Tomato Grilled Cheese, 112
Buffalo Chicken Tenders, 115
Cashew Chicken with Noodles, 99
Chicken, Nectarine & Avocado Salad, 427
Chicken with Pineapple, 91
Copycat Chicken Salad, 121
Crispy Dill Tilapia, 105
Curried Chicken Salad, 123
Easy Asian Glazed Meatballs, 121
Easy Caribbean Chicken, 127
Game-Night Nacho Pizza, 106
Garlic Bread Pizza Sandwiches, 124
Garlic Bread Tuna Melts, 106
Garlic Toast Pizzas, 94
Ginger-Glazed Grilled Salmon, 118
Gnocchi Chicken Skillet, 87
Grilled Brats with Sriracha Mayo, 88

Grilled Greek Pita Pizzas, 104
Grilled Hummus Turkey Sandwich, 98
Grilled Salmon with Nectarines, 101
Gumbo in a Jiffy, 102
Haddock with Lime-Cilantro Butter, 102
Havarti Turkey Hero, 87
Italian Patties, 116
Lemon-Garlic Pork Chops, 124
Lemon-Parsley Tilapia, 97
Mediterranean Tilapia, 109
Mexican Hot Dogs, 101
Mushroom Hunter's Sauce, 88
Oktoberfest Brats with Mustard Sauce, 93
Pesto Fish with Pine Nuts, 111
Pesto Halibut, 115
Pico de Gallo Black Bean Soup, 111
Pierogi Quesadillas, 98
Pumpkin Soup, 104
Roast Beef Pasta Skillet, 422
Rotisserie Chicken Panini, 93
Sesame-Orange Salmon, 116
Shrimp Asparagus Fettuccine, 123
Skillet Pork Chops with Apples & Onion, 122
Sloppy Cheesesteaks, 118
Spice-Rubbed Chicken Thighs, 97
Spinach & Tortellini Soup, 91
Spinach Dip Burgers, 109
Sweet Chili & Orange Chicken, 112
Tomato-Artichoke Tilapia, 127

30-MINUTE MAINS

Asian Barbecue Chicken Slaw, 206
Asian Pork Linguine, 213
Bacon, Lettuce & Tomato Pizza, 210
Bean & Rice Burritos, 218
Beef & Bacon Gnocchi Skillet, 239
Beefy Mushroom Soup, 422
Bistro Turkey Sandwich, 247
Blackened Halibut, 225
BLT Skillet Supper, 205
Cashew Mango Grilled Chicken, 209
Chicken & Broccoli with Dill Sauce, 229
Chicken & Vegetable Curry Couscous, 221
Chicken Cordon Bleu Stromboli, 253
Chicken Pasta Caesar Salad, 250
Cheddar Ham Soup, 431
Cod & Asparagus Bake, 200
Cola BBQ Chicken, 235
Country Chicken with Gravy, 212
Country Ham & Potatoes, 235
Creamy Chicken Soup, 427
Creamy Lentils with Kale Artichoke
  Saute, 205
Creamy Noodle Casserole, 429

Dad's Cola Burgers, 248
Dill Pickle Hamburger Pizza, 236
Easy Chicken & Dumplings, 239
Easy Sweet-and-Sour Meatballs, 199
Egg Roll Noodle Bowl, 222
Fast Refried Bean Soup, 209
Five-Spice Glazed Smoked Chops, 232
Ginger Salmon with Green Beans, 217
Glazed Smoked Chops with Pears, 199
Grilled Garden Pizza, 203
Hamburger Steaks with Mushroom Gravy, 212
Homemade Barbecues, 434
Italian Sausage & Zucchini Soup, 195
Jalapeno Burgers with Gorgonzola, 240
Jamaican Ham & Bean Soup, 200
Lemon-Dill Salmon Packets, 214
Lemon Pork with Mushrooms, 230
Lemony Greek Beef & Vegetables, 247
Mango Salsa Chicken with Veggie Hash, 240
Meatball Flatbread, 221
Meatball Submarine Casserole, 217
Mediterranean Shrimp Orzo Salad, 195
One-Pan Chicken Rice Curry, 210
Pepperoni Pizza Baked Potatoes, 222
Po'Boy Tacos, 236
Pressure-Cooker Lentil Pumpkin Soup, 213
Pressure-Cooker Risotto with Shrimp &
  Asparagus, 232
Pretzel-Crusted Catfish, 230
Pulled Pork Grilled Cheese, 203
Quick Antipasto Salad, 430
Quick Chicken & Dumplings, 243
Quick Pepperoni Calzones, 225
Quinoa & Black Bean-Stuffed Peppers, 196
Quinoa-Stuffed Squash Boats, 244
Ramona's Chilaquiles, 253
Roasted Sweet Potato & Chickpea Pitas, 196
Salsa Verde Chicken Casserole, 206
Scallops with Snow Peas, 244
Skillet Nachos, 204
Southwest Turkey Burgers, 214
Spicy Egg Bake, 437
Spinach & Gouda-Stuffed
  Pork Cutlets, 251
Steak & Mushroom Stroganoff, 251
Stovetop Cheeseburger Pasta, 231
Sun-Dried Tomato Pasta, 226
Taco Pizza Squares, 438
Tequila Lime Shrimp Zoodles, 229
Thai Peanut Naan Pizzas, 226
Turkey a La King, 248
Veggie Fajitas, 231
What's in the Fridge Frittata, 218
Zesty Corkscrews, 243

45-MINUTE MAINS

60-MINUTE MAINS

ALPHABETICAL RECIPES INDEX

A

B